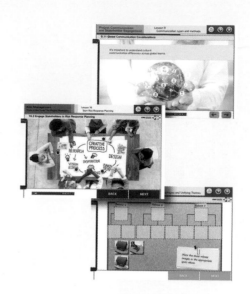

Rita Mulcahy's™

CAPM® Exam Prep

Rita's Course in a Book® for Passing the Certified Associate in Project Management (CAPM)® Exam

Rita Mulcahy, PMP, et al.

Printed in the United States of America

Fourth Printing

ISBN 978-1-943704-13-2

Library of Congress Control Number: 2018961536

Tricks of the Trade, RMC Learning Solutions, and PM FASTrack are registered trademarks of RMC Project Management, Inc. Rita's Process Chart, Rita's Process Game, and RMC Publications, Inc. are trademarks of RMC Project Management, Inc.

PMI, PMP, PMBOK, CAPM, and OPM3 are registered marks of the Project Management Institute, Inc.

This publication contains material from *A Guide to the Project Management Body of Knowledge (PMBOK® Guide)—Sixth Edition*, which is copyrighted material of, and owned by, Project Management Institute, Inc. (PMI), copyright 2017. This publication has been developed and reproduced with the permission of PMI. Unauthorized reproduction of this material is strictly prohibited.

This publication uses the following terms trademarked by the Project Management Institute, Inc.: Project Management Institute (PMI)®, Project Management Professional (PMP)®, *A Guide to the Project Management Body of Knowledge (PMBOK® Guide)*, Certified Associate in Project Management (CAPM)®.

Phone: 952.846.4484
Fax: 952.846.4844
Email: info@rmcls.com
Web: www.rmcls.com

This and all editions of this book are dedicated to Rita Mulcahy.

Her vision made RMC the company it is today. She had a profound influence on so many people—her readers, her students, and, not least, her employees. May we all apply what we learned from her and embody her passion for improving our organizations, our communities, and our world through effective project management.

Table of Contents

Acknowledgments

The following people made invaluable contributions to this book:

Subject Matter Expert

Margo Kirwin, CAPM, CPLP, PMP, PMI-ACP, PMI-PBA

Project Manager/Content Editor

Tori Turnquist

Production Editors

Patti Frazee

Rose Brandt

Content Reviewers/Contributors

Elaine Marans, PMP, CBAP

Jean McKay, PMP, MSCIS, PMI-ACP, PMI-RMP

Mary Pat Shaffer, CAPM

Nah Wee Yang, PMP, PMI-ACP, SCPM

Additional Contributors

Jen Weers

Ellen Sundell

Rich Conniff

Free Updates The purchase of this book includes access to updates regarding the CAPM exam, as well as additional tricks, tips, and information to help you prepare for the exam. Access this information at rmcls.com. Have this book with you when you go to the website as you'll need to verify your product purchase.

We Need You to Help Us Stop Copyright Infringement As the publisher of the best-selling CAPM exam prep book on the market, RMC is also, unfortunately, the most illegally copied. It is true that many people use our materials legally and with our permission to teach CAPM exam preparation.

However, from time to time, we are made aware of others who copy our exam questions, Tricks of the Trade®, and other content illegally and use them for their own financial gain.

If you recognize any of RMC's proprietary content being used in other CAPM exam prep materials or courses, please notify us at copyright@rmcls.com. Please also contact us for clarification on how to use our materials in your class or study group without violating any laws.

Contact Us We love to hear your feedback. Is there anything in this book that you wish was expanded? Is there anything that we focus on too much, or is there anything not covered that you think should be here? We would love to hear from you. Send us an email at info@rmcls.com.

Tricks of the Trade® for Studying for This Exam

O N E

You are about to go on a journey, not just to pass an exam, but to learn about what it takes to be a truly great project manager. The CAPM exam is designed to test your knowledge of PMI's book *A Guide to the Project Management Body of Knowledge* (also known as the *PMBOK® Guide*). The exam doesn't test real-world project management or your project management experience. However, to pass the exam, you will need to understand the project management concepts covered in the *PMBOK® Guide*. This book will prepare you to do that—and along the way, you will also learn a great deal about real-world project management.

To get the most out of this book, we suggest that you let the book do the work for you. Follow all pointers and complete all exercises. All aspects of this book are designed to help you shorten your study time and pass the exam. Imagine thousands of people coming before you and contributing to the topics described here, and you'll see how valuable this book will be to you. Trust the information, exercises, and tricks presented here, and you'll pass the exam.

Although you'll learn a lot about managing a project by reading this book, it is not intended to teach you all you need to know to manage a project or the art and science of project management. If you have had training in project management, the only materials you should need to pass the CAPM exam are this book, our CAPM FASTrack® Cloud exam simulator, our *CAPM Hot Topics* flashcards, and the *PMBOK® Guide*, *Sixth Edition*.

In order to get the most out of your efforts and save time studying, this book has been specifically designed to help you:

- Pass the exam on your first try
- Learn, not just memorize
- Shorten your study time
- Determine the gaps in your knowledge
- Gain insider tips on the exam that are not readily available elsewhere
- Make sense of the topics on the exam

Qualifying to Take the CAPM Exam

To take the CAPM exam, you must meet requirements as outlined by the Project Management Institute. Currently, test takers must have a high school diploma, associate's degree, or global equivalent, and 23 hours of project management education.

Applying to Take the Exam
You must submit an application to PMI to take the CAPM exam. Applications may be submitted online or by mail. Submit online if at all possible, since PMI's response time is faster for electronic submissions. In addition, the online application process makes it easier for you to document your project management training or experience while adhering to the application guidelines. After submitting your application, you'll receive a notice that will confirm your application has been accepted; you will then be prompted to pay for your exam appointment. Once payment is received, you'll receive an email authorizing you to make an appointment to take the exam. You may be subject to an audit of your application before it's approved. Be aware that an audit will delay your authorization to take the exam.

Once you receive your authorization notice, you must pass the exam within one year. You can take the exam up to three times within that year; if you fail all three times, you must wait one year to reapply for the exam.

How to Use This Book

Be Sure You Have Current Materials for the Exam
Before you begin using this book, you should make sure it's the correct edition. RMC products are updated to give you the most current information available, and they take into account the latest changes to the exam. Previous editions of this book are out of date and should not be used to try to pass the exam. This edition of the *CAPM Exam Prep* book is in alignment with the *PMBOK® Guide, Sixth Edition* that was published September 6, 2017, and is meant to be used to study for exams taken after May 21, 2018.

How This Book Is Organized
Most of the chapters in this book have been organized the same way: a list of Quicktest topics (generally listed in order of importance), an introduction to the knowledge area, a discussion of the key inputs, tools and techniques, and outputs for that knowledge area; exercises and review materials; and a practice exam. Let's review these key components of the chapters.

Quicktest The list at the beginning of each chapter indicates the topics covered in the chapter and our impression as to their general order of importance. To test your knowledge of the chapter contents and to review what's most important, refer back to this list when you're finished with each chapter.

Introduction The introduction provides an overview of the knowledge area covered in the chapter. It may also include key concepts and information you will need to understand the material.

Discussion of Key Inputs, Tools and Techniques, and Outputs The discussion highlights the key inputs, tools and techniques, and outputs for each knowledge area, with page references to the *PMBOK® Guide, Sixth Edition*. The content primarily focuses on the most important and difficult aspects, and it addresses particular areas that are the most troublesome for test takers. Also note that tips and tricks that can shorten your study time and improve your exam score have been incorporated into the material as well.

Note: All page references in this document refer to the *PMBOK® Guide, Sixth Edition* unless otherwise stated.

The chapters also include a wealth of tips for passing the exam called Tricks of the Trade® (a registered trademark of RMC). The tricks are designated by this logo, and they will give you extra insight into what you need to know for the exam.

 Our method of helping you prepare for the exam does not focus on rote memorization. However, the few things you need to memorize are designated by this "memory finger" logo.

Exercises and Review Materials

This book contains extensive review materials and many exercises. These materials, which can be found within each chapter, have been developed based on accelerated learning theory and an understanding of the difficult topics on the exam. Make sure you do the exercises, rather than jumping right to the answers. Do not skip the exercises, even if their value does not seem evident to you. The exercises and activities are key benefits of this book. They will help you pass the exam. The answers are listed immediately following the exercises. We have found that it is most effective to place the answers right after the exercises rather than later in the book. If you want to keep yourself from seeing the answers, keep a blank piece of paper handy to cover the answers until you have completed each exercise and are ready to review them.

Each chapter also includes games to help you understand and review the key inputs, tools and techniques, and outputs of each knowledge area. Again, these tools only include the key items that you need to understand for the exam. This will save you study time and help you focus on the most important information.

Practice Exams

The practice exam at the end of each chapter allows you to review the material and test your understanding. Please refer to the "How to Study for the CAPM Exam" section on page 9 to understand how and when to use these practice exams as part of your overall study plan. On the following page, you will find a score sheet to use as you take the practice exams. Make a copy of it for each practice exam.

Bear in mind that the practice exam questions in this book are simply intended to test your understanding of the chapter content. They do not simulate the complete range and depth of the CAPM exam questions. For exam simulation, use RMC's PM FASTrack® Cloud for the CAPM exam (described below).

However, note that you cannot simply practice answering questions to prepare for the CAPM exam. The questions in this book and in PM FASTrack® Cloud are provided to help you assess your knowledge and get familiar with the types of questions that are on the exam. Make sure you focus your study efforts on reading this book, doing the exercises and review activities, and filling gaps in your project management knowledge.

Score Sheet

Make a copy of this score sheet for each practice exam. Each time you take a practice exam, use this form to see where you need to focus your study efforts. (Note that if you are using RMC's full CAPM Exam Prep System, please see the study plan instructions "How to Study for the CAPM Exam" on page 9.)

Question Number	First Time	Why I Got the Question Wrong	Second Time	Why I Got the Question Wrong
1.				
2.				
3.				
4.				
5.				
6.				
7.				
8.				
9.				
10.				
11.				
12.				
13.				
14.				
15.				
Total Score	First Time		Second Time	
How will I improve how I take the exam next time?				

Other Materials to Use to Study for the CAPM Exam

You can use this book as a stand-alone prep tool or combine it with the following products for a comprehensive exam prep experience.

Rita Mulcahy's™ PM FASTrack® Cloud Exam Simulator

Our PM FASTrack® Cloud exam simulator offers over 700 questions—including tricky questions with more than one "right" answer. In addition to this book, PM FASTrack® is the most important tool for passing the exam. The online subscription allows you to create sample exams by knowledge area, process group, keyword, and CAPM simulation. It also saves you a huge amount of time by automatically scoring and keeping records of exams, and it includes comprehensive grading and reporting capabilities. All questions are cross-referenced with this book or the *PMBOK® Guide*, making it easy to go back to the topics on which you need more studying.

Rita Mulcahy's™ *Hot Topics* Flashcards (flipbook or eBook)

Are you looking for a way to prepare for the CAPM exam that fits into your busy schedule? Now you can study at the office, on a plane, or even in your car, with RMC's portable and extremely valuable *Hot Topics* flashcards—in flipbook or eBook format. Over 500 of the most important and difficult-to-recall CAPM exam-related terms and definitions are now available for study as you drive, fly, or take your lunch break. Add instant mobility to your study routine.

CAPM® Exam Prep eLearning Course

This self-directed eLearning course for the CAPM exam offers bite-size mobile-friendly interactive lessons, hundreds of audio clips, dozens of exercises and games, digital *Hot Topics* flashcards, unlimited timed and scored practice exams with the PM FASTrack® exam simulator, and all 23 contact hours necessary to apply to sit for the CAPM exam. It also includes a comprehensive document library, along with an abridged digital copy of this exam prep book.

PMBOK® Guide, Sixth Edition   The *PMBOK® Guide, Sixth Edition* (2017) is the international standard for project management from the Project Management Institute (PMI).

Project Management Training   Many of those who fail the CAPM exam do not have adequate project management training. If you need more training, try our *PM Crash Course™* book or Project Management Tricks of the Trade® course. Visit rmcls.com for more details.

What Is the CAPM Exam Like?

The CAPM exam tests your knowledge of the information in the *PMBOK® Guide* through a series of 150 questions over a three-hour testing period. PMI has two administration methods: an online proctored test and a center-based test. Test takers have the option of taking the CAPM exam on a computer at a designated testing site, or they may take their exam online, either at work or at home. For more information, visit pmi.org and download the Certified Associate in Project Management (CAPM)® Handbook.

As mentioned in the previous paragraph, the exam includes 150 multiple-choice questions with four answer choices per question. Fifteen (15) of the 150 exam questions are experimental questions, meaning they are not included in your score for the exam. These questions will be randomly placed throughout the exam. You will not know which ones are which. The experimental questions are included by PMI to validate questions for future inclusion in their master database. Your score will be calculated based on your response to the remaining 135 questions. PMI has not published what it considers to be a passing score. Based on the exam history, however, we estimate a passing score to be approximately 88 questions out of the 135 answered correctly, or 65 percent.

The questions are randomly generated from a database containing hundreds of questions. The questions may jump from topic to topic, and a single question may integrate multiple concepts. You get one point for each correct answer. There is no penalty for wrong answers.

The following table breaks out the number and percentage of the 150 questions on the exam in each knowledge area, mapped to the chapters in the *PMBOK® Guide*.

PMBOK® Chapter	Knowledge Area	Number of Questions	Percent of 150 Questions
1	Introduction to Project Management	9	6%
2	Project Environment	9	6%
3	Role of the Project Manager	10 to 11	7%
4	Integration Management	13 to 14	9%
5	Scope Management	13 to 14	9%
6	Schedule Management	13 to 14	9%
7	Cost Management	12	8%
8	Quality Management	10 to 11	7%
9	Resource Management	12	8%
10	Communications Management	15	10%
11	Risk Management	12	8%
12	Procurement Management	6	4%
13	Stakeholder Management	13 to 14	9%

Also note the introduction to each knowledge area within the *PMBOK® Guide,* as you may encounter exam questions that relate to the following sections:

- Key concepts
- Trends and emerging practices
- Tailoring considerations
- Considerations for agile/adaptive methods (pay special attention to agile/adaptive considerations in relation to scope, schedule, cost, resource, and communications management)

PMI occasionally makes changes to many aspects of the exam, including the qualification requirements, the application process, the passing score, and the breakdown of questions in each knowledge area. For the latest information, please visit pmi.org and read your authorization notice carefully. Any differences between what is listed here and what is communicated by PMI should be resolved in favor of PMI's information.

Before You Take the Exam

Many people fail the exam because they don't adequately prepare. You can avoid that mistake. Read the following tips carefully, and honestly assess how each one applies to you.

1. Know the exam material covered in this book, focus on the processes, knowledge areas, and process groups, as well as the inputs, tools and techniques, and outputs of each process.

2. Aim for a broad understanding of these concepts that will allow you to work through exam questions logically. For the CAPM exam, this will be much more helpful than memorizing specific technical details.

3. Read the *PMBOK® Guide*. Be sure to dedicate some time to the table on page 25, which shows how each process group relates to each knowledge area.

4. If you have PM FASTrack®, practice using analysis to select the best answer from what appears to be two or more "right" answers. (See the next section for more information.)

5. Decide in advance what notes you will write down at the beginning of your exam. This may include formulas or gaps in your project management knowledge. Practice creating this "download sheet" before taking the exam. (See the next section for more information.)

6. Deal with stress before you take the exam. If you are a nervous test taker, using PM FASTrack® can give you an opportunity to practice stress control.

7. Plan and use a strategy for taking the exam. This may mean you will take a ten-minute break after every 50 questions, or that you will answer all exam questions as quickly as possible and then take a break before you review, and potentially adjust, your answers.

8. Expect that there will be questions you cannot answer or even understand. This happens to everyone. Be prepared so you don't get anxious or doubt your abilities during the exam.

9. Visit the exam site before your exam date to determine how long it will take to get there, see what the testing room looks like, and learn how you will be able to access any food or beverages that you may bring to the testing center. This is particularly helpful if you are a nervous test taker.

10. Don't expect the exam site to be quiet. A student from one of RMC's PMP® Exam Prep courses had to deal with a band playing outside the testing center for three hours. Others have had someone taking an exam that required intensive typing, and thus more noise, right next to them. Many testing sites will have earplugs or headphones available. If you have PM FASTrack®, practice answering questions in an environment that is not 100 percent quiet.

11. Do not overstudy. Getting completely comfortable with all the material in this book is just not possible. It's not worth studying for hundreds of hours. It's a waste of time and will not guarantee you'll pass the exam.

12. Don't study the night before you're scheduled to take the exam. Instead, do something relaxing and get extra sleep. You want to be fresh and well rested.

© 2018 RMC Publications, Inc.™ • 952.846.4484 • info@rmcls.com • www.rmcls.com

Tricks for Taking and Passing the CAPM Exam

TRICKS OF THE TRADE® This book has presented what you should do and know before you take the exam. Now, let's prepare you for the big day. The following are some tips for taking—and passing—the exam. Note that some of these tips are specific to a center-based test, in which the test taker goes to a designated testing site to take the exam. To prepare for the online proctored exam, visit pmi.org.

1. You must bring your authorization email or letter from PMI to the test site, as well as two forms of ID with exactly the same name you entered on the exam application.

2. Make sure you're comfortable during the exam. Wear layered clothing so you can remove outer layers if you become too warm. (Note, however, that some testing centers may require you to store any layers of clothing removed during the exam outside the exam room.)

3. Bring something to eat and drink in case you need either during the exam. You will not be able to take food or beverages into the exam room, but you will be able to access your things outside the exam room. You don't want to be distracted by being hungry.

4. You will be given paper and pencils to make notes during the exam. The type, size, and amount of paper varies based on each testing center. Some locations may instead provide a marker and erasable board or laminated paper. Note that the testing center will require you to exchange your used paper if you need more during the exam.

5. After you start your exam, consider taking no more than five to seven minutes of your test time to create your "download sheet," which is where you write down anything you have trouble remembering. It will free up your mind to handle exam questions once the information you are most concerned about is written down.

6. When you take the exam, you will see one question on the screen at a time. You can answer a question, mark it to return to later, or skip it. You will be able to move back and forth throughout the exam.

7. After you are shown to your assigned space in the testing center, you'll typically have two computer tutorials (general testing center and CAPM test-specific) to complete prior to the start of the exam. This will help you become familiar with the computer-based test functionality. You need to start and complete those tutorials prior to starting the exam.

8. You will have access to a calculator during the exam. With computer-based testing, the computer may have a calculator function (and a tutorial to show you how to use it), or you may be given a physical calculator. Contact the testing center ahead of time if you have a question about this.

9. The exam does not adapt to your answers. This means 150 questions are selected when your exam starts, and those 150 questions will not change.

10. Use deep breathing techniques to help you relax and focus. This is particularly helpful if you are very nervous before or during the exam or when you notice yourself reading the same question two or three times. Breathing techniques can be as simple as breathing deeply five times, to provide more oxygen to your brain.

11. Smile when taking the exam. This may sound hard to do when you're stressed and taking an exam for three hours, but studies show that smiling relieves stress and makes you feel more confident.

12. Use all the exam time. Do not submit your exam early unless you have reviewed every question you skipped or marked for review.

13. Everyone has their own unique test-taking quirks and style. If you have PM FASTrack®, pay attention to your quirks while you work through the exam simulations. You may have to create a plan to ensure your style will not negatively impact you while taking the exam.

14. Control the exam; don't let it control you. How would you feel if you read the first question and didn't know the answer? And then the same thing happened after you read the second and third questions as well? This can happen because you're just not ready to answer questions and your level of stress is not allowing you to think. So what do you do? If you do not immediately know the answer to a question, leave it blank, or use the Mark for Review function and come back to it later.

15. One common reason people answer questions incorrectly is that they don't read all four answer choices. Do not make this mistake. Make sure you read the question and all four choices. This will help you select the best answer. If you find yourself forgetting to read all answer options, start reading the choices backwards (choice D first, then C, etc.).

16. There may be more than one "correct" answer to each question, but only one "best" answer. Make sure you're looking for the best answer.

17. Be alert to the fact that the answer to one question is sometimes given away in another question. Write down things you do not understand as you take the exam (also note the question number so you can easily go back to it). Use any extra time at the end of the exam to go back to these questions.

18. Almost all the answer choices will be the same length for each question. Therefore, do not follow the old "rule" that the longest answer is likely to be the right one.

19. Do not confuse inputs and outputs. Remember that an input is something you need before you can complete a process, and an output is something you have when the process is completed.

The exam will not be scored until you indicate you are ready, or three hours are up. You will also be asked if you're certain you want to score your exam after you submit it. You will receive a printed summary of your test results. If you pass, the testing center will print out a certificate, and you will officially be certified. If you do not pass, PMI will send you information about retaking the exam. You will have to pay an additional fee to retake the exam.

How to Study for the CAPM Exam

Some people believe you need to read every resource available and spend as much time as possible preparing for the CAPM exam. Do not make that mistake. You should not read every book you can find, and there is a risk in overstudying. Instead, we recommend the approach outlined in the following sections.

The Magic Three
Studies have shown that if you visit a topic three times, you will remember it. Therefore, you should read this book once and then skim through it two more times, focusing most on the activities you do not do in the real world and on the concepts you have trouble understanding.

Be in Test-Taking Mode
The actual exam will not present questions in order based on process groups. Get used to jumping from one topic to another. You'll also need to practice answering questions for three hours. You can do this by skipping all the practice exams in this book until you feel ready to answer the questions. Then take all the practice exams in one sitting (see step 1 in plan B later in this chapter). Do not underestimate the physical, mental, and emotional aspects of taking an exam for that long. You can also get into test-taking mode using our PM FASTrack® exam simulator.

Your Step-by-Step Study Plan
We recommend you use one of the following study plans. Follow Plan A if you own RMC's complete CAPM Exam Prep System. Follow Plan B if you do not own the entire system.

Plan A: Using This Book with the CAPM Exam Prep System (*CAPM® Exam Prep* book, PM FASTrack® Cloud Exam Simulator, and *Hot Topics* Flashcards) One common mistake made by people who purchase the CAPM Exam Prep System is to spend most of their time answering question after question in PM FASTrack®, thinking that will prepare them to pass the exam. This approach won't work. As we mentioned earlier, you need to focus your study efforts on reading this book, completing the exercises and review activities, and filling the gaps in your project management experience. To do this, follow the steps listed here to study this book in conjunction with using PM FASTrack® and the *Hot Topics* flashcards:

1. Before you read this book, test yourself on 20 questions in each knowledge area using PM FASTrack®. This will help you determine how much study time you need and which chapters to read more carefully. This step will also give you a baseline from which to track your progress as you study.

   WARNING: You might be tempted to test yourself on more than 20 questions, but this isn't a good idea. Twenty questions should be sufficient to help you assess your knowledge.

2. Read this book for the first time and complete all exercises, but don't do the practice exams at the end of each chapter. Focus on the chapters where you had the most errors in step 1. As you read each chapter, also read the corresponding chapter in the *PMBOK® Guide*. Read both descriptions carefully to make sure you understand all the material covered in that knowledge area.

3. As you finish each chapter, review the Quicktest terms listed on the first page of the chapter to make sure you know the meaning of each term or concept. Use the *Hot Topics* flashcards to improve recall and test your understanding of that chapter.

4. If it's at all possible, form a study group after you have read the book for the first time on your own. This will actually make your study time shorter and more effective. You will be able to ask questions, and the studying (and celebrating afterward) will be more fun. A study group should consist of only three or four people. (See the "How to Use This Book in a Study Group" section later in this chapter.)

5. Skim through this book again.

6. Make sure you really know the material, and then take a full exam simulation in PM FASTrack®. This step will give you a baseline against which to track your progress as you continue to study.

   WARNING: You should limit yourself to no more than two full exam simulations before you take the actual exam. Otherwise, you diminish the value of PM FASTrack® by memorizing questions and answers that will not be presented in the exact same way on the exam.

   WARNING: If you do not score over 70 percent the first time you take a full exam simulation (not just an individual knowledge area or process group exam), you may need a refresher in core project management concepts. If you have taken a basic project management class, review the materials you received from that class. If you have not had such a class, consider taking one.

7. Review each question you got wrong in PM FASTrack®, writing down the specific reasons for each wrong answer. Assess why the correct choice is correct and the other answers are wrong.

8. Use your list of why you got each question wrong (from step 7) to determine which material to study further. This will help you determine how much more study time you need and which chapters to read more carefully. Continue to study this book, focusing on the areas in which you have gaps in your knowledge, and skimming the sections or chapters on which you did well. Correct any errors in your understanding of the concepts discussed in this book. Review the *PMBOK® Guide* to focus on these gaps.

9. If you had difficulty with certain knowledge areas, process groups, or concepts and you have studied your gap areas, you may want to answer a small sample of questions (no more than 20) using the Knowledge Area, Process Group, or Keyword function in PM FASTrack®. Analyze why you answered any questions wrong, and continue to study your gap areas.

WARNING: You might be tempted to answer more than 20 questions, but that number should be sufficient to help you assess whether you have progressed in the particular knowledge area, process group, or concept—or whether you need to study more. Answering more than 20 questions in a particular area can diminish the value of PM FASTrack® and will not prepare you properly for the breadth of the exam experience.

10. Take your final simulation exam. You should score over 75 percent before you take the real exam. If you see many of the questions repeated, you are overusing PM FASTrack®.

11. Use the *Hot Topics* flashcards and other materials to retain the information you have learned until you take the exam.

12. PASS THE EXAM!

Plan B: Using This Book as a Stand-Alone Study Tool

1. Before you read this book, take all the practice exams at the end of each chapter in one sitting. This will help you determine how much study time you need and which chapters to read more carefully. This step will also give you a baseline from which to track your progress as you study.

2. Read this book for the first time and complete all exercises, but skip the practice exams at the end of each chapter. Focus on the chapters where you had the most errors in step 1. As you read each chapter, also read the corresponding chapter in the *PMBOK® Guide*. Read both descriptions carefully to make sure you understand all the material covered in that knowledge area.

3. As you finish each chapter, review the Quicktest terms listed on the first page of the chapter to make sure you know the meaning of each term or concept.

4. If it is at all possible, form a study group after you have read the book for the first time on your own. This will actually make your study time shorter and more effective. You will be able to ask questions, and the studying (and celebrating afterward) will be more fun. A study group should consist of only three or four people. (See the "How to Use This Book in a Study Group" section later in this chapter.)

5. Spend more time reviewing any topics you scored poorly on before moving to step 6. Many people want to just jump into testing. This is a mistake. In order to decrease your study time and increase your probability of passing the exam, learning must come before testing.

6. Make sure you really know the material, and then retake the practice exams in this book. A trick here is to take the exams in random order, not following the chapters, so that you can make sure the chapter heading is not leading you toward the correct answer.

7. Review each question you got wrong in the chapter practice exams, writing down the specific reasons for each wrong answer on the Score Sheet provided in this chapter. Assess why the correct choice is correct and the other answers are wrong.

8. Use your list of why you got each question wrong (from step 7) to determine which material to study further, and then study this material, focusing on the areas in which you have gaps in your knowledge, and skimming the sections or chapters on which you did well. Correct any errors in your understanding of the concepts discussed in this book. Review the *PMBOK® Guide* to focus on these gaps.

   WARNING: If you do not score 70 percent or higher overall on the chapter practice exams, you may need a refresher in core project management concepts. If you have taken a basic project management class, review the materials you received from that class. If you have not had such a class, consider taking one. You cannot rely on these practice questions alone to prepare you for the exam. Make sure you're confident you have filled your gaps before taking the exam.

9. PASS THE EXAM!

Tricks of the Trade®

How to Use This Book in a Study Group Each time you meet as a group, go over questions about topics you do not understand and review the key topics on the exam using the *Hot Topics* flashcards, if you have them. To get started, pick someone to lead the discussion of each chapter (preferably someone who is not comfortable with the chapter, because the presenter often learns and retains the most in the group). Most groups meet for one hour per chapter. Either independently or with your study group, do further research on questions you do not understand or answered incorrectly.

Each member of the study group should have their own copy of this book, which provides exercises, homework, and even class activities. (Please note that it is a violation of international copyright laws to make copies of the material in this book or to create derivative works from this copyrighted book.)

PMI-isms

RMC has been helping people pass the CAPM exam for more than 20 years. During that time, we have developed the following list of things that the exam emphasizes but that may not be commonly known. Rita coined the term "PMI-isms" as a way to refer to these concepts that are underlying assumptions. For the CAPM exam, you don't need to worry too much about these assumptions, since this exam does not focus on applied knowledge or situational questions. However, many people who take the CAPM exam do so as a first step toward PMP certification. With that in mind, it may be helpful to read through the following list and consider PMI's take on project management as you study for the CAPM exam.

General PMI-isms
Project managers are the center of the project universe. Without a skilled project manager, a project is destined to fail. With a person educated in the skills of project management, regardless of title (whether they carry the title of project manager or not), a project will succeed.
The project manager puts the best interests of the project first—not their own interests.
It's helpful to assume, unless stated otherwise, that the project manager is working on a large project that involves more than 200 people from many countries, will take at least one year to complete, has never been done before in the organization, and has a budget of $10 million or more.
Project managers have all the power described in the *PMBOK® Guide* and perform all the stated activities in the real world.
The project manager is assigned during project initiating, not later in the life of the project.
The project manager understands the process of project management (i.e., what to do first, second, etc., and why).
Team members are motivated, empowered, and engaged, and come prepared with suggestions; they don't require micromanagement from the project manager.
The project manager spends time planning, managing, assessing, and monitoring and controlling scope, schedule, cost, quality, risk, resources, and customer satisfaction.
Organizations have a project management office (PMO), and that office has important, clearly defined responsibilities regarding projects across the organization.
Organizations have project management policies, which the project manager adapts for use on their project. These policies may include project management methodologies, risk procedures, and quality procedures.

Organizations have records (historical information and lessons learned) for all previous projects that include what the work packages were, how much each work package cost, and what risks were uncovered (referred to in the *PMBOK® Guide* as part of organizational process assets). The project manager uses this history from other projects to plan the current project. As the project progresses, the project manager feeds historical records and lessons learned from the current project back into the organization's knowledge base.

The project manager works within the existing systems and culture of a company (enterprise environmental factors), and one of a project's results is to provide input to improve those systems.

Every project has a project charter, which authorizes the project and the role of the project manager.

A work breakdown structure (WBS) and WBS dictionary are used on every project.

A project management plan is not a bar chart, but rather a series of management plans. The project manager knows what is involved in creating a project management plan.

The project manager creates and keeps current other documents (project documents) in addition to the project management plan to help plan, manage, and monitor and control a project.

Stakeholders are involved throughout the project. Their needs are taken into account while planning the project and creating the communications management plan and the stakeholder engagement plan. They may also help identify and manage risks.

Gold plating (adding extra functionality) is not in the best interests of the project and should be prevented.

The project manager has a professional responsibility to properly use the tools and processes of project management.

Planning the Project

Planning is important, and all projects must be planned.

The project manager plans the project with input from the team and stakeholders, not on their own.

Part of planning involves deciding which processes in the *PMBOK® Guide* should be used on each project and how to tailor those processes to the project. The approach (plan-driven or change-driven) to the project should also be determined and recorded.

There are plans for how the knowledge areas of scope, schedule, cost, quality, resources, communications, risk, procurement, and stakeholder management will be planned, managed, and monitored and controlled. These are called management plans, and every project has one for every knowledge area. Note that the length and detail of these plans may vary by size and importance to the project.

If at all possible, all the required work and all the stakeholders are identified before the project work actually begins.

The project manager determines metrics to be used to measure quality.

The project manager plans to improve project processes.

The project manager creates a system to reward team members and stakeholders.

All roles and responsibilities are clearly documented and assigned to specific individuals on the project. These may include things such as reporting responsibilities, risk management assignments, and meeting attendance, as well as project work.

The project manager focuses extensively on identifying risks.

The stakeholders, as well as team members, are assigned risk identification and risk management duties.

The project manager realizes that managing risks saves the project time and money.

Project cost and schedule cannot be finalized without completing risk management.

The project manager creates realistic estimates for the overall project schedule and its associated costs.

The project manager assesses whether the project can meet the end date and other project constraints and objectives. They meet with management to resolve any differences before the project work starts. A project manager knows that an unrealistic schedule is their fault, because they have the tools and skills to solve it.

The project manager plans when and how to measure performance against the performance measurement baseline, as documented in the project management plan, but they also have other measurements to use to determine how the project is performing while the work is being done.

The project management plan is realistic, and everyone believes it can be achieved.

While the Project Work Is Being Done

The project is managed to the project management plan, which is realistic and complete.

The project manager measures against the project management plan to help determine project status throughout the life of the project.

Projects are reestimated throughout the life of the project to make sure the end date and cost objectives will be met. Therefore, the project manager almost always knows if the project can meet the agreed-upon end date and budget.

Delays must be made up by adjusting future work, rather than by asking for more time.

The project manager has authority and power. They can say no and work to control the project for the benefit of the customer.

The project manager lets others know they cannot get something for nothing. A change in scope must be evaluated for its impacts on the project's schedule, cost, quality, risk, resources, and customer satisfaction. The project manager has enough data about the project to do this analysis.

The project manager understands, and takes seriously, the human resource responsibilities on a project.

The project manager spends time on such activities as team building and ensuring high team performance.

The project manager is proactive, and finds problems early, looks for changes, and prevents problems.

The project manager spends more time focusing on preventing problems than on dealing with problems.

Most problems that occur have a risk response plan already created to deal with them.

Risks are a major topic at every team meeting.

Team meetings do not focus on status. That can be collected by other means.

All changes to the project management plan flow through the change management process and integrated change control.

The project manager ensures that organizational policies are followed on the project.

The project manager recommends improvements to the performing organization's standards, policies, and processes. Such recommendations are expected and welcomed by management.

Quality should be considered whenever there is a change to any component of the project.

Quality should be checked before an activity or work package is completed.

The project manager works closely with the quality department in performing some of the quality activities discussed in the *PMBOK® Guide*.

The project manager is actively involved with the procurement process and assists in managing procurements.

The project manager understands contract language.

The project manager makes sure all the terms of the contract are met, including those that do not seem important.

Closing the Project
The project manager archives all project records.
No project is complete unless there has been final acceptance from the customer.
All projects produce a final report that gives the project team a chance to announce that the project objectives have been met.

Since many of the assumptions listed above are likely to be different from your real-world project experience, this list can serve as an introduction to PMI's perspective on project management. Again, you don't need to worry about these assumptions for the CAPM exam, but they can help you understand the approach outlined in the chapters that follow. With that in mind, let's move on to the project management framework.

Project Management
Framework

T W O

*There are 28 to 29 questions on the CAPM exam that address
the topics covered in this chapter and chapter 3.*

This chapter covers the fundamental project management terms and concepts you'll need to have a firm grasp of for the CAPM exam. In fact, the largest single category of exam questions will be focused on making sure you understand the concepts covered in this chapter and the project management processes chapter that follows. Don't worry, these questions will be fairly straightforward—even when you aren't sure of the answers, you should be able to figure them out logically if you understand this material. Also note that you should review this chapter, along with chapter 3, shortly before you take the exam, to refresh your memory of these definitions.

> ## QUICKTEST
>
> - Definition of a project
> - Project management
> - Project team
> - Project management team
> - Stakeholders and stakeholder management
> - Governance
> - Project management office (PMO)
>   - Supportive
>   - Controlling
>   - Directive
> - Organizational structure
>   - Matrix
>   - Functional
>   - Project-oriented
> - Operations versus project
> - Enterprise environmental factors
> - Organizational process assets
>   - Processes, procedures, and policies
>   - Organizational knowledge repositories
> - Assumptions
> - Assumption log
> - Constraints
> - Work performance data, information, and reports
> - Program management
> - Portfolio management

Terms and Concepts

We'll start with some of the basic concepts and terms of project management. For example, what is a project? How does a project differ from ongoing operations? What does it mean to manage a project?

Definition of a Project   PAGE 4*   Because the art and science of project management revolves around projects, knowing the definition of a project—as the term is used on the exam—is essential to your overall knowledge and understanding of project management.

On the exam, a project is assumed to have the following characteristics:

- It is a temporary endeavor—with a beginning and an end.
- It creates a unique product, service, or result.

*All page number references are to the *PMBOK® Guide, Sixth Edition*

So, what is a project? If your manager walked into your office today and said, "The system is broken. Can you figure out what's wrong with it and fix it?" Would this be a project?

Are you reading on before you have thought through the question? If so, read the question again, and think about your answer. This is an important concept, both for the exam and in the real world.

Of the thousands of students RMC has taught, very few came into our classes understanding that you must first take what you are given and organize the work into appropriate projects, phases, and a life cycle. The project planning process will produce schedules and budgets. Can you schedule "fix it" if you don't know what's wrong? You can't; in fact, there are at least two projects in the previous scenario. The Project Management Processes chapter goes into more detail about dividing work into projects and life cycle phases.

Are you really working on projects? If you work at a help desk and someone contacts you about a problem they are having, you may be able to use a work breakdown structure (WBS), but do you need a network diagram? Do you need to use earned value management? How about management plans for scope, schedule, and cost? Probably not. Some activities are simply part of the company's normal operations, rather than a project.

TRICKS OF THE TRADE® In preparing for the exam, make sure your definition of a project is in alignment with the *PMBOK® Guide*. You should have a large, plan-driven project in mind when you are studying for the exam and answering exam questions. Think of a project that is new to an organization (it has not been done before), utilizes resources from many countries, has more than 200 people on the team, lasts longer than one year, and has a budget of over $10 million. Such an initiative would require you to use many of the tools of project management.

Regardless of whether you currently work on large projects, you will need to answer questions on the exam as if you do. There is a big difference between managing small and large projects. A large project requires using the full breadth of project management processes and tools.

On a small project, when you have an issue to resolve, you walk over to the person you need to speak to. On a large project, you may have spent weeks planning communications. When there is an issue, you have to figure out who is involved and where they are located, look up their contact information and preferred method of communication, and then communicate with them in that way. If you keep this large-project focus in mind as you read this book, you will see that all the elements being described here as part of project management make sense, are necessary, and add value. And if the concepts make sense to you, you do not have to memorize them—you can use logic to answer questions on the exam.

Why Projects Exist

Projects are created to provide business value and deliver the benefits defined in the business case and the benefits management plan. Projects are designed to bring a positive change to the organization, usually to add or improve products or services, and, in some cases, to satisfy legal or other regulatory requirements.

Operations and Projects PAGE 16

Most work done in organizations can be described as either operational or project work. Operational work is ongoing work to support the business and systems of the organization, whereas project work ends when the project is closed. It's important to understand the difference for the exam. You may see instances where the real problem in the question is that someone is attempting to manage ongoing (operational) work, such as manufacturing, as a project.

Although these are two distinct areas of work, they are closely connected. When a project is finished, the deliverables are transitioned to ongoing business operations so the benefits of the project work can be incorporated into the organization. A successful transition may require employee training or adjustments to operational processes. For example, when an insurance company's internal project to develop a new caseload tracking system is completed, employees will need to learn how to use the system and adjust their processes to incorporate it into their daily work so the benefits can be realized.

Governance   PAGE 16   Organizational governance refers to the overall structure of an organization, and it involves setting the policies and procedures for how work will be performed to meet high-level strategic goals. Also note that there are multiple levels of governance within an organization. Generally, a board of directors is responsible for ensuring that work throughout the organization conforms to external (government or regulatory) and internal standards and requirements. Internal requirements include policies and procedures regarding portfolio, program, and project work, which help ensure that these endeavors are within the strategic plan of the organization and contribute to the delivery of specific benefits or value. Every organization is different, and governance is designed to support the specific culture and attributes of the organization.

What Is Portfolio Management?   PAGE 15   A portfolio includes programs, individual projects, and other related operational work that is prioritized and implemented to achieve a specific strategic business goal (see fig. 2.1). Combining programs, projects, and operations into one or more portfolios helps optimize the use of resources, enhances the benefits to the organization, and reduces risk. The programs and projects that make up a portfolio may not be related, other than by the fact that they are helping to achieve a common strategic goal. The work of an organization can comprise one or multiple portfolios. A project is included in a portfolio based on potential return on investment, strategic benefits, alignment with corporate strategy, and other factors critical to organizational success.

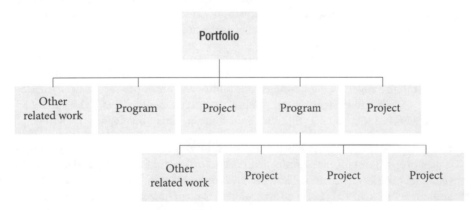

Figure 2.1 Portfolio management

What Is Program Management?   PAGE 14   By grouping related projects into a program, an organization can coordinate the management of those projects (see fig. 2.2). The program approach focuses on the interdependencies between the projects and may help decrease risk, achieve economies of scale, and improve management. In addition to the work required to complete each individual project, the program also includes efforts such as the program manager's coordination and management activities. So, when you discover that your work encompasses more than one project, you can manage all the projects as a program if there is a benefit to doing so. However, this should be done only when the program approach adds value. Projects are combined into programs to provide coordinated control, support, and guidance. The program manager works to ensure projects and programs achieve the benefits for which they were initiated.

If you want to learn more about program management, visit rmcls.com for information about RMC's courses on this topic.

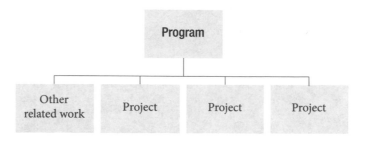

Figure 2.2 Program management

What Is Project Management? Why Is It Important? PAGE 10   Project management is both a science and an art. The science is the systematic process of managing work efficiently and effectively to deliver planned results. This includes tailoring efforts to meet the needs of the project and using the appropriate processes and tools to accomplish the work. The art of project management relates to how a project manager uses skills such as influencing, organizing, and strategizing, in addition to other interpersonal and team skills.

The *PMBOK® Guide* breaks project management into process groups and knowledge areas. The project management process groups are initiating, planning, executing, monitoring and controlling, and closing. Each of these process groups is discussed more fully in the Project Management Processes chapter. The knowledge areas are integration, scope, schedule, cost, quality, resource, communications, risk, procurement, and stakeholder management. The work of these process groups and the knowledge areas within them can occur simultaneously, and is iterated as the project progresses.

Chances are, there are some key aspects of project management you do not know. The answer to the question, "What is project management?" is described throughout this book. It can involve technical terms and processes, but it also involves roles and responsibilities and authority levels. Applying the practices, tools and techniques, and knowledge and skills of project management increases the likelihood of project success. As you read this book, you may find that project management involves more than you thought.

Effective use of project management ensures that the organization is focused on the most important work and, because of appropriately tailored planning efforts, the work is done correctly and in the most time- and cost-effective manner. Risks are identified and planned for before they occur, communication is managed effectively, and quality is achieved. These efforts result in stakeholder satisfaction and the achievement of business objectives.

Project Management Office (PMO)   PAGE 48   The project management office (PMO) is a departmental unit within the organization that provides or ensures compliance with project governance. The office oversees and standardizes the management of projects. A PMO may take one of three forms—supportive, controlling, or directive.

- **Supportive** A supportive PMO provides the policies, methodologies, templates, and lessons learned for managing projects within the organization. It typically exercises a low level of control over projects.

- **Controlling** A controlling PMO provides support and guidance on how to manage projects, trains others in project management and project management software, assists with specific project management tools, and ensures compliance with organizational policies. It typically has a moderate level of control over projects.

- **Directive** A directive PMO provides project managers for different projects and is responsible for the results of those projects; all projects, or projects of a certain size, type, or influence, are managed by this office. A directive PMO has a high level of control over projects.

The PMO may:

- Manage the interdependencies among projects, programs, and portfolios.
- Integrate information from all projects to assess whether the organization is achieving its strategic objectives.
- Help provide resources.
- Recommend the termination of projects, when appropriate.
- Monitor compliance with organizational processes.
- Help gather lessons learned into a repository and make them available to other projects.
- Provide templates for documents such as work breakdown structures (WBS) or communications management plans.
- Provide guidance and project governance.
- Provide centralized communication about the projects.
- Be more heavily involved during project initiating than later in the project.
- Have representation on the change control board.
- Be a stakeholder.
- Prioritize projects.

Organizational Structure PAGE 45 A project does not operate in a vacuum. Projects are impacted by, and have an impact on, the cultural norms, management policies, and procedures of the organizations of which they are a part. These factors are increasingly important in global organizations in which team members are often located in different offices and in multiple countries. The best project managers look for these influences and manage them for the benefit of the project and the organization.

One of the primary forms of influence is how the company is organized. The organizational structure will dictate who the project manager goes to for help with resources, how communications must be handled, and many other aspects of project management. This influence is so important that an answer to a question on the exam can change depending on the structure of the organization being discussed.

Questions on the exam are often phrased in terms of the project manager's level of authority and how the form of organization impacts their management of projects. For example, exam questions may deal with who has the power in each type of organization (the project manager or the functional manager), or they may require you to understand the advantages and disadvantages to the project manager in each type of organization.

As you read through the following sections defining the different organizational structures, take the time to think about how each form would impact a project manager's work and how a project manager would solve problems in different situations within each structure.

- **Functional** This is a common organizational structure. Functional organizations are grouped by areas of specialization within functional areas, such as accounting, marketing, or manufacturing. When you see "functional" on the exam, think "silo." Projects generally occur within a single department. If information or project work is needed from another department, employees transmit the request to the head of the department who communicates the request to the other department head. Otherwise, communication stays within the project. Team members complete project work in addition to normal departmental work.

- **Project-Oriented** In a project-oriented, or projectized, organization, the entire company is organized by projects, and the project manager has control of the project. Personnel are assigned and report to a project manager. When you see "project-oriented" on the exam, think "no home." Team members complete only project work, and when the project is over, they do not have a department to go back to. They need to be assigned to another project or get a job with a different employer. Communication primarily occurs within the project. This type of organization can also be referred to as composite or hybrid.

- **Matrix** This form is an attempt to maximize the strengths of both the functional and project-oriented structures. When you see "matrix" on the exam, think "two managers." The team members report to two managers: the project manager and the functional manager (for example, the engineering manager). Communication goes from team members to both managers. Team members do project work in addition to normal departmental work.

In a *strong* matrix, power rests with the project manager. In a *weak* matrix, power rests with the functional manager, and the power of the project manager is comparable to that of a coordinator or expediter. In a *balanced* matrix, the power is shared between the functional manager and the project manager.

As stated in the previous paragraph, the project manager's role in a weak matrix or in a functional organization might be one of the following:

- **Project expediter** The project expediter acts primarily as a staff assistant and communications coordinator. The expediter cannot personally make or enforce decisions.
- **Project coordinator** This position is similar to the project expediter, except that the coordinator has some authority and power to make decisions and reports to a higher-level manager.

 The exam typically does not identify the form of organization being discussed. When it does not specify a form, assume matrix. If you remember this, you should get a few more questions right.

 A tight matrix has nothing to do with a matrix organization. It simply refers to colocation—the practice of locating the work spaces for the project team in the same room. Because it sounds similar to the other forms of organization, it has often been used as a fourth choice for these questions on the exam.

Now that we have discussed the terms and concepts to know for the CAPM exam, let's look at specific roles within projects.

Project Roles

For the exam, it's important to understand who is involved in the project and what they should be doing. Some people actually fail the exam because they are not clear about the roles within a project and don't really know what a project manager does, or at least don't understand how the exam expects the role to be performed. They may also have problems differentiating between what the team, project manager, and management should be doing.

This exercise will help you focus on roles and responsibilities within the context of the exam. The answers may provide you with new information or simply refresh your memory.

Exercise

The Role of the Project Sponsor/Initiator   Test yourself! Describe the role of the project sponsor/initiator.

```
┌─────────────────────────────────────────────────────────────┐
│                                                             │
│                                                             │
│                                                             │
│                                                             │
│                                                             │
│                                                             │
│                                                             │
│                                                             │
│                                                             │
│                                                             │
│                                                             │
│                                                             │
│                                                             │
│                                                             │
└─────────────────────────────────────────────────────────────┘
```

Answer

The Role of the Project Sponsor/Initiator   A basic definition of a sponsor is one who provides the financial resources for the project. However, the exam has attributed additional duties to the sponsor—including providing support for the project and protecting the project from unnecessary changes. The role of the sponsor may be filled by two or more individuals, working together.

Think about your company's management as you read this. Do they know what their role is on projects? Without having the sponsor or someone in management performing the functions detailed in the lists that follow, the project will suffer, wasting time and resources. Management must serve as a protector of the project (so long as the project continues to meet the organization's strategic goals). Management is anyone senior to the project manager in the organization, including program or portfolio managers.

Read the following list carefully to understand the role of the sponsor and senior management in an organization. Since the list is so long—and since many project managers have gaps in their knowledge here—we have organized this section by process group.

During or prior to project initiating, the sponsor:

- Has requirements that must be met
- Is a project stakeholder
- Participates in developing the business case for the project
- Helps define the measurable project objectives
- Advocates for or champions the project, especially while the project concept is being put together

- Serves as a voice of the project or spokesperson to those who do not know about the project, including upper management
- Gathers the appropriate support for the project
- Ensures buy-in throughout the organization
- Provides funding
- Provides high-level requirements
- Provides information regarding the initial scope of the project
- May dictate milestones, key events, or the project end date (along with the customer)
- Determines the priorities between the constraints (if not done by the customer)
- Provides information that helps develop the project charter
- Gives the project manager authority as outlined in the project charter
- Sets priorities between projects
- Encourages the finalization of high-level requirements and scope by the stakeholders
- Guides the process to get the project approved and formalized, assisted by the project manager as necessary

During project planning, the sponsor:

- Provides the project team with time to plan
- May review the WBS
- Identifies risks
- Determines the reports needed by management to oversee the project
- Provides expert judgment
- Helps evaluate trade-offs during crashing, fast tracking, and reestimating
- Approves the final project management plan

During project executing and project monitoring and controlling, the sponsor:

- Supports the efforts of the project manager
- Protects the project from outside influences and changes
- Enforces quality policies
- Provides expert judgment
- Helps evaluate trade-offs during crashing, fast tracking, and reestimating
- Resolves conflicts that extend beyond the project manager's control
- Approves, rejects, or defers changes, or authorizes a change control board to do so
- May direct that a quality review be performed
- Clarifies scope questions
- Works with the project manager to monitor progress

During project closing, the sponsor:

- Provides formal acceptance of the deliverables (if they are the customer)
- Enables an efficient and integrated transfer of deliverables to the customer
- Supports the collection of historical records from the project

Exercise

The Role of the Project Team   Test yourself! Describe the role of the team.

```




```

Answer

The Role of the Project Team   The project team is a group of people, including the project manager, who will complete the work of the project. The team members can change throughout the project as people are added to and released from the project.

Generally, it is the team's role to help plan what needs to be done by creating the WBS and schedule estimates for their work packages or activities. During project executing and monitoring and controlling, the team members complete activities to produce the deliverables represented in work packages and help look for deviations from the project management plan. More specifically, the team may help:

- Identify and involve stakeholders
- Identify requirements
- Identify constraints and assumptions
- Create the WBS
- Decompose the work packages for which they are responsible into schedule activities
- Identify dependencies between activities
- Provide schedule and cost estimates
- Participate in the risk management process
- Comply with quality and communications plans
- Enforce ground rules
- Execute the project management plan to accomplish the work defined in the project scope statement
- Attend project team meetings
- Recommend changes to the project, including corrective actions
- Implement approved changes
- Share new knowledge
- Contribute to the lessons learned knowledge base

In agile environments, team members are responsible for clarifying user stories with the customer so they can estimate and plan the releases and iterations, hold reviews and retrospectives, and update the project information using tools such as Kanban boards and burndown charts.

On large projects, there may be too much project management work for one person to perform. Therefore, the project manager may select some project team members to help perform the project management activities. The *PMBOK® Guide* refers to these people as the project management team. Members of this team must have project management training. Keep all this information in mind when the exam uses the term "project management team" versus "project team" or "team."

Exercise

The Role of the Stakeholders   Test yourself! Describe the role of the stakeholders as a group.

Answer

The Role of the Stakeholders   A stakeholder is anyone who will be impacted by the project or can positively or negatively influence the project. This includes the customer or end user, the project manager and team, the project's sponsor, program and portfolio managers, the project management office, functional or operational managers within the organization, other departments or groups within the organization (such as business analysis, marketing, procurement, quality, or legal), and external sellers that provide services or materials for the project. Questions about the role of stakeholders and how they should be managed appear throughout the exam.

The stakeholders' role on a project is determined by the project manager and the stakeholders themselves. Stakeholders should be involved in planning the project and managing it more extensively than many people are used to on their real-world projects. For example, stakeholders may be involved in the following activities.

- Creating the project charter and the project scope statement
- Developing the project management plan
- Approving project changes and being on the change control board
- Identifying constraints and assumptions
- Identifying requirements
- Managing risk

In an agile environment, the project owner role is someone from the business who is responsible for working with the agile team to prioritize features and functions. This person may also:

- Attend reviews and accept the deliverables presented
- Be a risk owner
- Participate in phase gate reviews
- Be involved with governance
- Identify issues
- Document lessons learned
- Provide expert judgment

Exercise

The Role of the Functional or Resource Manager   Test yourself! Describe the role of the functional or resource manager.

Answer

The Role of the Functional or Resource Manager   A functional or resource manager manages and is responsible for the human and physical resources in a specific department, such as IT, engineering, public relations, marketing, etc. They are responsible for working with the project manager to meet the needs of the project. As managers of people, facilities, or equipment, functional or resource managers maintain a calendar indicating availability of these resources for projects and other organizational work, and they coordinate with project managers who need the resources. This might involve negotiation if people, facilities, or equipment are needed by more than one project at the same time. If the project manager has issues with resources provided by the functional manager, the managers collaborate to resolve the issues.

The degree to which functional managers are involved in a project depends on the organizational structure. In a matrix organization, the functional managers and project manager share responsibility for directing the work of individuals and managing the physical resources needed on the project. In a project-oriented organization, the project manager does all the directing of team resources. In contrast, the project manager does little directing in a functional organization, where that responsibility falls to functional managers. To avoid conflict, the project manager and functional managers must balance their respective needs regarding the use of resources to complete project and functional work. It is generally the responsibility of the project manager to manage this relationship by using clear communication and interpersonal and team skills, such as conflict management and emotional intelligence.

The specific activities performed by functional managers on a project vary greatly based on the type of organizational structure, as well as the type of project, but may include the following:

- Assigning specific individuals to the team and negotiating with the project manager regarding team and physical resources
- Letting the project manager know of other projects or departmental work demands that may impact the project
- Participating in initial planning until work packages or activities are assigned
- Providing subject matter expertise
- Approving the final schedule during schedule development when it involves team or physical resources under their control
- Approving the final project management plan during project management plan development when it involves team or physical resources under their control
- Recommending changes to the project, including corrective actions
- Managing activities within their functional area
- Assisting with problems related to team or physical resources under their control
- Improving resource utilization
- Participating in rewards and recognition of team members
- Participating in risk identification
- Participating in quality management
- Sitting on the change control board

Exercise

The Role of the Project Manager   Test yourself! Describe the role of the project manager.

Answer

The Role of the Project Manager   To put it simply, the project manager is responsible for managing the project to meet project objectives and deliver value and benefits to the organization. Imagine you are a project manager, and think about your role on projects. Do you have the knowledge, abilities, and authority described in this book? Do you fully plan and control your projects? Are you leading and managing your projects effectively?

Remember that as a project manager, you must come up with a project management plan that people agree to and believe is realistic, and, even more importantly, that you can stake your reputation on. A project manager is responsible for ensuring that a project is completed according to the project schedule and budget, including approved changes, and that it meets the other project objectives. The project manager is held accountable for delivering project benefits.

In today's project environments, people managing projects may not realize they lack knowledge of what proper project management involves, and many companies don't understand why project management is so important in delivering the benefits they want to realize. People with the title of project manager are often not really project managers at all; instead, their role is more of a project coordinator. Before taking the exam, it's important that you understand not only the project manager's role but also all the roles of other people involved in projects.

Remember that the work of the project manager may be shared by members of the project team, referred to as the project management team. This is described in the "Role of the Project Team" exercise.

The project manager's level of authority can vary depending on the structure of the organization and other factors, such as whether they are assigned part-time or under contract. On the exam, however, the authority of the project manager has generally been interpreted to mean that the project manager:

- Is assigned to the project no later than project initiating
- Helps write the project charter
- Is in charge of the project, but not necessarily the resources
- Does not have to be a technical expert
- Identifies and analyzes constraints and assumptions
- Leads and directs the project planning efforts
- Selects appropriate processes for the project
- Identifies dependencies between activities
- Analyzes unrealistic schedule requirements, and takes action to produce a realistic schedule
- Develops time and cost reserves for the project
- Has the authority and accountability necessary to accomplish the project management work
- Says no when necessary
- Integrates the project components into a cohesive whole that meets the customer's needs
- Finalizes and gains approval of the project management plan
- Influences the project team and the atmosphere in which the team works by promoting good communication, insulating the team from politics (both internal and external to the project), enhancing the positive aspects of cultural differences, and resolving team issues
- Spends more time being proactive than dealing with problems (being reactive)
- Understands how cultural differences may impact the project, particularly in the case of global teams, virtual teams, or projects involving multiple organizations
- Ensures professional interactions between the project team and other stakeholders
- Coordinates interactions between the project team and key stakeholders
- Understands and enforces professional and social responsibility
- Assists the team and other stakeholders during project executing
- Identifies and delivers required levels of quality
- Identifies stakeholders, supports stakeholder engagement, and manages stakeholder expectations throughout the project
- Manages project knowledge, including sharing lessons learned
- Demonstrates ethics and leadership
- Manages and controls resources
- Maintains control over the project by measuring performance and determining variances from the plan
- Monitors risk, communications, and stakeholder engagement to ensure they are in conformance with expectations
- Determines the need for change requests, including recommended corrective and preventive actions and defect repair
- Approves or rejects changes as authorized, manages the change control board, and frequently sits on the change control board
- Uses metrics to identify variances and trends in project work, and is responsible for analyzing the impact of these variances and trends
- Works with team members to resolve variances from the project management plan
- Keeps the team members focused on risk management and possible responses to the risks
- Performs project closing at the end of each phase and for the project as a whole
- Performs or delegates most of the activities outlined in this book
- Applies project management knowledge and uses personal and leadership skills to achieve project success
- Communicates
- Solves problems
- Makes decisions
- Develops the team
- Uses rewards and recognition
- Is accountable for project success or failure

In addition to understanding the basic points just listed, it is also important to become familiar with many terms you will see used in the rest of this book. Many of them are used in multiple processes and for different purposes throughout a project.

Organizational Process Assets (OPAs) PAGE 39

Most organizations maintain two types of OPAs: processes, procedures, and policies and organizational knowledge repositories.

Processes, Procedures, and Policies
Over time, organizations develop or adopt processes, procedures, and policies for projects. Collectively, these processes, procedures, and policies are referred to as organizational process assets, and they apply to aspects of the project such as quality, procurement, and resource management, as well as change control, safety, compliance, and more. Projects may recommend changes or ways to increase the efficiency of these processes and procedures, but they are generally owned by the project management office or other departments responsible for organizational governance.

Organizational Knowledge Repositories
The other type of organizational process asset is organizational knowledge repositories, which include information on many facets of projects.

Historical knowledge bases are maintained and updated for every project, and made accessible to the rest of the organization as part of the historical information repository. They can be used to plan and manage future projects, thereby improving the process of project management and avoiding challenges experienced by past projects.

Historical information can include:

- Activities
- WBSs
- Benchmarks
- Reports
- Risks and risk response plans
- Estimates
- Resources used
- Project management plans
- Project documents
- Baselines
- Correspondence

Another part of historical information is lessons learned. We will discuss lessons learned in more detail in the Integration Management chapter. For now, you need to know that lessons learned, which are created throughout projects, document what went right, what went wrong, and what the team would do differently if they had the opportunity to start the project over again. The lessons learned register from each project becomes part of the lessons learned repository after project closure.

Other organizational knowledge repositories include:

- Configuration management, including file structure, file naming conventions, baselines of organizational standards, and templates of project documents
- Financial data, including budgets and actual costs of completed projects

- Issue logs and documentation regarding defects on projects
- Metrics that may be useful for other projects
- Project management plans and baselines, as well as project documents, such as network diagrams, risk registers, and stakeholder registers

When answering questions on the exam, assume the organization has information such as historical records and lessons learned from previous projects and that the company has incorporated these records into an indexed organizational knowledge repository available to all.

Enterprise Environmental Factors PAGE 38

Enterprise environmental factors (EEFs) are similar to organizational process assets as they provide a context within which to plan the project. However, enterprise environmental factors are generally outside the control of the project team.

Enterprise environmental factors external to the organization include governmental or other rules and regulations that apply to the performing organization.

Internal enterprise environmental factors include the structure, culture, systems, and geographic location(s) of the organization. Resource-related EEFs include the technology and resources available for assignment to projects, such as documentation of the skills and abilities of internal and preapproved external resources that are available through approved agreements. EEFs related to project management may include a resource management system, a procurement system, and a quality management system.

When answering questions on the exam, assume that the impacts and limitations imposed by enterprise environmental factors are taken into consideration during planning and as the work is carried out.

EEFs are inputs to many planning, executing, and monitoring and controlling processes. The project may suggest improvements to the EEFs, particularly in the area of resource management.

Assumption Log

The assumption log is a repository of both assumptions and constraints. It is started at the time the project charter is developed. Assumptions and constraints are first identified at a high level in the business case and project charter. They will receive further attention as the project progresses. The assumption log is an input to many project processes, and assumption log updates are a frequent output.

Assumptions
It is an important part of communication to understand what your management and stakeholders believe to be true about the project—these are assumptions. Assumptions are comparable to expectations, as they may not be entirely based on fact. Stakeholders may not realize they are making assumptions, and therefore may not articulate them when communicating their requirements. Incorrect assumptions introduce risk to the project, so they must be identified and managed by the project manager. The assumption log is a frequent input to planning processes, and updates to the log are outputs of many planning and control processes.

Constraints
Constraints are easier to identify than assumptions, as they are usually clearly imposed by management or the sponsor. Constraints limit options during planning and beyond. A project manager must juggle many things on a project, including project constraints such as schedule, cost, risk, scope,

quality, resources, customer satisfaction, and any other factors that limit options (see fig. 2.3). For example, the date a milestone deliverable is due, the date by which the project must be completed, and the maximum allowable risk a project is allowed to have are all constraints. Constraints can be a challenge to manage.

Figure 2.3 Project constraints

Management directly or indirectly sets the priority of each constraint. This prioritization is then used to plan the project, evaluate the impact of changes, and prove successful project completion. It's important to evaluate the effect a change to one constraint has on another. In other words, you probably cannot shorten the schedule without causing a negative impact on cost, risk, etc. This comes into play both in planning and as the project manager deals with change requests. For example, an additional activity may only take one day, but the cost of adding the activity must be evaluated, along with the impact to the critical path. The risk of adding or rejecting the requested activity must also be evaluated. Changes to the project plan generally impact multiple constraints. The project manager and team can assess them, but change requests that impact approved parts of the plan must go through integrated change control.

Constraints are discussed in many areas of this book. Take time to really understand the discussion of integrated change control in the Integration Management chapter, including how it relates to constraints. Understanding the relationship between the constraints and how they impact a project can help you get several questions right on the exam.

Stakeholders and Stakeholder Management

Stakeholders include more than the project manager, customer, sponsor, and team; stakeholders are any people or organizations whose interests may be positively or negatively impacted by the project or the product of the project. They can include individuals and groups you may not have thought about before, such as the project management team, the project management office, portfolio managers, program managers, other departments or groups within the organization (marketing, legal, or customer service, for example), functional or operational managers, and business analysts. Stakeholders may be actively involved in the project work or may fill an advisory role. Stakeholders may also be external to the organization, including government regulators, consultants, sellers, end users, customers, taxpayers, banks, and other financial institutions. People or groups who could exert positive or negative influence over the project but would not otherwise be considered part of the project are also considered stakeholders.

Think about how a project manager would involve stakeholders on a project. Proper stakeholder management means the project manager keeps stakeholders informed, solicits their input, and works to satisfy their needs and expectations. Without this effort, the project may fail.

The topic of stakeholders is discussed throughout this book because a project manager should analyze and manage the needs and levels of influence of stakeholders throughout a project. The Stakeholder Management chapter includes an in-depth discussion of the concept of stakeholder management. Also note that the Resource Management and Communications Management chapters include a special focus on this topic.

Work Performance Data, Information, and Reports PAGE 26

A great deal of data and information is generated, considered, and communicated throughout the life of a project, from initial observations and measurements to analyzed content and reports. The *PMBOK® Guide* uses three different terms to identify the stages through which this data and information move. Work performance data includes the initial measurements and details about activities gathered during the Direct and Manage Project Work process in executing. When monitoring and controlling a project, work performance data is analyzed to make sure it conforms to the project management plan. It is also assessed to determine what the data means for the project as a whole. The result is known as work performance information. Work performance information can then be organized into work performance reports, which are distributed to the various stakeholders who need to receive and possibly act on the information.

For example, let's say a project team performs their assigned work according to the project management plan. They provide information and data on their progress: a certain activity took 10 hours and was completed on July 21st. This is work performance data. The next step is to look at how this data compares to the project management plan (in this case, the project schedule). The activity in this example was estimated to take 12 hours, with an estimated completion date of July 22nd. You need to analyze why this activity took less time than planned and what this will mean for the rest of the project. Why was the work completed early? Will this mean improved performance for the rest of the project? Did the team follow the communications management plan and notify resources assigned to successor activities about the anticipated early completion so they could start their work early? Should future activities be reestimated if similar resources will be performing similar work? The result of this analysis is work performance information. This information can then be organized into work performance reports that are distributed through the Manage Communications process. If the activity was on the critical path and had taken longer than scheduled, a formal change request might have been required to adjust the rest of the schedule.

Frequently Used Tools and Techniques

There are over 100 tools and techniques in the *PMBOK® Guide,* and there are many more that we discuss in this book. The key is to use the right ones for the right purposes under the right conditions. It is also important to realize that tools and techniques can have multiple applications throughout the project management process.

You will see tools and techniques described throughout this book, in the knowledge area chapter(s) where they are primarily used. You don't have to be an expert at using all of them, but you do need to understand the purpose of each. The following tools and techniques are categorized by their function.

Data Gathering
If a project manager needs to collect input from stakeholders, they can use one or more of the following data-gathering tools and techniques:

- Benchmarking
- Brainstorming
- Prompt lists
- Checklists
- Interviews
- Market research
- Questionnaires and surveys

Data Analysis
Depending on the type of data a project manager is working with and the depth of analysis they need to do, they can choose from many data analysis tools and techniques, including the following:

- Alternatives analysis
- Assumptions and constraints
- Cost-benefit analysis
- Document analysis
- Earned value analysis
- Performance reviews
- Reserve analysis
- Root cause analysis
- Simulation
- Strengths, weaknesses, opportunities, and threats (SWOT)
- Trend analysis
- Variance analysis
- What-if analysis

Data Representation
Throughout the project, the project manager will gather and generate data from various sources for a number of purposes. They will likely need to communicate that information to others. This category includes options for representing, or communicating, data. Some tools and techniques are designed for a specific purpose. The project manager will need to choose which ones to use based on the type and amount of data they are working with, the audience with whom they will be communicating, and, possibly, other considerations, such as the knowledge area they are working in. Data representation tools and techniques include the following:

- Affinity diagrams
- Cause-and-effect diagrams
- Control charts
- Flow charts
- Hierarchical charts
- Histograms
- Logical data models
- Matrix diagrams/charts
- Mind mapping
- Probability and impact matrices
- Scatter diagrams
- Stakeholder engagement assessment matrices
- Stakeholder mapping/representation
- Text-oriented formats

Decision Making

Throughout the project, the project manager will have to make countless decisions, often with the input of the project team. There are many approaches to decision making, including the following techniques, which are used in many project management processes:

- Multicriteria decision analysis
- Voting

Communication

As you will read later in this book, a great deal of a project manager's time is spent communicating with management, the team, the customer, and other stakeholders. The following are several important communication techniques and concepts a project manager may use throughout the project:

- Active listening
- Feedback
- Presentations
- Meeting management
- Communication methods
- Communications technology

Interpersonal and Team Skills

Interpersonal and team skills are elements of the art of project management. Closely related to the communication techniques and concepts listed above, the following skills are essential for project success:

- Conflict management
- Cultural awareness
- Decision making
- Emotional intelligence
- Facilitation
- Influencing
- Leadership
- Meeting management
- Motivation
- Negotiation
- Networking
- Observation and conversation
- Political awareness
- Team building

Estimating

The project manager is responsible for leading estimating efforts for many aspects of the project, including schedule, cost, and resources. In this book, you will learn about the following common estimating techniques.

- Analogous
- Bottom-up
- Top-down
- Expert judgment

Project Management Information System (PMIS) An organization's project management information system is part of its enterprise environmental factors. The PMIS includes automated tools, such as scheduling software, a configuration management system, shared workspaces for file storage or distribution, work authorization software, time-tracking software, and procurement management software, as well as repositories for historical information. The PMIS is used in many planning, executing, and monitoring and controlling processes.

Expert Judgment Sometimes, the easiest way to get information is to consult experts. Often, those with expertise needed by the project are working on the team, or at least within the organization. Expert judgment is a common tool of the project management planning processes, although it is not frequently discussed in this book.

Meetings Meetings are often used in the planning processes of a project, although you will not always see meetings discussed in this book as a planning tool. Meetings can be an effective way to get input or feedback from groups of people, but they can be overused. The project manager is responsible for determining whether a meeting is worth the time of those who would attend it, or if there is a more efficient way to achieve an objective. The value of meetings, as well as some suggested ground rules for meetings, is discussed in the Resource Management chapter.

Make sure you are comfortable with all the concepts in this chapter before reading further; these concepts provide a basis for understanding much of the material presented in the remainder of this book.

Practice Exam

1. All the following are characteristics of a project except:
   A. It is temporary.
   B. It has a definite beginning and end.
   C. It creates a unique product.
   D. It repeats itself every month.

2. Which of the following statements about the project manager is true?
   A. The project manager provides subject matter   expertise.
   B. The project manager ensures buy-in and gathers support for the project throughout the organization.
   C. The project manager is responsible for managing the project to meet project objectives and deliver value.
   D. The project manager determines the priorities between project constraints.

3. Who has the most power in a project-oriented organization?
   A. The project manager
   B. The functional manager
   C. The team
   D. They all share power equally.

4. What is a program?
   A. The same thing as a project
   B. A group of related projects
   C. A type of organizational structure
   D. Ongoing operations rather than project work

5. A project team member is concerned because many people are asking him to do things. If he works in a functional organization, who has the power to give him direction?
   A. The project manager
   B. The functional manager
   C. The team
   D. The PMO

6. Operational work is different from project work in that operational work is:
   A. Unique
   B. Temporary
   C. Ongoing and repetitive
   D. A part of every project activity

7. In a project-oriented organization, the project team:
   A. Reports to many managers
   B. Has no loyalty to the project
   C. Reports to the functional manager
   D. Will not always have a "home"

8. Which of the following statements about the project management office (PMO) is true?
   A. The PMO standardizes the management of projects.
   B. A supportive PMO directly manages most projects within an organization.
   C. A directive PMO allows the project manager to control most aspects of the project.
   D. A directive PMO provides project managers but is not responsible for the results of projects.

9. What is the main difference between a matrix organization and a functional organization?
    A. In a functional organization, project managers have more authority than they do in matrix organizations.
    B. More people work full-time on projects in a functional organization than in a matrix organization.
    C. Project team members usually report to two managers in a matrix organization—the functional manager and the project manager.
    D. Most companies have found that a functional organizational structure provides the most flexibility for managing projects.

10. A collection of programs and projects managed as a group to achieve a specific strategic business goal is called:
    A. Operational work
    B. A portfolio
    C. A baseline
    D. A life cycle

11. A project manager is trying to complete a software development project but cannot get enough attention for the project. Resources are focused on completing process-related work, and the project manager has little authority to properly assign resources. What form of organization must the project manager be working in?
    A. Functional
    B. Matrix
    C. Expediter
    D. Coordinator

12. Which of the following is a responsibility of the project manager?
    A. Providing funding for the project
    B. Helping to write the project charter
    C. Protecting the project from outside influences and changes
    D. Setting priorities among different projects

13. The organization's management has decided that all orders will be treated as "projects" and that project managers will be used to update orders daily, resolve issues, and ensure that the customer formally accepts the product within 30 days of completion. The project manager will not be required to perform planning or provide documentation other than daily status updates. Which of the following statements about this situation is true?
    A. Because each individual order is a "temporary endeavor," each order is a project.
    B. This is an example of program management since there are multiple projects involved.
    C. This is an example of a recurring process, not a project.
    D. The orders described here are both temporary and complex enough that they require proper project management.

14. Which of the following is one of the seven project constraints?
    A. Change requests
    B. Sellers
    C. Organizational structure
    D. Customer satisfaction

15. During project planning in a balanced matrix organization, the project manager determines that additional human resources are needed. From whom would she request these resources?
    A. The PMO manager
    B. The functional manager
    C. The team
    D. The project sponsor

Answers

1. **Answer** D
   Explanation "It repeats itself every month" implies that the whole project repeats every month. Generally, the only things that might repeat in a project are some activities. The entire project does not repeat.

2. **Answer** C
   Explanation The project manager is responsible for managing the project to meet project objectives and deliver value to the organization. The functional or resource manager may provide subject matter expertise, and the project sponsor is responsible for ensuring buy-in, gathering support, and determining the priorities among the project constraints.

3. **Answer** A
   Explanation In a project-oriented organization, the entire company is organized by projects, giving the project manager the most power.

4. **Answer** B
   Explanation A program is a group of related projects. Grouping such projects into a program can help an organization reduce risk and achieve economies of scale. Programs also improve management by providing coordinated control, support, and guidance across multiple projects.

5. **Answer** B
   Explanation In a functional organization, the team members report to the functional manager. The project manager probably reports to the functional manager as well.

6. **Answer** C
   Explanation Operational work is work that is done on an ongoing basis to sustain an organization, while a project is a temporary endeavor, with a beginning and an end, that creates a unique result.

7. **Answer** D
   Explanation The main drawback of the project-oriented organization is that at the end of the project, the team is dispersed, and the team members do not have a functional department ("home") to go back to.

8. **Answer** A
   Explanation The PMO oversees and standardizes the management of projects within an organization. Supportive PMOs exercise a low level of control over projects; they focus on providing methodologies, templates, and lessons learned rather than on directly managing projects. A directive PMO exerts a high level of control over projects; it is responsible for the results of the projects for which it supplies project managers.

9. **Answer** C
   Explanation In a matrix organization, team members typically report to a functional manager as well as the project manager. Project managers have less authority in a functional organization than in a matrix organization. The amount of time people work on projects depends on the needs of the organization, not on how the organization is structured. Functional organizations do not provide more flexibility for managing projects.

10. **Answer** B
    Explanation A portfolio may include programs and individual projects, as well as related operational work, that are managed together to achieve a specific strategic business goal. Note that the projects or programs included in the portfolio may not be related except for the common strategic goal that they are intended to accomplish.

11. **Answer** A
    Explanation In a functional organization, projects often do not have strong support, and the project manager has little authority to assign resources. The project expediter and project coordinator are roles in a weak matrix organization.

12. **Answer** B
    Explanation The project manager is assigned in project initiating, and one of their roles is to help write the project charter. Providing project funding, protecting the project from outside influences or changes, and setting priorities among different projects are responsibilities of the sponsor.

13. **Answer** C
    Explanation Because these orders are ongoing, repetitive, and of short duration, this is a recurring process, not a project.

14. **Answer** D
    Explanation The seven project constraints are scope, schedule, cost, quality, risk, resources, and customer satisfaction. These constraints must be balanced by the project team throughout the project.

15. **Answer** B
    Explanation In a balanced matrix organization, power is shared between the functional manager and the project manager, so the project manager needs to negotiate with the functional manager for the resources.

Project Management
Processes

*There are 28 to 29 questions on the CAPM exam that address
the topics covered in this chapter and chapter 2.*

This chapter will help improve your understanding of the processes involved in managing a project. It will also examine the project management process, both at a high level and in more detail. As you read this chapter and complete the exercises, identify the gaps in your knowledge. This will help you know which areas to focus on to reduce your study time. Understanding the process of managing a project and knowing what should be done at what times will provide a framework for understanding all the inputs, tools and techniques, and outputs that will be tested on the CAPM exam.

Before we discuss the actions that take place in each of the project management process groups, let's go through the definition of a project life cycle and the project management process.

QUICKTEST

- What is done during each of the project management process groups
  - Initiating
  - Planning
  - Executing
  - Monitoring and controlling
  - Closing
- Project life cycle
  - Plan-driven
  - Change-driven

Project Life Cycles and the Project Management Process

For the exam, you should understand the difference between the project life cycle and the project management process. Both are necessary to complete a project. The project life cycle is what you need to do in order to *do* the work, and the project management process is what you need to do in order to *manage* the work.

Project Life Cycle PAGE 19
A life cycle is a progression of phases through a series of developmental stages. The project life cycle is the performing organization's or department's methodology for managing a project. It is the logical breakdown of what a project manager will need to do to produce the deliverables of the project. The project life cycle for a particular project is selected based on factors such as the type of product being developed, the industry, and the organization's preferences.

Project life cycles can be either plan driven or change driven. Within a project life cycle, there are generally one or more phases. These phases are collectively referred to as the development life cycle of a project. The development life cycle is used to ensure that the expected or planned result of each phase is achieved. An example of a development life cycle for a software project might include the following life cycle phases: research, design, code, test, and implement.

Plan-Driven Project Life Cycle
Plan-driven projects have predictive development life cycles (sometimes referred to as waterfall or traditional life cycles) that require scope, schedule, and cost to be determined in detail early in the life of a project—before the work begins—to produce the project deliverables. For example, a construction project would typically be managed using a predictive life cycle.

Change-Driven Project Life Cycle
Change-driven projects use iterative, incremental, or adaptive (agile) development life cycles, and have varying levels of early planning for scope, schedule, and cost.

Incremental and iterative life cycles involve early planning of high-level scope sufficient enough to allow for preliminary estimates of time and cost; scope is developed a little more with each iteration.

An incremental development life cycle delivers a complete, usable portion of the product for each iteration. For example, a project to build a website using an incremental life cycle would involve prioritizing requirements into iterations that deliver a fully functioning portion of the website at the end of each iteration.

With an iterative development life cycle, the complete concept is built in successive levels of detail to create the end result. To build a website using an iterative life cycle, planning for the first iteration would focus on planning to create a prototype of the entire website. After the basic skeleton of the site is built, each successive iteration would be planned to add more detail until a complete and fully functioning site is achieved.

Note that a project may use a combination of incremental and iterative life cycles throughout the project or for phases of the project.

Adaptive development life cycles involve a fixed schedule as well as fixed costs. Scope is broadly defined with the understanding that it will be refined throughout the life of the project. The customer's requirements are documented and prioritized in a backlog, which can be adjusted as the project progresses. Work is planned in short increments to allow the customer to change and reprioritize requirements within the time and cost constraints. A new software development project may follow an adaptive approach, using phases that might include high-level feasibility, design, and planning, followed by short, iterative phases of detailed design, coding, testing, and release.

Hybrid Development Life Cycle
A hybrid life cycle is a combination of a predictive and an adaptive development life cycle. With such an approach, a predictive life cycle is used to manage the project requirements that are well defined, while an adaptive life cycle is used to manage the requirements that are more uncertain.

TRICKS OF THE TRADE® The processes, tools and techniques, and concepts discussed in this book can be modified based on the nature of the project, the characteristics of the organization, and other factors, including the project and development life cycle. As you read through this book and prepare for the exam, think in terms of a plan-driven project life cycle. Just remember that many of the same processes, tools, and techniques can be used on change-driven projects as well. Tailoring project management practices to fit the needs of the project and the organization is the responsibility of the project manager.

Project Management Process PAGE 23 First, let's review the project management process
at a high level. The steps in this process consist of:

- Initiating the project (Start)
- Planning the project (Plan)
- Executing the project (Do)
- Monitoring and controlling the project (Check and Act)
- Closing the project (End)

Figure 3.1 shows how the project management process groups fit together:

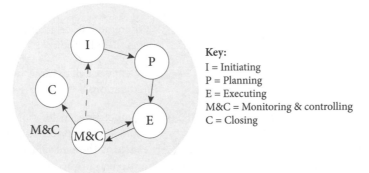

Key:
I = Initiating
P = Planning
E = Executing
M&C = Monitoring & controlling
C = Closing

Figure 3.1 Project Management Process

As noted earlier, the project management process is what you need to do to manage the work throughout the project life cycle. It includes managing the efforts related to initiating, planning, executing, monitoring and controlling, and closing the project.

Figure 3.2 shows how the project management process groups interact.

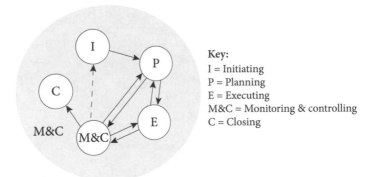

Key:
I = Initiating
P = Planning
E = Executing
M&C = Monitoring & controlling
C = Closing

Figure 3.2 Project management process

The process groups are described in detail later in this chapter, but let's take some time now to discuss the difference between the project management process and the project life cycle—including how the overall project management process interacts with the project life cycle. For small projects following a plan-driven (or predictive) life cycle, the project manager may go through the overall project management process (initiating through closing) once for the entire project, although portions of the process may be iterated or repeated throughout the project life cycle (see fig. 3.3).

Project Management Processes

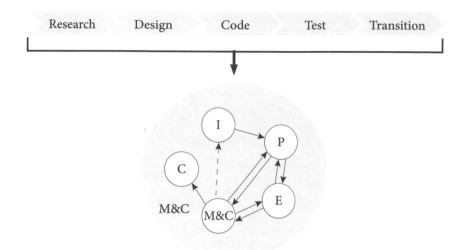

Figure 3.3 Small project with a predictive life cycle

Large projects often require each life cycle phase to be managed through the project management process groups. The example illustrated in figure 3.4 is for a large construction project. In this project, the development life cycle phases of feasibility, planning, design, production, turnover, and start-up are all extensive, requiring separate planning and management of each phase. This means there would be an overall initiating effort in which the project manager would help create a charter and do high-level planning for the entire project to get charter approval. Then, a separate initiating process for the feasibility phase would take place, followed by a planning effort for the work that will be done in the feasibility phase, the execution and control of that work, and, finally, a closeout of the phase, which typically includes a handoff of deliverables (in this example, the results of the feasibility analysis). This would then be repeated for each of the life cycle phases.

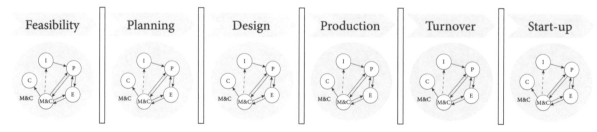

Figure 3.4 Large project with a predictive life cycle with phase gates (indicated by the vertical bars)

At the end of each phase, an event called a phase gate may take place. A phase gate involves analyzing the results of the completed phase by comparing the results of the phase with the business documents, the project charter, and the project management plan. Based on that analysis, a decision is made. Options include redoing the same phase, moving forward with the next phase, or choosing not to continue with the project. If the decision is made to move forward, the project would begin initiating work on the next phase and progress through the project management process groups for that phase.

Large change-driven projects may also be broken into phases and then into smaller releases and iterations within those phases. The project management processes of initiating, planning, executing, monitoring and controlling, and closing are done for each phase. This process is typically done within each release and iteration as well. The level of detail and the time spent on each of the project management process groups may vary based on the phase of the project the project manager is working on, but the entire project management process is typically followed, as indicated in figure 3.5, which depicts an adaptive life cycle.

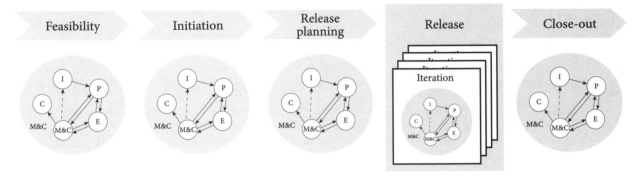

Figure 3.5 Large project with an adaptive life cycle

The project life cycle varies depending on the industry, the organization, and the type of product, service, or result being developed. The project manager works with the project management team and project governance to select the right approach for the project.

The rest of this chapter examines the project management process, both at a high level and in more detail with Rita's Process Chart™. Carefully review the information in the chapter, especially the process chart, and complete all the exercises. These are valuable tools for helping you identify the gaps in your knowledge and will significantly cut down your study time. Understanding the process of managing a project and knowing what should be done and when provides a framework for understanding all the inputs, tools and techniques, and outputs involved in project management.

The illustration that appeared in figure 3.2 is shown again here as figure 3.6 for your reference as you read the following section.

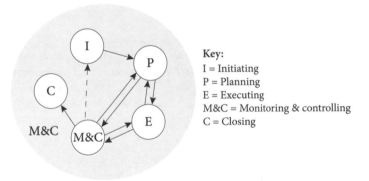

Key:
I = Initiating
P = Planning
E = Executing
M&C = Monitoring & controlling
C = Closing

Figure 3.6 Project management process

In initiating, the project manager determines whether the business case and the benefits management plan can be achieved and does some high-level planning to verify that it is likely the project can be completed within the given constraints of scope, schedule, cost, etc. Stakeholders are identified, and stakeholder analysis is performed to assess each stakeholder's potential involvement and influence on the project.

The project is formally authorized in project initiating, when the sponsor signs the project charter. After the project charter has been approved, the project moves from initiating into detailed planning, where a project management plan (including plans for how to plan, execute, monitor and control, and close the project) is developed. When the project management plan includes the appropriate amount of detail for the project life cycle and development approach, it is approved by the sponsor.

The project then moves into executing, where the team completes the work according to the processes and procedures detailed in the project management plan.

While the work is being done, the work results (or work performance data) are fed into monitoring and controlling, to make sure the project is progressing according to the baselines established in the project management plan.

If variances from the plan require changes, the change requests are evaluated in the Perform Integrated Change Control process (part of monitoring and controlling) to determine their impact on the project, identify the best options for dealing with them, and decide whether they should be approved, rejected, or deferred.

For approved changes that require adjustments to the baselines and project management plan, a replanning effort must be completed before the team can start working from the updated version of the plan and baselines in executing. This replanning effort is done as part of the Perform Integrated Change Control process in monitoring and controlling. After the plan and baselines are modified, the revised plan is provided to the team in executing, and the project is executed according to the updated plan, and monitored and controlled to the revised baselines. If the project gets so far off the baselines that it requires an analysis of whether the project should continue at all, or if significant changes are suggested that are outside the project charter, it may move back into initiating while that decision is made (since the charter, which is created in initiating, would have to change in such a situation). Ultimately, when the work is done (or the project is terminated), the project moves into closing.

Throughout the project, it may be necessary to revisit project planning. For example, if a stakeholder is identified and their requirements are analyzed after work has begun, or if a new risk that needs to be analyzed using qualitative risk analysis is identified in a risk review, the project will return to planning. The project also returns to planning to do rolling wave planning. Another instance when the project returns to planning is when new information becomes available through progressive elaboration (for example, more accurate estimates are generated that could impact the project schedule and budget).

There's one last point to keep in mind about the illustration shown in figure 3.1 and figure 3.6. Did you notice the large monitoring and controlling circle encompassing all the project management processes? It's there to illustrate that all the work of the project and project management must be monitored and controlled. This is an important concept to remember for the exam: throughout the life of the project, the project manager will be monitoring and measuring the outcomes of the project and any project management efforts, and analyzing them to help identify variances from the plan so that they can make proactive decisions to keep the project on track.

As explained in the Project Management Framework chapter, for small projects, this process might be exactly what a project manager needs to use to manage a project. For large projects that are broken into phases, this process may be repeated multiple times. For example, on a project with a research phase, the project manager would complete initiating through closing for that phase, and then repeat the process from initiating to closing for the next phase.

Now let's look at the project management process in more detail, using Rita's Process Chart™.

Rita's Process Chart™   This chart (shown on the next page) is designed to help you put the knowledge areas and process groups into perspective. It will give you an overview of project management and help you see when each process is done and the potential interactions between the processes. If you want to see the "big picture" of project management in the real world, this chart will help. Many of the items in the process chart are the responsibility of the project manager.

Project Management Processes

INITIATING	PLANNING	EXECUTING	MONITORING & CONTROLLING	CLOSING
	(This is the only process group with a set order.)			
Select project manager	Determine development approach, life cycle, and how you will plan for each knowledge area	Execute work according to the project management plan	Take action to monitor and control the project	Confirm work is done to requirements
Determine company culture and existing systems		Produce product deliverables (product scope)	Measure performance against performance measurement baseline	Complete final procurement closure
Collect processes, procedures, and historical information	Define and prioritize requirements	Gather work performance data	Measure performance against other metrics in the project management plan	Gain final acceptance of product
Divide large projects into phases or smaller projects	Create project scope statement	Request changes		Complete financial closure
Understand business case and benefits management plan	Assess what to purchase and create procurement documents	Implement only approved changes	Analyze and evaluate data and performance	Hand off completed product
Uncover initial requirements, assumptions, risks, constraints, and existing agreements	Determine planning team	Continuously improve; perform progressive elaboration	Determine if variances warrant a corrective action or other change request(s)	Solicit customer's feedback about the project
Assess project and product feasibility within the given constraints	Create WBS and WBS dictionary	Follow processes	Influence factors that cause change	Complete final performance reporting
Create measurable objectives and success criteria	Create activity list	Determine whether quality plan and processes are correct and effective	Request changes	Index and archive records
Develop project charter	Create network diagram	Perform quality audits and issue quality reports	Perform integrated change control	Gather final lessons learned and update knowledge bases
Identify stakeholders and determine their expectations, interest, influence, and impact	Estimate resource requirements	Acquire final team and physical resources	Approve or reject changes	
Request changes	Estimate activity durations and costs	Manage people	Update project management plan and project documents	
Develop assumption log	Determine critical path	Evaluate team and individual performance; provide training	Inform stakeholders of all change request results	
Develop stakeholder register	Develop schedule	Hold team-building activities	Monitor stakeholder engagement	
	Develop budget	Give recognition and rewards	Confirm configuration compliance	
	Determine quality standards, processes, and metrics	Use issue logs	Create forecasts	
	Determine team charter and all roles and responsibilities	Facilitate conflict resolution	Gain customer's acceptance of interim deliverables	
	Plan communications and stakeholder engagement	Release resources as work is completed	Perform quality control	
	Perform risk identification, qualitative and quantitative risk analysis, and risk response planning	Send and receive information, and solicit feedback	Perform risk reviews, reassessments, and audits	
	Go back—iterations	Report on project performance	Manage reserves	
	Finalize procurement strategy and documents	Facilitate stakeholder engagement and manage expectations	Manage, evaluate, and close procurements	
	Create change and configuration management plans	Hold meetings	Evaluate use of physical resources	
	Finalize all management plans	Evaluate sellers; negotiate and contract with sellers		
	Develop realistic and sufficient project management plan and baselines	Use and share project knowledge		
	Gain formal approval of the plan	Execute contingency plans		
	Hold kickoff meeting	Update project management plan and project documents		
	Request changes			

Rita's Process Chart™
Where are we in the project management process?

51

Project Management Processes   THREE

Now here's some great news: you don't have to memorize this chart for the CAPM exam! So why are we including it here? Because it's a tool that can help you pass the exam. Reading through this chart and comparing the activities listed here to your real-life project experiences will improve your intuitive understanding of what happens in PMI's approach to project management. For the CAPM exam, that kind of general familiarity will be very helpful, allowing you to figure out the answers to many of the questions logically.

The questions on the CAPM exam are relatively straightforward and primarily aim to test whether you have a good understanding of the material covered in the *PMBOK® Guide*. Rita's chart can prepare you for that by helping you see where the actions, inputs, and outputs occur in the overall process. In other words, this chart translates PMI's matrix of knowledge areas and process groups (as shown on page 25 of the *PMBOK® Guide*) into the actual activities that must be done, to help you understand how it actually works. We won't go into a lot of detail about this chart here—if you want to learn more about it, see our book *PMP® Exam Prep*. However, here are a few key points to bear in mind:

- In the Planning column, note the first box: "Determine development approach, life cycle, and how you will plan for each knowledge area." Each knowledge area (scope, schedule, cost, etc.) requires management plans as well as additional plans for configuration, change, and requirements management. The first thing a project manager will need to do as they start planning is figure out how they are going to plan, execute, and control for each knowledge area. This will help guide the remaining planning efforts.

- Look at the phrase "Go back—iterations" in the Planning column. This is an important concept. When planning a project, the project manager and the team complete each item listed in the Planning column above this point to the best of their ability. However, a project will evolve as each item is planned, and much of the earlier planning work will need to be modified or added to. For example, it is only after completing the risk management planning efforts that the WBS and the other items can be finalized. The important thing to remember is that planning should lead to a realistic, bought-into, approved, and formal project management plan that is updated throughout the project to reflect approved changes. Iterations help to create and maintain such a plan.

- On a related note, the Planning column includes a reminder that planning is the only process group with a set order. Occasionally, however, a planning process will require an input that, according to this column, won't be available yet. The risk register, for example, is an input to several processes leading to the creation of the schedule. The schedule is developed before the project manager performs risk management activities in the Planning column, so how can the risk register be an input? In such situations, the project manager will start off using a preliminary version of the input. Initial risks are uncovered during initiating, so although the risk register will by no means be complete by the time the project manager is creating the schedule, the known risks can be factored into planning. Then, after performing risk management activities, the project manager will have a more complete risk register that they can use to refine their schedule through iterations.

- As project executing progresses, the project manager may determine that a change to the project is needed. The same could happen while the project manager is monitoring and controlling the work. That's why changes can be requested in both the executing and the monitoring and controlling process groups. Change requests may also be generated in planning as a result of rolling wave planning that occurs after the plan has been approved and work has started. Change requests are evaluated and approved or rejected as part of the Perform Integrated Change Control process (see the Integration Management chapter).

- Do the project management process groups occur sequentially? No; they all overlap. For example, the project manager could be using monitoring and controlling processes to control the identification of stakeholders, the adherence to organizational requirements for project planning, or the creation of baselines and project documents. Defects could be identified in executing that will require work in executing to fix them, as well as work in monitoring and controlling to decide if the defects require a change to the plan to prevent future rework and delays. Controlling procurements and the final closure of procurements can occur simultaneously on projects because some sellers will complete their contractual obligations to the project while others are still producing deliverables.

How to Use the Rest of This Chapter

For many people, this is the hardest chapter in this book, and it uncovers the most gaps in their knowledge. If this chapter is difficult for you, trust us to help you; carefully follow along and try to complete each exercise. Then look for gaps in your knowledge. Do not simply skip to the answers.

The exercises in this chapter are extensive and are designed to help you explore what a project manager needs to do during each of the project management process groups. Take your time completing each exercise and reviewing the answers. Note your gaps on a separate sheet. Then spend some time making sure you research each knowledge gap as you read the rest of the book and clear it from your list.

Again, we encourage you to complete all exercises as they are intended to be completed. The exam includes common project management errors as choices and will focus on things most people don't know they should be doing. RMC has helped people all over the world find their knowledge gaps, and we have determined which gaps are most common. We then created exercises to fill those gaps. So, approach these exercises with the intent of discovering your personal gaps, and make sure you are thinking of a large, plan-driven project when you complete each exercise.

Also remember that you should read each chapter in this book more than once. When you go through this chapter the second time, focus on filling the gaps you discovered in the first pass through the chapter, rather than recreating the complete list for each exercise.

Initiating Process Group

The processes in the initiating process group formally start a new project or project phase. The initiating process group involves identifying and analyzing stakeholders to align their expectations about the project. It also provides a guiding vision for the project in terms of the organization's strategic objectives, the benefits the project will help achieve, the project's high-level scope, and any known constraints. The project is officially authorized through project initiating, and this process group provides the project manager with the authority and information necessary to begin the project. The project charter and the stakeholder register are the outputs of this process group.

Let's start by looking at the inputs to this process group. If you know what efforts are involved in project initiating (such as drafting the project charter and identifying and analyzing stakeholders), the inputs are easier to identify logically. To initiate a project, a project manager will need to know or have the following:

- The business case and the benefits management plan for the project
- The product description and requirements as they are known up to this point; in other words, what is the project supposed to do?
- How the project fits into or supports the company's strategic plan
- A list of likely stakeholders
- Any known constraints (such as imposed schedule, budget, or resources), risks, and assumptions

- Any relevant agreements, including contracts, if any of the work will be done under contract
- Industry standards
- Marketplace trends and legal, regulatory, or compliance factors
- The company's change control system
- Defined processes and procedures for how the company operates
- Relationships with the sponsor of the project, likely stakeholders, and possible team members
- Templates from past projects
- Historical WBSs
- Historical estimates
- Lessons learned from previous projects
- What is currently going on in the company, including major projects and the potential impact that current and planned initiatives could have on this project
- An understanding of the company's culture
- A list of people who may be good team members
- Information on organizational and project governance

Bear in mind that you don't need to memorize this list; instead, use it to improve your understanding of the initiating process. Compare these inputs to your real-world project management experiences, and make a note of anything that is different for further review.

Now let's turn to the first exercise, which reviews the processes that are included in the initiating process group.

Exercise

According to the *PMBOK® Guide*, what specific processes are part of project initiating?

Answer

The processes of project initiating that are covered in the *PMBOK® Guide* are:

- Develop Project Charter (Integration Management chapter)
- Identify Stakeholders (Stakeholder Management chapter)

Now let's move beyond the *PMBOK® Guide* to get a better understanding of the initiating process. The table below lists the actions required to complete project initiating, from the time the project manager is assigned. Remember that what needs to be done on a project varies based on the specific project, its life cycle, development approach, and the industry, so it may not be practical to do all of these actions on every project.

The purpose of this list of actions is to help you identify gaps in your knowledge where your project management experience differs from PMI's approach. As you read through this list, bear in mind that these actions are not listed in any particular order. Try not to lose focus, just spend about ten minutes thinking about these activities.

	Actions Involved in Project Initiating
1	Sponsor(s) selects the project manager.
2	Sponsor(s) determines the authority of the project manager.
3	Collect historical information.
4	Divide large projects into phases. Use project governance rules and apply them to the project.
5	Identify stakeholders, and determine their influence, expectations, and impact. Document that information in a stakeholder register.
6	Determine high-level requirements, constraints, assumptions, and risks.
7	Turn high-level stakeholder needs, wants, and expectations into requirements.
8	Make sure the business case and the analysis supporting the need for the project are documented and understood.
9	Use the benefits management plan to understand the benefits the project is expected to deliver to the business.
10	Ensure the high-level product scope is documented with as much detail as is practical.
11	Understand how the project supports the organization's strategic objectives.
12	Collect and use any relevant, existing agreements (including contracts) that might be generating the project or that will be required during the project.
13	Determine success criteria and measurable project and product objectives.
14	Facilitate the resolution of conflicting objectives.
15	Become familiar with the company culture and structure as they relate to the project.
16	Find existing processes, standards, and compliance requirements that affect the project.
17	Understand how the organization does business (business knowledge) and what governance, procedures, and policies are already in place to use on the project.
18	Do planning on a high-level basis.
19	Perform high-level estimating for the project schedule and budget.
20	Use the high-level planning and estimating data to determine whether the project objectives can be achieved within the given constraints and whether the expected benefits can be realized.
21	Determine what form the project charter will take, including its level of detail.
22	Coordinate project initiating efforts with stakeholders, including the customer.
23	Work with the customer and others to determine high-level acceptance criteria and clarify what is and what is not in the project.
24	Determine the initial project organization.
25	Identify any inherent or required milestones on the project.
26	Finalize the project charter.
27	Obtain formal approval of the project charter.
28	Define the exit criteria for the project (when and why the project or phase should be closed).
29	Involve subject matter experts in developing the project charter and identifying stakeholders.
30	Develop project documents such as the risk register, the stakeholder register, and the assumption log, including data on identified risks and stakeholders.
31	Use stakeholder mapping to analyze data on identified stakeholders to understand their power, interest, and influence.

The following are some points from the previous list of actions that could use further clarification.

Progressive Elaboration

You may notice that many of the items in the previous list (including estimates, product scope description, etc.) start in the initiating process group and then are iterated or refined into plans that can be used to manage the project. Although the project management plan is finalized in planning, items such as detailed estimates and project scope and product scope descriptions may be clarified as the work is being done during the executing and monitoring and controlling processes. The process of continually refining estimates and scope definition is called progressive elaboration.

Rolling Wave Planning

The technique of rolling wave planning is a form of progressive elaboration. The earliest parts of the project are planned in sufficient detail for work to begin. Later phases of project work are planned at a high level. As the project progresses, and more information impacting the work becomes available, plans are elaborated in sufficient detail to accomplish the work.

Project Manager Assigned

You should notice in the previous list that the project manager is assigned early in the process. This means the project manager is involved in project initiating. Is this true on your projects? For the exam, assume the project manager is involved this early in the project, and make sure you understand what is going on during initiating.

Business Documents

Imagine you're a project manager managing a project. Do you know why your project was selected? Does it matter? As noted in the discussion of Rita's Process Chart™, the project manager needs to keep in mind throughout the project the reason the project was started. It will influence how the project is planned, what changes are allowed, and how the project scope is defined. The business case and the benefits management plan are inputs to developing the charter. (See the Develop Project Charter discussion in the Integration Management chapter for more about the importance of project business documents.)

High-Level Planning Is Done during Project Initiating

The other important thing to notice in the previous exercise is that high-level planning is done during project initiating. Such planning may include creating a high-level WBS, performing order-of-magnitude estimating, and doing high-level risk identification. A project manager may use this information to determine whether the product of the project can be delivered by the end date and within the organization's established budget for the project. In other words, they need to assess whether the project has a chance of being successful before the organization commits money and resources to it. This high-level planning effort is part of creating the project charter, which documents measurable project objectives, success criteria, milestone schedules, and an initial budget for the project.

Figure 3.7 shows the reasons why project initiating is begun.

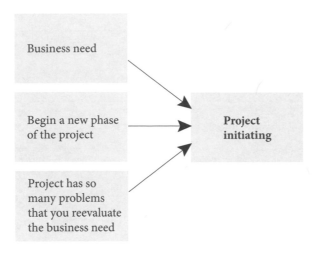

Figure 3.7 Reasons for entering project initiating

Planning Process Group

Imagine you are a project manager who has just completed a difficult project. If you could magically do your last project over again, how much better would it be? This is the power of planning. Project planning entails walking through the project using a consistent process, iterating plans, and getting the project organized in sufficient detail before actually doing the work to produce the product of the project. Planning efforts save resources, time, and money, and encourage increased stakeholder buy-in and commitment to the project.

In project planning, the project manager and the team perform a detailed analysis of whether the objectives in the project charter and the expected business benefits can be achieved. They then decide how the project objectives will be accomplished, addressing all appropriate project management processes and knowledge areas. This means determining what processes are appropriate for the needs of the project and tailoring them to the needs of the project.

Exercise

According to the *PMBOK® Guide*, what specific processes are part of project planning?

| |
| |
| |
| |
| |
| |
| |
| |
| |
| |

Project Management Processes

Answer

The processes of project planning that are covered in the *PMBOK® Guide* are:

- Develop Project Management Plan (Integration Management chapter)
- Plan Scope Management (Scope Management chapter)
- Collect Requirements (Scope Management chapter)
- Define Scope (Scope Management chapter)
- Create WBS (Scope Management chapter)
- Plan Schedule Management (Schedule Management chapter)
- Define Activities (Schedule Management chapter)
- Sequence Activities (Schedule Management chapter)
- Estimate Activity Durations (Schedule Management chapter)
- Develop Schedule (Schedule Management chapter)
- Plan Cost Management (Cost Management chapter)
- Estimate Costs (Cost Management chapter)
- Determine Budget (Cost Management chapter)
- Plan Quality Management (Quality Management chapter)
- Plan Resource Management (Resource Management chapter)
- Estimate Activity Resources (Resource Management chapter)
- Plan Communications Management (Communications Management chapter)
- Plan Risk Management (Risk Management chapter)
- Identify Risks (Risk Management chapter)
- Perform Qualitative Risk Analysis (Risk Management chapter)
- Perform Quantitative Risk Analysis (Risk Management chapter)
- Plan Risk Responses (Risk Management chapter)
- Plan Procurement Management (Procurement Management chapter)
- Plan Stakeholder Management (Stakeholder Management chapter)

Now let's move beyond the *PMBOK® Guide* to get a better understanding of the planning process. The table below lists the actions required to complete project planning. Review this list and try to identify any gaps in your knowledge compared to PMI's approach, bearing in mind that these actions are not listed in any particular order. Try not to lose focus, just spend about 15 minutes thinking about the activities on this list.

	Actions Involved in Project Planning
1	Determine how you will plan the planning, executing, and monitoring and controlling efforts for stakeholders, requirements, scope, schedule, cost, quality, resources, communications, risk, procurement, changes, and configuration, and put that information into the beginnings of management plans.
2	Refine the high-level requirements from project initiating so they are more specific and detailed, and look for additional requirements, being sure to consider any internal or external analysis, reports, or regulations; analyze and prioritize requirements.
3	Expand on the assumptions identified in project initiating, looking for new assumptions and documenting the details of the assumptions.
4	Refine the high-level constraints (such as resources, schedule, and cost) from project initiating so they are more specific and detailed.
5	Create a description of the project deliverables, the work required to complete those deliverables, and their acceptance criteria (project scope statement).
6	Use the project scope statement to gain approval of the "final" scope from stakeholders before further planning is done.
7	Assess what may need to be purchased on the project. Identify any pieces of work that may be outside the organization's abilities to complete, and determine if new equipment or technology is needed to perform the project work.
8	Select the procurement strategy for each contract. Create a draft of the procurement documents for necessary contracts, including bid documents, procurement statements of work, source selection criteria, and contract provisions.
9	Determine what subject matter experts you will need on the project team to help with project planning.
10	Break down the deliverables into smaller, more manageable pieces (WBS).
11	Create descriptions of each work package in a WBS dictionary so the work can be understood and produced without gold plating.
12	Break down the work packages from the WBS into lists of activities to produce them.
13	Sequence activities and determine predecessors and successors in the network diagram.
14	Estimate resource requirements (such as staff, facilities, equipment, and materials).
15	Meet with managers to gain resource commitments.
16	Decide what level of accuracy is needed for estimates.
17	Use historical data to support estimating time and cost.
18	Involve experts or those who will work on activities to estimate time and cost.
19	Determine how long the project will take without compressing the schedule (determine critical path).
20	Develop a schedule model, evaluate it against the schedule constraint in the project charter, and use schedule compression techniques to reconcile the two to come up with a final schedule for the project management plan.
21	Develop a preliminary budget and compare it to the budget constraint in the project charter. Then, develop options to reconcile the two to come up with the final budget for the project management plan.

	Actions Involved in Project Planning
22	Determine quality policies, practices, and standards, and then determine metrics to measure quality performance.
23	Determine processes to fulfill quality requirements and conform to organizational standards and policies.
24	Determine how you will improve the processes in use on the project.
25	Create a system for recognizing and rewarding the efforts of project team members to help keep them motivated and engaged in project efforts.
26	Plan for acquisition, team building, training, assessment, and release of team members. Plan for physical resources requirements, including acquisition and logistics.
27	Clearly determine all roles and responsibilities so team members and stakeholders know their roles on the project and what work they will need to do.
28	Work with the project team to develop a team charter defining their commitments and interactions with each other, including ground rules for meetings, conflict resolution processes, etc.
29	Determine what information you need from other projects and what information you will share with the organization and other projects.
30	Plan what will be communicated on the project, to whom, by whom, when, and how.
31	Plan how to involve stakeholders and manage their expectations during the project.
32	Complete detailed risk identification, subjectively analyze risks (qualitative risk analysis), perform quantitative risk analysis as necessary, and do risk response planning.
33	Iterations—go back and update project plans and documents as necessary to work toward a project management plan that is bought into, approved, realistic, and formal.
34	Finalize the procurement statement of work and other bid documents for each contract.
35	Look for potential positive and negative interactions with other projects that could affect the project.
36	Determine the processes that will be used to request, approve, and manage changes on the project.
37	Develop the configuration management plan, outlining naming conventions and processes for document versioning, storage, and retrieval.
38	Plan ways to measure project performance, including determining the measurements to be used, when they will be taken, and how the results will be evaluated.
39	Determine what meetings, reports, and other activities you will use to control the project to the project management plan.
40	Finalize the "execute" and "monitor and control" aspects of all management plans. Document closing requirements and actions.
41	Develop the final project management plan, project documents, and performance measurement baseline by performing schedule network analysis, looking for options, and confirming that project objectives can be met.
42	Gain formal approval of the project management plan from the sponsor, team, and managers of resources.
43	Hold a kickoff meeting with key stakeholders, team members, managers of team members, and the customer to make sure everyone is on the same page and gain buy-in.
44	Throughout the project, return to the planning processes to do rolling wave planning (progressive elaboration or iteration) as more information becomes available. Results will likely require change requests and updates to the project management plan and project documents.

Project planning is iterative. Each planning process may use the results of the previous processes, and each process may affect or cause changes to the previous processes. The idea, in the real world, is to attempt to complete each planning process as completely as possible. Then, after risk identification, qualitative and quantitative risk analysis, and risk response planning, the project manager goes back to finalize all the components of the project management plan and project documents. This approach to planning saves time and is efficient. It is only after risk management planning is completed that the final cost and schedule can be determined. Risk management could also result in iterations to the scope, the deliverables, the project resources (including when they are used), the sequence in which activities are performed, and almost all other parts of the project. The results of the planning effort are the project management plan and project documents that will guide the execution and control of the project.

Notice the references to management plans in the previous table. As described in chapter 1, management plans are a PMI-ism. Too often, project managers jump right into whatever they are doing without analyzing or planning. Such actions lead to inefficiencies, rework, mistakes, conflict, and needless overtime. Project managers are supposed to think about things before they do them. The exam assumes you are a project manager who takes a more formal approach that includes considering how you will do the work and documenting that information in a management plan.

There are many components to management plans, but generally they answer questions such as: "How will we go about planning scope, schedule, cost, etc.?" "How will we manage and monitor and control scope, schedule, cost, etc., now that we have planned what needs to be done?" "How will we perform the closing of project phases and the overall project?" The answers to these questions are determined as part of project planning. For clarity, the previous table groups management plans together instead of listing each management plan separately. It also accounts for the iterations of the management plans by separating them into the planning, executing, and monitoring and controlling parts of each plan. The individual management plans are combined into the overall project management plan. We will further discuss the project management plan and its components in the Integration Management chapter.

Another important concept to understand about planning is that the amount of time the team spends in project planning and the level of detail achieved in the plan should be appropriate to the needs of the project. The appropriate level of detail is dictated by the selected development approach and project governance. If a high-priority project has a tight schedule that does not allow much room for variance, the project will require more planning than a low-priority project with a fairly flexible schedule.

Some projects cannot be fully planned to a detailed degree prior to starting work. Often, such projects are organized by phases (such as test phase, install phase, etc.), or they use an adaptive life cycle approach. Using an adaptive life cycle, only the first part of the project may be fully planned, while the later pieces are planned at a higher level and then progressively elaborated when more is known about the project. Detailed planning for the next phase is done as the previous phase nears completion.

Everyone is involved in the planning processes. The project manager compiles the project management plan and project documents with input from stakeholders. The project manager may also use information gathered from resources such as historical records from previous projects, company policies, governance, regulatory and compliance policies and procedures, and other such sources to plan the project.

Figure 3.8 shows the reasons for entering project planning.

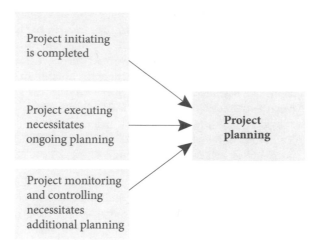

Figure 3.8 Reasons for entering project planning

For descriptions of each of the individual planning processes, see the rest of this book—particularly the Integration Management chapter, which discusses the development of the project management plan.

Executing Process Group

The purpose of project executing is to complete the project work as defined in the project management plan to meet the project objectives and achieve the expected business value. In other words, the goal is to produce the project deliverables within the project's planned budget and schedule to deliver the agreed-upon benefits. The focus is on leading and managing the project; that includes engaging stakeholders, working with the team to complete work, following processes, and communicating according to the plan. During executing, the project manager essentially has a guiding, proactive role, and uses the project management plan and project documents as reference points in managing the work.

Many project managers do not create management plans that include specific plans (for scope, schedule, cost, etc.) that are realistic and have the support of management. Without experience in using such a plan, they do not realize the value a project management plan can provide in properly managing and executing a project. They may find exam questions about executing with this type of project management plan to be extremely difficult because it is so different from their daily work practices.

Exercise

According to the *PMBOK® Guide*, what specific processes are part of project executing?

<table>
<tr><td></td></tr>
<tr><td></td></tr>
<tr><td></td></tr>
<tr><td></td></tr>
</table>

Answer

The processes of project executing that are covered in the *PMBOK® Guide* are:

- Direct and Manage Project Work (Integration Management chapter)
- Manage Project Knowledge (Integration Management chapter)
- Manage Quality (Quality Management chapter)
- Acquire Resources (Resource Management chapter)
- Develop Team (Resource Management chapter)
- Manage Team (Resource Management chapter)
- Manage Communications (Communications Management chapter)
- Implement Risk Responses (Risk Management chapter)
- Conduct Procurements (Procurement Management chapter)
- Manage Stakeholder Engagement (Stakeholder Management chapter)

Now let's move beyond the *PMBOK® Guide* to get a better understanding of the executing process. The table below lists the actions required to complete project executing. Review this list and try to identify any gaps in your knowledge compared to PMI's approach, bearing in mind that these actions are not listed in any particular order. Try not to lose focus, just spend about 15 minutes thinking about the activities on this list.

	Actions Involved in Project Executing
1	Communicate your expectations for stakeholders and the project, and manage the involvement and needs of all stakeholders throughout the project to ensure everyone has a common understanding of the work.
2	Implement the most up-to-date version of the project management plan, including revisions made as a result of control activities.
3	Complete work packages.
4	Collect, document, and share lessons learned.
5	Establish and manage communication channels.
6	Evaluate how effectively the team members function as a team.
7	Implement approved changes, including corrective actions, preventive actions, and defect repair.
8	Confirm that practices and procedures are being followed and are still appropriate for the project.
9	Produce and distribute reports on project performance.
10	Hold team-building activities.
11	Use the team charter for guidance on team interactions. Follow ground rules at team meetings.
12	Obtain needed training for team members.
13	Exchange information about the project according to the plan, and solicit feedback to ensure communication needs are being met.

	Actions Involved in Project Executing
14	Remove roadblocks.
15	Achieve work results that meet requirements.
16	Meet with managers to reconfirm resource commitments.
17	Keep managers apprised of when their resources will be needed on the project.
18	Commit, manage, and release physical and team resources in accordance with the project management plan.
19	Guide, assist, communicate, lead, negotiate, facilitate, and coach.
20	Use your technical knowledge.
21	Hold meetings to identify and address issues, assess risks, and keep the project work moving forward.
22	Manage stakeholder engagement and expectations, increase project support, and prevent possible problems.
23	Focus on preventing problems rather than just dealing with them as they arise.
24	Make sure all team members have the skills, information, and equipment needed to complete their work.
25	Look for exceptions to the approved project management plan in team members' performance, rather than checking up on every person's work.
26	Recommend changes to be evaluated in the Perform Integrated Change Control process.
27	Follow organizational policies, processes, and procedures.
28	Increase the effectiveness of processes.
29	Make updates to the project management plan and project documents to reflect current information about the project.
30	Create recommendations for the performing organization to increase its effectiveness.
31	Ensure continued agreement from the stakeholders to the project management plan.
32	Keep everyone focused on completing the project to the project charter and project management plan.
33	Keep the project's business case and benefits management plan in mind while managing the project, especially when problems occur.
34	Solve problems.
35	Determine where project changes are coming from and what you can do to eliminate the root cause of the need for change.
36	Determine final team members and other resources, and bring them onto the project as needed.
37	Recognize and reward the team and individuals for their work and performance on the project.
38	Gather initial measurements and details about activities of project work (work performance data).
39	Implement approved process improvements.
40	Use an issue log to record project issues and details about their resolution, including who is responsible for resolving each issue and the expected timeline.
41	Obtain seller responses to bid documents.
42	Review proposals, bids, and quotes; negotiate contract terms with prospective sellers; and manage the evaluation and selection of sellers.
43	Manage the integration of sellers' work and deliverables into the overall work and deliverables of the project; manage any seller-related conflicts or challenges.

© 2018 RMC Publications, Inc.™ • 952.846.4484 • info@rmcls.com • www.rmcls.com

	Actions Involved in Project Executing
44	Expend and manage project funds.
45	Facilitate conflict resolution using conflict resolution techniques.
46	Assess individual team member performance.
47	Update human resource records of team members to reflect new skills acquired while working on the project.
48	Carry out contingency plans in response to risk triggers.

Did you notice that "solve problems" is only one of 48 items on the list of actions to be done during project executing? Project managers should focus on preventing problems so they don't have to deal with them. With proper project management, problems occur less often, and should not have a major impact on the project. Assume that risk management efforts have identified and evaluated risks, and that contingency plans are in place to deal with risks that have high probability or impact ratings. Instead of handling risk events, a project manager can spend time engaging stakeholders and encouraging team members.

Also note that meetings are certainly part of executing a project, but many people don't realize that proper planning can decrease the number of needed meetings. If you were thinking about "go around the room and report what you have done" types of meetings, realize that status can also be collected through other means. Effective agile teams have focused daily stand-up meetings to keep the team on track to complete their commitments for the iteration. The occasions when the team gets together are too important to just focus on collecting status. How about reviewing risk triggers and upcoming contingency plans during meetings? Having too many meetings can cause a project manager to lose buy-in from their team if the team feels the project manager is wasting time.

The processes of project management are not always performed in the same sequence. Executing means working with the latest revision of the project management plan. In other words, the project manager is always executing according to the project management plan, but the plan might change over time. Figure 3.9 illustrates the reasons for entering project executing.

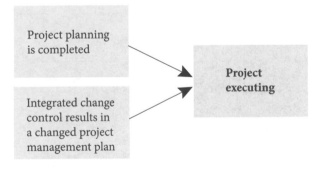

Figure 3.9 Reasons for entering project executing

Monitoring and Controlling Process Group

Many test takers who are new to the *PMBOK® Guide* find the concept of monitoring and controlling to be more difficult to understand than the other process groups. However, monitoring and controlling is an essential concept in PMI's approach to project management. So be sure to spend more time with this section, and pay special attention to the additional information we've included, as it will help you develop a better overall understanding of what "monitoring and controlling" is.

Project Management Processes

It's important to know that monitoring and controlling are combined into one process group, but each has a different focus. Monitoring requires the project manager to focus their attention on how the project is progressing. The project manager will need to assess how stakeholders are participating, communicating, and feeling about the project, the work, and the uncertainties that have been identified. Controlling requires evaluating hard data on how the project is conforming to the plan and taking action to address variances that are outside of acceptable limits. This is done by recommending changes to the way the work is being done, or possibly adjusting baselines to reflect more achievable outcomes. In this context, the term "changes" encompasses corrective and preventive actions and defect repair.

Did the above paragraph make sense to you? If not, go back and read through the paragraph again before moving on to the following exercise.

Exercise

According to the *PMBOK® Guide*, what specific processes are part of project monitoring and controlling?

Answer

The processes of project monitoring and controlling that are covered in the *PMBOK® Guide* are:

- Monitor and Control Project Work (Integration Management chapter)
- Perform Integrated Change Control (Integration Management chapter)
- Validate Scope (Scope Management chapter)
- Control Scope (Scope Management chapter)
- Control Schedule (Schedule Management chapter)
- Control Costs (Cost Management chapter)
- Control Quality (Quality Management chapter)
- Control Resources (Resource Management chapter)
- Monitor Communications (Communications Management chapter)
- Monitor Risks (Risk Management chapter)
- Control Procurements (Procurement Management chapter)
- Monitor Stakeholder Engagement (Stakeholder Management chapter)

Now let's move beyond the *PMBOK® Guide* to get a better understanding of the monitoring and controlling process. The table below lists the actions required to complete project monitoring and controlling. Review this list and try to identify any gaps in your knowledge compared to PMI's approach, bearing in mind that these actions are not listed in any particular order. Try not to lose focus, just spend about 15 minutes thinking about the activities on this list.

	Actions Involved in Project Monitoring and Controlling
1	Measure project performance according to the planned measures in the management plans.
2	Measure against the performance measurement baseline.
3	Analyze and evaluate work performance data.
4	Determine variances.
5	Use your judgment to determine what variances are important and if they warrant recommending a change or corrective action.
6	Recommend changes, including defect repair and preventive and corrective actions. Do not just wait for others to recommend them.
7	Make or obtain a decision in integrated change control about whether changes should be approved, rejected, or deferred.
8	Track and evaluate naming conventions, version control processes, the storage and retrieval system (configuration management), and the use of the PMIS. This ensures everyone knows which version of the project or product documentation is the latest version.
9	Control scope, schedule, and cost to their baselines.
10	Perform procurement inspections and reviews of seller performance to the contract.
11	Refine control limits as needed.
12	Identify the root causes of problems with the help of techniques such as process analysis (for example, Lean, Kanban, and Six Sigma).
13	Obtain formal acceptance of interim deliverables from the customer.
14	Identify the need for replanning.
15	Replan and make updates to the project management plan and project documents to reflect approved changes and updates to the project.
16	Evaluate stakeholder relationships and involvement to determine if they require improvement.
17	Manage the schedule and cost reserves.
18	Recalculate how much the project will cost and how long it will take, and create forecasts.
19	Obtain additional funding if needed.
20	Prepare work performance reports from the analyzed data and measurements.
21	Hold periodic quality inspections.
22	Make decisions to accept or reject completed deliverables.
23	Evaluate the effectiveness of implemented corrective actions.
24	Assess the effectiveness of project control systems.
25	Spend time trying to improve quality.
26	Determine if project controls need to be updated.
27	Identify and analyze trends.
28	Evaluate the effectiveness of risk responses in a risk review.
29	Look for newly arising risks.

	Actions Involved in Project Monitoring and Controlling
30	Reanalyze identified risks.
31	Use milestones as a project control tool.
32	Observe and analyze.
33	Use variance reports to help correct small problems before they become serious.
34	Calculate estimate to complete.
35	Use and interpret earned value calculations.
36	Use quality control tools such as inspections, histograms, performance reviews, and cause-and-effect diagrams.
37	Influence any factors that could result in the project's change control and configuration management measures being bypassed.
38	Control changes.
39	Control to make sure that only approved changes are implemented.
40	Work with the change control board.
41	Evaluate stakeholder satisfaction.
42	Control procurements through actions such as reviewing, approving, and paying invoices, administering claims, and performing inspections and audits.
43	Validate defect repair.
44	Determine where project changes are coming from and what you can do to eliminate the root cause of the need for change.
45	Consider the project's business case and the organization's strategic objectives when analyzing change requests.
46	Use active listening, inquiry, and data gathering to confirm that communications and stakeholder engagement efforts are effective and working as planned. Make or recommend needed adjustments.
47	Evaluate the use, cost, and other aspects of physical resources. Make appropriate changes and adjustments.
48	Close procurements after final deliverables are accepted.
49	Update the risk report to keep key stakeholders informed about the status of overall project risk and the highest-ranked individual risks.

Does this list of actions make sense? Take a moment to go back and look again at the above table, envisioning how each item is done in the real world. Spend some time on this list to make sure you have a solid understanding of the overall project management process as it relates to monitoring and controlling.

Not all monitoring and controlling efforts result in the discovery of variances that warrant preventive or corrective action, defect repair, or changes to the baselines or plan. When a project has been planned appropriately, most control efforts result in information that proves work is being done according to the plan and that scope is being produced to the agreed-upon standards and metrics. Results of measurements (whether positive or negative) and outcomes of other monitoring and controlling efforts are added to the project management plan and project documents as updates. In fact, updates to the project management plan and project documents are outputs of every monitoring and controlling process. Records of the work, measurements, and lessons learned are used for reference and comparison throughout the life of the project. In addition to identifying variances, measurements can be useful in trend analysis, forecasting, and estimating the remaining work.

Note: Because this is one of the most challenging process groups for many test takers, you should spend a considerable amount of time reviewing the following lists. Remember that monitoring and controlling is an essential concept in PMI's approach to project management. It is important to pay special attention to the additional information we've included here, as it will help you develop a better overall understanding of what "monitoring and controlling" is, as mentioned earlier in this section.

Control Scope
- Follow the change management plan.
- Measure scope performance against the performance measurement baseline.
- Influence the factors that cause changes.
- Control scope changes and the impacts of those changes.
- Analyze work performance data and variances.
- Request changes.
- Update the scope baseline, other parts of the project management plan, and requirements documentation with approved changes.
- Validate changes to make sure they do not over- or undercorrect problems.
- Document lessons learned.

Control Schedule
- Follow the change management plan.
- Measure schedule performance against the performance measurement baseline.
- Influence the factors that cause changes.
- Control schedule changes and the impacts of those changes.
- Analyze work performance data and variances.
- Request changes.
- Update the schedule baseline, other parts of the project management plan, and schedule-related documentation with approved changes.
- Document lessons learned.
- Manage the schedule reserve.
- Use earned value analysis to create schedule forecasts.
- Validate changes to make sure they do not over- or undercorrect problems.

Control Costs
- Follow the change management plan.
- Measure cost performance against the performance measurement baseline.
- Influence the factors that cause changes.
- Control cost changes and the impacts of those changes.
- Analyze work performance data and variances.
- Request changes.
- Update the cost baseline, other parts of the project management plan, and cost estimates.
- Document lessons learned.
- Manage the cost reserve.
- Use earned value analysis to recalculate the estimate at completion and other cost forecasts.
- Obtain additional funding when needed.
- Validate changes to make sure they do not over- or undercorrect problems.

Control Quality
- Hold periodic inspections.
- Ensure the deliverables are meeting the standards.
- Influence the factors that cause changes.
- Request changes or improvements to work and processes.
- Make decisions to accept or reject work.
- Assess the effectiveness of project quality control systems.
- Analyze work performance data and variances.
- Update the quality management plan, as well as quality- and process-related documentation.
- Validate changes to make sure they do not over- or undercorrect problems.
- Document lessons learned.

Control Resources
- Confirm that the type and quantity of resources used are consistent with what was planned.
- Evaluate the effectiveness of the physical resources.
- Analyze work performance data and variances.
- Request changes.
- Validate changes to make sure they do not over- or undercorrect problems.
- Update the resource management plan, as well as resource-related documentation.
- Document lessons learned.

Monitor Communications
- Ensure information is being communicated to the appropriate people in the right way and at the right time.
- Analyze work performance data and variances.
- Request changes.
- Analyze information about communications to make sure they are meeting stakeholder needs.
- Validate changes to make sure they do not over- or undercorrect problems.
- Document lessons learned.

Monitor Risks
- Reassess risks, planned risk responses, and risk reserves.
- Identify new risks.
- Watch for the occurrence of risk triggers.
- Create and implement workarounds.
- Perform risk audits to evaluate the effectiveness of risk management processes. Analyze work performance data, work performance reports, and variances.
- Request changes.
- Evaluate the effectiveness of implemented risk response plans.
- Document lessons learned.

Control Procurements
- Monitor performance to make sure both parties to the contract meet contractual obligations.
- Inspect and verify the contract deliverables.
- Protect your legal rights.
- Follow the defined procurement management procedures, including the contract change control system.
- Analyze work performance data, seller work performance reports, and variances.
- Request and manage changes.
- Authorize contract-related work.
- Issue and review claims.
- Maintain comprehensive records.
- Report on seller performance compared to the contract.

- Review invoices and make payments.
- Update the project management plan and procurement documentation.
- Validate contract changes, control contracts to updated versions, and evaluate effectiveness of changes.
- Document lessons learned.
- Close out contracts as final deliverables are completed and accepted.

Monitor Stakeholder Engagement
- Analyze work performance data and variances.
- Evaluate stakeholder engagement and stakeholder relationships, and look for opportunities for improvement.
- Assess whether stakeholders' expectations are aligned with the project.
- Resolve conflicts.
- Maintain an issue log.
- Request changes.
- Update the stakeholder management plan and stakeholder register.
- Document lessons learned.
- Validate success of changes to stakeholder engagement strategy.

Project management does not progress sequentially from initiating to planning to executing to monitoring and controlling to closing; the processes overlap. In fact, the project manager will do some level of monitoring and controlling throughout the project—from initiating to closing. Figure 3.10 illustrates key project outputs that trigger a focus on monitoring and controlling. It also shows that the project manager might go from monitoring and controlling to other process groups, depending on the needs of the project.

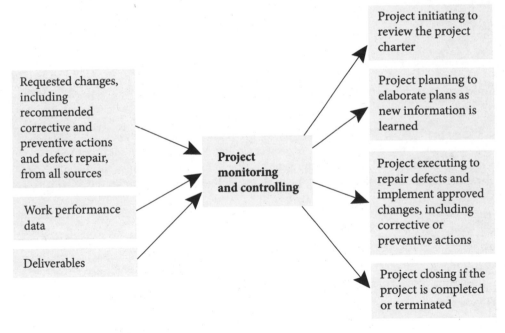

Figure 3.10 Key outputs that trigger project monitoring and controlling, and potential next steps

Closing Process Group

The project or phase is not over when the product scope is completed; there is one more process to be done—project closing, where the project is finished. The closing effort includes administrative activities such as collecting and finalizing all the paperwork needed to complete the project, and technical work to confirm that the final product of the project is acceptable. It will also include any work needed to transfer the completed project to those who will use it and solicit feedback from the customer about the product and the project.

In many real-world situations, projects never seem to officially finish. Sometimes the project manager gets pulled off a project to do other things. Sometimes work on the project just stops. Sometimes the project priority decreases. Because all projects are unique, there is no universal way in which a project officially ends; however, all projects must follow the closing process and complete the required closing activities.

The work done during closure is extremely important to the performing organization and to the customer. The exam asks questions in this area to see if you know what those valuable activities are and when a project is really finished.

Exercise

According to the *PMBOK® Guide*, what specific processes are part of project closing?

Answer

The processes of project closing that are covered in the *PMBOK® Guide* are:

- Close Project or Phase (Integration Management chapter)

Now let's move beyond the *PMBOK® Guide* to get a better understanding of the closing process. The table below lists the actions required to complete project closing. Review this list and try to identify any gaps in your knowledge compared to PMI's approach, bearing in mind that these actions are not listed in any particular order. Try not to lose focus, just spend about 5 minutes thinking about the activities on this list.

	Actions Involved in Project Closing
1	Confirm that all project requirements have been met.
2	Verify and document that the project or project phase meets completion or exit criteria set in place during project planning.
3	Obtain formal (legal) sign-off and final acceptance of the product of the project from the customer.
4	If any issues prevent final acceptance by the customer, negotiate a settlement or other resolution.
5	If the project was terminated before completion, document the reasons for termination and the status of the project and deliverables.
6	Make final payments, and complete cost records.
7	Gather final lessons learned and share with the organization.

	Actions Involved in Project Closing
8	Update project records.
9	Ensure all the project management processes are complete.
10	Update corporate processes, procedures, and templates based on lessons learned.
11	Complete project (or phase) closure.
12	Analyze and document the success and effectiveness of the project.
13	Create and distribute a final report of project (or phase) performance.
14	Index and archive project records.
15	Evaluate customer satisfaction regarding the project and the deliverables.
16	Hand off the completed project deliverables to the appropriate stakeholders (the customer, operations and maintenance, etc.).
17	Confirm all contracts have been formally closed; update and archive records.
18	Celebrate!

Because many organizations do not require formal closure procedures, let's take a moment to discuss some of the key actions listed in the previous table that many people miss.

Confirming that all the requirements have been met may seem unimportant; however, most studies show that many requirements are not met on projects, especially on projects with numerous pages of requirements. This confirmation needs to take place and can be done by reviewing the project management plan and accepted deliverables.

What about handing off the completed project deliverables to operations and maintenance? Work involved in completing such a transfer is considered part of the project. The work could include meetings to explain the project nuances, training, documentation for maintenance, and other activities as needed.

Now let's think about formal sign-off and acceptance. These are important because they confirm that the customer considers the project completed and accepts the whole project. Without that acceptance, the project manager cannot be sure the project was finished. Imagine that the team never gains formal acceptance on a project for an external customer, but moves on to other projects. Then the customer calls for additional scope to be added to the project. How difficult would it be to regroup the team to perform the work? Gaining formal acceptance helps ensure this won't be necessary.

Measuring customer satisfaction is another important part of project closing. It's highly beneficial for the project manager to solicit feedback from the customer about both the project and the product, and to evaluate the customer's satisfaction level during project closing. Just like lessons learned, measuring customer satisfaction should be ongoing throughout the project, but it must occur during project closing. The satisfaction level of stakeholders should also be assessed, and they should be asked for input to improve processes and procedures on future projects.

In the first chapter of this book, we noted that historical records are a PMI-ism. For the exam, make sure you understand the value of these records and the project manager's and team's responsibility for creating them. Historical information is collected throughout the project, but it is during project closing that the final versions of the lessons learned are compiled and archived in the lessons learned repository. In addition, project closing involves a concerted effort to index all files, letters, correspondence, and other records of the project into an organized archive that is stored for use on future projects.

Some project managers consider completing the final project performance report and holding an end-of-the-project celebration to be unimportant. But there is good reason for these activities, both of which recognize the team's efforts. The final report communicates to all stakeholders and the entire organization the benefits achieved by the team members' efforts on the project.

After the administrative pieces of project closure are completed and the customer, sponsor, and other stakeholders provide formal sign-off that the product of the project is acceptable, the project is closed. At that point, any team members utilized to close the project or project phase are released.

Figure 3.11 illustrates the reasons a project might enter the closing process group.

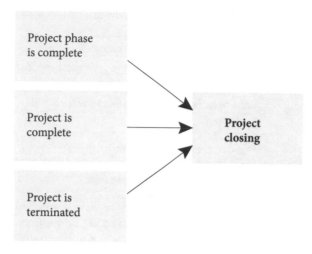

Figure 3.11 Reasons for entering project closing

Inputs and Outputs

Inputs and outputs are logical and should not require memorization if you have a good understanding of the actions involved in each of the knowledge area processes. Test your understanding by answering the following question: What is an input to a WBS? Make sure you read the Create WBS discussion carefully in the Scope Management chapter, and pay attention throughout this book to when and how a WBS is used.

Why worry about inputs and outputs? Here is a trick to help you gain confidence in your understanding of the project management processes.

An input means:

"What do I need before I can. . ."

An output means:

"What will I have when I am done with. . ."

Or, *"What am I trying to achieve when I am doing. . ."*

Project Management Processes Review

Exercise

During the CAPM exam, you'll have to answer questions about each of the project management processes. In this exercise, list which knowledge area processes are done in which project management process groups. The goal is to practice working with the processes and help identify your gaps.

Note: The Shuffle Game that follows offers another approach to this material. You can use either or both of these study tools, depending on your preference.

Initiating

Planning

Executing

Monitoring and Controlling
Closing

Answer   Here are the answers to the project management processes review exercise.

Initiating	
Develop Project Charter	Identify Stakeholders

Planning	
Develop Project Management Plan	Determine Budget
Plan Scope Management	Plan Quality Management
Collect Requirements	Plan Resource Management
Define Scope	Estimate Activity Resources
Create WBS	Plan Communications Management
Plan Schedule Management	Plan Risk Management
Define Activities	Identify Risks
Sequence Activities	Perform Qualitative Risk Analysis
Estimate Activity Durations	Perform Quantitative Risk Analysis
Develop Schedule	Plan Risk Responses
Plan Cost Management	Plan Procurement Management
Estimate Costs	Plan Stakeholder Engagement

Executing	
Direct and Manage Project Work	Manage Team
Manage Project Knowledge	Manage Communications
Manage Quality	Implement Risk Responses
Acquire Resources	Conduct Procurements
Develop Team	Manage Stakeholder Engagement

Monitoring and Controlling	
Monitor and Control Project Work	Control Quality
Perform Integrated Change Control	Control Resources
Validate Scope	Monitor Communications
Control Scope	Monitor Risks
Control Schedule	Control Procurements
Control Costs	Monitor Stakeholder Engagement

Closing	
Close Project or Phase	

Shuffle Game

Some people learn best by doing, which is why we have developed this alternate approach to reviewing integration management. To save you time, only the most important topics for the exam—those covered in this chapter—have been included.

Instructions

1. Cut out the cards on the next pages.
2. Lay out the bold title cards as column headers.
3. Shuffle the remaining cards and try to put them in the columns where they belong. Check your answers against the material covered in this chapter or the *PMBOK® Guide*, and make note of any gaps in your knowledge.

Note: Be sure to keep all cards for each chapter shuffle game as you will use them again for the final Shuffle Game in chapter 14.

Initiating	**Planning**	**Executing**
Monitoring and Controlling	**Closing**	Develop Project Charter
Identify Stakeholders	Develop Project Management Plan	Plan Scope Management
Collect Requirements	Define Scope	Create WBS
Plan Schedule Management	Define Activities	Sequence Activities

Estimate Activity Durations	Develop Schedule	Plan Cost Management
Estimate Costs	Determine Budget	Plan Quality Management
Plan Resource Management	Estimate Activity Resources	Plan Communications Management
Plan Risk Management	Identify Risks	Perform Qualitative Risk Analysis
Perform Quantitative Risk Analysis	Plan Risk Responses	Plan Procurement Management

Plan Stakeholder Engagement	Direct and Manage Project Work	Manage Project Knowledge
Manage Quality	Acquire Resources	Develop Team
Manage Team	Manage Communications	Implement Risk Responses
Conduct Procurements	Manage Stakeholder Engagement	Monitor and Control Project Work
Perform Integrated Change Control	Validate Scope	Control Scope

Control Schedule	Control Costs	Control Quality
Control Resources	Monitor Communications	Monitor Risks
Control Procurements	Monitor Stakeholder Engagement	Close Project or Phase

Practice Exam

1. During which process group is the project work as defined in the project management plan completed?
   A. Initiating
   B. Executing
   C. Monitoring and controlling
   D. Closing

2. Which of the following activities takes place in the initiating process group?
   A. Ensuring that the high-level product scope is as detailed as is practical
   B. Ensuring continued understanding of the work
   C. Removing roadblocks
   D. Reviewing bids and selecting sellers

3. Which of the following is the most appropriate thing to do in project closing?
   A. Work with the customer to determine acceptance criteria.
   B. Collect historical information from previous projects.
   C. Confirm that all the requirements in the project have been met.
   D. Gain formal approval of the management plans.

4. Which of the following activities takes place during project planning?
   A. Creating the WBS dictionary
   B. Determining high-level requirements
   C. Refining control limits
   D. Validating scope

5. In which process group does the project manager focus on managing the project, engaging stakeholders, and communicating according to plan, while the team is completing the project activities?
   A. Monitoring and controlling
   B. Managing
   C. Executing
   D. Planning

6. Which of the following is the most appropriate thing to do in the executing process group?
   A. Evaluate individual team member performance.
   B. Evaluate customer satisfaction regarding the project.
   C. Determine acceptance criteria.
   D. Decide what level of accuracy is required for estimates.

7. Which of the following statements about change-driven development life cycles is true?
   A. With an adaptive development life cycle, work is planned in long increments, which lessens the need to change and reprioritize customer requirements.
   B. Change-driven projects use waterfall life cycles.
   C. Adaptive development life cycles involve fixed costs as well as a fixed schedule.
   D. Scope, schedule, and cost are all well-defined early in a project using an adaptive development life cycle.

8. During which process group should a procurement strategy be selected for each project contract?
   A. Initiating
   B. Planning
   C. Executing
   D. Closing

9. Project closing includes all of the following except:
   A. Determining performance measures
   B. Handing off the product of the project to the customer
   C. Making final payments on contracts
   D. Updating the company's organizational process assets

10. What is the status of a project when the project team has completed all the required work packages and the final deliverables have been sent to the customer?
    A. The project is completed.
    B. The project is in the closing process.
    C. The project is at the end of project executing.
    D. The project is in the Validate Scope process.

11. During which process group does the Perform Integrated Change Control process take place?
    A. Planning
    B. Closing
    C. Monitoring and controlling
    D. Executing

12. Which of the following takes place during project monitoring and controlling?
    A. Performing procurement inspections
    B. Facilitating the resolution of conflicting objectives
    C. Expending and managing project funds
    D. Creating a recognition and rewards system

13. The _____ is the logical breakdown of what a project manager needs to do to produce the project's deliverables.
    A. Project life cycle
    B. Product life cycle
    C. Organizational structure
    D. Executing process group

14. During which process group does the Direct and Manage Project Work process take place?
    A. Planning
    B. Closing
    C. Monitoring and controlling
    D. Executing

15. In which process group does the project manager establish and manage communication channels?
    A. Planning
    B. Closing
    C. Monitoring and controlling
    D. Executing

Answers

1. **Answer** B
   Explanation Project executing involves completing the project work as defined in the project management plan—with the goal of meeting the project objectives and achieving the expected business value.

2. **Answer** A
   Explanation Ensuring that the product scope is documented with as much detail as possible is done in project initiating. Ensuring continued understanding of the work, removing roadblocks, and reviewing bids in order to select sellers are all activities that take place in project executing.

3. **Answer** C
   Explanation Confirming that project requirements have been met occurs in project closing. Collecting historical information and determining high-level acceptance criteria are done in project initiating, while gaining approval of management plans is part of project planning.

4. **Answer** A
   Explanation In project planning, the project team creates a WBS dictionary, which includes descriptions of each work package so that the project work can be understood and produced without gold plating. High-level requirements are determined in project initiating (and refined in project planning). Refining control limits and validating scope take place in project monitoring and controlling.

5. **Answer** C
   Explanation The purpose of project executing is to complete the project work, and it is in this process group that the project manager is focused on managing the project, engaging stakeholders, and communicating according to plan.

6. **Answer** A
   Explanation Evaluating team member performance is done in the executing process group, as part of the Manage Team process. Evaluating customer satisfaction regarding the project is part of project closing. Determining high-level acceptance criteria occurs in project initiating. Establishing the required level of accuracy for estimates takes place in project planning.

7. **Answer** C
   Explanation Adaptive (also called agile) development life cycles involve fixed costs as well as a fixed schedule; however, on these types of projects, scope is typically only broadly defined early in the project and then refined over the course of the project. Change-driven projects use iterative, incremental, or adaptive development life cycles; waterfall life cycles are used in plan-driven projects. With adaptive life cycles, work is planned in short increments, which allows the customer to change and reprioritize requirements (within the project's time and cost constraints).

8. **Answer** B
   Explanation During project planning, a procurement strategy is selected for each required contract. Planning also involves creating draft procurement documents for each contract.

9. **Answer** A
   Explanation Handing off the product of the project to the customer, making final payments on contracts, and updating the company's organizational process assets all take place during project closing. Performance measures are determined early in the project—during project planning—so they can be used to measure progress during the project.

10. **Answer** B
    Explanation The project is not yet completed because formal acceptance has not been achieved, and the other activities in the Close Project or Phase process have not been performed. A project cannot be closed without getting customer acceptance of the deliverables.

11. **Answer** C
    Explanation The Perform Integrated Change Control process is performed during project monitoring and controlling.

12. **Answer** A
    Explanation Facilitating the resolution of conflicting objectives is part of project initiating. Expending funds is primarily done during project executing. A recognition and rewards system should be created during project planning, and procurement inspections are done during project monitoring and controlling.

13. **Answer** A
    Explanation The project life cycle provides the framework for managing a project, and it is the logical breakdown of what the project manager will need to produce the required deliverables on a project.

14. **Answer** D
    Explanation The Direct and Manage Project Work process is part of the executing process group.

15. **Answer** D
    Explanation Establishing and managing communication channels is done in project executing.

Integration Management

There are 13 to 14 questions on this knowledge area on the CAPM exam.
Also note, for a full list of all inputs, tools and techniques, and outputs within
this knowledge area, please see the table on page 71 in the PMBOK© *Guide.*

How would you respond if you were asked, "What is a project manager's primary role?" The correct answer is: to perform integration management—to pull all the pieces of a project together into a cohesive whole. This is so much a part of a project manager's job that it is arguably the reason for the project manager's existence in an organization and on a project.

While the work of the project is being done, the team members are concentrating on completing the work packages, and the project sponsor is protecting the project from changes and loss of resources. The project manager is responsible for integration—putting all the pieces of the project together into one cohesive whole that gets the project done faster, cheaper, and with fewer resources, while meeting the project objectives.

QUICKTEST

- Integration management process
- Integrated change control
- Process for making changes
- Project management plan
  - Knowledge area management plans
  - Baselines
  - Requirements management plan
  - Change management plan
  - Configuration management plan
- Project charter
- Assumption log
- Business documents
- Project documents
- Change requests
- Configuration management system
- Change control system
- Knowledge management
- Information management
- Change control board
- Corrective action
- Preventive action
- Defect repair
- Lessons learned register

TRICKS OF THE TRADE® Think about integration as balancing all the processes in all the knowledge areas (scope, schedule, cost, quality, resources, communications, risk, procurement, and stakeholder management) with each other. Project management processes don't happen independently. To complete a cost estimate, for example, factors should be taken into account such as the number of resources on the project, the scope being estimated, and the risk reserves. As another example, adding a new resource to the project may require cost or schedule changes. In dealing with each situation that develops during a project, the project manager is integrating the processes of project management.

The other knowledge area chapters in this book explain the detailed work of a project manager. This chapter, however, is about the high-level work a project manager needs to do. Read this chapter carefully; integration management is a difficult area on the exam.

Integration Management

The following should help you understand how each part of integration management fits into the overall project management process:

The Integration Management Process	Done During
Develop Project Charter	Initiating process group
Develop Project Management Plan	Planning process group
Direct and Manage Project Work	Executing process group
Manage Project Knowledge	Executing process group
Monitor and Control Project Work	Monitoring and controlling process group
Perform Integrated Change Control	Monitoring and controlling process group
Close Project or Phase	Closing process group

Integration management cannot be understood without a solid understanding of the process of project management, as well as the relationships between process groups and knowledge areas. Therefore, if you have limited project management training or experience, you might want to do a high-level review of this chapter now, read the rest of this book, and then come back and read this chapter again. It will make more sense the second time. Remember that integration management is the primary role of the project manager.

Figure 4.1 shows the relationship between the knowledge areas and process groups. All knowledge areas include processes that occur in planning and monitoring and controlling. Integration management is the only knowledge area that has processes occurring in all process groups, throughout the project management process. The project manager is always integrating.

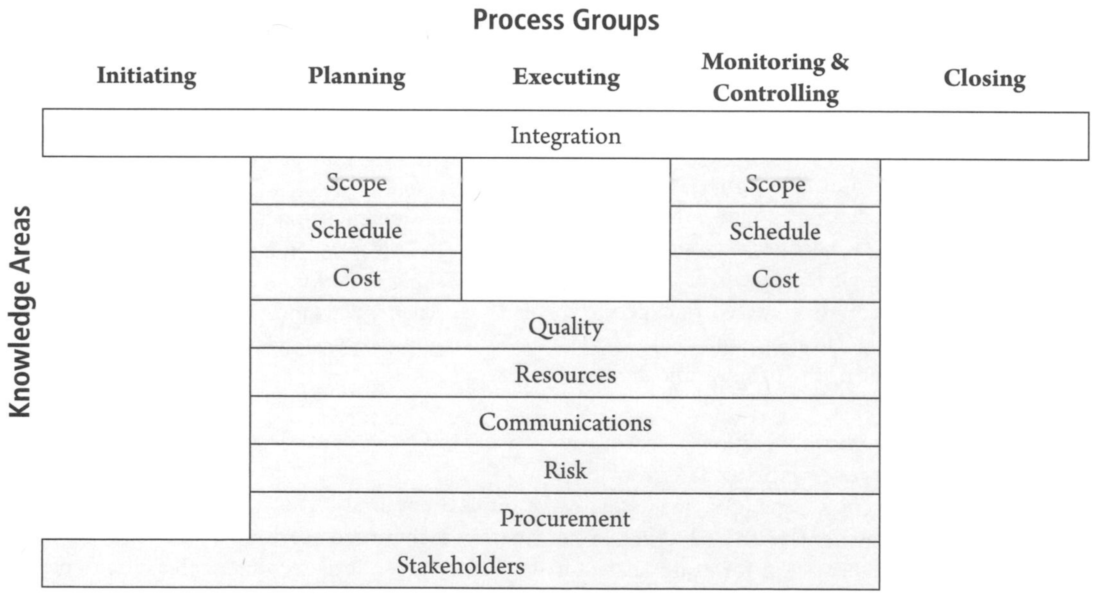

Process Groups

	Initiating	Planning	Executing	Monitoring & Controlling	Closing
Knowledge Areas					

Integration

	Scope		Scope	
	Schedule		Schedule	
	Cost		Cost	

Quality

Resources

Communications

Risk

Procurement

Stakeholders

Figure 4.1 The relationship between the knowledge areas and process groups

Make sure you fully understand the integration management process for the exam. In particular, remember that according to PMI the project manager's role is to manage the project, not to perform project work.

Next, we will go through the processes in this knowledge area, discussing the key elements you need to understand for the exam. In this book, we will not cover every topic that's listed in the *PMBOK® Guide*;

instead we will focus on the most important information you need to know, as well as the topics that tend to be more difficult for most people. This means you will need to read each chapter of the *PMBOK® Guide* and review the material covered in that book to make certain you don't miss anything.

Develop Project Charter PAGE 75

> **Process:** Develop Project Charter
> **Process Group:** Initiating
> **Knowledge Area:** Integration Management

The first part of integration management is developing a project charter. For the exam, you should understand what a project charter is, why it's important, and how it's used throughout the life of a project. Let's start by looking at what is included in a project charter. Although charters vary in length and level of detail, a typical charter might include the following sections:

- **Project title and description:** What is the project, and what will we call it?
- **Project manager assigned and authority level:** Who is given authority to lead the project? Can this person determine, manage, and approve changes to the budget, schedule, and team assignments?
- **Business case:** What is the purpose of this project? Why is it being done? On what financial or other basis can we justify doing this project?
- **Resources preassigned:** How many or which resources will be provided?
- **Key stakeholder list:** Who will affect or be affected by the project, as known to date?
- **Stakeholder requirements as known:** What are the requirements related to both the project and the product scope?
- **High-level product description/key deliverables:** What are the key product deliverables that are wanted, and what will be the end result of the project?
- **High-level assumptions:** What is believed to be true or reliable in this situation? What do we believe to be the case but do not have proof or data for?
- **High-level constraints:** What factors may limit our ability to deliver? What boundaries or parameters will the project have to function within?
- **Measurable project objectives:** How does the project tie into the organization's strategic goals? What project objectives support those goals? The objectives must be measurable and will depend on the defined priority of the project constraints.
- **Project approval requirements:** What items need to be approved for the project, and who will have sign-off authority? What designates success?
- **Overall project risks:** What are the overall potential threats and opportunities for the project?
- **Project exit criteria:** What needs must be met so that the project manager will be able to close or terminate the project or phase?
- **Project sponsors authorizing this project:** Who is approving this project to proceed?

The CAPM exam will expect you to understand the elements of a project charter in a general way, as outlined here. For example, notice that the charter includes the project's business case and its approval requirements, measurable objectives, and overall risks. Although some companies do expect a project charter to include information such as a detailed schedule and a full risk analysis, that level of detail is not available at this point in the project.

If your organization defines a project charter differently than PMI, remember for the exam that the project charter is not a project management plan. Creating the project charter involves planning the project at a high level to assess whether it's feasible within the given constraints, but detailed planning doesn't happen until after the charter is signed. In project initiating, the project manager may meet with key stakeholders and define the high-level objectives, constraints, requirements, scope, risks, and assumptions in an effort to assess the feasibility of the project. Much of this information will also be used for benefits analysis, in which the project manager and key stakeholders confirm that the project aligns with the organization's strategic goals and is likely to deliver the anticipated value. Detailed planning takes time and costs money, and this time and money should not be spent until the project is officially authorized by approval of the project charter.

Constraints and Assumptions
A quick note about constraints and assumptions. Constraints are factors—such as limits on resources, budget, schedule, and scope—that limit the team's options. (For example, management saying the project must be completed with only five resources.) Assumptions are things that are assumed to be true but that may not be true. (For example, "It is assumed that we will not need engineering department approval before we start the activity.") Both are identified at a high level in project initiating and then refined and documented in detail as part of the Define Scope process in project planning.

Once they are identified, constraints and assumptions need to be managed. The sponsor, the team, and other stakeholders may help identify constraints and assumptions and review them for validity throughout the life of the project. If the constraints change or the assumptions are proven wrong, the project management plan may need to change.

Inputs to Develop Project Charter PAGE 77
The following are the inputs to the Develop Project Charter process.

Business Documents
Business documents—including the business case and the benefits management plan—are key inputs to the development of the project charter. They provide critical information to the project manager and team, such as:

- Why the project was undertaken
- A summary of the relationship between the project objectives and the strategic goals of the organization

Business Case
The exam assumes that every project has a defined business case and that it is unacceptable to select a project based on anything but a sound business case. The business case captures the business need; it explains why the project was selected, how it fits into the organization's strategic goals, and how it will bring business value to the organization. (How each organization defines business value will vary, but such a definition could include quantifiable benefits, such as financial gain, as well as less obvious benefits, such as increased name recognition.)

Benefits Management Plan
The benefits management plan is a document that captures the organization's desired benefits from a project, whether economic or intangible, and explains how those benefits will be maximized and sustained. It also defines metrics and processes for measuring a project's benefits. As an input to the charter, the benefits management plan is important, as it provides information to be used to determine whether a project's deliverables will help the organization in meeting its strategic goals and objectives.

Agreements/Contracts
All projects should have charters, whether the project is an internal initiative or is being done for an external customer. The development of a charter often starts with some form of agreement or understanding. In the case of an internal project, the initial agreement may be as informal as an email or a conversation about what the project will entail. It could also take the form of a memorandum

of understanding or a letter of agreement. When the work is being done for an outside organization, a formal contract is typically involved. (See the Procurement Management chapter for more information about agreements and contracts.)

Enterprise Environmental Factors　　In the Develop Project Charter process, the relevant enterprise environmental factors may include the way the company is organized (organizational culture and political climate, for example). They may also include external factors such as government or industry standards, any legal and regulatory requirements, and marketplace conditions that could affect the product of the project.

Organizational Process Assets　　In the Develop Project Charter process, the relevant organizational process assets may include the organization's standard processes and policies, as well as templates, monitoring and reporting methods, historical information, and lessons learned from previous projects.

Tools and Techniques of Develop Project Charter PAGE 79

A project manager is expected to use their own expertise throughout the project, but they will also need to seek the advice or opinions of others who have specialized knowledge and experience. The project stakeholders, including the customer or sponsor, may be a source of such expertise, as well as others within the organization, such as the project management office (PMO), other departments, and other project managers. Other sources of expert judgment include outside experts uch as consultants and industry and professional organizations. Note that this all falls under the category of expert judgment.

Other tools and techniques that can be used during this process include data gathering (interviews, brainstorming, focus groups, etc.), interpersonal and team skills (conflict management, facilitation, meeting management, etc.), and meetings. During meetings with the sponsor and key stakeholders, the project manager can obtain needed information and work with experts to understand and address organizational strategy and develop measurable project objectives.

Outputs of Develop Project Charter PAGE 81

The results (or outputs) of the Develop Project Charter process are the project charter and the assumption log.

Project Charter　　The project charter is such an important document that a project cannot be started without it. The project charter is the project manager's target for the project and serves as a definition of how success will be measured. Without a project charter, the project and project manager cannot be successful.

The project manager may create the project charter, but it is issued (signed off on) by the sponsor as part of project initiating. The project charter should be broad enough that it doesn't need to change as the project progresses. (Any change to the project charter should call into question whether the project should continue.) It provides, at a minimum, the following benefits:

- The project charter formally recognizes (authorizes) the existence of the project, or establishes the project. This means that a project does not exist without a project charter.
- The project charter clarifies and encourages an understanding between the sponsor and project manager about the major deliverables and milestones. It also defines the key roles and responsibilities on the project.
- The project charter gives the project manager authority to spend money.
- The project charter gives the project manager authority to commit corporate resources to the project.
- The project charter provides the objectives, high-level requirements, and success criteria for the project.

- The process of creating the charter uncovers assumptions about the project, which the project manager may address at a later time.
- The project charter links the project to the strategic objectives and ongoing work of the organization.

Can you see that the creation of a project charter influences all the project management knowledge areas—scope, schedule, cost, quality, resources, communications, risk, procurement, and stakeholder management)?

Assumption Log The other output of the Develop Project Charter process is the assumption log, which contains a list of all assumptions and constraints that relate to the project. (Some project managers also include initial assumptions and constraints in the project charter.) The assumption log is typically added to during planning and updated throughout the project as assumptions and constraints change and new assumptions are uncovered.

Develop Project Management Plan PAGE 82

> **Process:** Develop Project Management Plan
> **Process Group:** Planning
> **Knowledge Area:** Integration Management

Project managers must plan before they act. The Develop Project Management Plan process involves creating a project management plan that is bought into, approved, realistic, and formal. In other words, the project management plan needs to be agreed to, it needs to be approved, everyone needs to believe it can be done according to plan, and it needs to be a formal document that is used and updated throughout the project.

If this is a new concept for you, think about how such a plan could be accomplished in the real world and what a plan like that would have to include. Then complete the following exercise.

Exercise   What should be described in the project management plan?

Answer This will be explained in more detail later in this section, but the project management plan should include information about the following:

- The project life cycle, including the phases of work required to produce deliverables
- The development approach that will be used throughout the life of the project (these approaches range from plan driven to change driven)
- How work will be performed throughout the life of the project
- How project performance will be monitored and controlled to the baselines
- Management reviews and any milestones built into the project management plan to indicate when project progress will be compared to what was planned
- Plans for managing changes, requirements, and configurations
- The project management processes that will be used on the project
- Baselines (performance measurement baseline)

Let's look at what management plans are, and then move on to discuss the output of the Develop Project Management Plan process.

Management Plans

For the exam, it's important to understand the concept of management plans. Management plans document the strategy and approach for managing the project and the processes related to the knowledge areas of scope, schedule, cost, quality, resources, communications, risk, procurement, and stakeholder management. This means there is a management plan for each knowledge area. These plans are, in essence, a set of documents with processes, procedures, practices, and standards the team will follow to ensure consistent results.

When creating a management plan, a project manager should pose the question, "How will I define, plan, manage (execute), and control scope (or schedule, cost, quality, etc.) for the project?" They should think ahead, and document how they will plan for each knowledge area (and ultimately the project) based on its particular needs, how they will manage each knowledge area during executing, and how they will monitor and control each knowledge area. This effort should cover all aspects of the project management process. A project manager will also need to think about who is involved in the project and how they will manage those people, evaluate their work, and keep them engaged. Management plans are, of necessity, unique to each project to address the project's particular needs. The format and level of detail of a management plan should be customized to fit the needs of the project, the style of the project manager, and the organizational influences.

Let's consider an example of how a project manager would address planning, executing, and monitoring and controlling cost management. The planning portion of a management plan is where a project manager defines the processes and procedures that will be followed when they are completing planning for a knowledge area. In our cost example, we need to address questions such as: How will we make sure all costs are identified and estimated? Who will be involved in estimating costs? What methods of estimating costs will we use? What historical records, processes, and organizational requirements will need to be used or met? What estimating tools and techniques will we employ? What level of accuracy is appropriate? How will funding and cost constraints be considered when establishing the budget? What data, metrics, and measurements do we need for planning cost?

The executing portion of a management plan focuses on the processes and procedures for doing the work. (Note that some knowledge areas, such as cost management, don't have separate executing processes; in such a case, the work performance data related to the knowledge area is gathered as part of Direct and Manage Project Work and must still be planned for.) The executing component of a cost management plan answers questions such as: What cost data is needed? Who is responsible for gathering it? Where will we capture the raw data that will later be used in monitoring and controlling?

The monitoring and controlling component of a management plan defines the processes and procedures that will be used to measure project progress, compare actual project results to what was planned, and determine how to handle variances that require a change.

 Here's a trick to understanding the topic of management plans for the exam. Know that management plans look forward in time and that there are management plans for all the knowledge areas. There are also the following management plans:

- Change management plan
- Configuration management plan
- Requirements management plan

Output of Develop Project Management Plan PAGE 86
The output of the Develop Project Management Plan process is the project management plan.

Project Management Plan
What do you currently think of as a project management plan or project plan? If you think of such a plan as just a schedule, then it's time to significantly expand your understanding of this concept.

The project management plan integrates all the individual management plans into a cohesive whole, creating a centralized document to describe what is involved in the project. The overall project management plan also includes the baselines for the project, which means a project management plan is a set of plans and baselines (not just a schedule). The key components of the project management plan are discussed in the following sections.

Project Life Cycle
The project life cycle describes the phases of work on a project required to produce the deliverables—for example, these phases might be "requirements, design, code, test, implement."

Development Approach
Development approaches to produce the project deliverables range from plan driven to change driven.

Management Reviews
Milestones will be built into the project management plan, indicating times when management and stakeholders will compare project progress to what was planned and identify needed changes to any of the management plans.

Project Management Processes That Will Be Used on the Project
Think about the science of project management for a moment. Would you want to use everything in the *PMBOK® Guide* to the same extent on every project? No! A project manager should determine the extent to which processes need to be used, based on the needs of the project. Tailoring the process to be followed is part of developing the project management plan.

Knowledge Area Management Plans
These are the management plans for scope, schedule, cost, quality, resources, communications, risk, procurement, and stakeholder management. The individual management plans are discussed in more detail in chapters 5 through 13 of this book.

For the CAPM exam, expect to see high-level questions about all the management plans listed above. As you read their descriptions throughout this book, don't try to memorize every detail of these plans. Instead, aim for a good general understanding that will enable you to use logic to answer the exam questions.

Baselines (Performance Measurement Baseline)   The project management plan includes scope, schedule, and cost baselines, against which the project manager will report project performance. These baselines are created during planning. They are a record of what the project manager had planned, scheduled, and budgeted for in terms of scope, schedule, and cost performance, and are used to compare the project's actual performance against planned performance. The following are the elements included in each baseline:

- **Scope baseline**   The project scope statement, work breakdown structure (WBS), and WBS dictionary
- **Schedule baseline**   The agreed-upon schedule, including the start and stop dates for each activity, and scheduled milestones
- **Cost baseline**   The time-phased cost budget—the spending plan indicating how much money is approved for the project and when the funds are required and will be available

Together these baselines are called the performance measurement baseline.

What do baselines mean for the project manager and team? The project manager must be able to clearly, completely, and realistically define scope, schedule, and cost to develop the baselines. That's not all, however. The project performance, and the performance of the project manager, will be measured against the baselines. The project manager and team will monitor and control for deviations from the baselines while the work is being done. If a deviation is discovered, they will assess whether adjustments can be made to the project to deal with the problem. These adjustments might involve submitting a change request for corrective or preventive action or defect repair. Depending on the extent and type of action required, the baselines themselves do not always change. If minor adjustments will not correct the deviation, however, a request to change the baselines might be necessary. A substantial part of project monitoring and controlling is making sure the baselines are achieved, which in turn helps ensure that the sponsor and the organization get the complete benefits of the project they chartered.

Baselines can be changed, but it should not be an easy thing to do. Requested changes to the baselines are evaluated and approved in the Perform Integrated Change Control process. Baseline changes are so serious that the evolution of the baselines should be documented to show why and when changes were made.

Requirements Management Plan   Part of the scope management process (which is described in the next chapter) involves defining and planning for stakeholders' needs, wants, expectations, and assumptions to determine the requirements for the project. The requirements management plan defines how requirements will be gathered, analyzed, prioritized, evaluated, and documented, as well as how the requirements will be managed and controlled throughout the project.

Change Management Plan   Controlling a project to the baselines and the rest of the project management plan is so important that a project manager needs to think in advance about where there might be changes and what to do to limit the negative effects of changes. Regardless of how small or large the project is, the project manager's role is not to just facilitate changes. Instead, they need to plan the project in a way that minimizes the need for changes and prevents unnecessary changes. The project manager will also need to proactively look for needed changes, thereby solving problems before they have a negative impact on the project. Because making changes is much more costly than including the work from the beginning, changes should not be undertaken lightly.

The change management plan describes how changes will be managed and controlled, and may include:

- Change control procedures (who and how)
- The approval levels for authorizing changes
- The creation of a change control board to approve changes, as well as the roles and responsibilities of those on the board (The change control board is described later in this chapter.)
- A plan outlining how changes will be managed and controlled
- Who should attend meetings regarding changes

- The organizational tools to use to track and control changes
- Information on reporting the outcome of change requests
- The emergency change process

Note that a change management plan will often have a separate process for addressing each of the knowledge areas, taking into account the specific needs within each knowledge area.

 Although the change management plan (as well as the configuration management plan, both described below) will not be addressed in the other chapters of this book, be sure that you understand these concepts and are prepared for questions about them on the exam..

Configuration Management Plan   With all the product and project documentation that is part of managing a project and all the changes to this documentation that will occur throughout the life of the project, it's essential to have a plan for making sure everyone knows what version of the scope, schedule, and other components of the project management plan is the latest version. This is the purpose of the configuration management plan. It defines the naming conventions, the version control system, and the document storage and retrieval system, and it details how you will manage the changes to the documentation, including which organizational tools you will use in this effort.

Related Systems   There are two systems that may relate to components of the project management plan.

Change Control System   Many organizations have a change control system as part of their project management information system (PMIS). This system includes standardized forms, reports, processes, procedures, and software to track and control changes. It is part of an organization's enterprise environmental factors.

Configuration Management System   Like the change control system, the configuration management system is part of the project management information system (PMIS). It contains the organization's standardized configuration management tools, processes, and procedures that are used to track and control the evolution of the project documentation.

Putting the Project Management Plan Together   The project management plan, including the individual management plans and the scope, schedule, and cost baselines, is created by completing the activities described in the Planning column of Rita's Process Chart™. Once the project management plan is complete, the sponsor or key stakeholders review and approve it. The Develop Project Management Plan process must result in a project management plan that is bought into, approved, realistic, and formal. In other words, the project management plan needs to be agreed to by those involved in the project, it needs to be formally approved, everyone needs to believe the project can be done according to the plan, and it needs to remain a formal document that is controlled and used throughout the project. If this is a new concept to you, make sure you spend time thinking about how to accomplish this in the real world.

Let's see how everything connects so far by looking at figure 4.2.

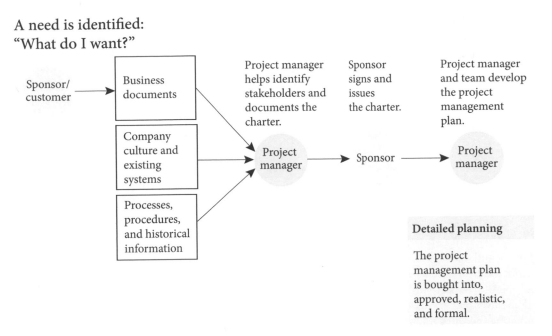

A need is identified:
"What do I want?"

Figure 4.2 Project initiating and planning

Once the project management plan has been completed, the project manager uses it as a tool to help manage the project on a daily basis. It is not just a document created for the sponsor and other key stakeholders. Although it may evolve over the life of the project through progressive elaboration or approved changes, the project management plan is designed to be as complete as possible when project executing begins.

Project Documents

A lot of information needs to be captured on a project, and not all of that information is recorded in the project management plan. The *PMBOK® Guide* uses the term "project documents" to refer to any project-related documents that are not part of the project management plan. They include the assumption and issue logs, cost and duration estimates, lessons learned register, project schedule, resource calendars, quality reports, resource requirements, requirements documentation, and other such documentation. (See page 89 in the *PMBOK® Guide* for a longer list of examples.) While the sponsor and key stakeholders will see and approve the project management plan, most project documents (excluding some documents such as the charter, agreements, contracts, and statements of work) are created by the project manager for use on the project and typically are not shown to or approved by the sponsor.

Due to the iterative nature of planning and the nature of the work throughout the rest of the project, project documents must be updated frequently. For the exam, know that project documents updates are an output of many of the project management processes, though this book will not cover these updates as an output of every process.

Project Management Plan Approval

Since the project management plan is a formal document that defines how the project will be managed, executed, and controlled and includes items such as the project completion date, milestones, and costs, etc., it typically requires formal approval by management, the sponsor, the project team, and other key stakeholders. Formal approval means sign-off (signatures). If the project manager has identified all stakeholders and their requirements and objectives, included the appropriate project and product scope in the plan, and dealt with conflicting priorities in advance, getting the project management plan approved should be relatively straightforward.

Kickoff Meeting

Before the Develop Project Management Plan process can be completed and project executing can begin, a kickoff meeting should be held. This is a meeting of the key parties involved in the project (customers, sellers, the project team, senior management, functional management, and the sponsor). The purpose of this meeting is to announce the start of the project, to ensure everyone is familiar with its details—including the project objectives and stakeholders' roles and responsibilities—and to ensure a commitment to the project from everyone. In other words, the meeting is held to make sure everyone is on the same page. In addition to introducing those involved in the project, the meeting may review such items as project milestones, project risks, the communications management plan, and the meeting schedule.

Direct and Manage Project Work PAGE 90

> **Process:** Direct & Manage Project Work
> **Process Group:** Executing
> **Knowledge Area:** Integration Management

This process represents the integration aspect of project executing.
In Direct and Manage Project Work, the project manager integrates all the executing work into one coordinated effort to accomplish the project management plan and produce the deliverables. In addition to completing the activities and deliverables in the project management plan, Direct and Manage Project Work involves gathering work performance data, creating and using the issue log, requesting changes, and completing the work resulting from approved change requests.

The Direct and Manage Project Work process involves managing people and keeping them engaged in the project, doing the work, finding ways to work more efficiently, requesting changes, and implementing approved changes. It is about being of service to the team to help them get the work completed, ensuring a common understanding of the project among stakeholders, and keeping everyone focused and informed by documenting and facilitating the resolution of issues. In other words, the project manager needs to do things such as facilitate meetings and technical discussions, make sure the stakeholders whose scope was not included in the project understand they will not receive that scope, use the work authorization system to keep the team and functional managers informed of upcoming work assignments and milestones, help remove roadblocks that would prevent the team from completing work, look at improving processes, and inform other departments within the organization how the project may affect their work.

There is another piece of the Direct and Manage Project Work process that you need to be aware of for the exam. When executing the project, the project manager takes time to focus on managing the schedule, budget, risks, quality, and all other knowledge areas. This way of thinking about project executing is not an approach that many project managers take. They just manage the project as a whole, rather than giving individual attention to each knowledge area. This can also mean they don't take the time to properly look at how issues relating to one knowledge area affect other knowledge areas (for example, how scope management issues can affect quality and resource management). They may forget to even think about some of the knowledge areas. Integration management requires project managers to keep all knowledge areas in mind at all times.

The project management information system (PMIS) is used to help the project manager keep track of the many aspects of the project. The PMIS includes automated tools, such as scheduling software, a configuration management system, shared workspaces for file storage or distribution, work authorization software, time-tracking software, procurement management software, and repositories for historical information.

The work authorization system is the project manager's system for authorizing the start of work packages or activities, and it is part of the PMIS. If you have never used such a system, imagine a large construction project with hundreds of people working on the project. Can you have a plumber and an electrician show up to work in one small area at the same time? No. Remember that a project is planned to the level of detail needed for that particular project. There might be instances when the project manager needs to manage at a detailed level, as in the case of the plumber and the electrician. To handle these types of situations, a work authorization system is put in place to make sure work is only started when a formal authorization is given. In many cases, this tool for authorizing work is a company-wide system used on the project, not created just for the project. There will likely only be one question about this on the exam, but the term may be included more frequently as an answer choice.

It is likely that the project manager will also make use of meetings as a tool for keeping the team and stakeholders informed and engaged in the project work during this process. Depending on the needs of the project and the project approach, the format of these meetings can range from informal stand-up sessions to structured meetings with an agenda and a focus on a specific aspect of the project. Within the Direct and Manage Work process, meeting topics may include project updates, lessons learned, upcoming project activities, and risk management.

The Direct and Manage Project Work process can be illustrated as shown in figure 4.3.

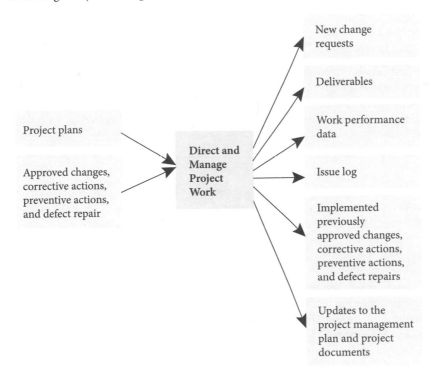

Figure 4.3   *The Direct and Manage Project Work process*

Inputs to Direct and Manage Project Work PAGE 92   The following are key inputs to the Direct and Manage Project Work process. Additional inputs may include project documents (such as the change log, project schedule, risk register, and risk report), enterprise environmental factors, and organizational process assets.

Project Management Plan   This process focuses on doing the project work according to the project management plan, which may include plans for requirements, scope, schedule, cost, and stakeholder management, for example.

Approved Change Requests   The Direct and Manage Project Work process includes implementing approved changes, including corrective actions, preventive actions, and defect repair, from the Integrated Change Control process.

Outputs of Direct and Manage Project Work PAGE 95   As shown in figure 4.3, the Direct and Manage Project Work process results in the following outputs.

 Deliverables   For the exam, you should realize that deliverables (meaning "completed work") are an output of integration management, not the other knowledge areas. There are other aspects to deliverables in Validate Scope (where deliverables are accepted by the customer) and Control Quality (where deliverables are verified), but the deliverables themselves are only done or completed as part of integration management.

Note: There are many time-saving tricks in this book based on feedback from hundreds of other test takers. Make sure you notice them all!

Work Performance Data   Once this process is completed, the project manager will have initial measurements and details about how the project is performing. You should understand that collecting this data is an integration management function. This data will be analyzed, and the resulting work performance information will be an input to the Monitor and Control Project Work process. In that process, the information is organized into reports. Work performance reports will be used in the Perform Integrated Change Control process to help assess the need for requested changes and the potential impacts of those changes on other areas of the project.

Issue Log   An issue log can be used to track and manage issues such as gaps, conflicts, or inconsistencies that may occur unexpectedly throughout the life of the project. This type of log may include a description of the issue, who raised the issue, a target resolution date, and the final solution.

Change Requests   Doing the work on the project will result in change requests. These requests can be related to many aspects of the project, including processes or policies, the project scope, the schedule, the budget, etc. Changes may be requested in the form of recommended corrective actions to address existing issues or preventive actions to address possible future issues. There may also be requests for defect repair. The need for changes can be identified by many different sources, including the project manager, the project team, the sponsor, other stakeholders, and even sources external to the project—for example, in response to changing industry or government regulations.

These change requests are either approved, rejected, or deferred in the Perform Integrated Change Control process. Those that are approved result in changes to the project management plan, and the project is then managed to the updated plan. Changes are described in more detail in the Monitor and Control Project Work and Perform Integrated Change Control sections of this chapter.

Project Management Plan and Project Documents Updates   Like change requests, doing the work on the project may also result in the need to make updates to any affected areas of the project management plan and project documents. Project management plan updates may include updates to any of the knowledge area management plans and any of the project baselines. Updates to the project documents include any updates to project management documents that are not part of the project management plan.

Updates to the project management plan and project documents are outputs of many project management processes. Although this book will not cover them each time, you should note these outputs when reading the *PMBOK® Guide*. For a study tool that can help you remember this, see the tables of commonly occurring inputs and outputs in chapter 14.

Manage Project Knowledge PAGE 98

Process: Manage Project Knowledge
Process Group: Executing
Knowledge Area: Integration Management

A project doesn't—or at least shouldn't—exist in a vacuum. Think of the tremendous amount of knowledge required to properly plan and execute a project. Project managers can benefit from the knowledge base of the organization, particularly from the experiences and discoveries of others on past, similar projects. The Manage Project Knowledge process provides a means to take advantage of the knowledge the organization has accumulated over time. In addition, it requires each project to actively contribute to that knowledge base. This includes sharing new processes and successes internally within the project, as well as making that knowledge accessible throughout the entire organization.

Successful knowledge management requires an organizational culture of trust, in which the project manager and stakeholders exchange knowledge without fear of judgment. Some of the knowledge to be shared will involve experiences that didn't work out as planned. But we can often learn more from mistakes than successes. Each mistake, each unidentified stakeholder, each missed risk trigger, and each unrealistic schedule teaches us something. What a valuable thing it is to share such information and save another project or individual from the same outcome!

This process includes two distinct types of knowledge—explicit and tacit:

Explicit knowledge   Explicit knowledge is fact-based, and can be easily communicated through words and symbols. However, it may need explanation or context to provide value to recipients of this information. Traditional lessons learned fall under this category of knowledge. Lessons learned are generated and shared as the project is ongoing, and consolidated as part of project closing.

Tacit knowledge   Tacit knowledge, on the other hand, includes emotions, experiences, and abilities, which are more difficult to communicate clearly. The sharing of this type of knowledge requires the atmosphere of trust discussed earlier.

In this process, the project manager is responsible for managing both knowledge and information.

Knowledge Management

Collaboration and knowledge sharing are key to successful projects. The project manager needs to plan and develop an environment within a project that will support the sharing of tacit knowledge (including the ways people do their work, their experiences and best practices, and how they solved problems encountered in their work). The availability of online knowledge-sharing tools helps facilitate knowledge sharing among distributed teams, enabling team members and others to benefit from a broad range of experience. Discussion forums and interactive events and meetings, whether in person or virtual, support the sharing of knowledge and experience.

Information Management

People on projects need to create and share information, or explicit knowledge, as efficiently as possible. Information management tools and techniques can help with this. The processes for capturing explicit knowledge include documentation in the lessons learned register and other repositories of explicit knowledge. Explicit knowledge is shared by making it available in the PMIS, through discussion, and via direct communication.

Other tools and techniques that may be used during the Manage Project Knowledge process include expert judgment and interpersonal and team skills such as active listening, facilitation, political awareness, networking, and leadership.

Inputs to Manage Project Knowledge PAGE 100   Enterprise environmental factors such as legal and regulatory requirements, and constraints such as nondisclosure agreements, may limit or impact the gathering or sharing of particular information due to confidentiality or privacy concerns, or may dictate the format and type of information that can be disseminated. Other factors may include organizational knowledge experts and geographic distribution of facilities and resources. Project documents and organizational process assets such as communication requirements specific to the organization and formal knowledge-sharing and information-sharing procedures may also be utilized during the Manage Project Knowledge process.

Also keep in mind that the entire project management plan is an input to the Manage Project Knowledge process. In particular, the communications, stakeholder engagement, and configuration management plans all provide direction for managing knowledge and information by the project manager, team members, and other stakeholders. Do you see why this is an integration process?

One input to this process that might seem confusing at first is deliverables. In fact, deliverables represent great amounts of knowledge regarding all aspects of what it will take to complete them. This might include new knowledge around standards or metrics, or the processes used to create the deliverables.

Outputs of Manage Project Knowledge PAGE 104   The outputs of the Manage Project Knowledge process include the lessons learned register and updates to the project management plan and organizational process assets.

Lessons Learned Register   Specific new knowledge shared through this process is referred to as lessons learned. You will see the topic of lessons learned mentioned often throughout this book, both as an input to and an output of many processes. As an input, it helps improve the current project. As an output, it helps make the organization better. Lessons learned are defined as "what was done right, what was done wrong, and what would be done differently if the project could be redone." Accurately and thoroughly documenting lessons learned is a professional responsibility.

A project manager should collect and review lessons learned from similar projects before starting work on a new project. Why make the same mistakes or face the same problems others have faced? Why not benefit from others' experience? Imagine reaching into a filing cabinet or accessing a database to see data for all the projects an organization has undertaken. How valuable would that be?

Lessons learned are collected and saved in a lessons learned register, which is the main output of this process. Do not underestimate the value of this shared information! Remember that the lessons learned register is a living document, which is shared throughout the project, as well as when the project is completed. New lessons learned may also be incorporated into the organization's recommended practices.

Lessons learned should include an overview of the situation, what was done, the impact of actions taken, and any updates to the project management plan or project documents necessitated by the action.

Exercise Test yourself! Lessons learned include what type of information?

| |
| |
| |
| |
| |
| |
| |

Answer The lessons learned register includes what was done right, what was done wrong, and what could have been done differently. Another way of saying this is that lessons learned include reasons why issues occur, change requests, workarounds, reestimates, preventive and corrective actions, and defect repair the project has faced, as well as the reasoning behind any implemented changes. They also include successes, such as new sources of information, newly developed processes, ways of tracking work, and even information on resources who demonstrate outstanding skills or are able to contribute to the project in unexpected ways.

To make lessons learned as valuable as possible, use categories to ensure that all are captured. Some categories that could be captured are:

- **Technical aspects of the project** What was right and wrong about how we completed the work to produce the product? What did we learn that will be useful in the future?

- **Project management** How did we do with WBS creation, risk planning, etc.? What did we learn that will be useful in the future?

- **Management** As a project manager, how did I do with communications and leadership? What did we learn that will be useful in the future?

  Many project managers don't understand the role of lessons learned on projects. Figure 4.4 helps explain their function.

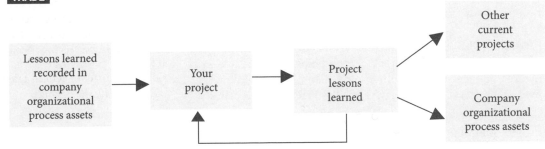

Figure 4.4 Lessons learned on a project

Monitor and Control Project Work PAGE 105

| Process: Monitor and Control Project Work |
| Process Group: Monitoring & Controlling |
| Knowledge Area: Integration Management |

The Monitor and Control Project Work process involves looking at what is happening on the project and comparing the actual and forecasted performance to what was planned. It is a monitoring and controlling function that's done from project initiating through project closing.

When you think of a large project, it makes sense that the project manager would make a formal effort to monitor and control how the project management and knowledge area processes are going. This process involves aggregating the work performance information from monitoring and controlling knowledge area processes to evaluate and assess how their individual process results are impacting the other knowledge areas and their plans and baselines. For example, the scope may be completed but the quality might not be acceptable, or the schedule might be met but at excessive cost. This process also involves monitoring any other performance requirements that were included in the project management plan. Monitoring and controlling project work encourages a holistic view of the project performance and enables the project manager to take appropriate action to keep the project on track.

The integration function of Monitor and Control Project Work also includes activities such as analyzing and tracking risks, performing quality control activities, assessing possible outcomes across the project using data analysis techniques (such as alternatives analysis, cost-benefit analysis, earned value metrics, root cause analysis, trend analysis, and variance analysis), reviewing changes and corrective actions made on the project to see if they were effective, creating work performance reports and additional change requests, and updating the project plan and project documents accordingly.

TRICKS OF THE TRADE® If the exam talks about monitoring and controlling project work, it might not be referring to the entire monitoring and controlling process group. Instead, it may be referring to this specific integration management process, Monitor and Control Project Work. Remember that monitoring and controlling means measuring against all aspects of the project management plan.

Many project managers don't control their projects to the project management plan. If the exam asks what you should do if a work activity on the project takes longer than estimated, the answer is to request corrective action (discussed later in this section) to make up for the delay. Such action keeps the project on or close to schedule and allows the project manager to feel comfortable that the scope will be completed according to the budget and schedule agreed to. This knowledge is the value of controlling the project.

Inputs to Monitor and Control Project Work PAGE 107

The following are key inputs to the Monitor and Control Project Work process. Agreements and organizational process assets may also be inputs to this process.

Project Documents There are several project documents that are considered inputs to the Monitor and Control Project Work process. For example, cost forecasts and schedule forecasts provide the project manager insight into any future project status. This insight is a valuable tool that can be used to compare how the project is progressing in comparison to the actual plan.

Project Management Plan In Monitor and Control Project Work, progress is compared to what was documented in the project management plan, including all knowledge area components. This allows the project manager to determine the actual status of the project and identify changes needed to keep the project on track.

Work Performance Information   Work performance information is fed into this process from the control processes of the other knowledge areas. This is the information that is compared to the project management plan.

Enterprise Environmental Factors   As stated earlier, enterprise environmental factors are the company culture and existing systems such as scheduling, cost, and resourcing tools, all of which can influence the Monitor and Control Project Work process.

Outputs of Monitor and Control Project Work PAGE 112   The results of the Monitor and Control Project Work process include work performance reports, change requests, and updates to the project management plan and project documents. Change requests from this and other processes are evaluated and approved, rejected, or deferred in the Perform Integrated Change Control process, described later in this chapter.

Work Performance Reports   Work performance reports include status reports or progress reports, which are used to communicate the analysis of work performance information that was performed in this process.

Change Requests   No matter how well you plan a project, there will always be changes. Change requests may have a different function, depending on which process they are generated in. The three main categories of change requests are corrective action, preventive action, and defect repair. Changes may involve additions to the project requested by the customer, changes to the plan that the team believes would make their work more efficient, or even changes to the policies and procedures used on the project.

The need for changes is identified as you manage the execution of the project and when you measure project performance against the performance measurement baseline in monitoring and controlling. See the "Perform Integrated Change Control" section later in this chapter for more about changes.

Related Concepts   The following sections highlight some important concepts related to the Monitor and Control Project Work process.

Corrective Action   A corrective action is any action taken to bring expected future project performance in line with the project management plan. Without a realistic performance measurement baseline and project management plan, including acceptable variances, you cannot determine when a variance has occurred and when corrective action is needed. Those who have problems with this in the real world will have problems on the exam. What do you do on your projects? Do you have predetermined areas to measure, and have you identified control limits for an acceptable range in which the measurements can fall to determine if a project is on schedule and on budget?

Typically, corrective actions are undertaken to adjust performance within the existing project baselines; the actions do not change the baselines. Corrective actions are reviewed and approved, rejected, or deferred as part of the Perform Integrated Change Control process. All changes that would affect the project management plan, baselines, policies or procedures, charter, contracts, or statements of work need the approval of the change control board or sponsor, as outlined in the change management plan.

As you may know, a significant portion of the project manager's time while the project work is being done is spent measuring performance (to determine the need for corrective action) and implementing corrective actions. Therefore, you can expect many scenario questions about this topic on the exam. Don't expect these questions to use the words "corrective action," however. One way to answer these types of questions would be to think of different situations that might arise on a project, such as the examples listed on the next page, and then match those situations with the name of the corresponding process or processes.

When	Process Name
When meeting with the customer to obtain acceptance of interim deliverables	Validate Scope
When measuring project performance against the performance measurement baseline	Control Scope, Control Schedule, Control Costs
When making sure people are using the correct processes	Manage Quality
When evaluating whether performance reports are meeting stakeholders' needs	Monitor Communications
When working with the project team	Manage Team
When assessing stakeholder relationships	Monitor Stakeholder Engagement
When you notice that there are many unidentified risks occurring	Monitor Risks
When evaluating a seller's performance	Control Procurements
When evaluating team members' performance	Manage Team
When making sure deliverables meet quality standards	Control Quality
When communicating with stakeholders to resolve issues and manage their perceptions about the project	Manage Stakeholder Engagement

Preventive Action   While taking corrective action involves dealing with actual deviations from the performance measurement baseline or other metrics, taking preventive action means dealing with anticipated or possible deviations from the performance measurement baseline and other metrics. The process for taking preventive action is not as clear as it is for taking corrective actions. Knowing when preventive action is needed requires more experience than calculation because the project manager is evaluating trends in the measurement analysis and anticipating that, if those trends continue, they could lead to deviation from the performance measurement baseline or other metrics. Examples of preventive actions include:

- Adjusting the project to prevent the same problem from occurring again later in the project
- Changing a resource because the resource's last activity nearly failed to meet its acceptance criteria
- Arranging for team members to gain training in a certain area to provide the necessary backup skills if a team member unexpectedly gets sick

Typically, preventive actions are undertaken to adjust performance within the existing project baselines; the actions don't change the baselines. All preventive actions should be reviewed and approved or rejected as part of the Perform Integrated Change Control process. Proposed changes that would affect the project management plan, baselines, policies or procedures, charter, contracts, or statements of work would likely have to go to the change control board or sponsor for approval, as outlined in the change management plan.

You will see preventive action mentioned throughout the *PMBOK® Guide*. Preventive action can be implemented at any time for any project management process.

Defect Repair   Defect repair is another way of saying "rework." Defect repair may be requested when a component of the project does not meet specifications. As with corrective and preventive actions, any defect repairs should be reviewed and approved or rejected as part of the Perform Integrated Change Control process.

Perform Integrated Change Control PAGE 113

> **Process:** Perform Integrated Change Control
> **Process Group:** Monitoring and Controlling
> **Knowledge Area:** Integration Management

At any time during the project, changes to any part of the project may be requested. Keep in mind, however, that just because a change is requested doesn't mean it has to be—or even should be—implemented. All change requests are evaluated and accepted, rejected, or deferred in the Perform Integrated Change Control process. A key focus of integrated change control is to look at the impact of each change on all the project constraints. For example, any scope change needs to be assessed for its impact on quality, risk, schedule, cost, resources, and customer satisfaction. The value of analyzing the impact of changes is to reduce the potential risk of not fulfilling project objectives.

For the changes that are accepted, updates and replanning efforts are required to make sure the project team is working with a current and integrated project management plan, performance measurement baseline, and project documents. These updating and replanning efforts take place during Perform Integrated Change Control. The approved changes are then implemented in Direct and Manage Project Work, Control Quality, and Control Procurements.

So do you need to go through Perform Integrated Change Control to make changes to processes or plans that haven't been finalized? No! When developing the project charter, project management plan, and baseline, changes can be made without a formal change request. But after the charter or the project management plan have been approved, requested changes need to be evaluated for resolution in integrated change control. Read exam questions carefully to understand whether a requested change pertains to something that is still in the process of being finalized or has already been finalized and approved. This will help you determine whether integrated change control is required.

To fully evaluate the impacts of a change, it is necessary to have:

- A realistic project management plan to measure against
- A complete product scope and project scope (see the definitions in the Scope Management chapter)

Change is inevitable on projects, but a project manager should work to prevent the root cause of changes whenever possible. And in many cases, the root cause may be that the project manager did not properly plan the project. The need for changes may indicate that the project manager didn't fully identify stakeholders and uncover their requirements or that they didn't properly complete other project management actions. All possible changes must be planned, managed, and controlled. Also note that you should read exam questions carefully that relate to change. Often, a required action might just entail looking at the project plan to determine how to handle an issue that has occurred on a project.

 Changes can be grouped into two broad categories—those that affect the project management plan, baselines, policies and procedures, charter, contracts, or statements of work, and those that do not. If a change doesn't affect any of these documents, the company's change management policies may allow the project manager to approve the change. If, on the other hand, the change does affect those key elements, the change typically needs to go to the change control board or sponsor for a decision.

Change Control Board (CCB) PAGE 115

Why should the project manager always have to be the one to deny a change request? They might not even have the knowledge or expertise to analyze a change request. Depending on the project manager's level of authority, their role might be to facilitate decisions about certain changes, rather than actually make the decisions. For these reasons, many projects have formally established a change control board that is responsible for reviewing and analyzing change requests in accordance with the project's change management plan. The CCB then approves, rejects, or defers the changes. The results of the board's decisions are documented in the project's change log. The board may include the project manager, the customer, experts, the sponsor, functional managers, and others. For the exam, assume that most projects have change control boards, with the exception of change-driven projects.

Process for Making Changes   Generally the change process should follow these steps:

1. **Evaluate the impact**   Evaluate (assess) the impact of the change on all aspects of the project. (For example, "This change will add three weeks to the project length, require $20,000 additional funding, and have no effect on resources.")
2. **Identify options**   This can include cutting other activities, compressing the schedule by crashing or fast tracking, or looking at other options. For example, you may be able to decrease the potential effect of the change on the project by spending more time decreasing project risk, or by adding another resource to the project team).
3. **Get the change request approved internally**.
4. **Get customer buy-in** (if required).

The above list provides a high-level overview of this process. It may also be helpful to understand a more detailed process for making changes:

1. Prevent the root cause of changes.
2. Identify the need for a change.
3. Evaluate the impact of the change within the knowledge area.
4. Create a change request.
5. Perform integrated change control.
   - Assess the change against all project constraints.
   - Identify options.
   - The change is approved, rejected, or deferred.
   - Update the status of the change in the change log.
   - Adjust the project management plan, project documents, and baselines as necessary.
6. Manage stakeholders' expectations by communicating the change to stakeholders affected by the change.
7. Manage the project to the revised project management plan and project documents.

Inputs to Perform Integrated Change Control PAGE 116   Inputs to the Perform Integrated Change Control process may include project documents, work performance reports, enterprise environmental factors, and organizational process assets. However, the key inputs to this process are the project management plan and change requests.

Project Management Plan   The key component of the project management plan that is needed for Perform Integrated Change Control is the change management plan, which documents how change requests will be managed. (See the discussion of the change management plan earlier in this chapter.) Remember that the change management plan may include change control procedures and approval levels for authorizing changes. Descriptions of roles and responsibilities of the Change Control Board (CCB) may also be included.

Change Requests   Change requests are created in numerous executing and monitoring and controlling processes. In Perform Integrated Change Control, each change request is evaluated for its impact on all aspects of the project. However, be aware that change requests may also be submitted in the context of any process group.

Outputs of Perform Integrated Change Control PAGE 120   Outputs of the
Perform Integrated Change Control process include approved change requests and updates to the project management plan and project documents.

Approved Change Requests   As noted previously, changes are approved, rejected, or deferred as part of integrated change control, and those decisions are recorded in a change log. The approved changes are then implemented in the Direct and Manage Project Work process.

Updates to Project Documents and the Project Management Plan   Approved changes require updates to the project management plan and project documents in order to keep the documentation realistic and ensure its continuing usefulness throughout the project.

Close Project or Phase PAGE 121

> **Process:** Close Project or Phase
> **Process Group:** Closing
> **Knowledge Area:** Integration Management

In terms of the Close Project or Phase process, it's important to understand that this effort finalizes all activities across all process groups to formally close out the project or project phase.

Is your project really done when the technical work is done? Not if you don't close it out! The Close Project or Phase process encompasses the actions of closing as outlined in the project management plan. For example, individual contracts are closed as part of the Control Procurements process, and all contracts must be closed out before the project is closed. The Close Project or Phase process ensures that final contract documentation and customer acceptance have been received.

A project manager must get formal acceptance of the project and its deliverables, issue a final report that shows the project has been successful, issue the final lessons learned, and index and archive all the project records. Make sure you become familiar with all the concepts and actions listed here—and if you don't currently do these things on your projects, imagine completing these activities in the real world on a large project. For the exam, be sure to remember that you always close out a project, no matter the circumstances under which it is terminated or completed.

There are financial, legal, and administrative efforts involved in closing. Let's look again at the activities listed in Rita's Process Chart™:

- Confirm work is done to requirements.
- Obtain formal confirmation that contracts are completed.
- Gain final acceptance of the product.
- Complete financial closure.
- Hand off completed product.
- Solicit customer's feedback about the project.
- Complete final performance reporting.
- Index and archive records.
- Gather final lessons learned, and update knowledge base.

Note that the Close Project or Phase process involves getting the final, formal acceptance of the project or phase as a whole from the customer, whereas the Validate Scope process in scope management (a monitoring and controlling process) involves getting formal acceptance from the customer for interim deliverables. A project needs both processes.

Does it make sense to you that the Close Project or Phase process is an integration management function? If not, think of the example of final performance reporting. Can you see how you would have to report on all knowledge areas? How about the example of indexing and archiving project records? You need to do so for records from all the knowledge areas.

Take some time to think about project closing and its necessity for proper project management of a large project before you take the exam.

Outputs of Close Project or Phase PAGE 127   The following are the outputs of the Close Project or Phase process.

Final Report   The final report for a project is a summary of the overall performance of the project. For example, this report may include information about objectives that relate to quality, cost, or scope. It may also include a description of the project or phase, as well as a summary of the validation information for the final product, service, or result.

Final Product, Service, or Result Transition   The final product, service, or result of the project is delivered as part of this process.

Updates to Project Documents and Organizational Process Assets   Assets such as operational and support documents, as well as the project or phase closure documents, may be updated as a result of the Close Project or Phase process. The lessons learned register, along with the lessons learned repository, may also be updated as well so other projects can access and benefit from the information.

© 2018 RMC Publications, Inc.™ • 952.846.4484 • info@rmcls.com • www.rmcls.com

Integration Management Review

Exercise

This exercise will help you review the key material you need to know for integration management. The Shuffle Game that follows offers another approach to this material. You can use either or both of these study tools, depending on your preference.

Instructions

1. Try to fill in the blanks in the below table using the knowledge and understanding gained after reading this chapter.
2. To review only the material contained in this chapter, focus on the cells that have asterisks. (These are the key topics you need to understand to pass the exam with the minimum amount of study time. The answer table will show only these topics.)
3. To review all the items listed in the *PMBOK® Guide*, fill in the entire table.

Key Inputs	Key Tools and Techniques	Key Outputs
Develop Project Charter Process group:		
*		*
Develop Project Management Plan Process group:		
		*
Direct and Manage Project Work Process group:		
*		*

Key Inputs	Key Tools and Techniques	Key Outputs
Manage Project Knowledge Process group:		
		*
Monitor and Control Project Work Process group:		
*		*
Perform Integrated Change Control Process group:		
*		*
Close Project or Phase Process group:		
		*

© 2018 RMC Publications, Inc.™ • 952.846.4484 • info@rmcls.com • www.rmcls.com

Answer
To save study time and focus on the most important information, this answer table only shows the topics that are covered in this chapter. If you tried to list all inputs, tools and techniques, and outputs, you'll need to check your answers against the *PMBOK® Guide*.

Key Inputs	Key Tools and Techniques	Key Outputs
Develop Project Charter Process group: Initiating		
Business documents • Benefits management plan • Business case Agreements/contracts Enterprise environmental factors Organizational process assets		Project charter Assumption log
Develop Project Management Plan Process group: Planning		
		Project management plan • Project life cycle • Development approach • Management reviews • Project management processes • Knowledge area management plans • Baselines • Requirements management plan • Change management plan • Configuration management plan
Direct and Manage Project Work Process group: Executing		
Project management plan Approved change requests		Work performance data Issue log Change requests Project management plan updates Project documents updates
Manage Project Knowledge Process group: Executing		
		Lessons learned register
Monitor and Control Project Work Process group: Monitoring and controlling		
Project management plan Project documents Work performance information Enterprise environmental factors		Work performance reports Change requests

Key Inputs	Key Tools and Techniques	Key Outputs
Perform Integrated Change Control Process group: Monitoring and controlling		
Project management plan Change requests		Approved change requests Project management plan updates Project documents updates
Close Project or Phase Process group: Closing		
		Final report Final product, service, or result transition Project documents updates Organizational process assets updates

Shuffle Game

Some people learn best by doing, which is why we have developed this alternate approach to reviewing integration management. To save you time, only the most important topics for the exam—those covered in this chapter—have been included.

Instructions

1. Cut out the cards on the next pages.
2. Lay out the bold title cards as column headers.
3. Shuffle the remaining cards and try to put them in the columns where they belong. Cards with italic terms must be matched to the corresponding group. For example, a *Cost of Quality* card in italics would match with a Data Analysis card, as cost of quality is a data analysis tool and technique.
4. Check your answers against the material covered in this chapter or the *PMBOK® Guide,* and make note of any gaps in your knowledge.

Note: Be sure to keep all cards for each chapter shuffle game as you will use them again for the final Shuffle Game in chapter 14.

Develop Project Charter *Key Inputs*	Develop Project Charter *Key Outputs*	Develop Project Management Plan *Key Outputs*
Direct and Manage Project Work *Key Inputs*	Direct and Manage Project Work *Key Outputs*	Manage Project Knowledge *Key Outputs*
Monitor and Control Project Work *Key Inputs*	Monitor and Control Project Work *Key Outputs*	Perform Integrated Change Control *Key Inputs*
Perform Integrated Change Control *Key Outputs*	Close Project or Phase *Key Outputs*	Business documents
Benefits management plan	*Business case*	Agreements/contracts

Enterprise environmental factors	Organizational process assets	Project charter
Assumption log	Project management plan	*Project life cycle*
Development approach	*Management reviews*	*Project management process*
Knowledge area management plans	*Baselines*	*Requirements management plan*
Change management plan	*Configuration management plan*	Project management plan

Approved change requests	Work performance data	Issue log
Change requests	Project management plan updates	Project documents updates
Lessons learned register	Project management plan	Project documents
Work performance information	Enterprise environmental factors	Work performance reports

Change requests	Project management plan	Change requests
Approved change requests	Project management plan updates	Project documents updates
Final report	Final product, service or result transition	Project documents updates
Organizational process assets updates		

© 2018 RMC Publications, Inc.™ • 952.846.4484 • info@rmcls.com • www.rmcls.com

Practice Exam

1. Which document gives the project manager the authority to spend money and commit corporate resources?
   A. Project charter
   B. Project management plan
   C. Work authorization plan
   D. Business case

2. An effective change management plan addresses all the following topics except:
   A. Procedures
   B. Approval levels
   C. Meetings
   D. Lessons learned

3. Which of the following is not an input to the Direct and Manage Project Work process?
   A. Approved corrective actions
   B. Project management plan
   C. Deliverables
   D. Defect repair orders

4. Managing project knowledge is a key integration management responsibility of the project manager. This responsibility includes managing two kinds of knowledge on a project: tacit and explicit. Which of the following statements about tacit knowledge is correct?
   A. Tacit knowledge is fact-based and can be easily communicated through words and symbols.
   B. Tacit knowledge may need explanation or context to provide value.
   C. Tacit knowledge includes emotions, experience, and abilities.
   D. Lessons learned are an example of tacit knowledge.

5. Which of the following best describes when a project baseline should be changed?
   A. A project baseline should be changed when a major delay occurs.
   B. A project baseline should be changed when a change to cost, schedule, or scope is approved.
   C. A project baseline should be changed when a cost increase occurs.
   D. Changes should never be made to a project baseline.

6. A company is making an effort to improve its project performance and create historical records of past projects. What is the best way to accomplish this?
   A. Create project management plans.
   B. Create lessons learned.
   C. Create network diagrams.
   D. Create status reports.

7. Which of the following is included in the performance measurement baseline?
   A. The agreed-upon schedule, including the start and stop times for each activity
   B. An analysis of the requirements and assumptions of each stakeholder
   C. The performance requirements that will be provided to sellers
   D. The metrics that will be used in the quality control system

8. Which of the following best describes a project management plan?
  A. The schedule and cost baselines for the project
  B. A description of the project's life cycle and the development cycle that will used on the project
  C. The project charter, WBS, and project scope statement
  D. A formal document showing a plan that is approved, realistic, and bought into

9. You are beginning a new project that has been attempted unsuccessfully several times in the past few years. The previous projects were cancelled because of "politics"—differing views and direction by key stakeholders on the project. This is an example of:
  A. Stakeholder analysis
  B. Scope management
  C. Historical information
  D. Risk identification

10. Which of the following is included in a project charter?
  A. A risk management strategy
  B. Work package estimates
  C. Detailed resource estimates
  D. The business case for the project

11. Which of the following is not included in the project management plan?
  A. Change management plan
  B. Integration management plan
  C. Configuration management plan
  D. Requirements management plan

12. When does the Monitor and Control Project Work process take place?
  A. Throughout the project, from project initiating through project closing
  B. During the monitoring and controlling process group
  C. Primarily during the executing and monitoring and controlling processes
  D. During project planning, executing, and monitoring and controlling

13. Which of the following best summarizes what happens during the Perform Integrated Change Control process?
  A. All requested changes are implemented, and any impacts on quality, risk, schedule, cost, resources, and customer satisfaction are documented.
  B. Change requests to the charter and project plan are implemented by the project manager, without the need for further approvals.
  C. Change requests are evaluated and accepted, rejected, or deferred to produce a list of approved change requests.
  D. The change control board reviews the impact of change requests on the project scope.

14. Which of the following is not included in a project charter?
  A. A detailed schedule and full risk analysis
  B. A description of overall project risks
  C. The high-level requirements for the project
  D. An explanation of how the project relates to the organization's strategic goals

15. Which of the following are all outputs of Monitor and Control Project Work?
  A. Change requests, change log, and issue log
  B. Work performance data, information, and reports
  C. Corrective action, preventive action, and defect repair
  D. Deliverables, change requests, and work authorization system

Answers

1. **Answer** A
   Explanation One of the primary functions of the project charter is to provide the project manager with the authority to spend money and commit corporate resources.

2. **Answer** D
   Explanation A change management plan describes how changes will be managed and controlled. It focuses on topics such as processes and procedures that will ensure the smooth evaluation and tracking of changes, the established approval levels for authorizing changes, and who should attend meetings related to changes. Lessons learned are reviews of the processes and procedures after the fact that are used to improve future projects.

3. **Answer** C
   Explanation In the Direct and Manage Project Work process, the work is completed according to the project management plan, and approved changes—including corrective actions and defect repair—are implemented, However, deliverables (completed project work) are outputs of Direct and Manage Project Work, not inputs.

4. **Answer** C
   Explanation Tacit knowledge includes emotions, experience, and abilities. The other choices relate to explicit knowledge, which is fact-based, can be easily communicated through words and symbols, and may need explanation or context to provide value. Lessons learned fall under the category of explicit knowledge.

5. **Answer** B
   Explanation Changes can be made to the baselines, but only after they are approved by the change control board. Delays or cost increases do not automatically result in changes to baselines.

6. **Answer** B
   Explanation Lessons learned help an organization avoid future pitfalls and use the good ideas developed on past projects. This leads to improvements on future projects.

7. **Answer** A
   Explanation The performance measurement baseline includes the scope baseline, the cost baseline, and the schedule baseline. The schedule baseline outlines the agreed-upon schedule, including the start and stop times for each activity.

8. **Answer** D
   Explanation The best option provided is the one that describes a project management plan as bought into, approved, realistic, and formal. Although the project management plan does include the schedule and cost baselines along with descriptions of the project life cycle and development approach, there are several other components of the plan, as well. The project charter is not part of the project management plan.

9. **Answer** C
   Explanation Although the word "stakeholder" is used in the question, this is not an example of stakeholder analysis, nor is it an example of scope management. The situation described relates to past projects. Such information can result in the identification of risks, but this is not an example of risk identification. The question describes historical information, which is extremely valuable to consider when planning a project.

10. **Answer** D

    Explanation The project charter is created in initiating, but a risk management strategy and work package estimates are not created until project planning. A project charter may include the names of some resources (such as the project manager), but not detailed resource estimates. Of the choices given, only the business case for the project, which captures the business need, is included in the project charter.

11. **Answer** B

    Explanation The project management process described in the *PMBOK® Guide* does not include an integration management plan. The change management, configuration management, and requirements management plans are all part of the project management plan.

12. **Answer** A

    Explanation Monitor and Control Project Work is done from project initiating through project closing because it involves monitoring and controlling all project efforts.

13. **Answer** C

    Explanation Not all change requests are implemented; they must first be evaluated and then accepted, rejected, or deferred. The project manager can only make changes to the charter and project plan without further approvals during the planning stages—before these documents are finalized. "The change control board reviews the impact of change requests on the project scope" describes one part of the Perform Integrated Change Control process, so this answer is somewhat correct; however, integrated change control evaluates the impact of a change on all aspects of the project, not just scope. Therefore, it is most correct to state that change requests are evaluated and accepted, rejected, or deferred to produce a list of approved change requests in Perform Integrated Change Control.

14. **Answer** A

    Explanation A description of overall project risks, high-level project requirements, and an explanation of how the project relates to the organization's strategic goals are all standard components of a project charter. If you got this question wrong, did you notice that it asked what is not in a project charter?

15. **Answer** C

    Explanation The key output of Monitor and Control Project Work is change requests, which may also involve corrective action, preventive action, or defect repair. The other choices all include at least one option that is not an output of this process.

Scope Management

F I V E

There are 13 to 14 questions on this knowledge area on the CAPM exam. Also note, for a full list of all inputs, tools and techniques, and outputs within this knowledge area, please see the table on page 130 in the PMBOK© Guide.

Think about a project that you worked on or are working on. How sure were you or the project manager about what work needed to be done? How many changes were made to what was to be done? The impacts to cost and schedule due to unclear or incomplete scope definition are greater once the project is underway than if the scope is clarified while planning the project.

Scope management is the process of defining what work is required and then making sure all of that work—and only that work—is completed. This is generally an easy topic, but we all have gaps in our knowledge, even for things, like scope management, that we deal with daily.

 Things to Know about Scope Management

- Scope must be clearly defined and formally approved before work starts.
- Requirements are elicited from all stakeholders, not just the person who assigned the project.
- Requirements elicitation can take a substantial amount of time, especially on large projects, which may involve obtaining requirements from hundreds of people.
- Requirements must be evaluated against the business case, ranked, and prioritized to determine what is in and out of scope.

QUICKTEST

- Scope management process
- Scope baseline
- Work breakdown structure (WBS)
- Project scope statement
- WBS dictionary
- Requirements documentation
- Requirements traceability matrix
- How to create a WBS
- Benefits of using a WBS
- Requirements management plan
- Scope management plan
- Work package
- Activity
- Product scope
- Project scope
- Decomposition
- Product analysis
- Interviews
- Focus groups

- Facilitation
- Unanimity
- Autocratic decision making
- Majority
- Plurality
- Consensus
- Brainstorming
- Voting
- Nominal group technique
- Multicriteria decision analysis
- Mind mapping
- Affinity diagrams
- Questionnaires and surveys
- Observation
- Prototypes
- Inspection
- Benchmarking
- Document analysis
- Control account
- Accepted deliverables
- Verified deliverables

- A work breakdown structure (WBS) is used on all projects. Using this tool enables a project manager to clarify identified scope as well as find additional scope.
- While the project is being completed, the project manager must check to make sure they are doing all the work included in the project management plan—and only that work.
- Gold plating a project (adding extras) is not allowed.
- Any change to scope must be evaluated for its effect on time, cost, risk, quality, resources, and customer satisfaction.
- Changes to scope require an approved change request.
- Scope changes should not be approved if they relate to work that does not fit within the project charter.

Note that creating a work breakdown structure (WBS) is a required part of project management. A WBS is not a list. If you have never created a WBS or do not currently use that tool, this chapter will help you understand how beneficial this tool is and what it can do for you. A WBS can help you clearly define requirements and more accurately plan how you will manage and control scope.

The following should help you understand how each part of scope management fits into the overall project management process.

Scope Management Process	Done During
Plan Scope Management	Planning process group
Collect Requirements	Planning process group
Define Scope	Planning process group
Create WBS	Planning process group
Validate Scope	Monitoring and controlling process group
Control Scope	Monitoring and controlling process group

You should understand the following concepts for the exam:

Product Scope PAGE 131   Product scope is another way to say "requirements that relate to the product, service, or result of the project." It can also be defined as the product deliverables with their associated features and functions. It answers the question, "What end result is needed?" There may be a separate, preliminary project to determine product scope, or you may define the requirements as part of your project.

Let's look at an example of product scope. On a project to build a new train terminal, the product scope is "a new train terminal that meets these technical specifications." To determine if the project successfully achieved the product scope, the resulting product (the new train terminal) is compared to the product requirements, which were recorded in the requirements documentation and the project scope statement for the project.

Project Scope PAGE 131   The project scope is the work the project team will do to deliver the product of the project; it encompasses the product scope. In the train terminal example, the project scope will be "a new train terminal that meets these technical specifications" plus all the work needed to deliver the train terminal. In other words, project scope includes the planning, coordination, and management activities (such as meetings and reports) that ensure the product scope is achieved. These efforts become part of the scope baseline and scope management plan, which are parts of the project management plan. To determine whether the project scope has been successfully completed, the work accomplished is measured against the scope baseline.

The Scope Management Process

There are a lot of acceptable ways to manage scope. If you do it differently than described here, you are not necessarily wrong—you may just be managing scope differently based on the needs of a project. For the exam, think of the scope management process as including the following steps:

1. Develop a plan for how you will plan, validate, and control scope and requirements on the project.
2. Determine requirements, making sure all requirements support the project's business case as described in the project charter.
3. Balance and prioritize the needs of stakeholders to determine scope.
4. Create a WBS to break the scope down into smaller, more manageable pieces, and define each piece in the WBS dictionary.
5. Obtain validation (signed acceptance) that the completed scope of work is acceptable to the customer or sponsor.
6. Measure scope performance, and adjust as needed.

Plan Scope Management PAGE 134

> **Process:** Plan Scope Management
> **Process Group:** Planning
> **Knowledge Area:** Scope Management

Each of the project management knowledge areas has a management plan. For scope, there are actually two—a scope management plan and a requirements management plan. Together these plans provide direction on how the project and product scope will be defined, managed, and controlled. Before we discuss these plans in more detail, let's look at the inputs to creating them.

Inputs to Plan Scope Management PAGE 135

The project charter, components of the project management plan (quality management plan, project life cycle description, and development approach), enterprise environmental factors, and organizational process assets are all inputs to the Plan Scope Management process. The project charter includes a high-level description of the product, service, or result the project is intended to produce. It also documents high-level project requirements.

The project life cycle description breaks the project into the phases needed to produce the product, service, or result. It's also important to note that scope management planning must be performed in accordance with organizational policies and procedures. Historical records and lessons learned from previous, similar projects may be useful for the team in their planning efforts.

In addition, every project has a development approach. This could be plan-driven (predictive or waterfall), change-driven (iterative, adaptive, or agile), or a combination (hybrid) approach. The development approach influences how requirements will be elicited as well as how the scope statement and WBS will be developed—for the entire project at once, or at a high level for the overall project, and then in more detail for each release.

Outputs of Plan Scope Management PAGE 137

As mentioned above, the outputs of the Plan Scope Management process include two management plans—the scope management plan and the requirements management plan. Let's look at each of these in more detail.

Scope Management Plan

The scope management plan, which is the primary output of the Plan Scope Management process, is part of the project management plan, and the project manager uses it to guide the project until closing. The scope management plan essentially contains three parts that detail how scope will be planned, executed, and controlled. It defines the following:

- How the scope will be achieved
- What tools will be used to plan how the project will accomplish the scope
- How the WBS will be created
- How scope will be managed and controlled to the project management plan
- How acceptance of deliverables will be obtained

Each project's scope management plan is unique, but it may cover topics that can be standardized for the company or the type of project. Therefore, companies often have templates, forms, and standards for scope management. These are valuable assets to have on a project.

Requirements Management Plan

The requirements management plan, the second and final output of the Plan Scope Management process, also falls under the PMI-ism of "plan before you do." This plan is also referred to as the business analysis plan. In addition to describing the methods you intend to use to identify requirements, the plan should answer the following questions: "Once I have all the requirements, what will I do to analyze, prioritize, manage, and track changes to them? What should I include in the requirements traceability matrix?" (The requirements traceability matrix is described later in this chapter.)

The scope management plan and the requirements management plan are parts of the project management plan. The next process, Collect Requirements, begins to put these plans into action.

Collect Requirements PAGE 138

> **Process:** Collect Requirements
> **Process Group:** Planning
> **Knowledge Area:** Scope Management

Requirements are what stakeholders need from a project or product.
Remember, work should not be included in a project just because someone wants it. Instead, requirements should relate to solving problems or achieving the objectives outlined in a project charter. Requirements may include requests about how the work is planned and managed. For example, a stakeholder could request that systems not be shut down to accommodate a project during peak business hours. Requirements may include the capabilities stakeholders would like to see in the product, such as a software application that allows multiple users to access it at the same time. Requirements can also relate to the following:

- **Quality** "The component D must be able to withstand 200 pounds of pressure."
- **Business processes** "You must track and report the project's expenses in this way."
- **Compliance** "By law, we have to meet this safety standard."
- **Project management** "We require risk management procedure X to be used on the project."

The Collect Requirements process looks for all requirements, not just those related to the product of the project. This process is critical to project success, as a missed requirement could mean significant changes and conflict throughout the remainder of a project—and even project failure.

The requirements gathering techniques are described briefly in this chapter to give you only what you need for the exam. If you want to learn more about defining and managing requirements, visit rmcls.com for information about courses on this topic.

Inputs to Collect Requirements PAGE 140

This process involves using the project charter, project documents (such as the stakeholder register, assumption log, and lessons learned register), agreements, and organizational process assets to create the requirements documentation and the requirements traceability matrix. Additional inputs may include the project management plan, business documents, and enterprise environmental factors. Review the key inputs to this process in the following paragraphs. Be sure to think through how each of these inputs might help a project manager collect requirements.

Project Charter   The high-level project and product descriptions are defined in the project charter, which is developed during initiating. The Collect Requirements process begins with these descriptions, and elicits more detailed input about what is required.

Assumption Log   The assumption log documents known stakeholder assumptions related to product and project requirements. Collect Requirements includes refining and adding to this list of assumptions, after an initial review at the beginning of this process.

Stakeholder Register   Remember that the stakeholder register was created in initiating. It includes a list of stakeholders identified thus far in the project, as well as their requirements and expectations.

Agreements   If the project includes procurements, the requirements of the buyers are documented in the contracts. Any agreed-upon requirements included in letters of agreement within an organization are also a source of requirements.

Organizational Process Assets   Organizational process assets, such as historical records and lessons learned, include requirements from past, similar projects and help identify relevant processes and expectations. For example, historical records may provide data about reporting requirements, project management requirements, system compatibility requirements, and compliance requirements. Lessons learned from other projects, which may identify commonly overlooked areas of scope, can be used to help ensure such requirements are not missed on the current project.

Tools and Techniques of Collect Requirements PAGE 142   The following are the tools and techniques of the Collect Requirements process. Pay special attention to the groups—which may also be referred to as categories—of these tools and techniques, as they are common concepts throughout the project management processes. For more information about how tools and techniques are represented, read pages 685 through 694 in the *PMBOK® Guide*.

Data Gathering

Brainstorming   Be careful here—many people think brainstorming is just a meeting where people discuss ideas, but it's more than that. The purpose of brainstorming is not so much to get individuals to share their thoughts on a topic as it is to encourage participants to build on each other's ideas. One person mentions an idea to solve a problem or, in this case, determine scope. That idea generates an idea from another participant, which leads to yet another idea, and so on. The results of brainstorming sessions vary depending on the participants. It can be highly beneficial to include people with different perspectives or backgrounds. The participants may be internal or external to the project or the organization. After all the ideas have been captured, the group can evaluate and rank them using the nominal group technique or multicriteria decision analysis, as described in the following sections.

Interviews   This technique is also referred to as expert interviews. The team or project manager interviews project stakeholders to elicit their requirements for a specific element of the product or project work, or for the overall project. These interviews can take place between two individuals or in group settings. Interviews can also be conducted via email or phone, or using virtual collaboration tools.

Focus Groups   A focus group technique is a way to elicit opinions and requirements for the product or an aspect of the project from stakeholders and subject matter experts. Members of a focus group are usually selected from a specific demographic group of customers. They discuss their ideas with each other, and the conversation is directed by a moderator.

Questionnaires and Surveys   Questionnaires and surveys are typically used for large groups. The questions are phrased in a way that is designed to elicit requirements from the respondents.

Benchmarking   Another way to help identify and define requirements is to look at what the competition is doing. Benchmarking focuses on measuring an organization's performance against that of other organizations in the same industry. There are limitations to this technique, however. Benchmarking can be time-consuming and costly. It may also inhibit the team's creativity because the focus is on studying solutions that have been used elsewhere, rather than on developing new, innovative ideas.

Data Analysis

Document Analysis   Most organizations have extensive documentation about what they do and why they do it. Reviewing such documentation allows the project manager to elicit requirements. Examples of such documents include agreements, issue logs, policies and procedures, and regulatory documentation.

Decision Making

Voting   Soliciting input about requirements from stakeholders often results in conflicting requirements. It is essential to resolve these conflicts, as well as to review, analyze, accept or reject, and prioritize requirements before recording them in project documents. Voting is commonly used to make decisions in a group setting. If the group agrees on a requirement unanimously (everyone agrees), the decision is easy. The decision-making process is also simplified if a single person is assigned to make the decision for the entire group. However, this autocratic method of decision making can have negative impacts on the project if the stakeholders don't buy into the decision.

When there are differing opinions, a group may take a majority approach. With this approach, the group chooses the decision that more than half of its members support. If there is no majority opinion, the group may go with the decision that has the largest number of supporters. This is known as the plurality approach.

Multicriteria Decision Analysis   Another way to rank ideas is through multicriteria decision analysis. With this technique, stakeholders quantify requirements using a decision matrix based on factors such as expected risk levels, schedule estimates, and cost and benefit estimates.

Data Representation

Affinity Diagrams   In this technique, the ideas generated from other requirements gathering techniques are grouped by similarities. Each group of requirements is then given a title. This sorting makes it easier to see additional areas of scope (or risks) that have not been identified (see fig. 5.1).

Affinity diagrams can also be organized by requirements categories. The following are some common categories used when collecting requirements:

- **Business requirements** Why was the project undertaken? What business need is the project intended to address?
- **Stakeholder requirements** What do stakeholders want to gain from the project?
- **Solution requirements** What does the product need to look like? What are its functional requirements (how the product should work) and nonfunctional requirements (what will make the product effective)?
- **Transition requirements** What types of handoff procedures or training are needed to transfer the product to the customer or organization?
- **Project requirements** How should the project be initiated, planned, executed, controlled, and closed?

- **Quality requirements** What quality measures does the product need to meet? What constitutes a successfully completed deliverable?
- **Technical requirements** How will the product be built? What are the product specifications?

Library Project Requirements

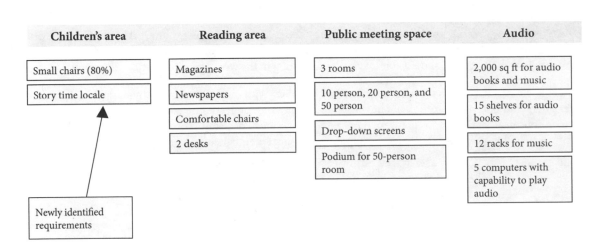

Book storage	Computers	Office space	Customer service
150,000 books	48 computers for public use	4 offices and 15 cubes	1 desk per area with computer and phone
15 different categories	12 computers for visitor service desks	1 director's office (12' × 12')	
Signage above for easy locating	20 computers for staff offices/cubes	3 managers' offices (7' × 7'), located near their areas of concern	
	Printer for each area; 7 printers for public use	5 cubes (6' × 4') for each manager's area	

Newly identified requirements (Computers)

Newly identified requirements (Customer service)

Children's area	Reading area	Public meeting space	Audio
Small chairs (80%)	Magazines	3 rooms	2,000 sq ft for audio books and music
Story time locale	Newspapers	10 person, 20 person, and 50 person	15 shelves for audio books
	Comfortable chairs	Drop-down screens	12 racks for music
	2 desks	Podium for 50-person room	5 computers with capability to play audio

Newly identified requirements (Children's area)

Figure 5.1 Affinity diagram

Mind Mapping   A mind map is a diagram of ideas or notes to help generate, classify, or record information. It looks like several trees branching out of a central core word or words (see fig. 5.2). Colors, pictures, and notations can be used to make the diagram more readable.

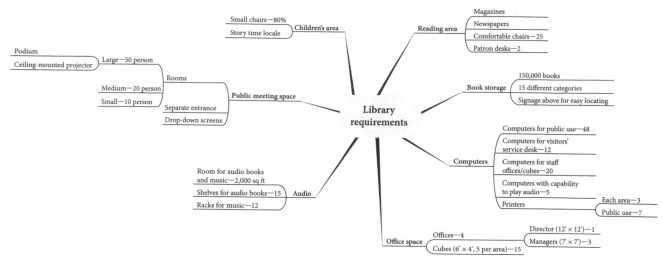

Figure 5.2 Mind map

Interpersonal and Team Skills

Nominal Group Technique   This technique is often done during the same meeting as brainstorming. It tends to be more structured than other techniques, and follows these four steps: a question or issue is posed, all meeting participants write down and then share their ideas, the group discusses what has been shared, and then ideas are ranked based on which ideas are the most useful.

Observation   Observation is a great way to learn about business processes and get a feel for the work environment of stakeholders. This technique generally involves job shadowing—watching a user of the potential product at work and, in some cases, participating in the work to help identify requirements.

Facilitation   Facilitation brings together stakeholders with different perspectives, such as product designers and end users, to talk about the product and, ultimately, define requirements. This technique uses a consensus approach to achieve general agreement about a decision. Those who would prefer another option are willing to accept the decision supported by most members of the group.

Stakeholders may develop user stories during these facilitated sessions. User stories describe functionality or features that stakeholders hope to see and are often written in the following format:

> *As a <role>, I want <functionality/goal> so that <business benefit/motivation>.*

For example: "As a community organizer, I want the new library to offer public meeting spaces so that we will have a central place to gather for neighborhood events."

Context Diagram   A context diagram, also known as a context level data flow diagram, is frequently used to define and model scope. It shows the boundaries of the product scope by highlighting the product and its interfaces with people, processes, or systems. Figure 5.3 shows an example of a context diagram for a payroll system upgrade.

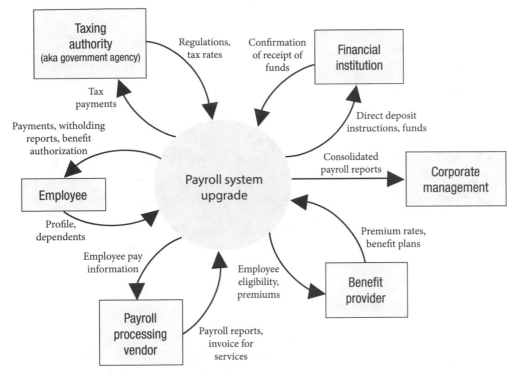

Figure 5.3 Context diagram

Prototypes   A prototype is a model of the proposed product that is presented to stakeholders for feedback. The prototype may be updated multiple times to incorporate stakeholders' feedback until the requirements have been solidified for the product.

Outputs of Collect Requirements PAGE 147   The following are the outputs of the Collect Requirements process.

Requirements Documentation   After requirements have been collected and finalized, they are documented. Imagine you have elicited requirements from hundreds of people. Can you see how documenting those requirements would be useful? This documentation helps to ensure all requirements are clear and unambiguous.

Requirements documentation can contain various types of information, but the one thing that must be included is acceptance criteria. To avoid having requirements that could easily be misunderstood, a great question to ask stakeholders is, "How will we know if our work meets this requirement?" Not only is this a good way to make sure you understand the stakeholder's requirement, it also helps to ensure the work being done will be acceptable.

It's also important to note that the level of detail of documentation is iterated until each requirement satisfies the criteria of being clear, complete, and measurable. Requirements must be described in such a way that associated deliverables can be tested or measured against the requirements in the Validate Scope process to confirm that the deliverables are acceptable.

Requirements Traceability Matrix   Have you ever worked on a project in which some requirements got lost in the details? In the process of determining requirements, one requirement often leads to additional, more refined, requirements and clarifications—especially on a large project. It can be difficult to remember where a requirement came from and what its significance is to the project. Losing focus on the reason for a requirement can result in a major strategic or project objective not being met. The requirements traceability matrix, another output of the Collect Requirements process, helps link requirements to the objectives (and other requirements) to ensure the strategic goals are accomplished (see fig. 5.4). The matrix is used throughout the project in analyzing proposed changes to project or product scope.

Information such as requirement identification numbers, the source of each requirement, who is assigned to manage the requirement, and the status of the requirement should be documented in the requirements traceability matrix. For a large project, however, including all this information in the matrix would make it cumbersome and difficult to use. Another option is to store this data in a separate repository, preserving the matrix as a reference tool. For the exam, simply understand that the requirements traceability matrix links requirements to objectives and other requirements, and that the requirements attributes, such as identification numbers, source, and status, also need to be documented.

Assigning responsibility for managing each requirement is similar to the concept of risk owners (described later in the Risk Management chapter). A requirement owner helps ensure that the customer receives what they asked for and the objectives are met. Assigning team members to manage requirements also helps free up the project manager's time. The role of requirement owner is another example of the type of work team members may do on a project in addition to their efforts to produce the product.

Objectives	Reading area				Book storage			Public meeting space			Children's area		Audio			Office space		Computers				
	Magazines	Newspapers	Comfortable chairs (25)	Patron desks (2)	Books (150,000)	Book categories (15)	Signage above	Rooms	Separate entrance	Dropdown screens	Small chairs (80%)	Story time corner	Room for audiobooks & music	Shelves for audiobooks (15)	Racks for music (12)	Offices (4)	Cubicles (15)	For public use (48)	For visitor service desk (12)	For staff (20)	With audio capability (5)	Printers
Improve access to job resources by 20%.		X		X				X		X								X	X			X
Improve local children's reading levels by two grade levels in one year.			X		X		X					X						X				
Provide a pleasant place for community members to meet.	X	X	X					X	X			X	X	X	X							
Replace the existing library by end of next quarter.	X	X	X		X	X	X					X		X				X	X	X	X	X

Figure 5.4 Requirements traceability matrix

Define Scope PAGE 150

The Define Scope process is primarily concerned with what is and is not included in the project and its deliverables. This process uses information from the project charter, the scope management plan, the requirements documentation (created in the Collect Requirements process), the assumption log, and the risk register to define the project and product scope.

Remember that planning is iterative. When the requirements have been determined and the scope is defined, the project manager follows the project management planning process to determine the schedule and budget. If the resulting schedule and budget do not meet the sponsor's or management's expectations for the project, the project manager needs to balance the requirements (scope) against the budget and schedule constraints. Through iterations, options for meeting the scope, schedule, and cost objectives of the project are developed. These options are then presented to management for a decision. This work may include compressing the schedule, identifying alternative ways to perform the work on the project, or adjusting the budget or scope. The result is a realistic schedule and budget that can achieve the project's agreed-upon scope.

It's also important to note that the process of Define Scope is iterated as the project progresses. Its purpose is always to determine what scope is and is not in the project.

Inputs to Define Scope PAGE 152   Inputs to the Define Scope process include the project charter, scope management plan, project documents, enterprise environmental factors, and organizational process assets. However, the key input to the Define Scope process is the requirements documentation that was created in the Collect Requirements process.

Requirements Documentation   In this process, the requirements are assessed to confirm that they are appropriate to the needs of the project. They are articulated as clearly as possible. Remember that the project scope includes many categories of requirements, including business, stakeholder, solution, transition, project, quality, and technical.

Tools and Techniques of Define Scope PAGE 153   Facilitation, expert judgment, alternatives analysis, and multicriteria decision analysis can be useful tools during the Define Scope process. Let's take a closer look at the key technique used in this process, product analysis.

Product Analysis   Part of defining scope is determining what the deliverables of the project are. Product analysis is used to analyze the objectives and description of the product, as stated by the customer or sponsor. That information is then used to define tangible deliverables. The work of product analysis may entail analyzing the product description and stated requirements, or using techniques such as systems engineering, value analysis, or value engineering. Product analysis is a critical tool that allows the project manager to make sure the product and project scope are understood and accurate.

Outputs of Define Scope PAGE 154   The primary output of the Define Scope process is the project scope statement.

Project Scope Statement   This document in effect says, "Here is what we will do on this project." Or it could say, "Here is the approved project and product or service scope for this project." On a plan-driven project, the development of the project scope statement can take a lot of time and involve the expert judgment of many stakeholders, and even experts from outside the organization. The project scope

statement for a change-driven project will be less detailed, but it will still have sufficient detail to define what is in and out of scope. Also note that the product scope will be progressively elaborated as needed. While defining requirements and scope, you should identify requested scope that was not approved. You should also clarify areas where scope information could easily be misunderstood. It is a waste of project time and money to create scope that's not needed or approved, yet it's easy for this to occur. One way to avoid this problem is to identify in the project scope statement what is not in the project, to make it clear that such additions are not allowed.

The project scope statement, along with the WBS and WBS dictionary (described in the next section), comprise the scope baseline, which is part of the project management plan. The project scope statement may include the following:

- Product scope
- Project scope, including a description
- Deliverables of the project
- Acceptance criteria
- What is not part of the project
- Assumptions and constraints

Create WBS PAGE 156

> **Process:** Create WBS
> **Process Group:** Planning
> **Knowledge Area:** Scope Management

What is a WBS? Correctly understanding this important project management tool is essential, both for successful projects and for passing the exam.

Exercise

Test yourself! What is a WBS?

Answer

The WBS is a required element of project management. This organizational tool shows all the scope of a project, broken down into manageable deliverables. Without a WBS, a project can and will take longer, deliverables and the work to produce them are likely to be missed, and the project will be negatively impacted. The WBS is part of the scope baseline for the project. All projects, even small ones, need a WBS. Read the rest of this section to learn more about the WBS and how it adds value to a project. Figure 5.5 shows a sample WBS.

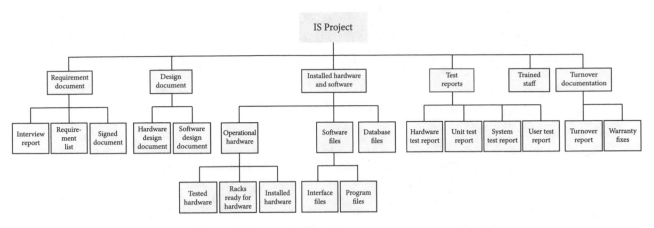

Figure 5.5   A sample WBS (on a summary level) for an IT project

Most commonly, the project name goes at the top of a WBS. The next level is typically the same as the development life cycle. The subsequent levels break the project into deliverables, which are then broken down again into smaller component deliverables, ultimately creating work packages (described next). Decomposition continues until we reach the level needed to manage the project.

Although a WBS may look like a corporate organizational chart, it serves a different function. A WBS allows you to break down a seemingly overwhelming project into pieces you can plan, organize, manage, and control. Decomposition can be done using a top-down approach (starting with the high-level pieces of a project), a bottom-up approach (starting at the work package level), or by following organizational or industry guidelines or templates.

On a WBS, the "work" refers not to an activity, but to the work packages or deliverables that result from an activity or group of activities. So, for the exam, each work package should consist of nouns—things (deliverables), rather than actions (activities). A WBS is deliverable-oriented. This doesn't mean that only customer deliverables are included. The complete scope of a project, including product scope, project scope, and project management efforts, are included as well.

TRICKS OF THE TRADE® Watch out for the word "task." What many people refer to as a "task" in the real world (and in some project management software) is generally called an "activity" on the exam. An activity is a particular piece of work scheduled for a project. For the exam, you should typically expect to manage to the activity level. Tasks are smaller components of work that make up an activity—they can be used to further break down an activity into smaller components of work.

Every WBS is unique, and every project manager will approach creating a WBS in their own way. However, there are a few guidelines that every project manager should follow when creating a WBS:

- The WBS should be created by the project manager using input from the team and other stakeholders.
- Each level of a WBS is a breakdown of the previous level.
- The entire project should be included in the highest levels of the WBS. Eventually, some levels will be further broken down.
- The WBS includes only project deliverables that are required; deliverables not included in the WBS are not part of the project.

During planning, the project management team and subject matter experts break down the scope description until the work package level is reached. This occurs when the deliverables:

- Can be realistically and confidently estimated (including the activities, duration, and cost associated with them)
- Can be completed quickly
- Can be completed without interruption and without the need for more information
- May be outsourced

At this point, you might enter the work packages—the items at the lowest level of the WBS—into some sort of project scheduling software. You would not try to finalize the list of work packages by using software, however. That list comes from the creation of the WBS.

The levels in the WBS are often numbered to make them easier to locate later. When the WBS is complete, identification numbers are assigned to help distinguish where a work package is in the WBS. There are many different numbering systems you can use. Figure 5.6 provides an example.

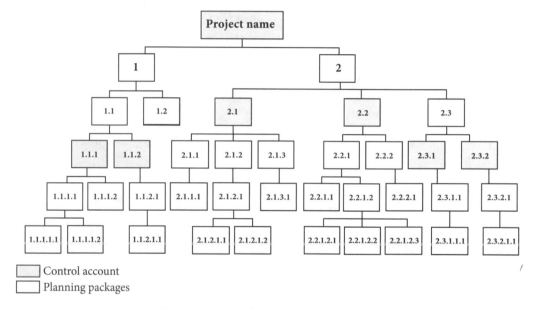

Figure 5.6   Sample WBS numbering system

You may see the terms "control account" or "planning package" on the exam. Sometimes found at higher levels within the WBS (as shown in figure 5.6), a control account is a tool that allows a project manager to collect and analyze work performance data regarding costs, schedule, and scope. Control accounts, which may include one or more planning package, provide a way to manage and control costs, schedule, and scope at a higher level than the work package. Each work package in a WBS is assigned to only one control account.

As planning progresses, the team breaks down the work packages from the WBS into the schedule activities (or "activities," for short) that are required to produce the work packages. Note that this further breakdown of the WBS into an activity list is done as part of the schedule management process of Define Activities. The team uses the project scope statement, WBS, and WBS dictionary (described later in this chapter) to help define which activities are required to produce the deliverables.

For example, on small projects, the WBS is often broken down into work packages that take between 4 and 40 hours to complete. Medium-sized projects may have work packages with 8 to 80 hours of work.

On large projects, however, the work packages may be much larger and could involve up to 300 hours of work. Therefore, the Define Activities process is especially important on large projects. Think about how this effort is different on a large project than on a small project.

If your company works on many similar projects, it's important to realize that the WBS from one project can be used as the basis for another. Therefore, the project management office should collect and share WBS examples and encourage the creation of templates. Project WBSs become part of the company's organizational process assets, and may be used by similar projects in the future.

Great project managers not only see the value of the information provided in the WBS, they also recognize the value of the effort involved in creating the WBS. Although the benefits of using a WBS won't be covered on the CAPM exam, they are important to understand to improve your real-world projects.

- Helps prevent work from slipping through the cracks
- Provides project team members with an understanding of how deliverables fit into the overall project management plan and gives the project team an indication of the impact of their work on the project as a whole
- Facilitates communication and cooperation between and among the project team and other stakeholders
- Helps manage stakeholder expectations regarding deliverables
- Helps identify risks
- Helps prevent changes
- Focuses the project team's experience on what needs to be done, resulting in increased quality and a project that is easier to manage
- Provides a basis for estimating resources, costs, and schedules
- Provides proof of the need for resources, funds, and schedules
- Helps with planning control efforts and establishing acceptance criteria for deliverables
- Gets team buy-in and builds the project team
- Helps people gain a better understanding of the project

A WBS is the foundation of a project. This means almost everything that occurs in planning after the creation of a WBS is related to the WBS. For example, project costs and schedules are estimated at the work package or activity level, and not for the project as a whole. Also note that a WBS can help a project manager identify more risks by examining the project at the work package level. Work packages are assigned to individuals or parts of the performing organization, depending on the size of the project.

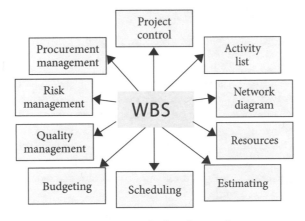

Figure 5.7 A WBS is the foundation of a project.

There may be many WBS references on the exam. To answer these questions correctly, remember that a WBS:

- Is a graphical picture of the hierarchy of a project that is part of the scope baseline
- Identifies all deliverables to be completed (if it's not in the WBS, it's not part of the project)
- Is the foundation upon which a project is built
- Should exist for every project
- Ensures that the project manager thinks through all aspects of a project
- Can be reused for other projects
- Does not show dependencies

 Many people confuse the terms "WBS" and "decomposition." The best way to think of decomposition is that decomposition is what you are doing, and a WBS is the means to do it. In other words, you decompose a project using a WBS.

 See figure 5.8 for another tip that can help you understand the relationships among control accounts, work packages, and activities on a project.

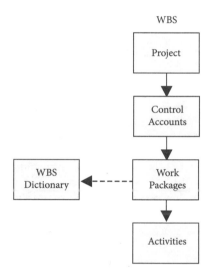

Figure 5.8 WBS relationships

WBS Dictionary PAGE 162

Think about how a work package is identified in a WBS. It's usually described using only one or two words, and assigning a deliverable with such a brief description to a team member allows for too much interpretation. In other words, it allows for scope creep (adding to product or project scope without adjusting time, cost, or resources). A WBS dictionary is the solution to this problem. This document provides a description of the work to be done for each WBS work package, and it lists the acceptance criteria for each deliverable, which ensures the resulting work matches what is needed. Therefore, a project manager can use a WBS dictionary to prevent scope creep before work even starts, rather than dealing with scope creep while the work is being done.

The WBS dictionary is an output of the Create WBS process. This document may be used as part of a work authorization system, which informs team members when their work package is going to start. A WBS dictionary can include descriptions of schedule milestones, acceptance criteria, durations, interdependencies, and other information about work packages. You can also use it to control what work is done when, to prevent scope creep, and to solidify a stakeholder's understanding of the effort required for each work package. The WBS dictionary essentially puts boundaries around what is included in a work package, similar to the way the project scope statement puts boundaries around what is included in a project. Note that some of the entries in a WBS dictionary, such as durations and interdependencies, may be filled in during iterations, rather than when it's first drafted.

A WBS dictionary may look similar to the example shown in figure 5.9.

WBS Dictionary			
Control Account ID #	Work Package Name/ Number	Date of Update	Responsible Organization/ Individual
Work Package Deliverable Description			
Work Involved to Produce Deliverable			
Acceptance Criteria (how to know if the deliverable/work is acceptable)			
Assumptions and Constraints			
Quality Metrics			
Technical Source Document			
Risks			
Resources Assigned			
Duration			
Schedule Milestones			
Cost			
Due Date			
Interdependncies Before this work package _____ After this work package _____			
Approved By: Project Manager _____ Date: _____			

Figure 5.9 WBS dictionary

Inputs to Create WBS PAGE 156
The following project documents are key inputs to the Create WBS process. Additional inputs include the scope management plan (which is part of the project management plan), enterprise environmental factors, and organizational process assets.

Project Scope Statement As explained earlier in this chapter, the project scope statement identifies what is and what is not included in the project. All project and product scope is broken down in the work breakdown structure.

Requirements Documentation This document includes detailed project requirements. It also depicts how the requirements will meet the business need for the project.

Tools and Techniques of Create WBS PAGE 158
The following is a key tool and technique of the Create WBS process.

Decomposition As previously mentioned, decomposition is used to break down the work of the project into smaller, more manageable pieces, or work packages. It is these pieces that are used to further plan and manage the project.

Outputs of Create WBS PAGE 161
The key output of the Create WBS process is the scope baseline, which encompasses the WBS, the WBS dictionary, and the project scope statement.

Scope Baseline As discussed in the Integration Management chapter, baselines help the project manager control a projects Baselines are simply the final and approved versions of certain pieces of the project management plan. For scope, the baseline is made up of the final versions of the WBS, the WBS dictionary, and the project scope statement that are approved at the end of planning, before the project work begins. As the work on the project is being done, the project manager reviews how the project is progressing and compares that data to the baseline by answering the following questions:

- How is my project going, and how does that compare to the baseline?
- What scope has been completed on the project?
- Does that scope match what is defined in the WBS, WBS dictionary, and project scope statement?

If scope is needed that isn't in the baseline, a change has to be formally approved through the integrated change control process, and a new item (or items) needs to be added to the WBS, WBS dictionary, and project scope statement to show the scope addition. This updated documentation becomes the new scope baseline for the project. Any other components of the project management plan and project documents that are affected by the change in scope also need to be updated, including requirements documentation and the assumption log.

A project's (and project manager's) measurements of success include whether the project has met all the requirements, including the scope baseline. Because a project manager's performance is evaluated along with the success of the project, it is essential to use the tools, techniques, and practices of project management in the real world.

© 2018 RMC Publications, Inc ™ • 952 846 4484 • info@rmcls.com • www.rmcls.com

Validate Scope PAGE 163

Many people are confused about what it means to validate scope. If you correctly understand scope validation, you can get five more questions right on the exam. These next few pages will clarify this process and help you find gaps in your knowledge.

TRICKS OF THE TRADE® First, think about the name of the process. Many people think Validate Scope means confirming the validity and appropriateness of the scope definition during project planning. This is incorrect, however. The Validate Scope process actually involves frequent, planned meetings with the customer or sponsor to gain formal acceptance of deliverables during project monitoring and controlling. That's a big difference, isn't it?

Let's look at the inputs to this process. Try this exercise.

Exercise

Can you list the inputs to Validate Scope? (Remember that the term *input* means, "What do I need before I can...?")

Answer

- Work must be completed and checked before each meeting with the customer; therefore, you must have what are called verified deliverables from the Control Quality process.
- It's helpful to have the approved scope with you when you meet with the customer, so you need the scope baseline from the project management plan.
- You'll also need to share information about the requirements of the project and show the customer how those requirements have been validated. This information can be found in the requirements management plan and the requirements traceability matrix.
- In addition, you should have the requirements documentation with you, in order to compare the requirements to the actual results. You can then determine whether any action or change needs to take place.
- Other project documents, such as quality reports and lessons learned, should also be reviewed at the start of this process. Quality reports can include information about open or closed issues as well as issue management, while lessons learned can be used to improve the process of validating project deliverables.

- Another component you should have from the project management plan is the scope management plan, which shows the previously agreed-upon deliverables and plans for gaining formal acceptance for them.
- Lastly, you will need to refer to work performance data from the Direct and Manage Project Work process to assess how well product deliverables are meeting the requirements.

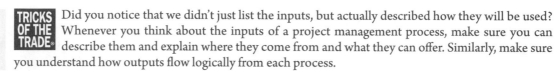 **TRICKS OF THE TRADE®** Did you notice that we didn't just list the inputs, but actually described how they will be used? Whenever you think about the inputs of a project management process, make sure you can describe them and explain where they come from and what they can offer. Similarly, make sure you understand how outputs flow logically from each process.

Now let's try outputs.

Exercise

Name the outputs of Validate Scope. (Remember that the term *output* means, "What will I have when I am done with…?")

Answer

Another way of looking at an output is to think about why you are doing this and what the expected result will be. Validate Scope is done to help ensure the project is on track from the customer's point of view during the project, rather than just hoping to get final acceptance in project closure. It's better to find changes and issues during the project than at the end. The customer will either accept the deliverables or make change requests. In either case, the project documents will need to be updated to reflect completion or changes. Therefore, the outputs are:

- Work performance information (analyzed work performance data)
- Accepted deliverables
- Change requests
- Updates to the lessons learned register, requirements traceability matrix, and requirements documentation

Beyond the potentially misleading name, there are a few more tricky aspects of the Validate Scope process. First, it can be done at the end of each phase of the project life cycle, to get formal acceptance of the phase deliverables. It can also be done at other points throughout the project as part of monitoring and controlling, to get formal acceptance of any deliverables that require approval in the middle of a phase, or the project. Therefore, the project manager validates scope with the customer multiple times throughout the life of a project. In a change-driven project, this will happen at the end of each iteration as part of the iteration review with the customer.

Second, the difference between the Validate Scope and the Close Project or Phase processes can also be a little tricky. Whereas the Validate Scope process results in formal acceptance by the customer of interim deliverables, part of the reason for the Close Project or Phase process is to get final acceptance or sign-off from the customer for the project or phase as a whole.

The third tricky aspect is understanding how Validate Scope relates to the Control Quality process. See the high-level diagram in figure 5.10.

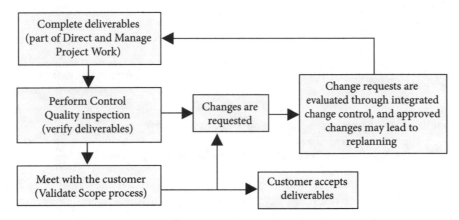

Figure 5.10 Relationship between Validate Scope and Control Quality

Although Control Quality is generally done first (to make sure the deliverable meets the requirements before it is shown to the customer), the two processes are very similar as both involve checking for the correctness of work. The difference is the focus of the effort and who is doing the checking. In Control Quality, the quality control department checks to see if the requirements specified for the deliverables are met and makes sure the work is correct. In Validate Scope, the customer checks and hopefully accepts the deliverables.

Inputs to Validate Scope PAGE 165
Verified deliverables are a key input to the Validate Scope process. Additional inputs may include components of the project management plan, project documents, and work performance data.

Verified Deliverables
In order to meet with the customer to gain formal acceptance of deliverables, you need to have the deliverables verified. "Verified" means the deliverable is checked as part of the process before it is submitted to the customer for approval.

Tools and Techniques of Validate Scope PAGE 166
The following technique is used during the Validate Scope process. Also note that voting is a decision-making technique that may be used during this process. Voting can be used to determine a final conclusion after scope validation. The project team and key stakeholders may participate in this voting.

Inspection   Inspection includes measurements, reviews, and possibly formal audits of work products and results. The purpose of inspections is to validate, before presenting the work product to the customer, that the work results conform to requirements. The person who produced the work product participates in the inspection, although the project manager may be responsible for overseeing the inspection process.

Outputs of Validate Scope PAGE 166
   The following are key outputs of the Validate Scope process. Additional outputs may include work performance information and updates to project documents such as the lessons learned register, requirements documentation, and the requirements traceability matrix.

Accepted Deliverables   What are accepted deliverables? They are deliverables that meet a set of conditions prior to acceptance. They are also formally signed off and approved by the customer or sponsor.

Change Requests   If the customer does not accept a deliverable, a change request may be issued. After the deliverable is corrected, it will be verified through the Control Quality process and then once again presented to the customer for approval in the Validate Scope process.

Control Scope PAGE 167

> **Process:** Control Scope
> **Process Group:** Monitoring & Controlling
> **Knowledge Area:** Scope Management

Control Scope involves measuring and assessing work performance data against the scope baseline and managing scope baseline changes. At any point in a project, the project manager must be sure that the scope is being completed according to the project management plan.

To control scope, the project manager needs to start with a clear definition of the scope (the scope baseline from the project management plan) and have work completed on the project. The project manager should also be aware of the original requirements recorded in the requirements documentation and the requirements traceability matrix (inputs to this process). At this point, the project manager can measure the completed work against the scope baseline, perform data analysis, including analyzing any variances, and determine whether the variances are significant enough to warrant changes. If necessary, the project manager would submit a change request through the Perform Integrated Change Control process to assess the impact the change would have on the project. New work performance information may result, along with updates to the project management plan and project documents.

Scope control feeds into and receives from the Perform Integrated Change Control process, as shown in figure 5.11.

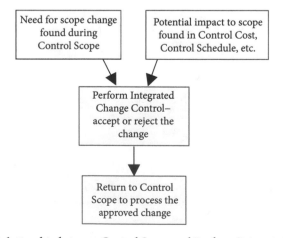

Figure 5.11   Relationship between Control Scope and Perform Integrated Change Control

Remember that the Control Scope process is extremely proactive. It includes thinking about where changes to scope are coming from on the project and what can be done to prevent or remove the need for any more changes from that source. Properly using project management tools, techniques, and practices will save you from unnecessary problems throughout the life of a project.

A project manager's job is not to just process other people's changes, but to control the project to the project management plan and meet all baselines. Therefore, a project manager should not be easily swayed or influenced, and should not let others add or change scope without following the approved change management process and ensuring the suggested changes are within the planned scope of the project. As discussed earlier, people who want work to be done will try to add it to the project whether it is logically part of the project or not. This is why it's so important that a project manager control the project scope.

Inputs to Control Scope PAGE 169   The following are key inputs to the Control Scope process.

Project Management Plan   The project management plan includes the scope baseline, which is an input to this process because it provides a clear definition of what the scope is on the project. The scope management plan is also relevant to this process because it provides an understanding of how scope is to be planned, managed, and controlled. The change and configuration management plans provide information about managing and controlling changes on the project and knowing which version of the scope is current. The requirements management plan is also an input, as it provides details about making changes to requirements and who is authorized to approve such changes.

Project Documents   Project documents such as the requirements documentation and requirements traceability matrix provide information about the history of requirements on the project, including who requested the requirement and how to know when a requirement is acceptable and completed. In addition to these documents, the lessons learned register may also be useful during the Control Scope process.

Tools and Techniques of Control Scope PAGE 170   Data analysis is a tool used in the Control Scope process.

Data Analysis   There are two types of data analysis techniques that may be used during the Control Scope process, variance analysis and trend analysis. Variance analysis simply means looking at the actual scope or technical performance on the project and comparing it to the planned performance (the scope baseline). If there are any differences, or variances, between what was planned and what is actually happening on the project, the project manager will need to decide if corrective or preventive action is necessary to bring the project back in line. Trend analysis examines project performance as a whole. This type of analysis will help a project manager determine whether performance is improving over time throughout the life of a project.

Outputs of Control Scope PAGE 170   The following are key outputs of the Control Scope process.

Work Performance Information   As a result of data analysis and other activities, work performance information is generated, including the status of the project compared to the scope baseline and projected future scope performance.

Change Requests   The analysis of project performance may result in requested changes, including recommendations for corrective or preventive action or defect repair. Change requests are a frequent output of monitoring and controlling processes. These requests are then approved, rejected, or deferred as part of the Perform Integrated Change Control process.

Project Management Plan and Project Documents Updates   The project management plan and project documents are not just created at the beginning of the project, and then forgotten about. They are used as day-to-day tools to manage the project and its activities. This documentation must be kept up to date to remain useful. The control processes for any knowledge area generally result in the same thing—updates to the project management plan and project documents.

Scope Management Review

Exercise

This exercise will help you review the key material you need to know for scope management. The Shuffle Game that follows offers another approach to this material. You can use either or both of these study tools, depending on your preference.

Instructions

1. Try to fill in the blanks in the below table using the knowledge and understanding gained after reading this chapter.
2. To review only the material contained in this chapter, focus on the cells that have asterisks. (These are the key topics you need to understand to pass the exam with the minimum amount of study time. The answer table will show only these topics.)
3. To review all the items listed in the *PMBOK® Guide*, fill in the entire table.

Key Inputs	Key Tools and Techniques	Key Outputs
Plan Scope Management Process group:		
		*
Collect Requirments Process group:		
*	*	*
Define Scope Process group:		
*	*	*

Scope Management

Key Inputs	Key Tools and Techniques	Key Outputs
Create WBS Process group:		
*	*	*
Validate Scope Process group:		
*	*	*
Control Scope Process group:		
*	*	*

Answer   To save study time and focus on the most important information, this answer table only shows the topics that are covered in this chapter. If you tried to list all inputs, tools and techniques, and outputs, you'll need to check your answers against the *PMBOK® Guide*.

Key Inputs	Key Tools and Techniques	Key Outputs
Plan Scope Management Process group: Planning		
		Scope management plan Requirements management plan
Collect Requirements Process group: Planning		
Project charter Assumption log Stakeholder register Agreements Organizational process assets	Data gathering • Brainstorming • Interviews • Focus groups • Questionnaires and surveys • Benchmarking Data analysis • Document analysis Decision making • Voting • Multicriteria decision analysis Data representation • Affinity diagrams • Mind mapping Interpersonal and team skills • Nominal group technique • Observation • Facilitation Context diagrams Prototypes	Requirements documentation Requirements traceability matrix
Define Scope Process group: Planning		
Requirements documentation	Product analysis	Project scope statement
Create WBS Process group: Planning		
Project scope statement Requirements documentation	Decomposition	Scope baseline
Validate Scope Process group: Monitoring and controlling		
Verified deliverables	Inspection	Accepted deliverables Change requests

Key Inputs	Key Tools and Techniques	Key Outputs
Control Scope Process group: Monitoring and controlling		
Project management plan Project documents	Data analysis	Work performance information Change requests Project management plan updates Project documents updates

Shuffle Game

Some people learn best by doing, which is why we have developed this alternate approach to reviewing scope management. To save you time, only the most important topics for the exam—those covered in this chapter—have been included.

Instructions

1. Cut out the cards on the next pages.
2. Lay out the bold title cards as column headers.
3. Shuffle the remaining cards and try to put them in the columns where they belong. Cards with italic terms must be matched to the corresponding group. For example, a *Cost of Quality* card in italics would match with a Data Analysis card, as cost of quality is a data analysis tool and technique.
4. Check your answers against the material covered in this chapter or the *PMBOK® Guide,* and make note of any gaps in your knowledge.

Note: Be sure to keep all cards for each chapter shuffle game as you will use them again for the final Shuffle Game in chapter 14.

© 2018 RMC Publications, Inc.™ • 952.846.4484 • info@rmcls.com • www.rmcls.com

Plan Scope Management *Key Outputs*	**Collect Requirements** *Key Inputs*	**Collect Requirements** *Key Tools and Techniques*
Collect Requirements *Key Outputs*	**Define Scope** *Key Inputs*	**Define Scope** *Key Tools and Techniques*
Define Scope *Key Outputs*	**Create WBS** *Key Inputs*	**Create WBS** *Key Tools and Techniques*
Create WBS *Key Outputs*	**Validate Scope** *Key Inputs*	**Validate Scope** *Key Tools and Techniques*
Validate Scope *Key Outputs*	**Control Scope** *Key Inputs*	**Control Scope** *Key Tools and Techniques*

Control Scope *Key Outputs*	Scope management plan	Requirements management plan
Project charter	Assumption log	Stakeholder register
Agreements	Organizational process assets	Data gathering
Brainstorming	*Interviews*	*Focus groups*
Questionnaires and surveys	*Benchmarking*	Data analysis

Document analysis	Decision making	Voting
Multicriteria decision analysis	Data representation	Affinity diagrams
Mind mapping	Interpersonal and team skills	Nominal group technique
Observation	Facilitation	Context diagrams
Prototypes	Requirements documentation	Requirements traceability matrix

Requirements documentation	Product analysis	Project scope statement
Project scope statement	Requirements documentation	Decomposition
Scope baseline	Verified deliverables	Inspection
Accepted deliverables	Change requests	Project management plan

Project documents	Data analysis	Work performance information
Change requests	Project management plan updates	Project documents updates

Practice Exam

1. Project requirements should be elicited from _____.
   A. The sponsor
   B. The project team
   C. All stakeholders
   D. The project manager

2. The project team has just discovered that work critical to the completion of a project deliverable was not done. This situation was most likely caused by a lack of:
   A. A good work breakdown structure
   B. A matrix organization
   C. Sponsor direction
   D. Effective status meetings

3. Which of the following statements about scope is correct?
   A. Project scope is defined as the project deliverables, with their associated features and functions.
   B. Product scope refers to the requirements that relate to the product, service, or result of the project.
   C. Product scope encompasses project scope.
   D. Product scope is the work the project will do to deliver a product, service, or feature.

4. Which of the following is not part of the Define Scope process?
   A. Facilitation
   B. Alternatives analysis
   C. Product analysis
   D. Inspection

5. Which of the following is not shown on a WBS?
   A. Control accounts
   B. Work packages
   C. Deliverables
   D. Workarounds

6. Which of the following is an output of the Collect Requirements process?
   A. Requirements traceability matrix
   B. Project scope statement
   C. Work breakdown structure
   D. Change requests

7. Which of the following is correct in regard to the Control Scope process?
   A. Effective scope definition can lead to a more complete project scope statement.
   B. The Control Scope process must be done before scope planning.
   C. The Control Scope process must be integrated with other control processes.
   D. Controlling the schedule is the most effective way of controlling scope.

8. Which of the following best describes product analysis?
   A. Working with the customer or sponsor to determine the product description during project initiating
   B. Mathematically analyzing the quality desired for the project as part of Plan Quality Management
   C. Analyzing the objectives and description of the product, as stated by the customer or sponsor, to define tangible deliverables
   D. Analyzing inspection data to determine whether the quality standards on the project can be met

9. If the team is performing variance analysis on the project, which process are they in?
   A. Collect Requirements
   B. Validate Scope
   C. Define Scope
   D. Control Scope

10. Which of the following is not required to create the scope management plan?
    A. A finalized requirements management plan
    B. Any historical records and lessons learned from previous projects
    C. Any existing templates, forms, or standards for scope management
    D. A good understanding of the project scope

11. Which of the following is not one of the rules for creating a WBS?
    A. Each level of the WBS shows a smaller piece of the level above it.
    B. If a deliverable isn't in the WBS, it isn't part of the project.
    C. The project team helps to create the WBS.
    D. All levels of the WBS are broken down to the same level of detail.

12. Two months into a design project, the customer requests a modification to the product. The change is made without notifying the project manager. During final testing, the results are different than what was planned for. This scenario can best be described as an example of which of the following?
    A. Poor scope control
    B. Poor adherence to the communications management plan
    C. Poor development of the quality management plan
    D. Poor definition of the test plan

13. What are the key outputs of the Plan Scope Management process?
    A. Accepted deliverables and change requests
    B. The scope management plan and the requirements management plan
    C. Constraints and assumptions
    D. Work breakdown structure and WBS dictionary

14. What is done during the Validate Scope process?
    A. The project manager measures and assesses work performance data against the scope baseline.
    B. The team confirms the validity and appropriateness of the project scope with key stakeholders.
    C. The project manager gains formal acceptance of deliverables from the customer or sponsor.
    D. The quality control department checks to see if the requirements specified for the deliverables have been met, and makes sure the work is correct.

15. What does the "work" in "work breakdown structure" refer to?
    A. The tasks that are being broken down from the required activities
    B. The processes involved in completing the work packages
    C. The activities or actions needed to complete the deliverables of the work packages
    D. The products or deliverables that will result from the activities

Answers

1. **Answer** C
   Explanation The project's sponsor, the project manager, and the project team are all stakeholders. Requirements must be elicited from all stakeholders, so that is the best answer here.

2. **Answer** A
   Explanation Although there could be other reasons than those presented, this situation was most likely caused by a lack of a good work breakdown structure, which identifies each work package so that they can be properly assigned, thus reducing the possibility that required work will slip through the cracks.

3. **Answer** B
   Explanation "Product scope" is the term for the requirements that relate to the product, service, or result of the project. Product scope—not project scope—is defined as the project deliverables. Project scope is the work the project team will do to deliver a product, service, or feature. Project scope encompasses product scope.

4. **Answer** D
   Explanation Facilitation, alternatives analysis, and product analysis are tools and techniques of Define Scope, which is part of the planning process group. Inspection is done during project monitoring and controlling—in the Validate Scope process—and is therefore the exception.

5. **Answer** D
   Explanation The only item listed here that is not shown on a WBS is workarounds.

6. **Answer** A
   Explanation The project scope statement is an output of the Define Scope process. The work breakdown structure is an output of the Create WBS process. Scope change requests are outputs of the Validate Scope and Control Scope processes. The requirements traceability matrix is an output of the Collect Requirements process. It links requirements to objectives and other requirements, and is used throughout the project.

7. **Answer** C
   Explanation Although it is correct that effective scope definition can lead to a more complete project scope statement, this cannot be the answer because it does not deal with controlling scope. Scope planning occurs before the Control Scope process, not after it. Controlling the schedule is not the best way to control scope. The control processes do not act in isolation. A change to one will most likely affect the others. Therefore, integrating the Control Scope process with other control processes is the best answer.

8. **Answer** C
   Explanation Product analysis involves analyzing the objectives and description of the product, as stated by the customer or sponsor. That information is then used to define tangible deliverables. Product analysis is a critical tool in the Define Scope process, which occurs during project planning. Product analysis allows the project manager to make sure the product and project scope are understood and accurate.

9. **Answer** D
Explanation Control Scope, which is a monitoring and controlling process, includes measuring the performance of the project to determine any variances from the scope baseline. Significant variances require corrective action by the team.

10. **Answer** A
Explanation This question is testing whether you understand the inputs to Plan Scope Management. A good understanding of the project scope is essential, and you'll also want to gather any available historical records and lessons learned, as well as any existing templates, forms, and standards for scope management. The scope management plan and the requirements management plan are outputs of the Plan Scope Management process, not inputs. Therefore, a finalized requirements management plan isn't needed to start creating the scope management plan.

11. **Answer** D
Explanation These are all valid rules for creating a WBS except for "All levels of the WBS are broken down to the same level of detail." The correct rule states that some levels on the WBS will be broken down further than others. Each level is broken down to the point at which the work package can be confidently estimated, so that it can be completed internally or outsourced without additional information.

12. **Answer** A
Explanation If the scope change had been properly communicated and recorded, the impact of the change could have been identified immediately. While poor communication is part of the problem here, poor scope control is still the best answer because making a modification is first and foremost a scope control issue. The question notes that testing apparently revealed the issue, so the problem is not related to poor test plan definition, and there no evidence of a quality management plan issue.

13. **Answer** B
Explanation The Plan Scope Management process results in the scope management plan and requirements management plan. Accepted deliverables and change requests are outputs of the Validate Scope process. Constraints and assumptions are included in the project scope statement, which is an output of the Define Scope process. The work breakdown structure and WBS dictionary are components of the scope baseline, which is an output of the Create WBS process.

14. **Answer** C
Explanation In the Validate Scope process, the project manager gains formal acceptance of interim deliverables from the customer or sponsor. A common misconception about the meaning of Validate Scope is that it involves confirming the project scope with stakeholders. Measuring and assessing work performance data is done during Control Scope. The quality control department checks to see if the requirements specified for the deliverables have been met, and during Control Quality, they make sure the work is correct. Remember that the difference between Validate Scope and Control Quality is the focus of the effort and who is doing the checking.

15. **Answer** D
Explanation The "work" in "work breakdown structure" refers not to the activities required to complete the deliverables, but to the deliverables that result from those activities. Since the other choices refer to tasks, processes, and activities, the correct answer is products or deliverables. Remember that a WBS is deliverable oriented.

Schedule Management

SIX

There are 13 to 14 questions on this knowledge area on the CAPM exam. Also note, for a full list of all inputs, tools and techniques, and outputs within this knowledge area, please see the table on page 174 in the PMBOK© Guide.

Imagine that your manager says they have a new project for you. You receive some information about the project, and then your manager asks you to create a schedule. What would you do first?

Most people would make a list of all the work or activities needed to complete the project, and then determine the duration for each activity or piece of work. If you have been carefully reading this book up until now, you may already realize that there are some planning steps that should be done prior to creating a schedule.

Let's assume, for this scenario, that you have completed some planning steps and developed a schedule for your project. Is the schedule realistic? Will any schedule that meets the requested end dates be acceptable? How is the schedule used to manage the project? What value does a detailed schedule have? These are questions you should be able to answer after reading this chapter.

 Schedule management is the process of developing a realistic project schedule and a schedule baseline. A project manager must first plan how they will do the work of schedule management. Then, they take the work packages in the WBS and make a list of the work (activities) that need to be done. The project manager then sequences those activities using a network diagram to determine how the project will flow from beginning to end. Also, activity durations are estimated for each activity.

QUICKTEST

- Schedule management process
- Schedule baseline
- Schedule compression
  - Crashing
  - Fast tracking
- Activity list
- Network diagram
- Dependencies determination
  - Mandatory
  - Discretionary
  - External
  - Internal
- Reserve analysis
- Alternatives analysis
- Activity attributes
- Milestone list
- Analogous estimating
- Parametric estimating
- Bottom-up estimating
- Precedence diagramming method (PDM)
- Critical path
- Float (schedule flexibility)
  - Total float
  - Free float
  - Project float
- Three-point estimating
  - Beta distribution
  - Triangular distribution
- Schedule model
- Schedule management plan
- Agile release planning
- Resource optimization
  - Resource leveling
  - Resource smoothing
- Critical path method
- Near-critical path
- Leads and lags
- Resource breakdown structure
- Reestimating
- Rolling wave planning
- Decomposition
- Bar charts
- Milestone charts
- Monte Carlo analysis

After all this is done, there may be meetings, negotiations, and adjustments to come up with not just a schedule, but a schedule that everyone can agree is realistic, given what is known at the time. Once the work starts, performance of the schedule is measured against the plan, and adjustments or changes are requested.

Did you notice how straightforward the process is, and how logical? If you thoroughly understand schedule management, you'll be able to answer exam questions that relate to inputs and outputs using your knowledge of the topic and concepts, instead of memorization.

The following table should help you understand how each part of schedule management fits into the overall project management process.

The Schedule Management Process	Done During
Plan Schedule Management	Planning process group
Define Activities	Planning process group
Sequence Activities	Planning process group
Estimate Activity Durations	Planning process group
Develop Schedule	Planning process group
Control Schedule	Monitoring and controlling process group

Plan Schedule Management PAGE 179

Process: Plan Schedule Management
Process Group: Planning
Knowledge Area: Schedule Management

The Plan Schedule Management process involves documenting how a project manager will plan, manage, and control the project to the schedule baseline, and how they will manage schedule variances. Many project managers just work on a project and hope the project meets the deadline; however, proper schedule management requires a project manager to develop and follow a plan, measuring progress along the way. During planning, the project manager will need to determine in advance what the measures of performance will be, how and when they will capture the data needed to evaluate schedule performance, how they will use the data to keep the project on track, and what they will do when variances occur. Plan Schedule Management answers questions such as, "Who will be involved, and what approach will we take to plan the schedule for the project?" and "What processes and procedures will we use to create the schedule?"

The project life cycle and development approach agreed on in the Develop Project Management plan process (in integration management) will influence the level and type of schedule management planning a project manager will do on a project. They will also consider existing enterprise environmental factors. Is there a work authorization system in place for the project to use? Does the organization have a preferred project management software to use for scheduling? If not, will the work of the project include creating a work authorization system or selecting a scheduling software product? How do the company culture and overall structure of the organization impact the work of scheduling the project?

Also keep in mind that expert judgment and data analysis techniques, such as alternatives analysis, may be used in planning the methodology a project manager will use to create the final schedule. To plan the schedule, a project manager might also need to review the project charter or hold meetings that include the project sponsor, team members, and other stakeholders.

© 2010 RMC Publications, Inc.™ • 952.846.4484 • info@rmcls.com • www.rmcls.com

Outputs of Plan Schedule Management PAGE 181   The output of the Plan Schedule Management process is the schedule management plan.

Schedule Management Plan   The key output of this process is a schedule management plan, which can be formal or informal. It is part of the project management plan, and it helps make the estimating and schedule development process faster by specifying the following:

- The scheduling methodology and scheduling software to be used on the project.
- Rules for how estimates should be stated; for example, should estimates be in hours, days, or weeks? Should estimators identify both the effort (the amount of labor involved in completing an activity—for example, 12 hours) and duration (the number of work periods the effort will span—for example, 1.5 days) needed to complete an activity?
- A schedule baseline for measuring against in project monitoring and controlling.
- A threshold for acceptable variance.
- Performance measures that will be used on the project to identify variances early.
- A plan for how schedule variances will be managed.
- A process for determining whether a variance must be acted upon.
- Identification of schedule change control procedures.
- Types of schedule reports required on the project.
- Format and frequency of project reporting.
- The number and timing of releases and iterations (in an adaptive life cycle).

Define Activities PAGE 183

> **Process:** Define Activities
> **Process Group:** Planning
> **Knowledge Area:** Schedule Management

This process involves taking the work packages created in the WBS and decomposing them into the activities that are required to produce the work package deliverables and thus achieve the project objectives. The activities should be at a level small enough to estimate, schedule, monitor, and control. These activities are then sequenced in the next process, Sequence Activities. (Note that breaking down the project work into the work packages in the WBS is part of scope management, and the identification of activities is part of schedule management.)

Defining activities is not always done as a separate process. Many project managers combine this effort with creating a WBS and WBS dictionary; they decompose work packages into the activities required to produce them, rather than stopping at the work package level.

Inputs to Define Activities PAGE 184   What does a project manager need in order to define activities? The schedule management plan, created in the previous process, gives the project manager important information about the approved methodology for scheduling. The scope baseline from scope management provides information about what is included in the project scope. This is the work they will now break down into project activities. The project manager may also refer to organizational process assets including existing templates, historical information (such as activity lists from other similar projects), and any standards (such as a prescribed scheduling methodology). Also note that involving the team in this process helps define the activities completely and accurately and therefore makes the estimates, created later in the planning process, more accurate.

The following are key inputs to the Define Activities process.

Project Management Plan
Components of the project management plan, such as the schedule management plan and scope baseline, may be useful during the Define Activities process. For example, the scope baseline includes the project scope statement, WBS, and WBS dictionary. The scope baseline is a critical input, as the project manager will need to know what is and what is not in scope for the project in order to define the activities. They also need the WBS and WBS dictionary to break the work packages into activities.

Enterprise Environmental Factors
Remember that these factors will be an input to many processes. The enterprise environmental factors relating to this process include the project management information system (PMIS) and any organizational cultures, as well as any structures that may impact the process of defining activities.

Organizational Process Assets
These assets are another repeated input. If you understand what each of these repeated topics are, you will be able to more easily determine if they are inputs or outputs on the exam. Organizational process assets relating to the Define Activities process include company policies and procedures, such as the scheduling methodology, as well as activity lists from other similar projects, which are part of lessons learned and historical information.

Tools and Techniques of Define Activities PAGE 184
The following are key tools and techniques used during the Define Activities process. It's important to note that expert judgment may be utilized as well.

Rolling Wave Planning
Have you ever worked on a project that seemed to have too many unknown components to adequately break down the work and schedule it? Be careful—when that's the case, there might be more than one project. Or, it might simply be a project for which it is better to not plan the entire project to the smallest detail in advance, but instead to plan to a higher level and then develop more detailed plans when the work is to be done. This practice is called "rolling wave planning," and it is a form of progressive elaboration. Remember that progressive elaboration refers to the process of clarifying and refining plans as the project progresses. With this method, the project manager plans activities to the level of detail needed to manage the work just before they are ready to start that part of the project. This technique is used to varying degrees on both change-driven and plan-driven projects. Iterations of rolling wave planning during the project may result in additional activities being added, and the further elaboration of other activities. Therefore, rolling wave planning may create the need for updates to the project management plan, specifically the schedule, scope, or cost baselines. These changes require integrated change control, beginning with a change request.

But remember—the option of rolling wave planning doesn't eliminate the need to identify all the scope that can be known before starting work.

Decomposition
Decomposition is used in this process, as well as in the Create WBS process in scope management. When you see this term used on the exam, it's important to look at the context of what is being decomposed. When deliverables are being decomposed into smaller deliverables (work packages), you know the question is referring to the Create WBS process. When work packages are being decomposed into the activities to produce them, the question is referring to the Define Activities process. Be sure to choose an answer choice that aligns with the appropriate process.

Outputs of Define Activities PAGE 185

The following key outputs are the result of the Define Activities process. Change requests and updates to components of the project management plan (such as the cost and schedule baselines, for example) may also occur as a result of this process. Note that Define Activities is one of only a few planning processes with an output of change requests specifically listed in the *PMBOK® Guide*. Refer back to the discussion of rolling wave planning, and you will see that, as the project progresses, early planning efforts may need to be iterated, potentially resulting in changes to the project baselines.

Activity List and Activity Attributes

When completed, the Define Activities process results in an activity list, which includes all activities required to complete the project, and activity attributes, or details regarding project activities. At this time, known attributes may be limited to the activity name and ID number. As the project progresses, additional attributes—such as planned completion date, leads and lags, and predecessor and successor activities—may be added.

Milestone List

The Define Activities process also involves determining milestones to use on the project. Milestones are significant events within the project schedule. They are not work activities and have no duration. For example, a completed design, a customer-imposed due date for an interim deliverable, or a company-required checkpoint, phase gate, or stage gate could be a milestone. Initial milestones are documented in the project charter. The project manager can also insert milestones as checkpoints to help control the project. If a milestone in the schedule is reached and any of the planned work has not been completed, it indicates the project is not progressing as planned. The milestone list is part of the project documents.

Sequence Activities PAGE 187

> **Process:** Sequence Activities
> **Process Group:** Planning
> **Knowledge Area:** Schedule Management

This process involves taking the activities and sequencing them in the order in which the work will be performed. The result is a network diagram (also referred to as a project schedule network diagram), which is illustrated in figure 6.1.

Figure 6.1 Network diagram

In its pure form, a network diagram just shows dependencies (logical relationships). If activity duration estimates and leads and lags are added to the diagram later in the schedule management process, it can also show the critical path. If plotted against time (or aligned with a calendar-based scale), the network diagram becomes a time-scaled schedule network diagram.

Inputs to Sequence Activities PAGE 188

The following is a key input to the Sequence Activities process. Additional inputs may include components of the project management plan (such as the schedule management plan and scope baseline), enterprise environmental factors, and any related organizational process assets.

Project Documents   Project documents that may be considered inputs to the Sequence Activities process include the activity attributes, the assumption log, the milestone list, and the activity list. The activity list includes all the activities required to complete the project, as well as documentation of the details of those activities (activity attributes).

Tools and Techniques of Sequence Activities PAGE 189   The following are key tools and techniques that may be used during the Sequence Activities process.

Precedence Diagramming Method (PDM)   In this method, nodes (or boxes) are used to represent activities, and arrows are added to show activity dependencies, as shown in figure 6.2.

Activity A ⟶ Activity B

Figure 6.2 Precedence diagramming method

This type of drawing can have four types of logical relationships between activities (see fig. 6.3):

- **Finish-to-start (FS)** An activity must finish before the successor can start. This is the most commonly used relationship. Example: You must finish digging a hole before you can start the next activity, planting a tree.
- **Start-to-start (SS)** An activity must start before the successor can start. Example: You must start designing and wait for two weeks' lag in order to have enough of the design completed to start coding.
- **Finish-to-finish (FF)** An activity must finish before the successor can finish. Example: You must finish testing before you can finish documentation.
- **Start-to-finish (SF)** An activity must start before the successor can finish. This dependency is rarely used.

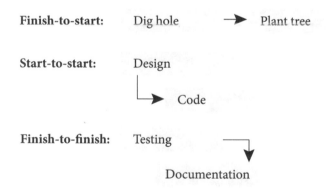

Finish-to-start: Dig hole ⟶ Plant tree

Start-to-start: Design ↳ Code

Finish-to-finish: Testing ↘ Documentation

Figure 6.3 Finish-to-start, start-to-start, and finish-to-finish dependencies

Dependencies Determination   The sequence of activities may be determined based on the following dependencies:

- **Mandatory dependency (hard logic)** A mandatory dependency is inherent in the nature of the work (for example, you must design before you can construct) or required by a contract.
- **Discretionary dependency (preferred, preferential, or soft logic)** This is how an organization may choose to have work performed. There are other ways it could be done, but this is the preferred approach. Whereas you cannot easily change the other types of dependencies, you can change a

discretionary dependency, if necessary. Discretionary dependencies are important when analyzing how to compress the schedule to decrease the project duration (i.e., fast track the project).

- **External dependency** This dependency is based on the needs or desires of a party outside the project (for example, government or suppliers).
- **Internal dependency** This dependency is based on the needs of the project and may be something the project team can control.

More than one dependency can be identified for the same work. Combinations include mandatory external, mandatory internal, discretionary external, and discretionary internal.

The project team identifies mandatory and discretionary dependencies; the project manager identifies external and internal dependencies. (Remember, when we use the term "project manager" in this book, we're referring to anyone doing project management activities on the project, which could include not just the lead project manager but also supporting members of the project management team.)

Leads and Lags

A lead may be used to indicate that an activity can start before its predecessor activity is completed. For example, web page design might be able to start five days before the database design is finished. A lag is waiting time inserted between activities, such as needing to wait three days after pouring concrete before constructing the frame for a house. When project activities are first being sequenced, the duration of the activities, and required leads and lags, may be uncertain.

Project Management Information System (PMIS)

Also keep in mind, when creating complex project schedule network diagrams that include leads and lags as well as other dependencies, an automated scheduling system that is part of the PMIS can be used. This is especially helpful on large projects.

Outputs of Sequence Activities PAGE 194

The following are the outputs of the Sequence Activities process.

Project Schedule Network Diagrams

A project schedule network diagram (which may also be referred to as a network diagram or an activity network diagram) is an image depicting the flow of project activities in the logical order in which they will be performed. All activities after Start should be connected to at least one predecessor activity. All activities on the network diagram before Finish should be connected to at least one successor activity. In addition to sequencing activities, the network diagram helps you to plan which activities can be completed in parallel and see where leads or lags are required. Of course, the more complex the project, the more likely it is that activities will overlap. When an activity has two or more activities directly preceding it, this is referred to as path convergence. When an activity has two or more successor activities directly following it, this is referred to as path divergence. Both path convergence and path divergence are indicators of greater risk within the impacted activities.

Benefits of Network Diagrams
- Help justify the time estimate for the project
- Aid in effectively planning, organizing, and controlling the project
- Show interdependencies of all activities, and thereby identify riskier activities
- Show workflow, so the team will know what activities need to happen in a specific sequence
- Identify opportunities to compress the schedule in planning and throughout the life of the project (explained later in this chapter)
- Show project progress (when used for controlling the schedule and reporting)

Project Documents Updates   In addition to a network diagram, the Sequence Activities process may result in updates to project documents such as the activity list, activity attributes, assumption log, and milestone list. Sequencing the activities can also reveal new risks, resulting in changes to the risk register.

Estimate Activity Durations PAGE 195

> **Process:** Estimate Activity Resources
> **Process Group:** Planning
> **Knowledge Area:** Schedule Management

When the activities have been defined and sequenced, the next step is to estimate how long each activity will take. This is the Estimate Activity Durations process. When possible, the estimators should be those who will be doing the work. On large projects, however, the estimators are more often the members of the project management team, as it is known during planning, who are most familiar with the work that needs to be done.

Inputs to Estimate Activity Durations PAGE 198   To come up with realistic time estimates, estimators need to have access to project documents such as the milestone list, project team assignments, resource calendars, and risk register. Additional documents may include the following:

- **Activity list and activity attributes**   The relevant inputs may include the time for required leads or lags between activities, which must be factored into duration estimates.
- **Assumption log**   Assumptions or constraints that contribute to risk within the activities to be estimated can be found in the assumption log.
- **Lessons learned register**   Information relevant to estimating the duration of schedule activities include lessons learned from earlier in the current project or from past, similar projects performed by the organization.
- **Resource breakdown structure**   Created in the Estimate Activity Resources process of Resource Management, the resource breakdown structure represents categories of resources required for the project.
- **Resource requirements**   These requirements indicate the skill levels required to perform specific project work.

The Estimate Activity Durations process also uses information from the project management plan, as well as any enterprise environmental factors and organizational process assets that may influence duration estimates.

Tools and Techniques of Estimate Activity Durations PAGE 200   Let's look at some of the different estimating techniques that may be used during this process.

Analogous (Top-Down) Estimating   Applicable to duration, cost, and resource estimating, analogous estimating uses expert judgment and historical information to predict the future. Management or the sponsor might use analogous estimating to create the overall project constraint or estimate that is given to the project manager as the project is chartered. The project manager may use analogous estimating at the project level, using historical data from past, similar projects. (For example, "The last five projects similar to this one each took eight months, so this one should as well.") Analogous estimating can also be used at the activity level, if the activity has been done on previous projects and there is substantial historical data to support the accuracy of such an estimate. (For example, "The last two times this activity was completed each took three days; since we have no other information to go on, we will use three days as the estimate for this activity and review the estimate when more details become available.")

Parametric Estimating   Parametric estimating involves creating a mathematical equation using data from historical records or other sources, such as industry requirements or standard metrics, to create

estimates. The technique analyzes relationships between historical data and other variables to estimate duration or cost. It can be applied to some or all of the activities within a project. For example, when estimating activity duration, the estimator may use measures such as time per line of code, time per linear meter, or time per installation. When used in cost estimating, the measures include cost as one of the variables. So the measures would be cost per line of code, cost per linear meter, and so on.

An estimator might create parametric estimates using the following:

- **Regression analysis (scatter diagram)** This diagram tracks two variables to see if they are related; the diagram is then used to create a mathematical formula to use in future parametric estimating (see fig. 6.4).
- **Learning curve** Example: The 100th room painted will take less time than the first room because of improved efficiency.

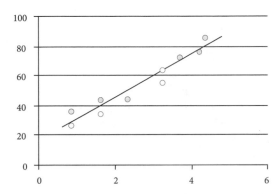

Figure 6.4 Regression analysis (scatter diagram)

Three-Point Estimating
Statistically, there is a very small probability of completing a project on exactly any one date. As we know, things don't always go according to plan. Therefore, it's often best to state estimates in a range, using three-point estimates. Analyzing what could go right (opportunities) and what could go wrong (threats) can help estimators determine an expected range for each activity. By analyzing the range of time or cost estimates, the project manager can better understand the potential variation of the activity estimates. With the three-point technique, estimators give an estimate for each activity: optimistic (O), pessimistic (P), and most likely (M). Three-point estimating allows more consideration of both the uncertainty of estimating and the risks associated with the activities being estimated. A wide range between the optimistic and pessimistic estimates can indicate uncertainty—and therefore risk—associated with the activity.

Three-point estimates can be used to calculate a risk-based expected duration estimate for an activity by taking either a simple average or a weighted average of three estimates. See the following information and formulas.

Triangular Distribution (Simple Average)
A simple average of the three-point estimates can be calculated using the formula $(P + O + M)/3$. The use of simple averaging gives equal weight to each of the three-point estimates when calculating the expected activity duration or cost. Using this formula, the risks (P and O estimates) are considered equally along with the most likely (M) estimate.

Beta Distribution (Weighted Average)
The use of a beta distribution (weighted average) gives stronger consideration to the most likely estimate. Derived from the program evaluation and review technique (PERT), this technique uses a formula to create a weighted average for the work to be done, which is $(P + 4M + O)/6$. Since the most likely estimate is multiplied by 4, this weights the average toward that estimate. This method of estimating leverages the benefits of risk management in reducing the uncertainty of estimates. When a good risk management process is followed, the most likely estimates are more accurate

because risk response plans have been developed to deal with identified opportunities and threats that have been factored into the pessimistic and optimistic estimates.

Bear in mind that both of these averages relate to activities, rather than the overall project; the team can use these formulas to define the ranges for activity durations and cost estimates. However, the project manager can also use this information to calculate an overall project estimate and standard deviation.

Bottom-Up Estimating
This technique involves creating detailed estimates for each part of an activity (if available) or work package (if activities are not defined). Doing this type of estimating well requires an accurate WBS. The estimates are then rolled up into control accounts and finally into an overall project estimate.

Data Analysis
Estimate Activity Durations uses two forms of data analysis—alternatives analysis and reserve analysis.

Alternatives Analysis
When activity estimates are not acceptable within the constraints of the project, alternatives analysis is used to look more closely at the variables that impact the estimates. For example, we might compare options such as outsourcing work versus completing it internally to meet a schedule constraint, or purchasing testing software versus taking the time to manually test components. Alternatives analysis involves evaluating the impact of each option on project constraints, including financial investment versus time saved and level of risk. This analysis will result in the determination of the best approach to complete project work within the constraints.

Reserve Analysis
Now let's connect the topics of estimating and risk management. Estimating helps to identify more risks. Risk management reduces the uncertainty in time and cost estimates. This is accomplished by evaluating and planning for significant opportunities and threats, including how they will be dealt with if they occur. Risk management saves time and money on the project.

Project managers have a professional responsibility to establish a reserve to accommodate the risks that remain after the risk management planning processes are completed. Often in the risk management process, an initial reserve is estimated, the Plan Risk Responses process is performed to reduce the risk, and then a revised reserve is created. This is another example of the iterative nature of project planning.

As described in the Risk Management chapter, two types of reserves can be added to the project schedule—contingency reserves and management reserves.

Contingency reserves for schedule are allocated for the identified risks remaining after the Plan Risk Responses process (that is, known unknowns). These reserves are included in the project schedule baseline.

Significant risks to critical path activities may be managed by allocating a specific amount of schedule reserve. The amount of this schedule reserve is based on the impact of identified risks on the activity, as well as the contingency plans to deal with it.

The expected values of each contingency plan are added together to create a schedule contingency reserve. The project manager employs the contingency plan and uses the contingency reserve when identified risks occur. This keeps the project within the schedule baseline. (See the Risk Management chapter for a more detailed discussion of reserves.)

Management reserves are additional funds and time to cover unforeseen risks that could impact the project's ability to meet the schedule. (These risks are referred to as unknown unknowns.) Management reserves are not part of the schedule baseline. These reserves may not be applied at the project manager's discretion, but rather require approval of a formal change request. The Risk Management chapter explains how these reserves are calculated.

For the exam, you should understand the major difference between creating reserves and padding. In creating reserves, the project manager has the information necessary to reliably calculate what additional time or funds the project may need; with padding, team members arbitrarily determine how much padding they want to add to their estimates.

Decision Making   Involving team members in estimating can be beneficial on many levels. Those doing the work are most likely to have a good understanding of the time required to complete the effort. Additionally, including team members in the estimating process increases their buy-in to the resulting schedule.

Voting is a method that can be used during decision making—giving every participant the opportunity to weigh in on a decision regarding an activity estimate or amount of reserve needed. On plan-driven projects, voting may result in a decision based on plurality, majority, or unanimity. A voting technique commonly used on change-driven projects is "fist of five," also called "fist to five." In this technique, team members are asked to raise their fingers to show their level of support for a decision. A closed fist indicates a zero (no support) and an open fist indicates five (full support). Team members who are not supportive, and show two or fewer fingers in the vote, are given a chance to share why they are not in support of the option. Voting is repeated until everyone in the group indicates their support by showing at least three fingers.

Outputs of Estimate Activity Durations PAGE 203   When the Estimate Activity
Durations process is completed, you will of course have estimates, including reserves. But remember that as a result of this process you may also update or make changes to the project documents, including the activity attributes, the assumption log, and the lessons learned register.

Another output of this process is the basis of estimates. The basis of estimates is an explanation of how the estimates were derived, what assumptions and constraints were included, and what risks were taken into consideration in the estimation process. Basis of estimates also includes the confidence level of the estimators, expressed as a range, such as plus or minus 20 percent within which the actual project results are expected to fall.

Develop Schedule PAGE 205

> **Process:** Develop Schedule
> **Process Group:** Planning
> **Knowledge Area:** Schedule Management

After network diagram and activity duration estimates are completed, it's time to put this information into the scheduling software within the project management information system (PMIS) to create a schedule model. The schedule model includes all the project data that will be used to calculate the schedule, such as the activities, duration estimates, dependencies, and leads and lags. The project schedule is the output of the schedule model, and it consolidates all the schedule data. Representations of the schedule include bar charts and milestone charts (described later in this chapter). The approved project schedule is the baseline (a version of the schedule model that can only be changed with change control procedures), and is part of the project management plan.

The project schedule is a primary output of the schedule management process, so it's worth spending some time thinking about what's needed to create it. The schedule should be calendar-based, approved, and realistic, as it includes all the activities needed to complete the work of the project, as well as contingency reserves to manage risk events. Also keep in mind that the Develop Schedule process is iterative and can occur many times over the life of a project (at least once per project life cycle phase on a large project).

Inputs to Develop Schedule   PAGE 207   Consider what is involved in creating a schedule, then complete the following exercise. Hint: Think about the outputs of the previous schedule management processes.

Exercise
What do you need before you can develop a schedule for a project?

Answer
To develop a schedule, a project manager needs the following:

- Historical records of previous, similar projects, including lessons learned
- The components of the project management plan needed to develop a realistic schedule (schedule management plan and scope baseline)
- Defined activities (activity list and attributes)
- Milestone list
- Assumption log
- The order in which the work will be done (network diagram)
- Basis of estimates
- An estimate of the duration of each activity (activity duration estimates)
- An estimate of the resources needed (resource requirements)
- An understanding of the availability of resources (resource calendars)
- The required resources by category (resource breakdown structure)
- A company calendar identifying working and nonworking days
- A list of resources already assigned to specific project activities by management or by agreement or contract (project team assignments)
- A list of risks that could impact the schedule (risk register)

Tools and Techniques of Develop Schedule PAGE 209   The following are some of the key tools and techniques that can be used to develop a project schedule.

Schedule Network Analysis   Schedule network analysis is used to create the schedule model, and, ultimately, to finalize the project schedule. This analysis may use one or more of the following techniques:

- Critical path method
- Schedule compression
- What-if/Monte Carlo analysis
- Resource optimization
- Agile release planning

Critical Path Method   The critical path method involves determining the longest duration path through the network diagram, the earliest and latest an activity can start, and the earliest and latest it can be completed.

To use this method, you need to understand the following basic concepts. It's important to note that the critical path:

- Helps prove how long the project will take
- Helps the project manager determine where to focus the project management efforts
- Helps determine if an issue needs immediate attention
- Provides a vehicle to compress the schedule during project planning, and whenever there are changes
- Shows which activities have float and can therefore be delayed without delaying the project

Critical Path   The critical path is the longest duration path through a network diagram, and it determines the shortest time it could take to complete the project.

The easiest way to find the critical path is to identify all paths through the network and add the activity durations along each path. The path with the longest duration is the critical path.

Near-Critical Path   In addition to the critical path, you should be familiar with the concept of a near-critical path. This path is closest in duration to the critical path. Something could happen that shortens the critical path or lengthens the near-critical path to the point where the near-critical path becomes critical. The closer in length the near-critical and critical paths are, the more risk the project has. It is important for a project manager to focus time and effort monitoring and controlling activities on both the critical and near-critical paths (yes, there can be more than one) so there is no delay to project completion.

Float (Schedule Flexibility)   You should understand the concept of float for the exam; you may need to perform calculations related to float. Note that the terms "float" and "slack" mean the same thing. Slack is an older term for this concept, and is rarely used in project management. It's unlikely that you'll see the term "slack" used on the exam.

There are three types of float:

- **Total float**   Total float is the amount of time an activity can be delayed without delaying the project end date or an intermediary milestone, while still adhering to any imposed schedule constraints. This is the primary type of float.
- **Free float**   Free float is the amount of time an activity can be delayed without delaying the early start date of its successor(s), while still adhering to any imposed schedule constraints.

- **Project float**   Project float (also referred to as positive total float) is the amount of time a project can be delayed without delaying the externally imposed project completion date required by the customer or management, or the date previously committed to by the project manager.

Activities on the critical path have zero float. Critical path activities that are delayed or have an imposed completion date can result in negative float. This must be addressed before the project begins, as the project manager is responsible for ensuring that the project schedule is realistic and achievable. Negative float analysis results in options to bring the schedule back within the baseline.

Float is an asset on a project, as it provides schedule flexibility. If a project manager knows where they have float, they can use it to help organize and manage the project.

When you know the critical path and any near-critical paths, you can use float as a way to focus your management of a project and achieve better allocation of resources. For example, if you have a resource who is not very experienced but whom you must use for the project, you can assign them (assuming they have the skill set) to work on the activity with the most float. This gives you some level of security; even if their activity takes longer, the project is less likely to be delayed.

Knowing the float also helps team members juggle their work on multiple projects. They of course need to get approval from the project manager for any delays from the plan, but the amount of float tells them how much time flexibility they may have for each activity they are working on.

Float is calculated using one of the following equations: Float = Late Start (LS) – Early Start (ES), or Float = Late Finish (LF) – Early Finish (EF). Either formula will result in the same answer.

 Use this trick to easily remember these formulas: "There is a start formula and a finish formula, and we always begin late." Notice that the two formulas use either two starts or two finishes, and each of them begins with "late."

Start Formula (used in forward pass)	Finish Formula (used in backward pass)
Float = LS – ES	Float = LF – EF

You determine whether to use the start or finish formula based on the information available. For example, if you have a late start of 30, an early start of 18, and a late finish of 34, how would you find the float? Using the previous trick, you know to subtract the two starts or the two finishes. Since you do not have two finishes, you use the equation 30 – 18, which equals 12.

Using the Critical Path Method   Now that we have discussed the basic concepts, let's look at how the critical path method works.

We'll use the network diagram in figure 6.5 as an example. Note that the critical path is identified by the bold arrows.

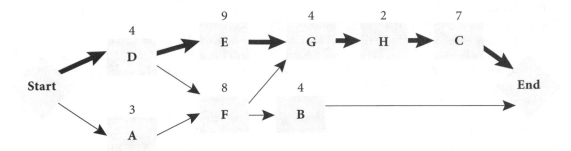

Figure 6.5   Critical path method

To determine the earliest and latest each activity can start and the earliest and latest each activity can be completed, you need to perform a forward and backward pass through the network diagram. The "early" figures are found by calculating from the beginning of the project to the end of the project, following the dependencies in the network diagram—a forward pass through the network diagram. The "late" figures are found by moving from the end of the project to the beginning of the project, following the dependencies in the network diagram—a backward pass.

The first activity in the diagram normally has an early start of zero. Some people, however, use 1 as the early start of the first activity. There is no right way to start calculating through network diagrams for the early and late starts; either method will get you the right answer. Just pick one method, and use it consistently.

Let's start with the forward pass. You need to move through the activities from the start until you reach the end, determining the early starts and early finishes, as illustrated in figure 6.6. This example uses zero as the early start for the first activities.

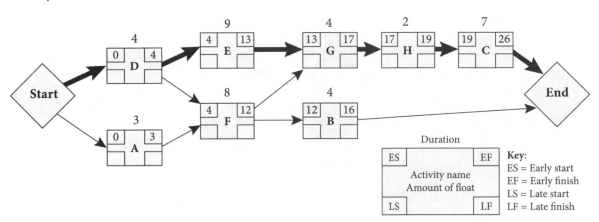

Figure 6.6   Forward pass through network diagram

It's important to look at where paths converge (path convergence). To compute the early start and the early finish in a forward pass, you have to take into account all the paths that lead into that activity (see activity F and activity G in figure 6.6). The same concept applies to the backward pass; to compute the late finish and late start, you need to consider all the paths that flow backward into an activity (see activity D and activity F in figure 6.6).

In this diagram, paths converge during the forward pass at activity F and activity G. So you need to do the forward pass on both paths leading up to activity F, calculating the early finishes for activities D (EF = 4) and A (EF = 3). You then select the later early finish of activities D and A to use as the early start for activity F, since activity F cannot start until both activities D and A are complete. Therefore, the early start of activity F is 4. You use the same process for calculating the early finish of activities E (EF = 13) and F (EF = 12) before determining the early start of activity G (ES = 13).

Once you have completed the forward pass, you can begin the backward pass, computing the late finish and late start for each activity. The backward pass uses the duration of the critical path (in this case, 26) as the late finish of the last activity or activities in the network. See figure 6.7 for the late start and late finish data.

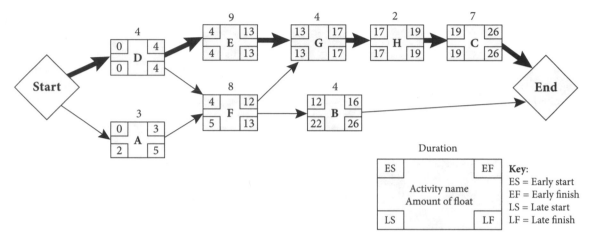

Figure 6.7 Backward pass through network diagram

Again, you need to be careful at points of convergence as you move through the network diagram. There is convergence at activity F and at activity D. You work from the end back to these by first computing the late start of activities B (LS = 22) and G (LS = 13). Select the earlier late start to use for the late finish of activity F, since activity F must be finished before either activity B or G can start.

Therefore, the late finish of activity F is 13. This same process should be used on activities E (LS = 4) and F (LS = 5) before calculating the late finish for activity D (LF = 4).

Once you finish calculating the starts and finishes, you have the data required to calculate float. It's time to use those formulas. What was that trick again? "There is a start formula and a finish formula, and we always begin late." Therefore, the formulas are:

Start Formula (used in forward pass)	Finish Formula (used in backward pass)
Float = LS – ES	Float = LF – EF

See figure 6.8 for the float of each activity. The activities with zero float are on the critical path (identified by the bold arrows).

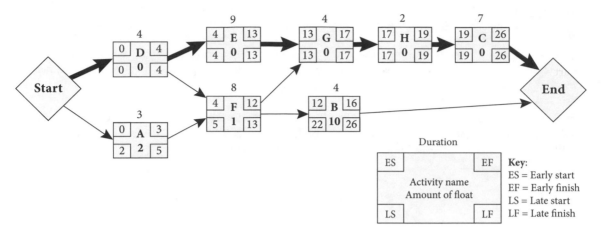

Figure 6.8 Float of activities on network diagram

 The following are good questions to test your knowledge about critical paths, float, and network diagrams:

- **Can there be more than one critical path?** Yes, there can be two, three, or many critical paths.

- **Do you want there to be?** No; having more than one critical path increases risk.

- **Can a critical path change?** Yes.

- **Can there be negative float?** Yes; it means the project is behind.

- **How much float does the critical path have?** In planning, the critical path generally has zero total float. During project executing, if an activity on the critical path is completed earlier or later than planned, the critical path may then have positive or negative float. Negative float on the critical path requires corrective action or changes to the project to bring it back in line with the plan.

- **Does the network diagram change when the end date changes?** No, not automatically, but the project manager should investigate schedule compression options such as fast tracking and crashing the schedule (both described in the next section) to meet the new date. Then, with approved changes, the project manager should change the network diagram accordingly.

- **Would you leave the project with negative float?** No; the project manager would compress the schedule. If schedule compression efforts do not result in zero or positive float, the project manager will need to request a change to adjust the baseline.

Schedule Compression   One of the most common problems on projects is an unrealistic timeframe. This problem can arise during project planning, when management or the customer requires a completion date that cannot be met, or during project executing, when the project manager needs to bring the project back in line with the schedule baseline or adjust the project for changes. As we discussed earlier, many project managers blame their sponsors or executives for unrealistic schedules, but project managers have a professional responsibility to push back, present options, and make sure the project is achievable by properly planning the project and using schedule network analysis techniques such as schedule compression.

Also keep in mind that schedule compression is a way to utilize float by fast tracking activities that are on the critical path. This means adjusting the network diagram so critical path activities that were originally planned to be completed in a series are replanned to be done in parallel. As we discuss below, fast tracking can save time, but it also adds risk to the project.

During project planning, schedule compression can help a project manager determine if the desired completion date can be met and, if not, what can be changed to meet the requested date.

Later in the project, schedule compression may be used during Perform Integrated Change Control and Control Schedule to evaluate options to manage the impacts of changes. The objective of this technique is to manage the schedule without changing the schedule baseline.

Fast Tracking   This technique involves taking critical path activities that were originally planned in a series and doing them instead in parallel for some or all of their duration (see fig. 6.9). Fast tracking often results in rework, usually increases risk, and requires more attention to communication.

Figure 6.9   Fast tracking

For example, which activity in figure 6.10 would you fast track to shorten the project length?

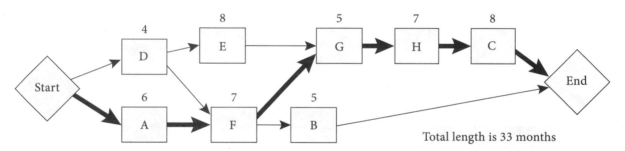

Figure 6.10   Which activity would you fast track?

Assuming the dependencies are discretionary, activity H could be fast tracked by making it occur at the same time as, or in parallel with, activity G. Any other pair of activities on the critical path could be fast tracked. Activities C and H could also be fast tracked by having part of activity C done concurrently with activity H.

Crashing   This technique involves adding or adjusting resources in order to compress the schedule while maintaining the original project scope. Crashing, by definition, always results in increased costs, and may increase risk.

For example, in the network diagram in figure 6.10, a contract resource could supplement the internal resource's efforts on a critical path activity (assuming this is logical, based on the nature of the work). Another option to crash the project might be to buy a software application; the purchase adds cost to the project but helps the team work more efficiently, thus saving time.

In crashing and fast tracking decisions, the project manager should consider all the potential choices and then select the option that will have the least negative impact on the project. So what are the impacts of the various options for shortening a project schedule? Let's take a look.

Option	General Impacts on the Project
Fast track	• Always adds risk • May add management time for the project manager
Crash	• Always adds cost • May add management time for the project manager • May add risk
Reduce scope	• May save cost, resources, and time • May negatively impact customer satisfaction
Cut quality	• May save cost, resources, and time • May increase risk • Requires good metrics on current and desired levels of quality to be effective • May negatively impact customer satisfaction

The best choice is to look at risks and then reestimate. Once it is known that the schedule (or budget) must be reduced, a project manager can investigate the activity estimates that contain the most unknowns, eliminate or reduce these risks, and thus decrease the estimate.

Data Analysis   In creating a finalized, realistic schedule, it's helpful to ask, "What if a particular factor changed on the project? Would that produce a shorter schedule?" The assumptions for each activity can change, and therefore the activity durations can also change. One of the ways to calculate the effect of these changes is through what-if scenario analysis and simulation. It's important to note that the most common simulation technique is called Monte Carlo analysis.

Monte Carlo Analysis   This technique uses computer software to simulate the outcome of a project, based on the three-point estimates (optimistic, pessimistic, and most likely) for each activity and the network diagram. The simulation can tell you:

- The probability of completing the project on any specific day
- The probability of completing the project for any specific cost
- The probability of any activity actually being on the critical path
- An indication of the overall project risk

Monte Carlo analysis is another way of putting together the details of three-point estimates into a project estimate. It's more accurate than other methods because it simulates the actual details of the project and calculates probability.

Monte Carlo analysis can help deal with "path convergence"—the places in the network diagram where multiple paths converge into one or more activities, thus adding risk to the project (see fig. 6.11). Monte Carlo analysis is also used as a risk management tool to quantitatively analyze risks (see the Risk Management chapter).

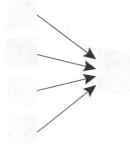

Figure 6.11 Path convergence

Resource Optimization

Resource optimization refers to finding ways to adjust the use of resources. There are two techniques that can achieve this outcome.

Resource Leveling

Resource leveling is used to produce a resource-limited schedule. Leveling lengthens the schedule and increases cost to deal with a limited number of resources, resource availability, and other resource constraints. A little-used function in project management software, this technique allows you to level the peaks and valleys of the schedule from one month to another, resulting in a more stable number of resources used on your project.

You might level the resources if your project used 5 resources one month, 15 the next, and 3 the next, or some other up-and-down pattern that was not acceptable. Leveling could also be used if you did not have 15 resources available and preferred to lengthen the project (which is a result of leveling) instead of hiring more resources.

Resource Smoothing

Resource smoothing is a modified form of resource leveling, where resources are leveled only within the limits of the float of their activities, so the completion dates of activities are not delayed.

Agile Release Planning

In agile—or change-driven—projects, work to develop the product of the project is broken down into iterations and releases. Agile release planning provides a high-level schedule that includes the timing of releases and the number of iterations that will be completed as a part of each release. The planning efforts result in a timeline, which indicates the features to be included in each release.

Outputs of Develop Schedule
PAGE 217   The Develop Schedule process results in the project schedule, the schedule baseline, schedule data, change requests, and updates to any related project documents. The following sections describe these outputs.

Project Schedule

The project schedule is the result of the previous planning processes and the schedule network analysis that is performed as part of the Develop Schedule process. As planning progresses, the schedule will be iterated in response to risk management and other parts of project planning until an acceptable and realistic schedule can be agreed upon. The iterated and realistic schedule that results from this effort is called the schedule baseline, which becomes part of the project management plan.

The project schedule includes project activities with assigned dates for each activity and the milestones inserted by the project manager or management. The project schedule may be represented in different formats, such as a bar chart or a network diagram.

The project schedule can be shown with or without dependencies (logical relationships), and it can be shown in any of the following presentations created from the schedule model, depending on the needs of the project:

- Network diagram (described earlier in this chapter)
- Milestone chart
- Bar chart

Milestone Charts

These are similar to bar charts (described next), but they only show major events. Remember that milestones have no duration; they simply represent the completion of activities. Milestones, which may include "requirements are complete" or "design is finished," are part of the inputs to the Sequence Activities process. Milestone charts are good tools for reporting to management and the customer. See the example in figure 6.12.

ID	Milestone	December	January	February	March	April
1	Start	◇12/14				
2	Requirements gathered		◇12/31			
3	Design complete		◇1/17			
4	Coding complete			◇2/15		
5	Testing complete				◇3/15	
6	Implementation complete					◇4/4
7	End					◇4/15

Figure 6.12 Milestone chart

Bar Charts   Bar charts are weak planning tools, but they are effective for progress reporting and control. They are not project management plans. Figure 6.13 shows a sample bar chart.

ID	Activity Name	Duration	Start	Finish	August	September	October
1	Start	0 days	Mon 8/26	Mon 8/26	◇		
2	D	4 days	Mon 8/26	Thu 8/29	▭		
3	A	6 days	Mon 8/26	Mon 9/2	▭		
4	F	7 days	Mon 9/2	Tue 9/10		▭	
5	E	8 days	Fri 8/30	Tue 9/10		▭	
6	G	5 days	Wed 9/11	Wed 9/18		▭	
7	B	5 days	Wed 9/11	Wed 9/18		▭	
8	H	7 days	Wed 9/18	Thu 9/26		▭	
9	C	8 days	Fri 9/27	Tue 10/8		▭	
10	Finish	0 days	Tue 10/8	Tue 10/8			◇

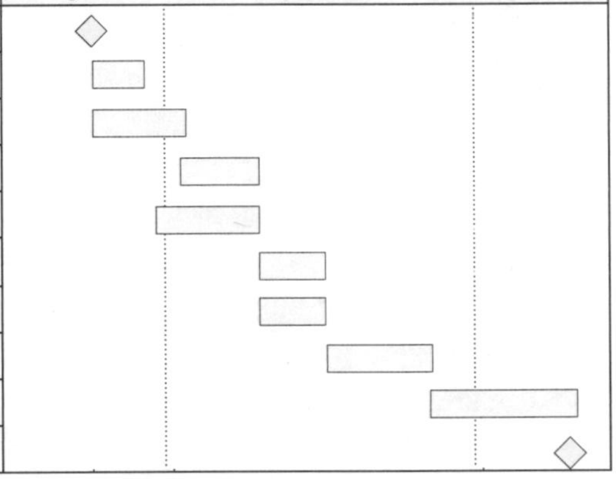

Figure 6.13 Bar chart

Notice that there are no lines between activities to show interdependencies, nor are assigned resources shown. Bar charts do not help organize the project as effectively as a WBS or network diagram. They are completed after the WBS and the network diagram in the project management process.

Schedule Baseline   The schedule baseline is the version of the schedule model used to manage the project; it is what the project team's performance is measured against. Remember that the baseline can only be changed as a result of formally approved changes. Meeting the schedule baseline is one of the measures of project success. If the project can be done faster than the customer requested, there may be a difference between the schedule baseline and the end date required by the customer. This difference is project float.

Schedule Data   Schedule data encompasses all the data used to create the schedule model, including milestones, project activities, activity attributes, duration estimates, dependencies, and the assumptions and constraints used in creating the schedule.

Change Requests   This is another planning process that has change requests as an output. As the project progresses, any changes to the schedule may necessitate changes to other parts of the project management plan. Change requests are addressed through the integrated change control process.

Project Documents Updates   The process of creating a final and realistic schedule could result in updates to project documents, including duration estimates, resource requirements, activity attributes, the risk register, the assumption log, and the lessons learned register.

Control Schedule PAGE 222

> **Process:** Control Schedule
> **Process Group:** Monitoring & Controlling
> **Knowledge Area:** Schedule Management

What does it mean to "control" a project schedule? Control means
measure; a project manager will need to measure against the plan to stay in control of their project. Measuring will show the project manager how the project is performing compared to the plan. Project managers measure against the plan and take action as needed to control the project.

Also make note of what is involved in schedule control. The project manager should protect the hard work of all those involved in planning to make sure what was planned occurs as close to the plan as possible. They should also be constantly on the lookout for anything that might affect the schedule.

The following are some additional activities that can be used to control the schedule:

- Access the PMIS to review current work performance data and compare actual progress to what was planned.
- Reestimate the remaining components of the project partway through the project (see the following discussion).
- Conduct performance reviews by formally analyzing how the project is doing.
- Perform data analysis of project performance (This can include earned value analysis, trend analysis, variance analysis, and what-if scenario analysis.)
- Confirm that critical path activities are being completed within the schedule baseline. If they are not, adjust the critical path by taking advantage of available float.
- Adjust future parts of the project to deal with delays, rather than asking for a schedule extension (using schedule compression techniques such as using leads and lags, crashing, and fast tracking).
- Consider making adjustments to optimize resources assigned to activities to improve the performance.
- Continue efforts to optimize the schedule.
- Adjust metrics that are not giving the project manager the information needed to properly understand performance and manage the project. Add new metrics if needed.
- Adjust the format or required content of reports as needed to capture the information necessary to control and manage the project.
- Identify the need for changes, including corrective and preventive actions.
- Follow the change control process.

Reestimating   One of the roles of a project manager is to make sure the project meets the project objectives. There are always changes that occur during a project. Therefore, it's standard practice to reestimate the remaining work at least once during the life of the project. This will ensure that the project manager can still satisfy the project objectives within the schedule, budget, and other project constraints, or adjust the project if needed.

Tools and Techniques of Control Schedule PAGE 226   The following are key tools and techniques that may be used during the Control Schedule process. Additional tools include the critical path method, resource optimization, leads and lags, and schedule compression.

Data Analysis   Data Analysis techniques such as earned value analysis, trend and variance analysis, and what-if scenario analysis can be used to examine and assess different aspects of a project. Burndown charts and performance reviews may also be useful.

Project Management Information System   Project management software is used to track planned versus actual results and perform "what-if" analysis to control the detailed schedule to the schedule baseline. Notice that the use of "project management software" is not called for early in the project; that's because it is, in fact, primarily a scheduling tool.

Outputs of Control Schedule PAGE 228   The Control Schedule process results in work performance information, schedule forecasts, and sometimes change requests. For example, a change to the schedule might require additional resources, or a change in scope. Such changes must be handled as part of the Perform Integrated Change Control process. Make sure you review this important process in the Integration Management chapter.

This process may also result in updates to the schedule management plan and performance measurement baseline in addition to project documents such as the assumption log, risk register, and lessons learned register, and changes to any other part of the project.

The following key outputs result from the Control Schedule process.

Work Performance Information   Earned value analysis produces work performance information, including the schedule variance and schedule performance index. This information can then be used to generate forecasts and progress reports.

Schedule Forecasts   Based on the results of earned value analysis and other work performance information to date, the project manager is able to create a forecast of future schedule performance. The forecast may be updated throughout the life of the project, as additional work is completed and additional information becomes available.

Change Requests   Formal change requests are an output of schedule control. Change requests may affect cost, risk, staffing, or any part of the project, in order to make sure the schedule baseline is met. These change requests can include recommendations for preventive and corrective actions.

Project Management Plan Updates   Efforts to control the schedule may include adjustments to other parts of the project. For example, they may result in scope changes or budget changes, in addition to changes to the schedule baseline.

Schedule Management

Schedule Management Review

Exercise

This exercise will help you review the key material you need to know for schedule management. The Shuffle Game that follows offers another approach to this material. You can use either or both of these study tools, depending on your preference.

Instructions

1. Try to fill in the blanks in the below table using the knowledge and understanding gained after reading this chapter.
2. To review only the material contained in this chapter, focus on the cells that have asterisks. (These are the key topics you need to understand to pass the exam with the minimum amount of study time. The answer table will show only these topics.)
3. To review all the items listed in the *PMBOK® Guide*, fill in the entire table.

Key Inputs	Key Tools and Techniques	Key Outputs
Plan Schedule Management Process group:		
		*
Define Activities Process group:		
*	*	*
Sequence Activities Process group:		
*	*	*

© 2018 RMC Publications, Inc.™ • 952.846.4484 • info@rmcls.com • www.rmcls.com

Key Inputs	Key Tools and Techniques	Key Outputs
Estimate Activity Durations Process group:		
	*	*
Develop Schedule Process group:		
	*	*
Control Schedule Process group:		
	*	*

Schedule Management

Answer   To save study time and focus on the most important information, this answer table only shows the topics that are covered in this chapter. If you tried to list all inputs, tools and techniques, and outputs, you'll need to check your answers against the *PMBOK® Guide*.

Key Inputs	Key Tools and Techniques	Key Outputs
Plan Schedule Management Process group: Planning		
		Schedule management plan
Define Activities Process group: Planning		
Project management plan Enterprise environmental factors Organizational process assets	Rolling wave planning Decomposition	Activity list Activity attributes Milestone list
Sequence Activities Process group: Planning		
Project documents	Precedence diagramming method Dependencies determination Leads and lags Project management information system	Project schedule network diagram Project documents updates
Estimate Activity Durations Process group: Planning		
	Analogous estimating Parametric estimating Three-point estimating Bottom-up estimating Data analysis • Alternatives analysis • Reserve analysis Decision making	Estimates Basis of estimates
Develop Schedule Process group: Planning		
	Schedule network analysis Critical path method • Critical path • Near-critical path • Float Schedule compression • Fast tracking • Crashing Data analysis • Monte Carlo analysis Resource optimization • Resource leveling • Resource smoothing Agile release planning	Project schedule • Milestone charts • Bar charts Schedule baseline Schedule data Change requests Project documents updates

Key Inputs	Key Tools and Techniques	Key Outputs
Control Schedule Process group: Monitoring and controlling		
	Data analysis Project management information system	Work performance information Schedule forecasts Change requests Project management plan updates

Shuffle Game

Some people learn best by doing, which is why we have developed this alternate approach to reviewing schedule management. To save you time, only the most important topics for the exam—those covered in this chapter—have been included.

Instructions

1. Cut out the cards on the next pages.
2. Lay out the bold title cards as column headers.
3. Shuffle the remaining cards and try to put them in the columns where they belong. Cards with italic terms must be matched to the corresponding group. For example, a *Cost of Quality* card in italics would match with a Data Analysis card, as cost of quality is a data analysis tool and technique.
4. Check your answers against the material covered in this chapter or the *PMBOK® Guide,* and make note of any gaps in your knowledge.

Note: Be sure to keep all cards for each chapter shuffle game as you will use them again for the final Shuffle Game in chapter 14.

Plan Schedule Management *Key Outputs*	**Define Activities** *Key Inputs*	**Define Activities** *Key Tools and Techniques*
Define Activities *Key Outputs*	**Sequence Activities** *Key Inputs*	**Sequence Activities** *Key Tools and Techniques*
Sequence Activities *Key Outputs*	**Estimate Activity Durations** *Key Tools and Techniques*	**Estimate Activity Durations** *Key Outputs*
Develop Schedule *Key Tools and Techniques*	**Develop Schedule** *Key Outputs*	**Control Schedule** *Key Tools and Techniques*
Control Schedule *Key Outputs*	Schedule management plan	Project management plan

Enterprise environmental factors	Organizational process assets	Rolling wave planning
Decomposition	Activity list	Activity attributes
Milestone list	Project documents	Precedence diagramming method
Dependencies determination	Leads and lags	Project management information system
Project schedule network diagram	Project documents updates	Analogous estimating

Parametric estimating	Three-point estimating	Bottom-up estimating
Data analysis	*Alternatives analysis*	*Reserve analysis*
Decision making	Estimates	Basis of estimates
Schedule network analysis	Critical path method	*Critical path*
Near-critical path	*Float*	Schedule compression

Fast tracking	*Crashing*	Data Analysis
Monte Carlo analysis	Resource optimization	*Resource leveling*
Resource smoothing	Agile release planning	Project schedule
Milestone charts	*Bar charts*	Schedule baseline
Schedule data	Change requests	Project documents updates

Data analysis	Project management information system	Work performance information
Schedule forecasts	Change requests	Project management plan updates

Practice Exam

1. Which of the following is a tool or technique of the Control Schedule process?
   A. Project management software
   B. Alternatives analysis
   C. Dependency determination
   D. Parametric estimating

2. What is the best project management tool to use to determine the longest time the project will take?
   A. Work breakdown structure
   B. Network diagram
   C. Bar chart
   D. Project charter

3. Which of the following statements is correct?
   A. Crashing always shortens the timeline but rarely increases risk.
   B. Fast tracking often results in rework, and crashing often results in increased cost.
   C. Crashing is only a viable alternative if earned value analysis indicates that the project is ahead of schedule and under budget.
   D. Fast tracking will result in fewer parallel activities than crashing the project.

4. All the following statements describe a schedule management plan except:
   A. It details the scheduling methodology that will be used on the project.
   B. It identifies schedule change control procedures.
   C. It must be issued as a formal and detailed document.
   D. It establishes a plan for managing schedule variances.

5. Using the average labor hours per installation from past projects to predict the future is an example of which of the following?
   A. Parametric estimating
   B. Three-point estimating
   C. Analogous estimating
   D. Monte Carlo analysis

6. Which schedule management output is used to measure the project team's progress throughout the project?
   A. Scope baseline
   B. Schedule baseline
   C. Cost baseline
   D. Performance baseline

7. What is shown on a project schedule network diagram?
   A. The external dependencies that affect the schedule
   B. The logical relationships among project activities
   C. The resource assignments for the project
   D. The schedule constraints and project milestones

8. What is the most commonly used logical relationship represented using the precedence diagramming method (PDM)?
   A. Start-to-start (SS)
   B. Finish-to-start (FS)
   C. Finish-to-finish (FF)
   D. Start-to-finish (SF)

9. Identifying and documenting the specific activities that must be performed to produce work packages is called:
   A. Define Scope
   B. Estimate Activities
   C. Define Activities
   D. Sequence Activities

10. What is the best method to use when estimating how long it will take to complete an activity that has not previously been done by your company?
    A. Analogous estimating
    B. Three-point estimating
    C. Monte Carlo analysis
    D. Parametric estimating

11. Which of the following activities isn't part of the schedule management knowledge area?
    A. Identifying the type and quantity of resources that will be required for each activity
    B. Organizing the activities and milestones in the order in which the work will be performed
    C. Estimating the amount of time required to complete each activity
    D. Decomposing the work packages created in the WBS into the activities required to produce the work package deliverables

12. In which schedule management processes are project schedule network diagrams created and analyzed?
    A. Develop Schedule; Control Schedule
    B. Sequence Activities; Develop Schedule
    C. Define Activities; Sequence Activities
    D. Estimate Activity Durations; Control Schedule

13. Your team is calculating triangular distributions. Which of the following processes are they engaged in?
    A. Control Schedule
    B. Estimate Schedule
    C. Sequence Activities
    D. Estimate Activity Durations

14. You have a project with four activities as follows. Activity 1 can start immediately and has an estimated duration of 1. Activity 2 can start after activity 1 is completed and has an estimated duration of 4. Activity 3 can start after activity 2 is completed and has an estimated duration of 5. Activity 4 has an estimated duration of 8. It can start after activity 1 is completed. Both activity 3 and activity 4 must be completed before the project is complete. What is the critical path of the project?
    A. Start, 1, 2, 3, End
    B. Start, 1, 4, 3, End
    C. Start, 1, 4, End
    D. Start, 1, 2, 3, 4, End

15. The critical path for your project is very close in length to the near-critical path. What does this tell you?
    A. Your project has higher risk because these two paths are of similar length.
    B. You don't need to worry about the length of the near-critical path; by definition, only the critical path is "critical."
    C. You should focus on increasing the length of the near-critical path; otherwise, it could threaten the team's ability to complete the critical path on schedule.
    D. Having two paths of similar length makes the project less risky.

Answers

1. **Answer** A

   Explanation Of the answer options provided, only project management software is a tool or technique of the Control Schedule process. The other tools listed are used in other schedule management processes.

2. **Answer** B

   Explanation The network diagram is used to determine the longest duration (critical) path for a project. The network diagram takes the activities from the activity list and adds dependencies, allowing us to look at the various paths through the diagram. The WBS breaks down the scope of the project into work packages, but it does not include information on how long each work package will take to complete. The bar chart may show an end date, but it is not used to determine dates. The project charter also may include a required end date, but not a logical determination of how long the project will take.

3. **Answer** B

   Explanation Both crashing and fast tracking are methods of schedule compression. Crashing often results in increased cost, and fast tracking usually increases the likelihood of rework.

4. **Answer** C

   Explanation The schedule management plan identifies the project's scheduling methodology, schedule change control procedures, and plan for managing schedule variances, among other things. It does not, however, need to be a formal, highly detailed document. It may be an informal, high-level plan.

5. **Answer** A

   Explanation Although you could use expert judgment and data from past projects to come up with the estimate (analogous estimating), the best answer is parametric estimating because past history is being used to perform a calculation to arrive at an estimate. Monte Carlo analysis is a modeling, or simulation, technique. Three-point estimating uses three time estimates per activity.

6. **Answer** B

   Explanation As the project continues, the project team's progress will be measured against the schedule baseline, which is an output of the Develop Schedule process. The other baselines listed here are not outputs of a schedule management process.

7. **Answer** B

   Explanation Project schedule network diagrams are schematic displays of the logical relationships among project activities.

8. **Answer** B

   Explanation Finish-to-start (FS) is the most commonly used relationship in PDM. In a finish-to-start relationship, an activity must finish before the successor can start.

9. **Answer** C

   Explanation The Define Activities process involves taking the work packages created in the WBS and decomposing them into the activities required to produce the work package deliverables.

10. **Answer** B

    Explanation Analogous estimating can be used when you have done similar work previously. Monte Carlo analysis is a schedule development technique. Parametric estimating includes the use of historical data and productivity rates for the work, which would not be available if you had not done the activity before. Three-point estimating is the best method to use in this case because it allows you to estimate in a range of three points: optimistic, pessimistic, and most likely.

11. **Answer** A

    Explanation Organizing the activities and milestones in the order in which the work will be performed describes the Sequence Activities process. Decomposing the work packages created in the WBS is done in the Define Activities process. Estimating the amount of time required to complete each activity is done during the Estimate Activity Durations process. All the processes mentioned so far are part of schedule management. Identifying the type and quantity of resources that will be required for each activity describes the Estimate Activity Resources process, which is part of the resource management knowledge area

12. **Answer** B

    Explanation Project schedule network diagrams are a key output of the Sequence Activities process, and schedule network analysis is one of the key tools and techniques of the Develop Schedule process.

13. **Answer** D

    Explanation Triangular distribution is a way of calculating three-point estimates, which means that the team is developing estimates. This narrows down the answer choices to Estimate Schedule or Estimate Activity Durations, as the other choices don't involve estimating. Since Estimate Schedule is not a valid schedule management process, they must be estimating activity durations.

14. **Answer** A

    Explanation The two possible paths in this question are Start, 1, 2, 3, End and Start, 1, 4, End. The Start, 1, 2, 3, End path would take 1 + 4 + 5 days, or 10 days to complete. The Start, 1, 4, End path would take 1 + 8 days, or 9 days to complete. To answer this type of question, carefully draw the network diagram, list all the possible paths, and then determine the duration of each path.

15. **Answer** A

    Explanation Of these statements, only "Your project has higher risk because these two paths are of similar length" is valid. If you picked one of the other answers, carefully review the explanation of critical and near-critical paths in this chapter to strengthen your understanding of this key topic.

© 2018 RMC Publications, Inc.™ • 952.846.4484 • info@rmcls.com • www.rmcls.com

Cost Management

S E V E N

There are 12 questions on this knowledge area on the CAPM exam. Also note, for a full list of all inputs, tools and techniques, and outputs within this knowledge area, please see the table on page 232 in the PMBOK© Guide.

Do you know how to create a budget for a project? Do you have experience managing and controlling project costs? Do you know how to use an agile approach if a project's scope is not completely defined? If you don't have a knowledge base of these efforts, make sure you read this chapter carefully and fully understand the concepts discussed.

On the exam, there is a strong connection between cost management and schedule management. Some topics covered in this chapter (including planning, estimating, and monitoring and controlling) also apply to the Schedule Management chapter. The Schedule Management chapter includes information on estimating techniques that can be used for both schedule and cost estimating. Earned value analysis, which is discussed in this chapter, is another example of a technique that can be used for both cost and schedule.

The Schedule Management chapter describes the decomposition of work packages into smaller components, or activities. For many projects, cost estimates are created at the activity level. However, based on the needs of a project, costs may also include higher levels in which costs are assigned

to control accounts. Control accounts do not affect overall cost estimates. They provide another level of control when costs need to be distributed to multiple stakeholder groups. For example, the cost of an internal project may be shared between two departments. Control accounts allow the project manager to apply the agreed-upon costs to each department. (See the Scope Management chapter for more on control accounts.)

The overall process of cost management includes planning, estimating costs for each activity, and compiling those estimates into a budget. It's also important to note that while project work is underway, cost performance will need to be measured (controlled) against the plan. Keep in mind that a variety of stakeholders and stakeholder groups typically help the project manager measure project costs.

The following table should help you understand how each part of cost management fits into the overall project management process.

The Cost Management Process	Done During
Plan Cost Management	Planning process group
Estimate Costs	Planning process group
Determine Budget	Planning process group
Control Costs	Monitoring and controlling process group

You should also be familiar with the following cost management concepts.

Value Analysis

This concept is sometimes referred to as value engineering. Its focus is on finding a less costly way to do the same work. In other words, this technique is used to answer the question, "How can we decrease cost on the project while maintaining the same scope?" Value analysis involves finding ways to provide required features at the lowest overall cost without loss of performance.

Cost Risk

The concept of cost risk involves cost, risk, and procurement management. This term means just what its name implies—cost-related risk. Because topics such as this one cross knowledge areas, the questions on the exam will, too. For example, here is a sample question:

> **Question:** Who has the cost risk in a fixed-price contract—the buyer or the seller?
> **Answer:** The seller

Plan Cost Management PAGE 235

> **Process:** Plan Cost Management
> **Process Group:** Planning
> **Knowledge Area:** Cost Management

The Plan Cost Management process involves identifying how to plan (including estimating and budgeting), manage, and monitor and control project costs, including the cost of the resources needed to complete project activities. This process answers the questions, "How will I go about planning cost for the project?" and "How will I effectively manage the project to the cost baseline, control costs, and manage cost variances?"

The project charter includes a high-level cost constraint as well as other requirements regarding cost management on the project. Organizational process assets used in this process include cost data and lessons learned from previous projects, as well as organizational standards and policies for estimating and budgeting.

In some organizations, the Plan Cost Management process can involve determining whether the project will be paid for with the organization's existing funds or will be funded through equity or debt. It can also include decisions about how to finance project resources—such as choosing whether to purchase or lease equipment. And it can include whether an agile or adaptive approach is more appropriate given the level of scope definition and project certainty. If a project is more high-level, a detailed approach to cost management may not be feasible. Instead, a project manager may need to utilize estimation methods that are less invasive, for example.

Outputs of Plan Cost Management PAGE 238   The output of this process is the cost management plan.

Cost Management Plan   The cost management plan, also known as the "budget management plan" or "budget plan," is similar to other management plans. ("Management plans" are a PMI-ism.) It can be formal or informal, and is part of the project management plan. This plan requires the project manager to think through, in advance, how they will plan, manage, and monitor and control project costs.

The cost management plan may include the following:

- Specifications for how estimates should be stated (in what currency)
- The levels of accuracy and precision needed for estimates
- Approved estimating techniques
- Reporting formats to be used
- Rules for measuring cost performance
- Whether costs will include indirect costs (costs not directly attributable to any one project, such as overhead costs) in addition to direct costs (costs directly attributable to the project)
- Guidelines for establishing a cost baseline for measuring against in project monitoring and controlling (the cost baseline will ultimately be established in Determine Budget)
- Control thresholds
- Cost change control procedures
- Information on control accounts or other ways to monitor spending on the project
- Funding decisions
- Methods for documenting costs
- Guidelines for dealing with potential fluctuations in resource costs and exchange rates
- Roles and responsibilities for various cost activities

Notice the inclusion of control thresholds. The creation of the cost management plan requires thinking ahead about how to control costs. If an actual cost comes in higher than expected, will the project manager need to take action? What if it's a two-dollar difference? Control thresholds are the amount of variation allowed before a project manager needs to take action. These thresholds are determined in planning while creating the cost management plan.

Estimate Costs PAGE 240

> **Process:** Estimate Costs
> **Process Group:** Planning
> **Knowledge Area:** Cost Management

This process involves coming up with cost estimates for all project activities and resources required to complete them. These estimates will be combined into one time-phased spending plan in the next process, Determine Budget.

So what costs should a project manager estimate? To put it simply, a project manager will need to estimate the costs of all the efforts needed to complete their project. This includes costs directly associated with the project, such as labor, equipment, materials, and training (for the project), as well as:

- Costs of quality efforts
- Costs of risk efforts
- Costs of the project manager's time
- Costs of project management activities
- Expenses for physical office spaces used directly for the project
- Overhead costs, such as management salaries and general office expenses

It is important to understand that part of the expense of a project comes from the costs of project management activities. Although project management efforts save money on projects overall, they also result in costs, and should be included in the project cost estimates. These include not only costs associated with the project manager's efforts, but also those associated with status reports, change analysis, and so on.

Types of Cost

There are several ways to look at costs when creating an estimate. However, you only need to understand two types of cost for the exam: direct and indirect. Read the descriptions below to fill any knowledge gaps you may have about these types of cost.

- **Direct costs** These costs are directly attributable to the work on the project. Examples are team wages, team travel and recognition expenses, and costs of material used on the project.
- **Indirect costs** Indirect costs are overhead items or costs incurred for the benefit of more than one project. Examples include taxes, fringe benefits, and janitorial services.

Inputs to Estimate Costs PAGE 241

The following inputs help a project manager create estimates more quickly and accurately. For example, imagine having access to a repository containing all the WBSs for previous, similar projects, along with the estimates and actual costs for each activity. Can you see how that might be helpful in creating more accurate estimates? Having highly accurate estimates will help a project manager better control the project later and, therefore, save time and effort. Read through the following list of inputs, and think through how each might help a project manager estimate costs.

Components of the Project Management Plan

Cost Management Plan   This plan documents the methods used to estimate costs, as well as the levels of accuracy and precision required for estimates.

Quality Management Plan   This plan outlines all the activities the team must perform (as well as any resources required) in order to achieve the expected level of quality. These quality activities have costs associated with them.

Scope Baseline   To create a cost estimate, the project manager will need to know the details of what project and product scope they are estimating for their project; this includes knowing what is out of scope and what cost-related constraints have been placed on the project scope. This information can be found by looking at all the components of the scope baseline (the project scope statement, WBS, and WBS dictionary).

Project Documents

Lessons Learned Register   If the project manager is using rolling wave planning, lessons learned from the estimates made in earlier phases of the current project should have been documented in the project's lessons learned register. Also, historical lessons learned regarding estimates from previous, similar projects should be available. The project manager can use these lessons to create more accurate estimates for the remaining parts of the project.

Project Schedule   The project schedule includes a list of activities, the resources needed to complete the work, and information about when the work will occur. There are two reasons a schedule is needed prior to budget development. First, the timing of when something is purchased may affect its cost. For example, the price of a material or a piece of equipment may vary due to factors such as availability, seasonal pricing fluctuations, or new model releases. If a project manager knows something will be more expensive at the time it is scheduled to be purchased, they might consider changing the schedule to purchase the material or equipment at a different time, for a lower price. Second, to monitor and control project expenditures in order to know how much money will be spent during specific periods of time (weeks, months, etc.), a time-phased spending plan may need to be developed. This is the process of iterative planning.

Resource Requirements   The resource management plan lists the human resources (including how many resources will be needed and their skills) required on the project, as well as all the other resources (such as materials and equipment) necessary to complete each activity. Of course, these resources have costs associated with them. The project manager should have access to the rates paid to everyone who works on the project. Recognition and rewards given to team members can increase productivity and save money, but they are still a cost item and need to be estimated. The resource management plan is discussed in more detail in the Resource Management chapter.

Risk Register   The risk management process can save time and money, but there are costs associated with the efforts to deal proactively with risks (both opportunities and threats). Risks are an input to this process because they influence how costs are estimated. They can also be an output because our choices related to estimating costs have associated risks. Again, planning is iterative.

Organizational Process Assets   As noted earlier, records from past projects can be highly beneficial in creating estimates for a current project. Organizational policies and standardized templates, such as the preferred estimation methods and forms for documenting estimates, can also make this effort faster and easier.

Enterprise Environmental Factors   For cost estimating, this includes marketplace conditions, commercial cost databases, exchange rates, and inflation. A project manager might review the sources and costs of supplies as part of estimating.

Accuracy of Estimates   Think about someone walking into your office and asking you to estimate the total cost of a new project. The first question you would probably ask is, "How accurate do you want me to be?" Estimates made earlier will be less accurate than those made later, when more is known about the project. Estimates should be in a range, as it's very unlikely an activity will be completed for the exact amount estimated. At first, a project manager will typically provide wide-ranging estimates, which are top-down in nature. Over time, as the project manager gathers more information about the project, they can narrow the estimate range. These top-down estimates evolve into bottom-up estimates.

Tools and Techniques of Estimate Costs PAGE 243   Costs can be estimated using three of the techniques described in the Schedule Management chapter: analogous estimating, parametric estimating, and three-point estimating. Review the discussion of these techniques under the Estimate Activity Durations process in the Schedule Management chapter and think about how they might be used for cost estimating. Costs can also be estimated using bottom-up estimating. This technique involves creating detailed estimates for each part of an activity (if available) or work package (if activities are not defined). To do this well requires an accurate WBS. The estimates are then rolled up into control accounts and finally into an overall project estimate, after reserves are factored in. (For additional information about contingency reserves and management reserves, review the Reserve Analysis section and the tools and techniques of the Determine Budget process on the following pages.)

The following are some other key cost estimating tools and techniques.

Data Analysis

Alternatives Analysis   In Estimate Costs, alternatives analysis is used to assess the cost of various ways to accomplish the project work. This could include make-or-buy analysis or other types of analysis regarding how to accomplish the project outcomes within cost constraints or practices of the organization.

Reserve Analysis   Proper project management requires the use of reserves to cover the risks to schedule, cost, and other areas in an estimate. As discussed in the Schedule Management chapter, reserve analysis involves identifying which activities on the project have significant risk and determining how much time and money to set aside to account for those known risks. Contingency reserves are used for known risks, which are identified risks. A management reserve is used to accommodate unknown, or unidentified, risks.

Cost of Quality The cost of work added to the project to accommodate quality efforts should be included in the project estimate.

Project Management Information System

A Project Management Information System (PMIS) is made up of tools to support information documentation, storage, and retrieval on the project. It includes estimating spreadsheets and software, and integrates finance and accounting, scheduling, quality, and risk tools. These tools can significantly speed up the calculations and analysis related to estimating.

Decision Making

As is the case with schedule estimates, involving team members in estimating costs improves accuracy because they are the ones most likely to understand what's involved in the effort. Examples of group decision-making techniques include voting, brainstorming, and the nominal group technique, all of which are described in the Scope Management chapter of this book.

Estimate Ranges

Organizations often have standard ranges for different types of estimates—such as preliminary, conceptual, feasibility, order of magnitude, and definitive estimates. These ranges tell you how much time and effort need to go into estimating to make sure the actual cost is within the range of the estimate. The usual standard ranges for the order of magnitude estimate, budget estimate, and definitive estimate are shown below.

- **Rough order of magnitude (ROM) estimate** This type of estimate is usually made during project initiating. A typical range for ROM estimates is –25 to +75 percent, but this range can vary depending on how much is known about the project when creating the estimates.

- **Budget estimate** As a best practice, it is a good idea to narrow the range of the estimate before you begin iterating the plan. A budget estimate is in the range of –10 to +25 percent.

- **Definitive estimate** As project planning progresses, the estimate will become even more refined. Some project managers use the range of +/–10 percent, while others use –5 to +10 percent.

Outputs of Estimate Costs PAGE 246

When completed, the Estimate Costs process results in cost estimates and an explanation of how those estimates were derived (which is known as the basis of estimates). It can also result in changes or updates to project documents, such as the risk register, assumption log, and lessons learned register.

Determine Budget PAGE 248

> **Process:** Determine Budget
> **Process Group:** Planning
> **Knowledge Area:** Cost Management

In this part of cost management, the project manager calculates the total cost of the project to determine the amount of funds the organization needs to have available for the project. The result of this calculation is the budget. The cost baseline is the portion of the budget the project manager will have control over. Meeting the cost baseline will be a measure of project success, so the budget should be in a form the project manager can use while the work is being done to control costs and, therefore, control the overall project.

© 2018 RMC Publications, Inc ™ • 952.846.4484 • info@rmcls.com • www.rmcls.com

Inputs to Determine Budget PAGE 250
To begin the Determine Budget process, the project manager should review the business case and the benefits management plan for the project. The business case includes the business need and the reason the project is being done. This may be expressed in financial terms, such as expected return on investment. The benefits management plan can be used to finalize the budget and compare it to the economic benefits expected from the project.

Many of the inputs to the Estimate Costs process are used here as well—the cost management plan, the scope baseline, the project schedule, the risk register, and organizational process assets (for example, the existing policies on cost control and cost budgeting). Two outputs from Estimate Costs—cost estimates and the basis of estimates—are also essential inputs to this process. You'll also need information about when and for how long resources will be needed (and at what rates—which can be found in the resource management plan), and any agreements regarding the purchase of services or products for the project.

Tools and Techniques of Determine Budget PAGE 252
The tools and techniques used to determine the budget for a project may include expert judgment, cost aggregation, reserve analysis, historical information review, funding limit reconciliation, and financing.

In estimating the total cost of a project (determining the project's budget), a project manager must perform risk management activities and include reserves in their estimates. The cost baseline includes contingency reserves; it represents the funds the project manager has authority to manage and control. The cost budget is the cost baseline plus the management reserves.

To create a budget, activity cost estimates are rolled up into work package cost estimates. Work package costs are then rolled up to control account costs and, finally, to project costs. This process is called cost aggregation. Contingency reserves are added to determine the cost baseline. These can be added at the project level, as described here and depicted in figure 7.1—but note that it is also possible to add contingency reserves at the activity level. In the final step, the management reserves are added.

After the cost baseline and cost budget are estimated, the project manager may compare these numbers to parametric estimates or expert judgment; alternatively, the project manager may perform a historical information review, comparing their estimates to those of past, similar projects. For example, a general rule for a high-level parametric estimate in some industries is that design should be 15 percent of the cost of construction. Other industries estimate the cost of design to be 60 percent of the project budget. The project manager needs to investigate and justify any significant differences between the project estimates and the reference data, to ensure the estimates are reasonable and as accurate as possible.

The next thing to check is cash flow (this is part of funding limit reconciliation). Funding must be available when it is needed on the project, or it will cause changes to other parts of the project and iterations of the project documents or project management plan. For example, if equipment that will cost $500,000 is scheduled to be purchased on June 1, but the money for the purchase is not available until July 1, the activities dependent on that equipment will have to be moved to later points in the schedule. The cost baseline, therefore, is time-phased and may be shown as an S-curve.

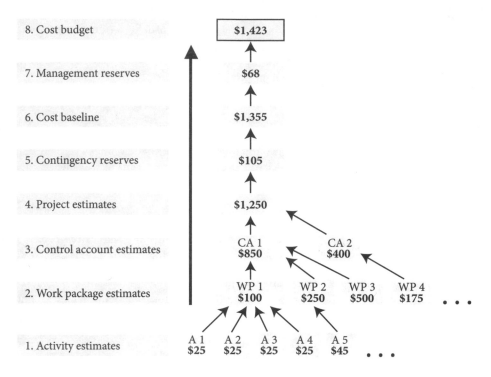

Figure 7.1 Creating a budget

The project manager needs to perform another reconciliation before the proposed cost baseline and cost budget can become final: reconciling with any cost constraints in the charter. If, after all of the project manager's work, the project estimate still exceeds the constraints, the project manager must meet with management, explain why their cost requirement cannot be met, and propose options to decrease costs. (Pay particular attention to that last sentence.)

Such actions are a required part of project management. If a proposed budget is unrealistic, it is the project manager's job to address it early in planning. As with the schedule, project managers have a professional responsibility to reconcile the budget in this way.

Financing refers to obtaining the needed funds for a project. This means all funds—both internal and external. External funds are obtained from sources outside the performing organization, and are typically needed for major long-term projects. These funds are included in the cost baseline. Also keep in mind that during funding limit reconciliation the project manager should reconcile the scheduled availability of and limits to funding dispersion.

Outputs of Determine Budget PAGE 254 When the Determine Budget process is complete, the cost baseline, including all funding requirements, is established. As in the other processes we have discussed, the efforts involved in determining the budget may create the need for updates to project documents including cost estimates, the risk register, and the project schedule.

Control Costs PAGE 257

Most of the project manager's activities while the work is being done should be focused on controlling the project. The Control Costs process is similar to the control part of any other knowledge area, with a focus on cost.

 As a rule, control-related processes are generally the same and have many of the same inputs and outputs. While you can save some study time if you understand what control is, it is still important to know what inputs and outputs are unique, and then apply that study practice to time, cost, quality, and so on.

Planning always comes before doing. The cost management plan includes the plan for controlling the costs of the project, such as the number and frequency of cost meetings, and the reports and measurements that will be needed. Also note that the control part of the management plan is customized to the needs of the project.

Inputs to Control Costs PAGE 259

Work performance data is a key input to the Control Costs process. Additional inputs may include components of the project management plan (such as the cost management plan, cost baseline, and performance measurement baseline), the lessons learned register, project funding requirements, and any organizational process assets that may impact how a project manager will control costs.

Work Performance Data

An important part of control is measuring to see if there are any variances from what was planned, and then deciding if those variances require change requests. Work performance data provides the information about project progress you need to analyze to determine if changes should be requested.

Tools and Techniques of Control Costs PAGE 260

The following are key tools and techniques of the Control Costs process.

Data Analysis

The primary data analysis techniques used to control costs are earned value analysis (which is part of earned value management), variance analysis, trend analysis, and reserve analysis.

Earned Value Analysis How valuable would it be to know how a project is really going? Knowing the true status of a project will allow a project manager to better focus on more critical management activities—and this is the primary benefit of earned value management. If a project manager relies on hope, guesses, or a general percent complete estimate to assess a project, they can expect to get an inaccurate analysis that will result in the need to work overtime at the end of the project because of the lack of control along the way.

Earned value analysis is used in performance reviews to measure project performance against the scope, schedule, and cost baselines. Note that earned value analysis uses a combination of these three baselines, known as the performance measurement baseline. The measurements resulting from an earned value analysis of the project indicate whether there are any potential deviations from the performance measurement baseline. Many project managers manage their project's performance by comparing planned to actual results. With this method, however, a project manager could easily be on time but overspend the plan. Using earned value analysis is ideal because it integrates cost, time, and the work done (or scope), and it can be used to forecast future performance and project completion dates and costs. Also keep in mind that a project manager should tailor their earned value management efforts to fit the needs of the project.

Cost Management SEVEN

Using the work performance information gathered through earned value analysis, a project manager can create reports, including cost forecasts, and other communications related to the project's progress. Earned value analysis may also result in change requests to the project.

Earned Value Terms to Know
Here are the basic earned value concepts that you need to understand for the CAPM exam.

Acronym	Term	Interpretation
PV	Planned value	As of today, what is the estimated value of the work planned to be done?
EV	Earned value	As of today, what is the estimated value of the work actually accomplished?
AC	Actual cost (total cost)	As of today, what is the actual cost incurred for the work accomplished?
BAC	Budget at completion (the cost baseline)	How much did we budget for the total project effort?
EAC	Estimate at completion	What do we currently expect the total project to cost? (a forecast)
ETC	Estimate to complete	From this point on, how much more do we expect it to cost to finish the project? (a forecast)
VAC	Variance at completion	As of today, how much over or under budget do we expect to be at the end of the project?

Formulas and Interpretations to Memorize
There are likely to be questions on the exam that require you to use some of the earned value formulas listed below. Be aware that knowing these formulas will only help you answer a few questions. If you choose to skip memorizing these formulas, still take note of the interpretations; that information may be easier to recall, and it may help you answer a few questions related to earned value.

Name	Formula	Interpretation
Cost variance (CV)	$EV - AC$	Negative is over budget; positive is under budget.
Schedule variance (SV)	$EV - PV$	Negative is behind schedule; positive is ahead of schedule.
Cost performance index (CPI)	$\dfrac{EV}{AC}$	We are getting \$ _____ worth of work out of every \$1 spent. Funds are (or are not) being used efficiently. Greater than one is good; less than one is bad.
Schedule performance index (SPI)	$\dfrac{EV}{PV}$	We are (only) progressing at _____ percent of the rate originally planned. Greater than one is good; less than one is bad.

© 2018 RMC Publications, Inc ™ • 952 846 4484 • info@rmcls.com • www.rmcls.com

Name	Formula	Interpretation
Estimate at completion (EAC)	AC + (BAC – EV)	This formula calculates actual costs to-date plus remaining budget. It is used when current variances are thought to be atypical of the future. It is essentially AC plus the remaining value of work to perform.
Estimate to complete (ETC)	EAC – AC	This formula calculates the total project cost as of today minus what has been spent to date.
Variance at completion (VAC)	BAC – EAC	How much over or under budget will we be at the end of the project?
Time variance (TV)	ES – AT	This is an emerging formula (which is an extension of EVM) that calculates schedule variances using earned schedule (ES) and actual time (AT).

 TRICKS OF THE TRADE® For the exam, you should understand the following about CV, SV, CPI, and SPI:

- EV comes first in each of these formulas.
- If it is a variance (difference), the formula is EV *minus* AC or PV.
- If it is an index (ratio), it is EV *divided by* AC or PV.
- If the formula relates to cost, use AC.
- If the formula relates to schedule, use PV.

People often answer questions incorrectly that involve interpreting earned value terms or acronyms because they fail to understand the meanings of the terms. Figure 7.2 illustrates some of the differences.

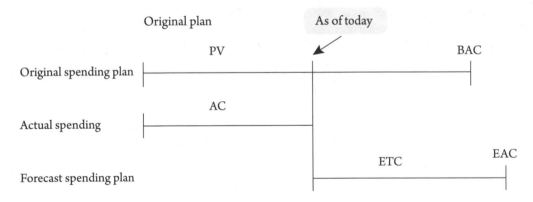

Figure 7.2 Understanding earned value concepts by looking backward and forward on a project

In figure 7.2, make note of the following key points:

- Planned value (PV—what the value was expected to be at this point in the project according to the plan) and actual cost (AC—what the cost has actually been on the project to this point) look *backward* at the project.

- Budget at completion (BAC), estimate to complete (ETC), and estimate at completion (EAC) look *forward*. BAC refers to the project's planned budget; it indicates what the end cost of the project would be if everything went according to plan.

- ETC and EAC forecast *future performance* based on what has actually occurred on the project, taking into account any variances from the plan that have already occurred. ETC is an estimate of how much more the remainder of the project will cost to complete. EAC indicates what the total project cost is forecasted to be.

Reserve Analysis   Remember the contingency reserves that get factored into the cost baseline to address known risks? Part of controlling costs involves analyzing whether those contingency reserves are still necessary, or whether new reserves are required. For example, let's say a project team identifies a highly ranked risk and sets aside a contingency reserve to address that risk, should the need arise. If the risk does not occur and it is determined the risk is no longer a threat, the contingency reserve can be removed from the cost baseline (as well as the cost budget). Or, a risk review on a project may identify new risks, which could lead to a decision to increase the contingency reserves. Both of these examples require a change request being submitted through integrated change control. It may also be necessary to reassess the amount of management reserve that was set aside to address unknown risks. Maybe too little or too much was set aside for management reserves in the cost management plan.

Reserve analysis allows a project manager to identify and apply lessons learned in the Control Costs process. Analysis of the management reserves may indicate that too many unknown risk events are occurring, suggesting that the risk management efforts in planning were inadequate and need to be redone. Management reserves, if you recall, are separate from the cost baseline, so changes to them will change the cost budget. If an unknown risk event occurs, management reserves will pay for the workaround; a change request is required to move those management reserve funds into the cost baseline and add any additional funds required to complete the reestimated project work within the new parameters of the project.

Variance Analysis   Variance analysis involves identifying the causes of variances and determining what to do about them. Remember, everything must be planned before it is done—so the cost management plan should have considered what variances from the baseline warrant a response.

Trend Analysis   Trend analysis includes at least two types of tools: charts and forecasting. In addition to measuring project performance, cost control includes forecasting the final cost of the project. Forecasting involves using earned value metrics to determine the likelihood of meeting the agreed-upon end date.

Outputs of Control Costs PAGE 268   The Control Costs process provides measurements that indicate how the work is progressing and allow the project manager to create reliable forecasts and take action to control the project. This process also results in change requests, including recommended corrective or preventive actions and updates to the project management plan and project documents. The project manager needs to make sure these changes and updates are communicated to stakeholders—including the team, to ensure they understand the revisions to the project and are implementing them correctly.

The Control Costs process results in the following key outputs.

Work Performance Information   The Control Costs process results in the analysis of measurements from the earned value calculations performed. This information can then be used to generate forecasts and progress reports.

Cost Forecasts   The results of estimate at completion (EAC) or bottom-up EAC calculations are used to forecast the final costs of the project.

Change Requests   Most project managers think of change requests in terms of time (requesting more time for the project), but changes may also be requested for cost, communication, or risk. However, changes to cost should be requested only for good reasons, not just because the cost was not properly managed. Not all cost overruns can be fixed by asking for more funds through a change request. Some cost overruns need to be made up by adjusting future components of the project. Change requests for this process can include recommendations for corrective or preventive actions.

Project Management Plan and Project Documents Updates   The Control Costs process may result in updates to the cost management plan as well as updates to the cost baseline. These updates may result from approved changes in scope, time, or cost estimates and should be communicated to the team and all stakeholders.

Cost Management Review

Exercise

This exercise will help you review the key material you need to know for cost management. The Shuffle Game that follows offers another approach to this material. You can use either or both of these study tools, depending on your preference.

Instructions

1. Try to fill in the blanks in the below table using the knowledge and understanding gained after reading this chapter.
2. To review only the material contained in this chapter, focus on the cells that have asterisks. (These are the key topics you need to understand to pass the exam with the minimum amount of study time. The answer table will show only these topics.)
3. To review all the items listed in the *PMBOK® Guide*, fill in the entire table.

Key Inputs	Key Tools and Techniques	Key Outputs
Plan Cost Management Process group:		
		*
Estimate Costs Process group:		
*	*	*
Determine Budget Process group:		
*	*	*

Key Inputs	Key Tools and Techniques	Key Outputs
Control Costs		
Process group:		
*	*	*

Cost Management

SEVEN

Answer To save study time and focus on the most important information, this answer table only shows the topics that are covered in this chapter. If you tried to list all inputs, tools and techniques, and outputs, you'll need to check your answers against the *PMBOK® Guide*.

Key Inputs	Key Tools and Techniques	Key Outputs
Plan Cost Management Process group: Planning		
		Cost management plan
Estimate Costs Process group: Planning		
Project management plan • Cost management plan • Quality management plan • Scope baseline Project documents • Lessons learned register • Project schedule • Resource requirements • Risk register Enterprise environmental factors Organizational process assets	Data analysis • Alternatives analysis • Reserve analysis • Cost of quality Project management information system Decision making	Cost estimates Basis of estimates
Determine Budget Process group: Planning		
Project management plan Project documents Business documents Agreements Enterprise environmental factors Organizational process assets	Expert judgment Cost aggregation Reserve analysis Historical information review Funding limit reconciliation Financing	Cost baseline Project funding requirements Project documents updates
Control Costs Process group: Monitoring and controlling		
Project funding requirements Work performance data	Data analysis • Earned value analysis • Variance analysis • Trend analysis • Reserve analysis	Work performance information Cost forecasts Change requests Project management plan updates Project documents updates

Shuffle Game

Some people learn best by doing, which is why we have developed this alternate approach to reviewing cost management. To save you time, only the most important topics for the exam—those covered in this chapter—have been included.

Instructions

1. Cut out the cards on the next pages.
2. Lay out the bold title cards as column headers.
3. Shuffle the remaining cards and try to put them in the columns where they belong. Cards with italic terms must be matched to the corresponding group. For example, a *Cost of Quality* card in italics would match with a Data Analysis card, as cost of quality is a data analysis tool and technique.
4. Check your answers against the material covered in this chapter or the *PMBOK® Guide,* and make note of any gaps in your knowledge.

Note: Be sure to keep all cards for each chapter shuffle game as you will use them again for the final Shuffle Game in chapter 14.

Plan Cost Management *Key Outputs*	**Estimate Costs** *Key Inputs*	**Estimate Costs** *Key Tools and Techniques*
Estimate Costs *Key Outputs*	**Determine Budget** *Key Inputs*	**Determine Budget** *Key Tools and Techniques*
Determine Budget *Key Outputs*	**Control Costs** *Key Inputs*	**Control Costs** *Key Tools and Techniques*
Control Costs *Key Outputs*	Cost management plan	Project management plan
Cost management plan	*Quality management plan*	*Scope baseline*

Project documents	*Lessons learned register*	*Project schedule*
Resource requirements	*Risk register*	Enterprise environmental factors
Organizational process assets	Data analysis	*Alternatives analysis*
Reserve analysis	*Cost of quality*	Project management information system
Decision making	Cost estimates	Basis of estimates

| Project management plan | Project documents | Business documents |

| Agreements | Enterprise environmental factors | Organizational process assets |

| Expert judgment | Cost aggregation | Reserve analysis |

| Historical information review | Funding limit reconciliation | Financing |

| Cost baseline | Project funding requirements | Project documents updates |

Project funding requirements	Work performance data	Data analysis
Earned value analysis	*Variance analysis*	*Trend analysis*
Reserve analysis	Work performance information	Cost forecasts
Change requests	Project management plan updates	Project documents updates

Schedule and Cost Game

This game will help you practice answering questions about schedule and cost management, which are two of the more difficult knowledge areas on the exam. You can play this game with a study group or study partner, or while studying on your own.

Instructions

1. Cut out the cards that follow these instructions. (Unlike the Shuffle Game cards, these cards are printed on both the back and the front.)
2. Play the game as follows:
    a. If you're studying on your own, read each question and then formulate your answer using the knowledge gained after reading the schedule and cost management chapters. Then flip the card over to see the answer. (You could also write down the answers, as if you were taking a test.)
    b. If you are working with a partner, ask your partner to read each question and check your answer.
    c. If you're working with a study group, have one person ask the questions while the other group members write down their answers. Keep track of the correct answers, and see who gets the highest score (one point for each correct answer).
3. Try to answer as many questions as you can in 10 minutes. If you can answer 10 questions correctly in 10 minutes, you are working at the pace needed to pass the exam. (The exam allows about 1 minute and 15 seconds per question.)
4. Make a note of your gaps for further review.

Question: What is the formula for cost performance index (CPI)?	Question: What estimating method would use optimistic, pessimistic, and most likely activity estimates?	Question: "The estimated value of the work that will be done" has what earned value name?
Question: What is the critical path method?	Question: When should a project manager estimate how long each activity will take?	Question: What does the schedule variance tell a project manager?
Question: What scheduling technique involves crashing?	Question: What does a finish-to-start relationship mean?	Question: What does the estimate at completion tell a project manager?
Question: Why would a project manager crash a project?	Question: What is the name of the software that simulates a project's outcome?	Question: What does a start-to-start relationship mean?
Question: What does a milestone chart show?	Question: What is the duration of a milestone?	Question: What is another name for analogous estimating?

Answer:

Planned value

Answer:

Three-point estimating

Answer:

EV / AC

Answer:

How far behind or ahead of schedule a project is

Answer:

Estimate Activity Durations

Answer:

The longest duration path in the network diagram

Answer:

What a project manager can now expect the total project to cost

Answer:

One activity must finish before the next can start

Answer:

Schedule compression

Answer:

One activity must start before the next can start

Answer:

Monte Carlo analysis

Answer:

To compress the schedule and save time

Answer:

Top-down estimating

Answer:

Zero; they simply represent the completion of activities

Answer:

Dates of significant events within a project schedule

Question: What is the primary range of a definitive estimate?	Question: What are direct costs?	Question: What is the earned value term for the actual cost incurred for the work accomplished?
Question: What is value analysis?	Question: What is a management reserve?	Question: What is the cost variance formula?
Question: Who has more cost risk in a fixed-price contract—the buyer or the seller?	Question: What does agile release planning provide?	Question: What are the three types of float?
Question: What formulas are used to calculate float?	Question: Why would a project manager want to use resource leveling?	Question: What does a lead indicate?
Question: A critical path activity will generally have how much float?	Question: What is parametric estimating?	Question: What is a typical range for ROM estimates?

Answer: Actual cost	Answer: Costs incurred directly by the project	Answer: +/− 10 percent
Answer: EV − AC	Answer: An amount of time or money set aside to cover unforeseen risks	Answer: Finding a less costly way to do the same work without loss of performance
Answer: Total float, free float, and project float	Answer: A high-level schedule that includes the frequency of releases and the number of iterations for each release	Answer: The seller
Answer: That an activity can start before its predecessor is completed	Answer: To level the peaks and valleys of the schedule to get a more stable number of resources used on a project	Answer: LS − ES or LF − EF; this is the amount of time an activity can be delayed without delaying the project
Answer: −25 to +75 percent	Answer: Analyzing the relationships between historical data and other variables to estimate duration or cost	Answer: Zero

Practice Exam

1. Which of the following is an input to the Estimate Costs process?
    A. Reserve analysis
    B. Quality management plan
    C. Basis of estimates
    D. Cost forecasts

2. If the team is using earned value analysis and variance analysis, they are performing:
    A. Cost control
    B. Qualitative risk analysis
    C. Dependency determination
    D. Cost budgeting

3. As a rule, which of the following is a true statement about estimates that are made early in a project?
    A. They cost more to create than estimates that are made later.
    B. They are more likely to accurately predict the final results than estimates that are made later.
    C. They take more time to put together than estimates that are made later.
    D. They should be expressed as a wider range than estimates that are made later.

4. During project executing, the forecasted remaining hours exceed planned remaining hours. Consequently, the project takes on a negative variance. Which calculation is the project manager likely to use as a measurement tool to validate this information?
    A. EV – PV
    B. EV/AC
    C. EV/PV
    D. EV – AC

5. Which of the following are components of cost management?
    A. Float calculations, estimate at completion, and dependency determination
    B. Analogous estimating, basis of estimates, and earned value analysis
    C. Earned value analysis, dependency determination, and basis of estimates
    D. Dependency determination, float calculations, and earned value analysis

6. A cost baseline is an output of which cost management process?
    A. Estimate Activity Resources
    B. Estimate Costs
    C. Determine Budget
    D. Control Costs

7. Which of the following would not be part of a cost management plan?
    A. Approved estimating techniques
    B. How the project resources will be allocated
    C. Rules for measuring cost performance
    D. Change control procedures

8. An estimate that is –25/+75 percent of actual is an example of a _____ estimate.
    A. Budget
    B. Rough order of magnitude (ROM)
    C. Definitive
    D. Parametric

9. Which of the following represents the estimated value of the work actually accomplished?
   A. Earned value (EV)
   B. Planned value (PV)
   C. Actual cost (AC)
   D. Cost variance (CV)

10. The project manager is allocating overall cost estimates to individual activities to establish a baseline for measuring project performance. What process is this?
    A. Plan Cost Management
    B. Estimate Costs
    C. Determine Budget
    D. Control Costs

11. A project team accomplished $3,000 worth of work and has spent $4,000 to date. If they budgeted $5,000 for the work scheduled, what is the cost variance (CV)?
    A. ($1,000)
    B. $2,000
    C. $1,000
    D. ($2,000)

12. In which cost management process are cost forecasts developed?
    A. Estimate Costs
    B. Plan Cost Management
    C. Determine Budget
    D. Control Costs

13. Which of the following formulas would be used during Control Costs to estimate how much more the remainder of the project will cost to complete?
    A. EV – PV
    B. EV – AC
    C. EV/PV
    D. EAC – AC

14. What is least likely to be included in the key output of Plan Cost Management?
    A. Control thresholds
    B. Roles and responsibilities for cost activities
    C. Earned value analysis
    D. Funding decisions

15. If planned value (PV) is $29,000, actual cost (AC) is $32,000, and earned value (EV) is $30,000, what is the schedule variance (SV)?
    A. 0.938
    B. $1,000
    C. 1.034
    D. ($2,000)

Answers

1. **Answer** B

   Explanation The quality management plan outlines all the activities the team must perform to achieve the expected level of quality, and it is an input to Estimate Costs. Reserve analysis is a technique used in Estimate Costs, while the basis of estimates is an output of that process. Cost forecasts are an output of Control Costs.

2. **Answer** A

   Explanation Earned value analysis and variance analysis are data analysis techniques used in the Control Costs process to track the status of the project budget, comparing the actual costs to those budgeted.

3. **Answer** D

   Explanation As a rule, estimates that are made early in a project should be expressed as a wider range than estimates that are made later, when we have more data and know more about the project. The other statements are not valid generalizations.

4. **Answer** A

   Explanation The measurement tool described here is the schedule variance calculation. Earned value (EV) minus planned value (PV) equals schedule variance (SV), or $SV = EV - PV$. A negative SV means the project is behind schedule; a positive SV means the project is ahead of schedule.

5. **Answer** B

   Explanation Analogous estimating, basis of estimates, earned value analysis, and estimate at completion are all components of cost management. Float calculations and dependency determination are both part of schedule management.

6. **Answer** C

   Explanation A cost baseline is an output of the Determine Budget process.

7. **Answer** B

   Explanation Of the options presented, the only one not included in the cost management plan is how the project resources will be allocated.

8. **Answer** B

   Explanation A rough order of magnitude (ROM) estimate, which is usually made during project initiating, typically has a range of −25/+75 percent of actual.

9. **Answer** A

   Explanation In earned value analysis, earned value (EV) is the estimated value of the work completed to date.

10. **Answer** C

    Explanation Plan Cost Management may include work to define how costs will be estimated, but that process does not involve working with actual estimates. In the situation described, the estimates are already created, so the answer is not Estimate Costs. The answer is not Control Costs, because the baseline has not yet been created. The work described is the Determine Budget process.

11. **Answer** A

    Explanation A question like this requires you to know the meaning of earned value terms in common terminology. The relevant formula is EV – AC = CV. In this scenario, EV (earned value) is $3,000 and AC (actual cost) is $4,000. That means that the CV (cost variance) is $3,000 – $4,000 = ($1,000).

12. **Answer** D

    Explanation During Control Costs, the results of the estimate at completion (EAC) or bottom-up EAC calculations are used to forecast the final costs of the project.

13. **Answer** D

    Explanation An estimate of how much it will cost to finish the remaining project work is developed using the estimate to complete (ETC) formula: ETC = EAC (estimate at completion) – AC (actual cost). EV – PV is used to calculate schedule variance, while EV – AC calculates the cost variance. EV/PV is the formula for calculating the schedule performance index (SPI).

14. **Answer** C

    Explanation Control thresholds, roles and responsibilities for cost management activities, and funding decisions are all components of the cost management plan, the key output of Plan Cost Management. Earned value analysis happens later, during Control Costs.

15. **Answer** B

    Explanation Schedule variance is calculated using the formula EV – PV, or $30,000 – $29,000 = $1,000. The positive schedule variance shows that this project is ahead of schedule.Question:

Quality Management

EIGHT

There are 10 to 11 questions on this knowledge area on the CAPM exam. Also note, for a full list of all inputs, tools and techniques, and outputs within this knowledge area, please see the table on page 272 in the PMBOK© Guide.

Some people argue that project managers don't have time to spend managing quality, and many organizations don't require their project managers to have quality management plans. But think about the impact of managing quality. A lack of attention to quality results in rework or defects. The more rework a project manager has to do, the more time and money they are wasting, and the less likely they are to meet the project schedule and cost baselines. With a focus on quality, a project manager can spend time preventing—rather than dealing with—problems. They can actually save time on the project that they would have otherwise spent on rework and problem solving.

Projects and organizations sometimes determine the approach to quality management. For some, that may mean simply responding to customer complaints about the quality of deliverables. For others, it may mean that they need to inspect deliverables for quality before the deliverable reaches the customer. More informed organizations not only inspect their deliverables, they also evaluate and adjust their quality management processes in an effort to identify the causes of defects. An even better approach includes these quality management and process improvements, as well as planning quality into projects. Ideally, an organization embraces all these efforts as part of a total commitment to providing the required level of quality.

QUICKTEST

- Quality management process
- Definition of quality
- Quality metrics
- Quality management plan
- Continuous improvement
- Control charts
- Cause-and-effect diagrams
- Checklists
- Checksheets
- Flowcharts
- Mind mapping
- Logical data models
- Scatter diagrams
- Histograms
- Pareto charts
- Affinity diagrams
- Matrix diagrams
- Multicriteria decision analysis
- Prioritization matrices
- Interviews
- Brainstorming
- Benchmarking
- Test and inspection planning
- Inspections
- Meetings
- Document analysis
- Process analysis
- Audits
- Cost-benefit analysis
- Cost of quality
- Alternatives analysis
- Performance reviews
- Root cause analysis
- Costs of conformance and nonconformance
- Statistical sampling
- Questionnaires and surveys
- Prevention over inspection
- Gold plating
- Just in Time (JIT)
- Responsibility for quality
- Design of experiments
- Design for X
- Problem solving
- Grade

Let's look at an overview of quality management to help you understand how each part fits into the overall process. Remember that everything must be planned before it's done. In quality management, we must first determine how we will plan, manage, and control quality. We then make sure we are using all the necessary processes on the project. Finally, we measure quality compared to the plan.

The following should help you understand how each part of quality management fits into the overall project management process:

The Quality Management Process	Done During
Plan Quality Management	Planning process group
Manage Quality	Executing process group
Control Quality	Monitoring and controlling process group

Before we start discussing these three processes in detail, let's look at some basic quality management concepts you should understand for the exam.

Definition of Quality

What is quality? Quality is defined as the degree to which the project fulfills requirements. Memorize this phrase, as it may help you with a handful of questions on the exam.

If the definition of quality is the degree to which the project fulfills requirements, can you achieve quality in a plan-driven or predictive environment if you do not have all the stated and unstated requirements defined in the project scope statement and requirements documentation? Of course not. This makes the requirements-gathering effort (from scope management), the project scope statement, and requirements documentation very important to the quality management effort.

In a change-driven, or adaptive, environment, a project manager captures quality requirements and acceptance criteria in user stories (a written summary that may include details such as the requesting stakeholder's role and what the stakeholder needs to achieve). As user stories are prioritized, quality efforts are planned in detail for releases and iterations.

Whereas *quality* is defined as the degree to which a project (or deliverable) fulfills requirements, *grade* refers to a general category or classification of a deliverable or resource that indicates common function, but varying technical specifications. For example, a low-grade concrete that supports limited weight might be sufficient for a project's needs and could be of acceptable quality if it meets the established quality requirements, such as having zero defects. Likewise, a high-grade concrete intended to sustain more weight could be of unacceptable quality if it is mixed or poured to low standards, or otherwise fails to meet the established quality metrics.

Definition of Quality Management

Quality management includes creating and following organizational policies and procedures as well as applicable regulatory and industry standards, and tailoring them to ensure the project meets the needs of the customer. It's also accurate to say it means ensuring a project is completed in compliance with the project requirements. Quality management includes the processes of Plan Quality Management, Manage Quality, and Control Quality.

Quality-Related PMI-isms

Quality-related questions may be confusing if you don't know the difference between giving the customer extras, and the need to satisfy project requirements. Even though the CAPM exam may not directly test this approach, it's important to apply this concept to quality management to answer potential exam questions correctly. Know the following PMI-isms related to quality: Quality means meeting requirements, not adding extras.

- The project manager must determine the metrics to be used to measure quality before the project work begins.
- The project manager must define quality management processes for the project and put into place a plan for continually improving them.
- The project manager should recommend improvements to the performing organization's standards, policies, and processes. Such recommendations are expected and welcomed by management.
- Quality should be checked before an activity or work package is completed.
- Quality should be considered whenever there is a change to any of the project constraints.
- The project manager must ensure that authorized approaches and processes are followed.
- The project manager must ensure that the quality standards and processes on the project are adequate to meet quality requirements.
- Some quality activities may be performed by a quality department.

Additional Concepts

Let's briefly examine some additional concepts that show how quality management fits into PMI's project management process. Although these topics are not likely to be tested on the CAPM exam, they can help you understand the approach to quality described in the *PMBOK® Guide*.

Gold Plating

Gold plating refers to giving the customer extras. Although your company might have a policy that promotes gold plating (for example, "Meet and exceed customers' expectations"), proper quality management does not recommend "exceeding" as a best practice. Gold plating is often the team's impression of what is valued by the customer, and the customer might not agree. Since most projects have difficulty meeting the project objectives, all available effort should go into achieving those objectives, instead of into gold plating.

Prevention over Inspection

Is it better to inspect work to find problems or to prevent them in the first place? Which takes less effort? It is a PMI-ism that quality must be planned in, not inspected in.

Continuous Improvement

Continuous improvement involves continuously looking for ways to improve the quality of work, processes, and results. The terms "continuous improvement" and "kaizen" are taken to mean the same thing—however, "continuous improvement" is a general term, while "kaizen" is a quality movement that originated in Japan. The Japanese word *kaizen* means to alter *(kai)* in order to make better or improve *(zen)*. In the West, continuous improvement tends to focus on major improvements. In Japan, kaizen emphasizes smaller improvements. Continuous improvement of project management within an organization can include analysis of how quality management is planned and utilized on projects.

Just in Time (JIT)

Many companies find that holding raw materials or other resources in inventory is not only more expensive, but also unnecessary. Instead, they have their suppliers deliver resources just before they are needed, thus decreasing inventory to nearly zero. A company using JIT must achieve a high level of quality in their practices; otherwise, there will not be enough materials or equipment to meet production requirements because of waste and rework. A JIT system forces attention on quality as well as schedule.

Responsibility for Quality   The project manager has the ultimate responsibility for the quality of the product of the project, but each team member must check their work by inspecting it themselves. It is not acceptable for team members to simply complete the work and then turn it over to the project manager or their manager to be checked. Work should meet the project requirements, and testing should be done whenever appropriate before submitting the work.

Understanding the Difference between Plan Quality Management, Manage Quality, and Control Quality   For the exam, here is a brief description of these three processes:

- **Plan Quality Management**   This process focuses on defining quality for the project, the product, and project management, and planning how it will be achieved.

- **Manage Quality**   Because it is an executing process, Manage Quality is focused on the work being done on the project. Its purpose is to ensure that the team is following organizational policies, standards, and processes as planned to produce the project's deliverables. The project manager also evaluates whether the quality management plan or processes need to be improved or modified.

- **Control Quality**   Control Quality, a monitoring and controlling process, includes examining the actual deliverables produced on the project to ensure they are correct and meet the planned level of quality, evaluating variances, finding the source of problems, and recommending ways to address them.

 The following chart presents a trick for understanding the three quality management processes. Study it to gain a clearer understanding of the focus of each process before reading the rest of this chapter. In the detailed descriptions, you will see combinations of actions and outputs. Can you spot them? You may want to review this chart after you read the in-depth discussion of each of the processes.

Plan Quality Management (Planning)	Manage Quality (Executing)	Control Quality (Monitoring and controlling)
High-Level Description of What Each Process Focuses On		
<ul><li>What is quality?</li><li>How will we ensure it?</li></ul>	<ul><li>Are we following the policies, metrics, procedures, and processes as planned?</li><li>Are the procedures and processes giving us the intended results?</li><li>Will we meet the quality objectives?</li></ul>	<ul><li>Are the results of our work meeting the standards and required metrics?</li><li>Is the variance within acceptable limits, or do we have to take action?</li></ul>

Plan Quality Management (Planning)	Manage Quality (Executing)	Control Quality (Monitoring and controlling)
More Detailed Description of What Each Process Focuses On		

• Review management plans and project documents to understand quality requirements on the project.
• Identify quality practices as well as internal and external standards relevant to the product, project, and project management efforts (OPAs and EEFs).
• Create additional project-specific processes, standards, and metrics.
• Determine the processes that will be used on the project.
• Determine what work you will do to meet the standards.
• Determine how you will measure to make sure you meet the standards.
• Plan for process improvement.
• Perform cost of quality, cost-benefit, and other analysis work to make certain the appropriate level of quality will be planned in.
• Determine roles and responsibilities for achieving quality requirements and objectives.
• Plan for testing and inspection to check that requirements, performance, reliability, and quality goals and objectives are achieved.
• Interface the quality management plan with other management plans to balance the needs of quality with scope, cost, time, risk, resources, and customer satisfaction requirements.
• Finalize a quality management plan as part of the project management plan.
	• Use measurements from Control Quality to confirm that:
	  – Policies and processes are being followed
	  – Policies, metrics, and processes are still appropriate for the project
	  – Policies and processes are effective in achieving planned quality results
	• Use data-representation techniques to analyze results of quality testing.
	• Determine the root cause of quality problems or variances from plan.
	• Perform continuous improvement to increase efficiency and effectiveness.
	• Create test and evaluation documents for use in Control Quality.
	• Determine if project activities comply with organizational and project policies, processes, and procedures (perform a quality audit).
	• Solve problems.
	• Produce reports.
	• Share good practices with others in the organization.
	• Submit change requests.
	• Update the project management plan and project documents.
		• Inspect and measure the quality of deliverables to determine whether they meet requirements.
		• Use the PMIS to track deviations from planned quality.
		• Identify the need for quality improvements (corrective or preventive action, and defect repair).
		• Complete checklists and checksheets, perform tests, and evaluate results.
		• Graphically document results of testing and evaluation using data-representation techniques.
		• Verify deliverables.
		• Validate approved changes.
		• Recommend improvements to testing processes.
		• Use and update lessons learned.
		• Submit change requests.
		• Update the project management plan and project documents.

Plan Quality Management PAGE 277

Process: Plan Quality Management
Process Group: Planning
Knowledge Area: Quality Management

The objectives of the Plan Quality Management process are to identify all relevant organizational or industry practices, standards, and requirements for the quality of the project, the product of the project, and the project management efforts, and then plan how to meet those quality standards and requirements. The main result of this process is a quality management plan.

It is important to keep in mind that the level of quality efforts should be tailored to fit the needs of the project. There is no reason to negatively impact project scope, time, or cost if higher quality is not required on the project. Quality must be balanced with the other project constraints. The project scope statement, WBS, and WBS dictionary (the scope baseline) help the project manager maintain the proper perspective needed to plan quality to the appropriate level.

The project manager must also plan the project so it meets the customer's quality standards. Quality requirements are documented, analyzed, and prioritized according to the requirements management plan. Examples of such standards are the acceptable number of software bugs per module, the strength of concrete, or the average time per installation. These measures of quality will help the project manager know when the project is out of control and when to request changes.

Once existing practices and standards are identified, the project manager creates any additional project-specific standards and procedures that are needed.

These standards and procedures may be created based on how quality is defined for each piece of work. After the standards and procedures have been identified or created, the project manager needs to determine what work is required to meet those standards. Additional testing may need to be planned into the project, resources may need to be adjusted, or the descriptions of products to be purchased may need to be changed. The project manager should also determine the specific measurements that will be made each week or each month, or for each deliverable, to ensure compliance with all standards.

Inputs to Plan Quality Management PAGE 279 The following are the key inputs of the Plan Quality Management process.

Project Management Plan, Project Documents, and Project Charter Components of the project management plan and project documents that influence quality planning include the scope baseline, the stakeholder engagement plan and stakeholder register, a list of the major project deliverables (requirements management plan), risk thresholds (risk management plan), and approval requirements (project charter). Also note that the assumption log provides insight into the level of quality that is assumed to be acceptable on the project, and the requirements traceability matrix shows the origin of requirements related to quality, which will be used to confirm that quality requirements have been achieved.

Enterprise Environmental Factors and Organizational Process Assets Organizational process assets (OPAs) and enterprise environmental factors (EEFs) inform the project manager of relevant standards, policies, and procedures. They include lessons learned from previous projects and the performing organization's idea of the best way to accomplish work.

Tools and Techniques of Plan Quality Management PAGE 281 The following are some tools and techniques used in the Plan Quality Management process. Remember that the objective of using these tools and techniques is to determine the quality requirements, procedures, and standards for the project and product.

Data Gathering   Data gathering tools and techniques that can be used to identify existing standards, processes, and metrics or create new ones include interviews, brainstorming, and benchmarking. Interviews and brainstorming can help identify appropriate ways to measure quality on the project along with the metrics or processes to be used. You may recall learning about these techniques in the Scope Management chapter.

Benchmarking was also discussed as a technique in the Scope Management chapter. Here, benchmarking is used to measure quality and review methodologies utilized by similar projects or organizations to establish quality metrics and acceptable variance ranges.

Decision Making   An important aspect of planning is determining priorities and choosing between options. In the Plan Quality Management process, key decisions might include selecting the most critical metrics or prioritizing quality requirements. Decision-making tools and techniques for planning quality include multicriteria decision analysis and prioritization matrices.

Data Analysis   Data analysis tools and techniques that may be used during the Plan Quality Management process include cost-benefit analysis and cost of quality.

Cost-Benefit Analysis   When performing a cost-benefit analysis, the project manager analyzes the benefits versus the costs of quality efforts to determine the appropriate quality level and requirements for the project. Note that if you have poor quality, you might also have:

- Increased costs
- Decreased profits
- Low morale
- Low customer satisfaction
- Increased risk
- Rework

Cost of Quality (COQ)   Evaluating the cost of quality means making sure the project is not spending too much to achieve a particular level of quality. It involves looking at what the costs of conformance and nonconformance to quality will be on the project and creating an appropriate balance. The following table provides some examples of the costs of conformance and nonconformance to quality.

Cost of Conformance	Cost of Nonconformance
Quality training	Rework of deliverables not meeting quality standards
Studies	Scrap
Measuring quality of interim deliverables	Inventory costs
Customer satisfaction surveys and work to respond to issues raised	Warranty costs
Efforts to ensure everyone knows the processes to use to complete their work	Lost business

The costs of conformance should be lower than the costs of nonconformance. Otherwise, why spend time improving quality?

Data Representation   Data Representation is another tool and technique group within the Plan Quality Management process. This group includes flowcharts, logical data model, matrix diagrams, and mind mapping.

Logical Data Models   The logical data model can be presented using an entity relationship diagram—a method of representing and analyzing data. A logical data model contains a description of the quality needs of the project. It is used to understand the requirements, clarify business rules, and define processes. It can be used to create and refine quality plans that best meet the needs of the project.

Matrix Diagrams   A matrix diagram is a visual representation of the relationship between two or more sets of items. In the Plan Quality Management process, matrix diagrams can be used to sort quality requirements and identify the requirements that are most critical to the project. With this information, appropriate metrics may be planned to track and measure project progress.

Mind Mapping   As discussed in the Scope Management chapter, a mind map is a diagram of ideas or notes to help generate, classify, or record information. It is used here to facilitate the gathering of quality requirements and illustrate their impacts on other parts of project planning.

Flowcharts   Flowcharts may also be referred to as process flows or process maps. They show how a process or system flows from beginning to end, how the elements interrelate, alternative paths the process can take, and how the process translates inputs into outputs. One common flowchart model is SIPOC, which shows the connections between the supplier, input, process, output, and customer in a process. Flowcharts can be used in many parts of project management. In the Plan Quality Management process, flowcharts can help determine the cost of quality by mapping the expected monetary value of pursuing paths of conformance and nonconformance to quality.

Flowcharts are also useful for defining and communicating processes that will be used on the project. They can also be analyzed to determine how processes will be measured for conformance and effectiveness.

You can use this tool in Plan Quality Management to visualize a process and find potential quality problems or quality control issues. Imagine that work results are passed to four departments for approval. Might this lead to quality problems? What about an unfinished fragile product in a manufacturing environment? Would the quality of the product be reduced if it needed to be passed by hand from person to person?

A generic example of a flowchart is shown in figure 8.1.

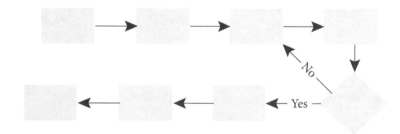

Figure 8.1 Flowchart

Test and Inspection Planning   Plan Quality Management includes determining how the team will confirm that the required level of quality has been achieved in the completed project deliverables, as well as how the deliverables will be evaluated for performance and reliability. Testing methods, which vary depending upon the type of product, service, or result being created, are used in the Control Quality process.

Meetings   Developing management plans requires the collaboration of the project manager and team. The project manager may hold meetings specifically focused on project planning. Note that any of the tools and techniques discussed in this section may be used within those meetings as part of quality management planning.

Outputs of Plan Quality Management PAGE 286   The following are key outputs of the Plan Quality Management process.

Quality Management Plan   Remember that the purpose of the Plan Quality Management process is to determine what quality is and put a plan in place to deliver that level of quality. This plan is called the quality management plan. It also includes analyzing processes to find ways to increase efficiency and prevent problems, which saves money and increases the probability that the customer will be satisfied.

Most quality management plans include the following:

- What quality practices and standards apply to the project
- Who will be involved in managing quality, what their specific duties will be, and when those activities need to be done
- What processes will be followed to help ensure quality
- A review of earlier decisions to make sure those decisions are correct
- What meetings will be held regarding quality
- What reports will address quality
- What metrics will be used to measure quality
- What parts of the project or deliverables will be measured, and when

Quality Metrics   Throughout the practice of proper project management, there is an underlying theme that the project manager must know how the project is performing compared to what was planned, and be able to determine when to request changes. The only way to effectively do this is to determine metrics in advance. This means the project manager needs to think through the areas on the project that are important to measure and (in most cases) decide what range of variation is acceptable. The following are some examples of quality metrics:

- The number of changes (to help measure the quality of the project management planning process)
- The variance related to resources utilization
- The number of items that fail inspection
- The variance of the weight of a product produced by the project compared to the planned weight
- The number of bugs found in software that is being developed as part of the project

The project manager must know what processes are being used on the project, analyze their effectiveness, and create additional processes as necessary, while also improving those processes as they are being used. This plan for analysis and improvement of these processes is included in the quality management plan. Improving existing processes saves time by increasing efficiency and preventing problems. It also saves money and increases the probability that the customer will be satisfied.

Project Management Plan and Project Documents Updates   The Plan Quality Management process will result in additions or changes to the project management plan and project documents. For example, quality management work may be added to the project. This work is documented in the scope baseline (WBS and WBS dictionary) as well as in the requirements traceability matrix, and may necessitate adjustments to the project activity list, schedule, budget, and resource assignments. Additional risks related to quality may be added to the risk register, and risk management efforts may be added to the project management plan.

Manage Quality PAGE 288

Manage Quality, an executing process, is performed while the project
work is being done. A group outside the project team, such as a quality department, often handles this
work on a project. The efforts of this process ensure that the project work, the processes followed, and the
deliverables produced conform to the quality management plan.

Processes to ensure that quality standards will be met are reviewed to make sure they are effective and are
being followed correctly. Quality audits, failure analysis, and design of experiments (described later in this
chapter) may be done to see if the quality management plan with the standards, metrics, processes, and
procedures may need to change. Test and evaluation documents are prepared in Manage Quality, for use
in Control Quality.

This process uses the quality management plan (which includes quality requirements) along with an
analysis of the measurements gathered in Control Quality to answer the following questions:

- Are the quality requirements, organizational policies, and processes identified in the quality
  management plan giving us the results we intended?
- Based on what we know now, is the work we planned the right quality for this project and the
  customer's requirements?
- Are we following the procedures and processes as planned?
- Can the processes and procedures be improved?
- How can we increase efficiency and prevent problems?

Inputs to Manage Quality PAGE 290
What do you think the key inputs to this process
might be? As you have likely noticed by now, the inputs to one process are often the outputs of a preceding
process. Therefore, you should be able to identify most of the inputs to this process by simply thinking of
the outputs of the Plan Quality Management process.

Project Management Plan
The quality management plan, which is part of the project management
plan, should be used as an input to the manage quality process. It includes key information about the level
of quality needed for both the project and product.

Project Documents
Project documents, such as quality metrics, quality control measurements, and the
lessons learned register, along with the risk report, should also be used as inputs to Manage Quality.

Tools and Techniques of Manage Quality PAGE 292
The following tools and techniques
are used to evaluate the success of all planning efforts. Many of these tools accomplish the same thing, but
in different ways. Not all of these tools and techniques will be used on every project. The choice depends
on the preferences of the project manager, the organizational requirements regarding quality management,
and the specific needs of the project.

TRICKS OF THE TRADE® As you read this next section, note that the CAPM exam is likely to test your knowledge of
specific tools and might not test your knowledge of the tools and techniques groups that we
reviewed in chapter 2 (which have also been reinforced throughout this book). Don't worry
about memorizing which tool belongs to which group, just try to get a basic understanding of
the tools and how they are used in this process.

Data Representation   Data representation is a tool and technique group that includes all tools and techniques used to represent or convey information.

Affinity Diagrams   We first saw this technique in the Collect Requirements process. In Manage Quality, affinity diagrams can help the project manager organize and group the results of a root cause analysis. For example, in Control Quality the project manager may have determined the cause of a variance, a product defect, or a deliverable not meeting requirements. They can use this information in the Manage Quality process to determine whether a change to the policies, procedures, or standards in the quality management plan could address the root cause of the problem.

Flowcharts   In the Plan Quality Management process, we discussed flowcharts (see fig. 8.1) as a tool to determine the cost of quality and identify potential quality problems. In Manage Quality, flowcharts may be used to study the steps of a process leading up to a quality defect. It is possible that this analysis would uncover confusion among the team or point out ways the process needs to be adjusted to make it more effective.

Matrix Diagrams   The matrix diagram is a visual representation of the relationship between two or more sets of items. There are several different types of matrix diagrams; the best matrix diagram to use will depend on the information that needs to be conveyed.

Cause-and-Effect (Fishbone, Ishikawa, or Why-Why) Diagrams   A project manager can use cause-and-effect diagrams to confirm that policies and procedures are being followed, metrics are being used correctly, and metrics are adequate to produce the required level of quality in project deliverables. Figure 8.3 in the Control Quality section of this chapter is an example of a cause-and-effect diagram.

Histograms   In this process, histograms are used to analyze the type and frequency of defects in order to identify where the quality plan and processes may need improvement as the project moves forward. Figure 8.4 in the Control Quality section of this chapter is an example of a histogram.

Scatter Diagrams   This diagram tracks two variables to determine their relationship to the quality of the results. Figure 8.2 in the Control Quality section of this chapter shows three examples of scatter diagrams.

Data Gathering   A data gathering technique that may be used as part of the Manage Quality process includes checklists.

Checklists   In Manage Quality, a checklist can be used to confirm that the steps of a process have been completed. It may also be used to analyze defects discovered in quality inspections, look for issues within the process, and assess whether a deliverable meets the acceptance criteria.

Data Analysis   There are multiple data analysis techniques that may be used as part of the Manage Quality process.

Document Analysis   Document analysis involves reviewing the results of testing and other quality reports to identify ways in which the quality management plan and processes might not be supporting the production of deliverables that meet the project quality requirements.

Alternatives Analysis   It is important to consider all the ways to solve an issue or problem. In Manage Quality, alternatives analysis may be used to evaluate which action would best impact the results of the quality management efforts or processes. For example, would a new automated testing tool be of more benefit than redefining the testing process?

Design of experiments (DOE) is a technique that can be used to analyze alternatives. Experimentation is performed to determine statistically what variables will improve quality; for example, DOE can be used to look for ways to deliver the same level of quality for less cost. DOE is a fast and accurate technique that allows you to systematically change the important factors in a process and see which combinations have an optimal impact on the project deliverables. For example, designers might use DOE to determine which combination of materials, structure, and construction will produce the highest-quality product. Performing DOE can help decrease the time and effort required to discover the optimal conditions in which to produce a quality deliverable. An alternative to DOE is to perform individual experiments for each variable in a process to assess their impacts on quality, but this can be time-consuming and can overlook interactions among variables.

Process Analysis   Have you ever worked on a project where some of the activities or work packages were repeated? This often happens when projects have multiple installations, such as a project to install software onto hundreds of computers. The lessons learned on the first few installations are used to improve the process for the remaining installations. Though this often happens naturally, formal process analysis should be planned in at certain points in the project (for example, after every 10 installations). Process analysis is a part of the continuous improvement effort on a project and focuses on identifying improvements that might be needed in project processes.

Root Cause Analysis   Root cause analysis in Manage Quality seeks to identify the processes, procedures, and policies within the plan that may not be working or that may need adjustment. Identifying the root cause of a quality problem or defect helps the team determine how to prevent it from recurring.

Failure analysis is a specific type of root cause analysis. It analyzes failed components of deliverables or failed processes to determine what led to that failure. Corrective action or change requests are likely outcomes of this type of analysis.

Decision Making   The project manager must facilitate a number of decisions regarding quality. There are several decision-making techniques that may be used.

Multicriteria Decision Analysis   Multicriteria decision analysis is a complex method of numerically assessing options based on criteria such as time, cost, and quality. It can be used throughout a project to help the team reach agreement regarding the best way to solve a problem or improve quality. For example, in Manage Quality, the team may use this technique when considering whether to adjust the quality management plan or specific processes or procedures.

Audits   Imagine a team of auditors walking into a project manager's office one day to check up on a project. Their job is to see if the project manager is complying with company policies, processes, practices, and procedures as defined in the quality management plan, and to determine whether those being used are efficient and effective. This scenario represents a quality audit, and it serves as an example of how seriously companies take quality. Don't think of a quality audit as a negative event. Instead, a good quality audit will look for new lessons learned and effective practices that the project can contribute to the performing organization. The work of a project is not only to produce the product of the project; it could also be said that a project should contribute to the best practices within the organization and, therefore, make the organization better. A quality audit may identify gaps or areas in need of improvement. Making these changes will enhance the project manager's ability to meet quality objectives.

If a project manager does not have a team of auditors from a quality department coming to check on their project, should they take on the responsibility of looking for opportunities to identify lessons learned and best practices on their project? Although quality audits are usually done by a quality department, a project manager can lead this effort if the performing organization does not have such a department.

Design for X   Design for X is another way of analyzing variables to evaluate both the effectiveness of the quality management plan and the team's ability to meet objectives. The X in this name can represent an attribute of quality, such as reliability, security, or serviceability. If the plan is not delivering the intended results in relation to the variable being analyzed, Design for X can help determine what changes or adjustments are needed.

Problem Solving   Gaining a good understanding of the real problem is the first step towards finding an effective and long-lasting solution. Problem solving can be used when considering quality improvements, or to determine how best to respond to deficiencies identified in quality audits.

The following are the steps used to analyze quality (and other) problems:

1. Define the real or root problem—not what is presented to you, or what appears to be the problem.
2. Analyze the problem.
3. Identify solutions.
4. Pick a solution.
5. Implement a solution.
6. Review the solution, and confirm that the solution solved the problem.

Outputs of Manage Quality PAGE 296   To understand the value of the Manage Quality process, you need to know that it leads to the following outputs.

Test and Evaluation Documents   Test and evaluation documents are identified or created in Manage Quality and used in Control Quality. They provide a format with which to evaluate whether quality objectives have been met. Control charts, checklists, test plans, or project documents such as a requirements traceability matrix from scope management, may also be used here. Larger organizations, or organizations that work on many similar projects, may develop templates for testing and evaluation work.

Quality Reports   These types of reports interpret and document the results of Manage Quality and Control Quality activities. They can present information in a number of formats. Information in quality reports is used to identify necessary changes to plans, policies, and processes to ensure that quality requirements will be met throughout the life of a project.

Change Requests and Project Management Plan Updates   Changes and updates to components of the project management plan—including the quality management plan and the scope, schedule, or cost baselines—may result from the work of this process.

Project Documents Updates   Newly discovered issues will be added to the issue log. The lessons learned register and risk register will be updated as needed.

Control Quality PAGE 298

> **Process:** Control Quality
> **Process Group:** Monitoring & Controlling
> **Knowledge Area:** Quality Management

Control Quality is the process of ensuring a certain level of quality in a deliverable, whether it be a product, service, or result. To *control* means to *measure*, and measurement is the major function of the Control Quality process. Aspects of products, services, or results are measured to determine whether they meet the quality standards. This process helps ensure customer acceptance, as it involves confirming and documenting the achievement of agreed-upon requirements.

It is important to note that Control Quality is closely related to the previous process, Manage Quality. Many of the tools and techniques used in Control Quality—as well as the resulting measurements—are also used in Manage Quality, but with a different focus. Control addresses the quality of the product—detecting and correcting defects. Manage Quality addresses the effectiveness of quality management plans, processes, and procedures, and whether the project is on track to meet its quality objectives. Quality defects are assumed to indicate issues with those plans, processes, and procedures.

Although a project manager must be involved and concerned about quality control, in large companies a quality department may complete much of this work. That department then informs the project manager about quality issues through change requests, which are accompanied by any necessary documentation and reports to detail the quality issues. The project manager must be able to read and understand quality measurement reports.

It is during Control Quality that the height of doors in a manufacturing process or the number of bugs per module will be measured. Quality control helps answer the following questions:

- Are the results of our work meeting the agreed-upon standards? Are they meeting project requirements?
- What is the actual variance from the standards?
- Is the variance from standards or processes outside acceptable limits?
- Are people using the checklists to support meeting the metrics established for the process?
- What changes in the project should be considered?

To better understand the Control Quality process, you should be familiar with the following inputs.

Inputs to Control Quality PAGE 300   The following are key inputs to the Control Quality process. Additional inputs include the quality management plan (a component of the project management plan), approved change requests, enterprise environmental factors, and any organizational process assets that may impact the project.

Deliverables   Deliverables are portions of the project scope that are produced in the Direct and Manage Project Work process. In the Control Quality process, we determine the level of quality for these deliverables.

Project Documents   Project documents that may be inputs to the Control Quality process include the lessons learned register, test and evaluation documents, and quality metrics. Quality metrics are documented in the quality management plan. They indicate what aspects of quality performance will be measured on the project, and what the level of acceptable quality will be.

Work Performance Data   While the Manage Quality process looks at whether standards and procedures are being followed, quality control looks at specific measurements (the height of doors in a manufacturing process or the number of bugs per module) to see if the project and its processes are in control. Work performance data also indicates how the actual progress compares to the planned cost or schedule for the project.

Tools and Techniques of Control Quality PAGE 302   There are many tools and techniques that may be used in this process. However, it is helpful to realize that regardless of the method used, the ultimate goal is the same: to test (verify) that each deliverable meets the metrics and requirements as stated in the plan. The following are the key tools and techniques of the Control Quality process.

Data Representation

Do you remember that this tools and techniques group was reviewed earlier in this chapter? If not, review the tools and techniques section of Plan Quality Management to fill any gaps you may have in your knowledge. When applied to Control Quality, this group may include control charts, cause-and-effect diagrams, histograms, and scatter diagrams.

Control Charts

In Manage Quality, control charts are established, and the parameters—such as the mean, specification limits, and control limits—are determined. Control charts are used in Control Quality to help determine if the results of a process are within acceptable limits.

To better understand the need for a control chart, imagine that a door manufacturer is undertaking a project to create a new production line. To make sure the production facility will create doors that meet quality standards, it's essential to monitor the processes and output so the new production line can become an ongoing business operation. Would each door be the same exact height? Weight? Not likely. Instead there is a range, however small, that is acceptable. Each door should be within the range of normal and acceptable limits.

During the Control Quality process, samples are taken and plotted on a control chart. The control chart shows whether the samples are within acceptable limits. If the data does not fall within the acceptable range, the results are considered to be "out of control," which indicates a problem that needs to be addressed.

A control chart can also be used to represent and monitor data on project performance, such as cost and schedule variances.

Scatter Diagrams

As discussed in Manage Quality, a scatter diagram is used to determine the relationship between variables and the quality of the results. In Control Quality, a scatter diagram can be used to compare actual results to what was anticipated, and estimate and forecast future outcomes of the process.

A scatter diagram tracks two variables to determine their relationship. Imagine that our door manufacturer has a project to develop a new painted door product line. Scatter diagrams may be used to determine the relationship of independent variables, such as paint quantity, dryer fan speed, and door weight, to the dependent variable of drying time, or to correlate defects with other variables in the process.

A regression line (or trend line) is calculated to show the correlation of variables, and can then be used for estimating and forecasting. Figure 8.2 depicts the possible resulting patterns: a *proportional,* or positive, correlation of paint quantity to drying time; an *inverse,* or negative, correlation of dryer fan speed to drying time; and *no correlation* between door weight and drying time.

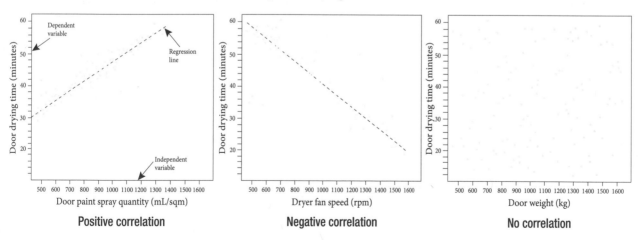

Figure 8.2   Scatter diagrams

Cause-and-Effect (Fishbone, Ishikawa, or Why-Why) Diagrams   Is it better to fix a defect or to get to its root cause? Think about this question for a moment.

The answer is that you should do both, and a cause-and-effect diagram can help you. In Manage Quality, we discussed the application of the cause-and-effect diagram in determining the root cause of quality issues relating to plans, processes, or procedures. In Control Quality, this tool can be used to look backward at what may have contributed to quality problems on the project, as well as analyze the impact of defects on the quality and acceptability of a deliverable.

Figure 8.3 shows the defect "system will not install" on the right and then lists the potential causes, such as hardware issues, software issues, etc. Various subcauses of each potential cause are also listed in an effort to find the root cause of the defect.

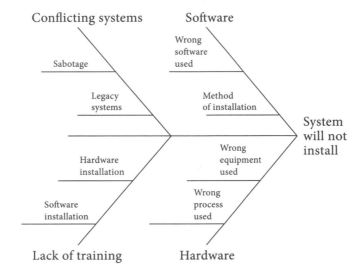

Figure 8.3 Cause-and-effect diagram

Histograms As shown in figure 8.4, a histogram shows data in the form of bars or columns. A typical histogram presents data in no particular order and without reference to time. The results of the measurements taken in Control Quality are displayed on a histogram to determine the problems that need the most immediate attention or are most likely to prevent the project from achieving its quality requirements. The Manage Quality process will analyze these problems and defects to determine if the cause is related to processes or the quality management plan.

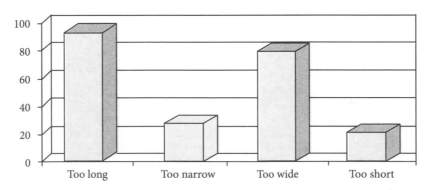

Figure 8.4 Histogram

Pareto Charts   A Pareto diagram or Pareto chart is a commonly used type of histogram that arranges the results from most frequent to least frequent to help identify which root causes are resulting in the most problems. Joseph Juran adapted Vilfredo Pareto's 80/20 rule to create the 80/20 principle (also known as the Pareto Principle), which states that 80 percent of problems are due to 20 percent of the root causes. Therefore, addressing the root cause of the most frequent problems makes the greatest impact on quality.

In Plan Quality Management, you can identify potential problems (using, for example, historical information from past projects) and document them on a Pareto diagram, as shown in figure 8.5. In Control Quality, you measure the data and represent it on the diagram to help analyze the situation and determine where to focus corrective action.

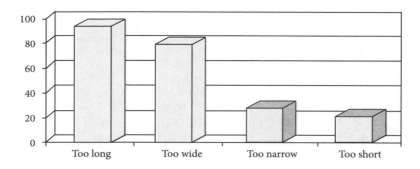

Figure 8.5 Pareto diagram

Data Gathering
There are several data gathering techniques that can be used during the Control Quality process. These techniques may include checklists, checksheets, statistical sampling, and questionnaires and surveys.

Checklists
Information about the quality of interim deliverables can be gathered using quality checklists. A quality checklist can be a list of items to inspect, a list of steps to be performed, or a picture of the item to be inspected, with space to note any defects found.

In Control Quality, checklists are used to determine that all required features and functions are included, and that they meet acceptance criteria. Checklists may be a part of the test and evaluation documents created in Manage Quality. Checklist templates for commonly performed work, deliverables, or processes may be organizational process assets of the organization.

Checksheets
A checksheet is a type of checklist that can be used to keep track of data, such as quality problems uncovered during inspections, as well as to document how often a particular defect occurs, as illustrated in figure 8.6.

Defect	Frequency
Too long	||||| ||
Too narrow	|||
Too wide	||||| |||
Too short	||

Figure 8.6 Checksheet

Statistical Sampling Let's think about the process of manufacturing doors. There would likely be some allowable variation in the height and weight of the doors being manufactured. Even so, the doors must be checked to see if they meet quality standards on the project. What if inspecting each door would cause damage or take too much time? Then you may need to take a statistically valid sample. It is best to take a sample of a population if you believe there are not many defects, or if studying the entire population would:

- Take too long
- Cost too much
- Be too destructive

The sample size and frequency of measurements are determined as part of the Plan Quality Management process, and the actual sampling is done in Control Quality. Keep in mind that statistical sampling can also be done for project management activities. For example, you may initially check the on-time status for 5 out of 50 of a group's activities. If you find issues in those 5 activities, you can assume there will be more issues in the remaining 45 activities.

Questionnaires and Surveys Questionnaires and surveys may be used in Control Quality to gather data on details of problems or defects, or to confirm that customers or end users are satisfied with the deliverables that have been deployed on the project. The results can be used to determine whether conformance to quality has been achieved.

Data Analysis Performance reviews and root cause analysis may be used as part of the Control Quality process. How would a project manager utilize these techniques when managing a project? Think through your answer before reading the next two descriptions.

Performance Reviews The project manager or quality department may conduct periodic performance reviews to formally assess how the project is doing in following the quality management plan and meeting quality requirements. This review involves comparing the results of control measurements to metrics identified in the quality management plan, and may uncover changes necessary to achieve quality requirements.

Root Cause Analysis Root cause analysis is used to identify the cause of quality problems, including defects, to determine how they can be resolved.

Meetings Lessons learned meetings and retrospectives are conducted in Control Quality to assess what was done right and what could have been done differently to make the project more successful. In an agile environment, retrospectives are held frequently to ensure that the quality process meets the needs of the project. Also note that approved change request reviews are meetings in which the team evaluates whether approved change requests have been completed, and whether they have returned the results intended.

Inspections Inspections are used to verify that deliverables meet the requirements. Inspections may be referred to as audits or walkthroughs, and they generally include measurement of project deliverables. Inspections are also used to check that previously approved changes have been made correctly, and that the changes have provided the intended results (validated changes).

Outputs of Control Quality PAGE 305
The following are key outputs of the Control Quality process. Additional outputs may include work performance information and updates to components of the project management plan, as well as project documents (such as the issue log, lessons learned register, risk register, and any test and evaluation documents).

Quality Control Measurements These measurements are the results of quality control activities. They may generate change requests, another output of the Control Quality process.

Verified Deliverables   Quality control involves confirming the correctness of deliverables. Which means deliverables are measured against the product scope. This step of validation results in verified deliverables (which ultimately become inputs to the process of Validate Scope).

Change Requests   The control processes, regardless of when they occur within the process of project management, all involve measurement. When completed, such measurements can lead to change requests, which are approved in the Perform Integrated Change Control process. Change requests can include recommendations for corrective or preventive actions or defect repair.

Putting It All Together

Do you think you understand quality management now? If not, review the following diagram carefully; it depicts how the quality management process (represented by the shaded area) fits into a project:

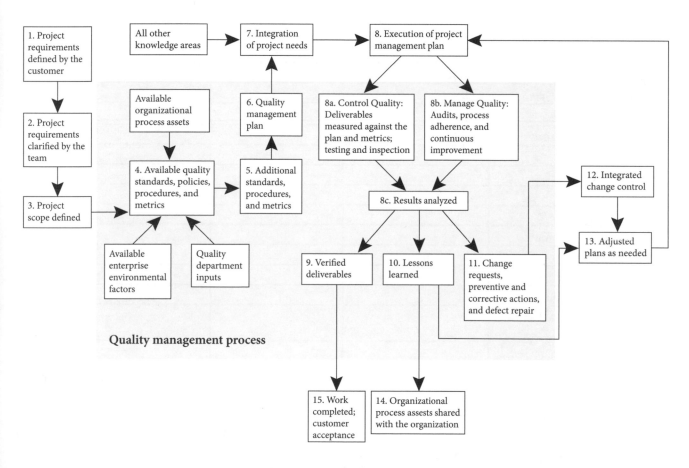

Figure 8.7: Quality management

Understanding the Tools and Techniques Used in Quality Management   In reading this chapter, have you found yourself asking, "When should all these tools and techniques be used?" People tend to struggle with this aspect of quality management. The following exercise will help fill any gaps you may have about the tools and techniques covered in this chapter.

Quality Management

Exercise

Take a moment to research in this chapter the different tools and techniques that are created or used in each of the quality management processes. Then complete the following table, indicating the process in which each tool is used. Remember that some tools and techniques are used in more than one quality management process. Think about how they are used in each process.

Tool	Used in Plan Quality Management	Used in Manage Quality	Used in Control Quality
Affinity diagrams			
Alternatives analysis			
Benchmarking			
Brainstorming			
Cause-and-effect diagrams			
Checklists			
Checksheets			
Control charts			
Cost of quality			
Cost-benefit analysis			
Design for X			
Document analysis			
Flowcharts			
Histograms			
Inspection			
Interviews			
Logical data model			
Matrix diagrams			
Meetings			
Mind mapping			
Multicriteria decision analysis			
Performance reviews			
Problem-solving			
Process analysis			
Questionnaires and surveys			
Root cause analysis			
Scatter diagrams			
Statistical sampling			
Test and inspection planning			
Testing/product evaluations			

© 2018 RMC Publications, Inc ™ ● 952.846.4484 ● info@rmcls.com ● www.rmcls.com

Answer

Tool	Used in Plan Quality Management	Used in Manage Quality	Used in Control Quality
Affinity diagrams		X	
Alternatives analysis		X	
Benchmarking	X		
Brainstorming	X		
Cause-and-effect diagrams		X	X
Checklists		X	X
Checksheets			X
Control charts			X
Cost of quality	X		
Cost-benefit analysis	X		
Design for X		X	
Document analysis		X	
Flowcharts	X	X	
Histograms		X	X
Inspection			X
Interviews	X		
Logical data model	X		
Matrix diagrams	X	X	
Meetings	X		X
Mind mapping	X		
Multicriteria decision analysis	X	X	
Performance reviews			X
Problem-solving		X	
Process analysis		X	
Questionnaires and surveys			X
Root cause analysis		X	X
Scatter diagrams		X	X
Statistical sampling			X
Test and inspection planning	X		
Testing/product evaluations			X

Quality Management

Quality Management Review

Exercise

This exercise will help you review the key material you need to know for quality management. The Shuffle Game that follows offers another approach to this material. You can use either or both of these study tools, depending on your preference.

Instructions

1. Try to fill in the blanks in the below table using the knowledge and understanding gained after reading this chapter.
2. To review only the material contained in this chapter, focus on the cells that have asterisks. (These are the key topics you need to understand to pass the exam with the minimum amount of study time. The answer table will show only these topics.)
3. To review all the items listed in the *PMBOK® Guide*, fill in the entire table.

Key Inputs	Key Tools and Techniques	Key Outputs
Plan Quality Management Process group:		
*	*	*
Manage Quality Process group:		
*	*	*
Control Quality Process group:		
*	*	*

Answer To save study time and focus on the most important information, this answer table only shows the topics that are covered in this chapter. If you tried to list all inputs, tools and techniques, and outputs, you'll need to check your answers against the *PMBOK® Guide*.

Key Inputs	Key Tools and Techniques	Key Outputs
Plan Quality Management Process group: Planning		
Project management plan Project documents Project charter Enterprise environmental factors Organizational process assets	Data gathering Decision making Data analysis • Cost-benefit analysis • Cost of quality Data representation • Logical data models • Matrix diagrams • Mind mapping • Flowcharts Test and inspection planning Meetings	Quality management plan Quality metrics Project management plan updates Project documents updates
Manage Quality Process group: Executing		
Project management plan Project documents	Data gathering • Checklists Decision making • Multicriteria decision analysis Data analysis • Document analysis • Alternatives analysis • Process analysis • Root cause analysis Data representation • Affinity diagrams • Matrix diagrams • Cause-and-effect diagrams • Flowcharts • Histograms • Scatter diagrams Audits Design for X Problem solving	Test and evaluation documents Quality reports Change requests Project management plan updates Project documents updates

Key Inputs	Key Tools and Techniques	Key Outputs
Control Quality Process group: Monitoring and controlling		
Deliverables Project documents Work performance data	Data representation • Control charts • Scatter diagrams • Cause-and-effect diagrams • Histograms Data gathering • Checklists • Checksheets • Statistical sampling • Questionnaires and surveys Data analysis • Performance reviews • Root cause analysis Meetings Inspections	Quality control measurements Verified deliverables Change requests

Shuffle Game

Some people learn best by doing, which is why we have developed this alternate approach to reviewing quality management. To save you time, only the most important topics for the exam—those covered in this chapter—have been included.

Instructions

1. Cut out the cards on the next pages.
2. Lay out the bold title cards as column headers.
3. Shuffle the remaining cards and try to put them in the columns where they belong. Cards with italic terms must be matched to the corresponding group. For example, a *Cost of Quality* card in italics would match with a Data Analysis card, as cost of quality is a data analysis tool and technique.
4. Check your answers against the material covered in this chapter or the *PMBOK® Guide,* and make note of any gaps in your knowledge.

Note: Be sure to keep all cards for each chapter shuffle game as you will use them again for the final Shuffle Game in chapter 14.

Plan Quality Management *Key Inputs*	Plan Quality Management *Key Tools and Techniques*	Plan Quality Management *Key Outputs*
Manage Quality *Key Inputs*	Manage Quality *Key Tools and Techniques*	Manage Quality *Key Outputs*
Control Quality *Key Inputs*	Control Quality *Key Tools and Techniques*	Control Quality *Key Outputs*
Project management plan	Project documents	Project charter
Enterprise environmental factors	Organizational process assets	Data gathering

Decision making	Data analysis	*Cost-benefit analysis*
Cost of quality	Data representation	*Logical data models*
Matrix diagrams	*Mind mapping*	*Flowcharts*
Test and inspection planning	Meetings	Quality management plan
Quality metrics	Project management plan updates	Project documents updates

© 2018 RMC Publications, Inc.™ • 952.846.4484 • info@rmcls.com • www.rmcls.com

| Project management plan | Project documents | Data gathering |

| *Checklists* | Decision making | *Multicriteria decision analysis* |

| Data analysis | *Document analysis* | *Alternatives analysis* |

| *Process analysis* | *Root cause analysis* | Data representation |

| *Affinity diagrams* | *Matrix diagrams* | *Cause-and-effect diagrams* |

| Flowcharts | Histograms | Scatter diagrams |

| Audits | Design for X | Problem solving |

| Test and evaluation documents | Quality reports | Change requests |

| Project management plan updates | Project documents updates | Deliverables |

| Project documents | Work performance data | Data representation |

Scatter diagrams	*Cause-and-effect diagrams*	*Histograms*
Data gathering	*Checklists*	*Checksheets*
Statistical sampling	*Questionnaires and surveys*	*Performance reviews*
Root cause analysis	Data analysis	Test and inspection planning

Quality control measurements	Verified deliverables	Change requests
Control charts	Meetings	

Practice Exam

1. Which statement about quality and grade is true?
   A. "Grade" refers to the degree to which a deliverable fulfills requirements.
   B. "Quality" is used to categorize deliverables or resources that have a common function but varying technical specifications.
   C. A low-grade resource could be of acceptable quality if it meets the established quality requirements.
   D. A resource is only of acceptable quality if it is high grade.

2. The purpose of a quality audit is to:
   A. Check if the customer is following their quality process
   B. Have the customer formally accept the quality of a particular deliverable
   C. Identify inefficient and ineffective policies
   D. Determine the quality processes that will be used on the project

3. What tool or technique in Plan Quality Management involves reviewing the quality practices used on other similar projects to establish quality metrics?
   A. Cost-benefit analysis
   B. Benchmarking
   C. Matrix diagrams
   D. Flowcharts

4. All the following are tools or techniques of Control Quality except:
   A. Cost of quality
   B. Inspection
   C. Control charts
   D. Checklists

5. Which of the following presents measurement results in order of frequency and helps the project team identify the root causes resulting in the most problems?
   A. Flowchart
   B. Fishbone diagram
   C. Control chart
   D. Pareto diagram

6. During _____, the project manager regularly evaluates project performance to ensure that quality standards are being followed.
   A. Plan Quality Management
   B. Manage Quality
   C. Control Quality
   D. Perform Quality Management

7. Identifying ways to eliminate the causes of quality problems would most likely lead to:
   A. Quality audits
   B. Work performance information
   C. Recommended corrective actions
   D. Statistical sampling

8. Which quality management process involves determining the definition of quality for the project and planning how to ensure that the project achieves that level of quality?
   A. Manage Quality
   B. Control Quality
   C. Plan Quality Management
   D. Plan Quality Assurance

9. Which of the following is not typically part of the Control Quality process?
   A. Checking to see whether the defined quality standards and procedures are being followed
   B. Using statistical sampling and inspections to confirm that quality standards are being met
   C. Evaluating a quality problem to see how it can be addressed
   D. Obtaining confirmation that the agreed-upon requirements have been met

10. One purpose of a fishbone diagram is to:
    A. Show how a process or system flows from beginning to end
    B. Confirm that quality policies and procedures are being followed
    C. Determine the organization of the project
    D. Show functional responsibilities and how they are related to one another and to the objectives of the project

11. Which of the following tools and techniques is not used in Plan Quality Management?
    A. Matrix diagrams
    B. Mind mapping
    C. Benchmarking
    D. Process analysis

12. Inputs to the Control Quality process include quality metrics, approved change requests, and:
    A. Control charts
    B. Work performance data
    C. Verified deliverables
    D. Work performance information

13. Which of the following tools or techniques would be the most useful for organizing the results of a root cause analysis in Manage Quality?
    A. Affinity diagram
    B. Audit
    C. Design for X
    D. Flowchart

14. What are quality checklists used for?
    A. To verify that a required action has taken place or a required item has been included
    B. To gather data, such as the number of quality defects found during inspections
    C. To document variances from the quality standards
    D. To measure the quality of the project management planning process

15. Which of the following is least likely to be included in the key outputs of Plan Quality Management?
    A. Which metrics will be used to control quality
    B. Which parts of the deliverables will be checked, and when
    C. Which practices and standards will be used to measure quality
    D. The schedule for the quality audits, including who will do them

Answers

1. **Answer** C
   Explanation Quality refers to the degree to which a deliverable fulfills requirements. Grade is used to categorize deliverables or resources that have a common function but varying technical specifications. Depending on the project, a resource could be of low grade but still be of acceptable quality.

2. **Answer** C
   Explanation One purpose of a quality audit is to identify inefficient and ineffective policies, as part of the Manage Quality process. A quality audit does not include checking on a customer's quality process because the seller generally cannot control or review the customer's processes. Customer acceptance of deliverables is part of the Validate Scope process, not a quality audit. Determining the processes that will be used on the project is done before any audits take place—in Plan Quality Management.

3. **Answer** B
   Explanation All the tools and techniques listed are used in Plan Quality Management; however, benchmarking is the technique that involves reviewing the quality practices used on other similar projects (or in other organizations) to establish quality metrics. Cost-benefit analysis involves analyzing the benefits versus the cost of quality efforts. Matrix diagrams are used to sort and prioritize quality requirements. In Plan Quality Management, flowcharts can be used to identify potential quality problems and determine the cost of quality by mapping the paths of conformance and nonconformance to quality.

4. **Answer** A
   Explanation Inspections, control charts, and checklists are all tools or techniques that can be used in the Control Quality process. Cost of quality is a technique used in the Plan Quality Management process to ensure that the project does not spend too much to achieve a particular level of quality.

5. **Answer** D
   Explanation A Pareto diagram is used in Control Quality; it shows measurement results in order of frequency, which helps the team identify which root causes are resulting in the most quality problems. A flowchart shows how a process flows from beginning to end. A fishbone diagram shows possible causes of problems, but not their frequency. A control chart shows whether samples are within acceptable limits.

6. **Answer** B
   Explanation The purpose of the Manage Quality process is to ensure that the project team is following quality standards, policies, and processes.

7. **Answer** C
   Explanation It is likely that recommended corrective actions would result from efforts to identify ways to eliminate the causes of quality problems. Quality audits, work performance information, and statistical sampling are all used to identify quality problems.

8. **Answer** C
   Explanation It is in the Plan Quality Management process that the project manager determines the definition of quality for the project and plans how to achieve that level of quality.

9. **Answer** A
   Explanation The Control Quality process involves all the activities listed except checking to see whether the defined quality standards and procedures are being followed; that activity is part of Manage Quality.

10. **Answer** B
    Explanation In Manage Quality, a fishbone diagram can be used to confirm that policies and procedures are being followed, that the project's established quality metrics are being used correctly, and that those metrics are adequate to produce the required level of quality.

11. **Answer** D
    Explanation Matrix diagrams, mind mapping, and benchmarking are all used in the Plan Quality Management process. Process analysis is used in Manage Quality to identify required process improvements.

12. **Answer** B
    Explanation Work performance data is used in Control Quality to determine if the project and its processes are in control. Although deliverables are an input to Control Quality, verified deliverables are a key output of this process. Work performance information is also an output of Control Quality, while control charts are a tool used in that process.

13. **Answer** A
    Explanation In Manage Quality, an affinity diagram can be used to organize the results of a root cause analysis. The other tools and techniques listed serve different purposes when used as part of Manage Quality. A quality audit is used to identify areas in need of improvement. Design for X can be used to determine why the quality plan is not delivering the intended results in relation to a particular variable (such as reliability or security). A flowchart is a useful tool for reviewing the steps of a process leading up to a quality defect.

14. **Answer** A
    Explanation A checklist can be used in Manage Quality to confirm that a required action has taken place. In Control Quality, checklists are used to determine that all required features are included, and that they meet acceptance criteria. (Don't confuse checklists with checksheets, which are used primarily to gather data.)

15. **Answer** D
    Explanation Quality metrics, the deliverables that will be checked, and the practices and standards for measuring quality are all components of a quality management plan, a key output of Plan Quality Management. Of the options presented, the schedule for quality audits is the least likely to be included in the quality management plan. Also, because such audits might be performed by another department, they might not be within scope for the project planning efforts.

Resource Management

NINE

There are 12 questions on this knowledge area on the CAPM exam. Also note, for a full list of all inputs, tools and techniques, and outputs within this knowledge area, please see the table on page 308 in the PMBOK© Guide.

As you might expect, resource management includes the project manager's responsibilities for planning, acquiring, and managing the project team. But there's more. In this chapter—and on the CAPM exam—the term "resources" refers to more than the team and other people from within or outside the organization who may be working on the project. It also encompasses the facilities, equipment, and materials (physical resources) that are required to perform the work of the project. You will see in this chapter that most of the processes of resource management include the project manager's responsibilities with regard to both human and physical resources.

Keep in mind that resource management responsibilities increase as the size of the project increases. The resource management process takes time and effort to plan. A project manager must do things such as identify all resources needed to complete the project (including the required skills of team resources and the required quality and grade of material or equipment), define everyone's roles, create reward systems, provide training and motivation for team members, manage the use of physical resources, and track performance.

QUICKTEST

- Resource management process
- Resource management plan
- Team charter
- Team building
- Conflict management
- Leadership
- Emotional intelligence
- Sources of conflict
- Individual and team assessments
- Personnel assessment tools
- Issue log
- Organizational Theory
- Responsibility assignment matrix (RAM)
- RACI chart
- Organizational breakdown structure
- Resource breakdown structure

- Work breakdown structure
- Text-oriented formats
- Resource histograms
- Ground rules
- Training
- Colocation
- Pre-assignment
- Negotiation
- Influencing
- Communication technology
- Multicriteria decision analysis
- Virtual teams
- Stages of team formation and development
- Recognition and rewards

 TRICKS OF THE TRADE® Let's look at the resource management process as a whole before we look at the details. First, of course, a project manager will need to plan their resource work, clearly determining roles and responsibilities, as well as determining what physical resources will be needed to complete all the project work. This information will help the project manager put a plan together for how resources will be managed. The project manager will then estimate activity resources and acquire the team and physical resources, which will result in physical resource and project team assignments. Once the work begins, the project manager will work to improve team member performance, managing individuals as project work continues throughout the life of the project.

Resource Management

The following should help you understand how each part of resource management fits into the overall project management process:

Resource Management Process	Done During
Plan Resource Management	Planning process group
Estimate Activity Resources	Planning process group
Acquire Resources	Executing process group
Develop Team	Executing process group
Manage Team	Executing process group
Control Resources	Monitoring and controlling process group

Roles and Responsibilities

Roles and responsibilities go far beyond a title. For example, if you know you are the project manager, what does that mean as the project work is being done? Do you know what decisions you can make and enforce, and when you need the approval of someone higher in the organization? Do you know what to expect from functional managers and your project sponsor? What about the team? Do they know their responsibilities, and when they need to escalate a situation?

Project roles and responsibilities, and the authority that goes with them, are agreed upon in planning, and documented in the resource management plan.

The following exercise tests your knowledge of some typical roles on a project.

Exercise

Did you complete the exercise on project roles in the Project Management Framework chapter? Your understanding of that content will impact how well you do on this exercise. You may want to review those pages before starting this exercise, or use the information in that exercise to fill your gaps.

This exercise is designed to help you answer questions on the exam dealing with project roles and responsibilities. If you disagree with some of the answers, make sure you are not reading something into the question, and assess whether it indicates a gap in your project management knowledge.

In the following table, write the initials of the key role responsible for solving each of the problems listed. Because much of the confusion of roles is between the team members (T), the project manager (PM), the sponsor (SP), and the functional manager (FM), this exercise is limited to those roles. Consider what you have learned about project roles, and remember to keep a matrix organization in mind when reading through these situations.

	Situation	Key Role
1	Two project team members are having a disagreement.	
2	There is a change to the overall project deliverable.	
3	A functional manager is trying to pull a team member off the project to do other work.	
4	The project manager does not have the authority to get things done.	
5	There are not enough resources to complete the project.	
6	The team is unsure of what needs to happen when.	

© 2010 RMC Publications, Inc.™ • 952.010.4404 • info@rmcls.com • www.rmcls.com

	Situation	Key Role
7	An activity needs more time and will cause the project to be delayed.	
8	An activity needs more time without causing the project to be delayed.	
9	A team member is not performing.	
10	The team is not sure who is in charge of the project.	
11	There is talk that the project may no longer be needed.	
12	The sponsor provides an unrealistic schedule objective.	
13	The team is in conflict over priorities between activities.	
14	The project is behind schedule.	
15	A team member determines that another method should be used to complete an activity.	
16	The project is running out of funds.	
17	Additional work that will increase cost and that was not identified during the risk management process is added to the project.	

Answer

	Situation	Key Role
1	Two project team members are having a disagreement.	T
2	There is a change to the overall project deliverable.	SP
3	A functional manager is trying to pull a team member off the project to do other work.	T
4	The project manager does not have the authority to get things done.	SP
5	There are not enough resources to complete the project.	SP/FM
6	The team is unsure of what needs to happen when.	PM
7	An activity needs more time and will cause the project to be delayed.	SP
8	An activity needs more time without causing the project to be delayed.	PM
9	A team member is not performing.	PM/FM
10	The team is not sure who is in charge of the project.	SP
11	There is talk that the project may no longer be needed.	SP
12	The sponsor provides an unrealistic schedule objective.	SP
13	The team is in conflict over priorities between activities.	PM
14	The project is behind schedule.	PM
15	A team member determines that another method should be used to complete an activity.	T
16	The project is running out of funds.	SP
17	Additional work that will increase cost and was not identified during the risk management process is added to the project.	SP

If you got many of the answers wrong, reread the discussion of roles and responsibilities in the Project Management Framework chapter, and review the exact wording of the situations presented here. With such a brief description, it can be easy to misinterpret a question. Although this exercise asked you to identify the key role responsible for solving the problems, you may have preferred the word "decide" or the words "make the final decision" to describe what should happen in some of the situations. This exercise should help prepare you to interpret questions on the exam. It is meant to make you think!

Plan Resource Management PAGE 312

> **Process:** Plan Human Resource Management
> **Process Group:** Planning
> **Knowledge Area:** Resource Management

The the Plan Resource Management process and the resource management plan encompass the management of human resources as well as physical resources. For both types of resources, the plan must answer questions such as the following:

- What resources are required?
- What quantity of each type of resource is needed to complete the work of the project?
- When and for how long will each resource be needed?
- How will the resources be acquired?
- Are these resources available internally, or will the procurement department need to be involved?
- What will be the cost of these resources?
- Is there a limited time during which the resources will be available for the project?
- How will resources be managed throughout the project?

Early in the project, the project manager will have to determine the approach they will take to manage the project, unless this has been determined in advance by management. As discussed earlier, in the Project Management Processes chapter, two common approaches to projects are plan-driven and change-driven. On a project following a plan-driven approach, as much resource management planning as possible will be done early in the project. On a project following a change-driven approach, planning and securing resources will likely occur as a part of each iteration or release.

A common complaint of team members is that roles and responsibilities are not clearly defined on a project. Therefore, the definition of roles and responsibilities is a critical part of the Plan Resource Management process. Project work often includes more than just completing work packages. It may also include responsibilities such as assisting with risk, quality, and project management activities. Team members need to know what work packages and activities they are assigned to, when they are expected to report, what meetings they will be required to attend, and any other work they will be asked to do on the project. In a functional or matrix environment, the managers of team resources also need to understand when and for how long these resources will be needed on the project.

In terms of physical resources, the project manager needs to determine what is needed and where the resources will come from. If the resources are available from departments within the organization, the project manager must work with the managers of those departments to reach an agreement on delivery dates as well as the quantity and quality of resources. If the resources will be obtained from external sources, the project manager must work with the procurement department, creating a purchase order or bid documents to facilitate the purchase. The project manager will likely be involved in the procurement process.

Inputs to Plan Resource Management PAGE 314   The following inputs may be used as part of the Plan Resource Management process.

© 2018 RMC Publications, Inc ™ • 952.846.4484 • info@rmcls.com • www.rmcls.com

Project Management Plan   The existing components of the project management plan will help a project manager plan resource management. Before they can define roles, responsibilities, reporting structure, and so forth, they'll need to consider information about the life cycle and processes already determined for the project, how work will be done, the communication needs of stakeholders, and other factors from the project management plan.

Project Charter   The project charter documents high-level requirements for the project. It may include a list of key stakeholders and preassigned resources, as well as budgetary constraints that must be considered when planning resource management.

Project Documents   Documents that can be used in planning resource management include requirements documentation, the project schedule, and the risk and stakeholder registers. These documents provide key information, such as the timeline for needed resources, what type of resources will be needed to complete project work, and how many resources will be required to get the work done.

Enterprise Environmental Factors   Before a project manager develops a resource management plan, they need to understand what enterprise environmental factors may come into play. Remember that the term "enterprise environmental factors" refers to the company culture and existing systems the project will have to utilize or work around. For this process, a project manager should take into account factors such as the following.

- What organizations will be involved in the project?
- Are there hidden agendas?
- Is there anyone who does not want the project?
- Are assigned and potential team members colocated or based in different offices or countries?
- What is the availability of contract help?
- What is the availability of training for project team members?

For most experienced project managers, this is common sense. They already consider such things on their projects, even if they have not called them enterprise environmental factors.

Organizational Process Assets   When developing the resource management plan, the project manager may use organizational process assets such as existing policies and procedures for resource management and a resource management plan template that describes the standard responsibilities on projects. These assets, along with historical information, such as lessons learned from similar projects, can help increase the efficiency of the Plan Resource Management process, as well as the effectiveness of the resulting plan.

Tools and Techniques of Plan Resource Management PAGE 315 A comprehensive
resource management plan includes documentation of all project responsibilities and assignments on the project. There are a lot of methods that can be used to document and communicate roles and responsibilities of management, team members, and other stakeholders. Examples include a responsibility assignment matrix (RAM), a RACI chart, an organizational breakdown structure, a resource breakdown structure (RBS), the WBS, and written position descriptions. Additional tools and techniques used in the plan resource management process include physical resource documentation and organizational theory.

Data Representation   Any roles and responsibilities that are expected of team members, such as project management team assignments, reporting requirements, or meeting attendance, need to be clearly assigned, in addition to the project activities the team members are expected to complete. In other words, all efforts the project team might expend should be determined in advance. While reading through this tools and techniques section, think about how much time this effort might take on a large project.

Resource Management

Responsibility Assignment Matrix (RAM)   This chart cross-references team members with the activities or work packages they are to accomplish. Figure 9.1 is an example of a RAM.

	Team Member			
Activity	Karla	Patrick	Muhammad	Trisha
A	P		S	
B		S		P

Key: P = Primary responsibility, S = Secondary responsibility

Figure 9.1   Responsibility assignment matrix

RACI Chart (Responsible, Accountable, Consult, and Inform)   This chart is a type of responsibility assignment matrix that defines role assignments more clearly than the example shown in figure 9.1. Instead of the P and S shown in the figure, the letters R for Responsible, A for Accountable, C for Consult, and I for Inform are used. Note that multiple resources may be responsible, informed, or consulted, but only one person is held accountable.

Organizational Breakdown Structure   An organizational breakdown structure can be used to assign project responsibilities to divisions or departments within the organization, such as marketing, product development, or IT. In a matrix organization, the project manager will have to interface with the managers of each department involved in the project to coordinate availability and scheduling of human and physical resources that will be used on the project. Figure 9.2 is an example of an organizational breakdown structure.

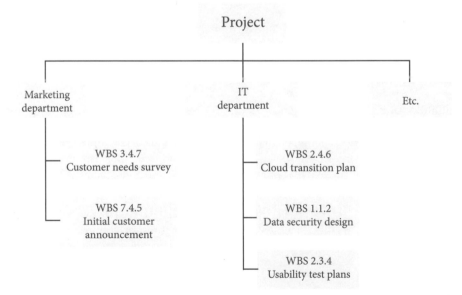

Figure 9.2   Organizational breakdown structure

Resource Breakdown Structure   The resource breakdown structure breaks the work down by type of resource (see fig. 9.3).

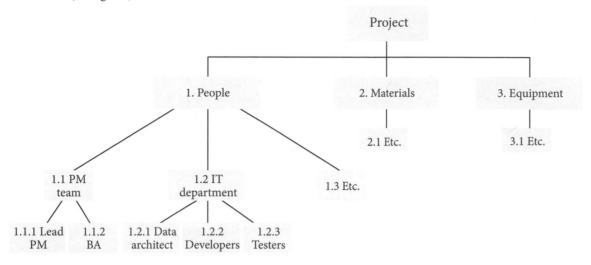

Figure 9.3 Resource breakdown structure

Work Breakdown Structure   Are you surprised to see the WBS here? Can you think of how the WBS could be a valuable tool in creating the resource management plan? Keep in mind that all project work must be represented in the WBS, as stated in the Scope Management chapter. This means that the WBS is a great tool to ensure that each work package has an "owner"—a team member responsible for completing that work.

Text-oriented Formats   Position descriptions are usually documented in text format rather than charts. If you are not familiar with this type of format, imagine a typical job description, but created only for project work.

Organizational Theory   Organizational theory studies organizations to identify how they solve problems, maximize efficiency and productivity, and meet the expectations of stakeholders. Such analysis helps the organization develop effective resource management policies and procedures for the acquisition, management, and evaluation of human and physical resources.

Outputs of Plan Resource Management PAGE 318   The Plan Resource Management
process results in the following outputs.

Resource Management Plan   The primary result (output) of the Plan Resource Management process is, of course, a resource management plan. If you have more experience with small projects, think for a moment about what the resource management effort would involve on a large project that has hundreds of assigned resources. Large projects require a plan for when and how resources will be added, managed, and released from the project. This is what the resource management plan provides.

Resource Management

Components of the resource management plan include the following:

- Human Resources
  - Identification of human resource requirements (who, when, how many, what skills, what level of expertise, duration)
  - Roles and responsibilities (described earlier in this chapter)
  - Project organizational charts (described earlier in this chapter)
  - Process for acquiring human resources (internal or procurement)
  - Training, team development, and recognition (goals, what, when)
  - Project team management (team charter, ground rules, engagement, communications)
  - Compliance (How will the project comply with any rules related to human resources?)
  - Safety (policies to protect the resources)
  - Release of human resources
- Physical Resources
  - Identification of physical resource requirements (what, when, how many, what type, quality, grade, duration)
  - Process for acquiring physical resources (internal or procurement)
  - Inventory management
  - Release of resources

Team Charter   This document is a working agreement developed by the members of the project team. It describes the approach the team will take regarding communications, decision-making, and conflict resolution, as well as ground rules for team meetings. The team charter is a project document and can be referenced at any time during the project.

Setting ground rules can help eliminate conflicts or problems with the team during the project because everyone knows what is expected of them. And if team members have input on the creation of the ground rules, they're more likely to follow them. Ground rules can be especially important when the team is managed virtually.

The ground rules may include items such as the following:

- How a team member should resolve a conflict with another team member
- When a team member should notify the project manager that they are having difficulty with an activity
- Rules for meetings
- Who is authorized to give direction to contractors
- How the team will decide work assignments
- When and how to provide status updates to the project manager
- Methods for coordinating and approving changes to team members' calendars, both in normal and emergency situations

Project Document Updates   The assumption log is updated to reflect assumptions made in planning regarding resources. These may include assumptions about the availability, quantity, quality, or type of human and physical resources. Other assumptions might relate to what type of rewards and recognition will be effective, and how the release of resources should be managed. Assumptions can change as the project progresses, and should be regularly assessed for validity. Incorrect assumptions may create risks for the project.

Another document that may need to be updated is the risk register. Risks related to resources should be added to the risk register, and then analyzed and prioritized along with other documented risks in the risk management process.

Estimate Activity Resources

Process: Estimate Activity Resources
Process Group: Planning
Knowledge Area: Resource Management

In the Estimate Activity Resources process, the project manager and team determine the type and quantity of resources needed to complete project work. This includes human resources to perform the work packages that were created in the WBS and broken down in the activity list. It also includes any equipment or materials needed, space in which to meet and perform project work, and anything else needed to fulfill the requirements of the project.

Inputs to Estimate Activity Resources PAGE 320

The resource management plan is an input to all the processes (with the exception of Plan Resource Management) within Resource Management. In Estimate Activity Resources, it provides documentation on the estimating methods to be used. Other inputs include the scope baseline (the project scope description, WBS, and WBS dictionary) and the activity list from Schedule Management. These enable the project manager to estimate needed resources at the work package level and activity level, respectively, and are important elements of creating accurate estimates. Another input from Schedule Management is activity attributes. Attributes provide specific information about each activity, such as the type and amount of human and physical resources expected to be required to complete them.

Cost estimates provide constraints in terms of resource estimating, as the resource costs must fall within the cost baseline. Resource calendars identify organizational work hours and company holidays, and show the availability of potential resources—both human and physical. Organizational process assets include policies the project must follow when arranging for staff and needed equipment.

Tools and Techniques of Estimate Activity Resources PAGE 324

In the Schedule and Cost Management chapters, we discussed the estimating techniques used to develop the schedule and budget. Several of those techniques may also be used to estimate activity resources. Let's briefly review them:

- **Bottom-up estimating**   This technique involves creating detailed estimates for each part of an activity or work package and then rolling the estimates into work packages and control accounts and, finally, into an overall project estimate.
- **Analogous estimating**   Analogous estimating uses expert judgment and historical information to predict the future.
- **Parametric estimating**   Parametric estimating creates an equation that uses historical information from other estimates, actual results, and variables (such as the number of hours to complete the work or the number of resources with the associated skill level, quality, or grade) to create estimates.
- **Alternatives analysis**   Bottom-up, analogous, and parametric estimating can be used to generate estimates for various options—such as the costs to make versus buy software for a project, the costs of internal versus external team members, or the impact of using various materials to produce components of the product of the project. Alternatives analysis can then be used to assess the impact of each option on project constraints such as schedule, cost, quality, and risk.

Another tool that can be used to estimate resources is a resource histogram. A resource histogram is a way to visualize resource requirements, and compare needed resources and their availability, to better enable estimating. As depicted in figure 9.4, a resource histogram is a bar chart that shows the number of resources needed per time period; it also illustrates where there is a spike in the need for resources. If the materials, equipment, or human resources are not available when they are needed, the project manager must evaluate available options, which may include negotiating with another department to provide the resources, procuring the resources from an external source, or adjusting the project schedule to do the work when the resources are available.

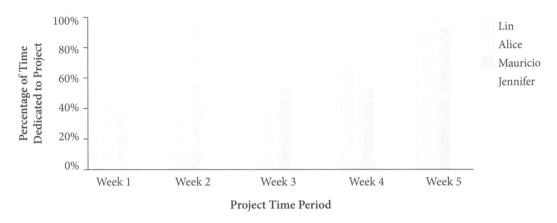

Figure 9.4 Resource histogram

Do you remember the discussion of resource leveling in the Schedule Management chapter? This is a technique to change the project to minimize the peaks and valleys of resource usage (level the resources). If resources are limited, the project manager could use a histogram to help perfom that activity.

Outputs of Estimate Activity Resources PAGE 325 At the end of the Estimate
Activity Resources process, the team will have determined the resource requirements for project activities, including the cost, quantity, and availability of human and physical resources. They may choose to document the requirements in a resource breakdown structure (RBS). You may remember that the RBS was also discussed as a Plan Resource Management tool that is used to break down the work by the type of resource required. As planning continues and more detail is gathered, the RBS is expanded and augmented in Estimate Activity Resources. The RBS in this process is an iteration of the document that was originally created in Plan Resource Management.

Acquire Resources PAGE 328

> **Process:** Acquire Resources
> **Process Group:** Executing
> **Knowledge Area:** Resource Management

The Acquire Resources process involves following the resource management plan to secure the human and physical resources needed for the project. The resource management plan describes how resources will be acquired and released, and the resource requirements documentation tells the project manager what types of resources are needed. The schedule and cost baselines provide essential information that detail when resources will be required and the amount of funds budgeted to pay for each resource.

To understand why this is an executing process, think of a large project that may last several years and require hundreds of people and lots of physical resources. A planning team is acquired early in planning to help the project manager. However, many of the people and other resources needed to do the work may not be needed until long after planning starts. The final list of resources might include contractors, sellers, and people who will work on the project years into the future and may not even be acquired by the company until needed. Likewise, the physical resources may be purchased closer to the time they are needed, to avoid the need to put inventory in a warehouse.

Therefore, you should read the process name "Acquire Resources" as "acquire the final resources." Acquiring resources includes the following:

- Knowing which resources are preassigned to the project, and confirming their availability
- Negotiating for the best possible resources
- Hiring new employees
- Hiring resources through the contracting process from outside the performing organization (i.e., outsourcing)
- Managing the risk of resources becoming unavailable

Inputs to Acquire Resources PAGE 330
Inputs to the Acquire Resources process may include components of the project management plan, enterprise environmental factors, organizational process assets, and project documents such as the resource requirements and stakeholder register.

Resource Management Plan
The resource management plan, a component of the project management plan, includes guidelines on how resources will be acquired.

Enterprise Environmental Factors
These factors may include resource availability as well as details about the cost and location of each resource. Can you think of any other factors that may impact the Acquire Resources process?

Organizational Process Assets
Assets that may be part of this process include hiring procedures, policies that relate to assigning resources to the project, and any historical information or lessons learned that could be useful when acquiring resources.

Tools and Techniques of Acquire Resources PAGE 332
The following tools and techniques may be used during the Acquire Resources process.

Preassignment
As noted earlier, sometimes resources are assigned before the project begins. Preassigned resources are documented in the project charter. This relates to both physical and team resources.

Negotiation
When resources are not preassigned, they may be acquired through negotiation. Note that negotiation relates to gaining resources from within your organization and in procurement situations. When resources must be acquired from outside the organization, such as from external vendors, suppliers, or contractors, the project manager is required to follow procurement and negotiating policies and procedures for the acquisition of resources.

Virtual Teams
Not all teams meet face-to-face. Virtual teams have to rely on other forms of communication to work together. Although virtual teams can be more challenging to manage because of communication issues and differences in the team members' schedules, languages, or cultures, they offer the opportunity to benefit from the expertise of team members who are in distant locations or are otherwise unavailable to participate onsite.

Decision Making
A decision-making technique that may be used as part of the Acquire Resources process is multicriteria decision analysis. When acquiring resources, the project manager may establish a set of criteria to help choose potential team members or physical resources. Factors that address the needs of the project, such as availability, cost, experience, location, or a required skill set, are weighted by importance, and potential resources are evaluated based on the selected criteria.

Outputs of Acquire Resources PAGE 333
The Acquire Resources process results in assignments for physical resources and the project team. Resource calendars, change requests, project management plan updates, project documents updates, and updates to enterprise environmental factors and organizational process assets may also be outputs to the Acquire Resources process.

Physical Resource Assignments and Project Team Assignments
While the process of Plan Resource Management determines what roles and responsibilities are needed on the project and identifies how to estimate what physical resources are needed to complete project work, it is in Acquire Resources that individuals are assigned to roles and responsibilities and physical resources are assigned to locations. These are called project team assignments and physical resource assignments.

Resource Calendars
It is important for a project manager to know when each resource is available. This gives the project manager enough information to adjust assignments on the project. For example, a resource may be assigned to the project for one week in May, but the same resource (either a physical resource or a project team member) might also be available in June for one week, if needed.

Project Management Plan Updates
As with most processes in the executing process group, updates to the project management plan are an output. Whenever resources are acquired for a project, the project management plan (especially the resource management plan) will need to be updated to reflect those adjustments to the project.

Develop Team PAGE 336

> **Process:** Develop Team
> **Process Group:** Executing
> **Knowledge Area:** Resource Management

The Develop Team process is done as part of project executing.
This process includes improving the knowledge and skills of team members, and enhancing teamwork and team member interactions. A project manager should lead, empower, and motivate the project team to achieve high performance and meet project objectives. This is accomplished by creating an environment conducive to building trust and cooperation, providing training and support for the team, and recognizing team members for their efforts.

A plan for making all this happen is included in the resource management plan. The project manager can also make use of lessons learned earlier in this project and on other similar projects to enhance their ability to effectively develop the team. Additional inputs to this process may include other project documents such as the project team assignments and team charter, enterprise environmental factors, and organizational process assets.

Tools and Techniques of Develop Team PAGE 340
The following tools and techniques may be used as part of the Develop Team process.

Interpersonal and Team Skills
In addition to understanding and following the project management process, a project manager also needs strong interpersonal skills to effectively lead the project team. These skills may include conflict management, influencing, team building, negotiation, and motivation.

Team Building   Team building can play a major role in team development—helping to form the project team into a cohesive group working for the best interests of the project and enhancing project performance. Team building, like many parts of project management, is, in part, a science. The Tuckman ladder model formally identifies the following stages of team formation and development:

- **Forming**   People are brought together as a team.
- **Storming**   There are disagreements as people learn to work together.
- **Norming**   Team members begin to build good working relationships and learn to trust the project manager and each other.
- **Performing**   The team becomes efficient and works effectively together. This is the point when the project manager can give the most attention to developing individual team members.
- **Adjourning**   The project ends, and the team is disbanded.

New teams may go through each step, while teams that have worked together before may experience a shortened version, possibly even skipping some of the early steps.

Negotiation   Negotiation can provide value in developing the team, while working to build consensus on project decisions. Including the team members in the decision-making process shows that the project manager values and considers their input.

Conflict Management   On any project, there may be conflicts among team members or between team members and the project manager. This is especially true as a team is moving through the forming and storming stages of development on the Tuckman ladder, discussed previously. It is a responsibility of the project manager to address such conflicts, and facilitate resolution in a way that satisfies everyone involved.

Influencing   Influencing is a rather ambiguous term, but it is an important aspect of a project manager's role that begins with actively listening to differing viewpoints expressed by team members. Acknowledging those different perspectives and using communication and persuasion skills helps the project manager develop mutual trust and, eventually, agreement within the team.

Training   Team members may require training to perform on the project or to enhance their performance. Such training can help team members while also decreasing the overall project cost and schedule through increased efficiency. If the training will benefit the organization in the long run or can be used on future projects, it may be covered as an organizational cost. Otherwise, it is paid for by the project and documented in the resource management plan and included in the project budget.

Colocation   A project manager might try to arrange for the entire team in each city to have offices together in one place or one room. This is called colocation, and it helps improve communication, decreases the impact of conflict (since all the parties are right there), and improves project identity for the project team (and, in a matrix organization, for management). These are also some of the reasons that colocation is suggested for adaptive or agile environments. The project charter, WBS, network diagram, and schedule may be posted on the walls to keep everyone focused on the work of the project.

Virtual Teams   The efforts of the project manager to develop the team have an added level of complexity when a team is not colocated. Extra efforts will be required to keep everyone on a virtual team informed, engaged, and committed to the project work. Such efforts include an emphasis on communication.

Communication Technology Technology provides many ways to keep in touch during a project, including the following:

- A shared portal, such as a website, enables access to current project documents at any time and from any location.
- Video or audio conferencing can be used to conduct virtual meetings when team members are working from remote locations.
- Email, text, and online chat are familiar ways for the project manager and team to communicate.

Recognition and Rewards In the Develop Team process, the project manager appraises performance and provides recognition and rewards in response to the work of the team or individual team members. To be effective, such rewards should be determined based on the project manager's understanding of what is valuable to the team member or group being recognized. In addition to recognizing past accomplishments, rewards provide incentive for ongoing achievement and efforts.

Individual and Team Assessments The more a project manager knows about each person on the project team, the easier it is to build trust, improve team communication, and encourage cooperation among team members. Personnel assessment tools can help the project manager learn more about team members by revealing how they make decisions, interact with others, and process information. This information can give the project manager insight into how to lead and guide the team. Formal and informal assessments of team members by the project manager should continue throughout the project.

The project manager completes formal and informal team performance assessments as part of developing the project team. These assessments are meant to evaluate and enhance the effectiveness of the team as a whole. They may include an analysis of how much team members' skills have improved over the course of the project; how well the team is performing, interacting, and dealing with conflict; and how they are progressing through the stages of team development. The assessments also help identify needed support or intervention by the project manager. Such assessments should be ongoing while project work is being done. The results of team assessments can be used to recognize the team's progress or motivate them to improve.

Outputs of Develop Team PAGE 343   The results of team performance assessments are an output of this process. They provide the project manager with insight into the team's performance. If the project manager determines that changes to any of the project plans are necessary, change requests are processed through integrated change control. Project documents, including the project schedule, team assignments, and resource calendars, may require such formal changes.

Organizational process assets updates may include changes to training requirements, newly adopted team-building exercises, and revisions to existing templates for individual and team assessments. This process may also result in updates to documents such as the team charter and lessons learned register.

Manage Team PAGE 345

> **Process:** Manage Team
> **Process Group:** Executing
> **Knowledge Area:** Resource Management

Like the Develop Team process, the Manage Team process is done during project executing. The Develop Team and Manage Team processes are performed simultaneously throughout the project.

The Manage Team process involves all the day-to-day management activities that a project manager is likely to do during a project. In this process, the project manager should perform the following activities to help challenge team members be part of a high performing team.

- Tracking and evaluating team performance
- Providing leadership
- Dealing with team issues
- Facilitating conflict resolution
- Negotiating and influencing
- Adjusting plans based on performance data
- Managing risks to team success
- Observing what is happening
- Using an issue log to track resolution
- Actively looking for and helping to resolve conflicts that team members cannot resolve on their own

Inputs to Manage Team PAGE 347

A primary input to the Manage Project Team process is the resource management plan. It is important to note that details related to team management activities are included in the resource management plan. Other inputs to this process include the issue log (described next), project team assignments (documented in a RACI chart), the lessons learned register, and the team charter. Work performance reports may also be used as an input to this process as they provide an indication of project progress compared to the project management plan. The project manager uses this information to identify necessary corrective actions. Also keep in mind that the results of team performance assessments from the Develop Team process may be analyzed to identify successes that need to be recognized, areas in which the team may need additional support or assistance, and issues or conflicts that need to be resolved.

Issue Log

Many project managers use issue logs, also known as issue registers or action item logs, to record problems and their resolutions. You have seen the issue log used in integration and quality processes, and you will also see it in other knowledge areas within this book. Because it is updated to reflect new issues as well as the resolution of issues, it is frequently an input and an output of the same process.

As part of managing team members and stakeholders, the issue log can be used to communicate about issues on the project. It facilitates the assessment of the causes of issues, the impact of issues on scope, schedule, cost, risk, and other aspects of the project, and the recommendation of corrective actions that could be taken. Such a log indicates to people that their needs will be considered, even if they are not addressed at the time the issue arises. Effective project managers control issues so they do not impact the project in a negative way. The issue log is updated as part of project documents updates throughout the project.

An issue log might look like the following:

Issue #	Issue	Date Added	Raised By	Person Assigned	Resolution Due Date	Status	Date Resolved	Resolution

Figure 9.5 Issue log

An issue log should be customized to meet the needs of the people who will be using it. For example, an issue log could include more detail—such as a description of the category of the issue (such as team, schedule, or technical)—as preferred by the team.

Tools and Techniques of Manage Team PAGE 348   Interpersonal and team skills and the project management information system may be used as part of the Manage Team process.

Interpersonal and Team Skills   Can you think of a few interpersonal and team skills that a project manager could use during this process? Some of the key skills include influencing, leadership, decision making, emotional intelligence, and conflict management.

Leadership   Project managers must be effective leaders and communicators and have the ability to inspire team members. There is no one right way to lead. Project managers should know the science of project management and should be able to utilize different leadership skills and styles based on any given situation throughout the project life cycle. This means they should also be able to make educated decisions about what they are doing, even when it comes to interacting with and managing people. They may sometimes need to coach team members, and at other times simply delegate work. In some cases, they may solicit the team's input or involve the team in making decisions. Whatever the case may be, a project manager must be intuitive when leading team members in order to achieve the best possible performance.

Emotional Intelligence   Emotional intelligence is the ability to recognize and express one's emotions appropriately and to perceive and manage the emotions of others by using observation, communication, and interpersonal skills. An emotionally intelligent project manager is able to establish and maintain positive relationships by adjusting communications and anticipating the needs of others. They understand how emotion can drive the behavior of others and are able to use this understanding when dealing with the issues and concerns of the team. Emotionally intelligent project managers are able to effectively use conflict resolution techniques—such as collaborating or smoothing, rather than forcing—because they are perceived as being trustworthy and fair.

Emotional intelligence enables a project manager to bring out the best in coworkers and team members by making them feel valued and important. Clearly, this trait is an asset for a project manager. Emotional intelligence can be developed and increased with study and practice.

Conflict Management   First, let's think about conflict. Is it bad? Should we spend time preventing the root causes of conflict? Who should resolve the conflict? Try to answer these questions before reviewing their answers, shown below.

- No, conflict is not inherently bad.
- Yes, it is important to identify and deal with the root causes of conflict.
- Conflict should be resolved by those who are involved, possibly assisted by the project manager.

Although we often think of conflict as a bad thing, it actually presents opportunities for improvement. Many people still have outdated beliefs about conflict. For the exam, make sure your understanding reflects the current (new) perspective.

| Changing Views of Conflict ||
Old	New
Conflict is dysfunctional and caused by personality differences or a failure of leadership.	Conflict is an inevitable consequence of organizational interactions.
Conflict is to be avoided.	Conflict can be beneficial.
Conflict is resolved by physical separation or the intervention of upper management.	Conflict is resolved through openness, identifying the causes, and problem-solving by the people involved and their immediate managers.

Conflict is inevitable, in part, because of the following factors.

- The nature of projects, which attempt to address the needs and requirements of many stakeholders
- Organizational limitations on the power of the project manager
- The necessity of obtaining resources from functional (resource) managers

The project manager has a professional responsibility as part of basic project management to attempt to avoid conflicts through the following actions:

- Keeping the team informed about the following:
  - Exactly where the project is headed
  - Project constraints and objectives
  - The contents of the project charter
  - All key decisions
  - Changes
- Clearly assigning work without ambiguity or overlapping responsibilities
- Making work assignments interesting and challenging
- Following good project management and project planning practices

Many people think the main source of conflict on a project is personality differences. They may be surprised to learn that this is rarely the case. It only becomes personal if the root cause of the problem is not resolved. On a project, the seven sources of conflict in order of frequency are as follows—note that personality is last.

1. Schedules (unrealistic)
2. Project priorities
3. Resources
4. Technical opinions
5. Administrative procedures
6. Cost
7. Personality

Conflict is best resolved by those involved in the conflict. The project manager should generally try to facilitate the resolution of problems and conflict as long as they have authority over those in conflict or over the issues in conflict. If not, the sponsor or functional managers may be called in to assist. There is one exception. In instances related to professional and social responsibility (someone breaking the law, not following policies, or acting unethically), the project manager must take the issue to someone higher in the organization.

The following are the main conflict resolution techniques to know for the exam. Notice that some have more than one title; you should know both.

- **Collaborating (problem-solving)**   With this technique, the parties openly discuss differences and try to incorporate multiple viewpoints to arrive at a consensus. Collaboration leads to a win-win situation.
- **Compromising (reconciling)**   This technique involves finding solutions that bring some degree of satisfaction to both parties. This is a lose-lose situation, since no party gets everything. Did you know that compromise is not the best choice, but rather second to collaborating?
- **Withdrawal (avoidance)**   With this technique, the parties retreat or postpone a decision on a problem. Dealing with problems is a PMI-ism; therefore, withdrawal is not usually the best choice for resolving conflict, though there may be situations where it is necessary.
- **Smoothing (accommodating)**   This technique includes making some concessions; it emphasizes agreement rather than differences of opinion. It does not result in a permanent or complete resolution of the conflict.
- **Forcing (directing)**   This technique involves pushing one viewpoint at the expense of another. It is a win-lose situation.

Resource Management

 TRICKS OF THE TRADE® Remember to look for collaborating or problem-solving choices as generally the best answers. Forcing is usually the worst, but the answer depends on the situation described. There could be situations in which withdrawal is the best option.

Exercise

Read each statement made to try to resolve a conflict, and determine which technique is being used.

	Description	Conflict Resolution Technique
1	"Do it my way!"	
2	"Let's calm down and get the job done!"	
3	"Let us do a little of what both of you suggest."	
4	"Let's deal with this issue next week."	
5	"Miguel and Kathleen, both of you want this project to cause as little distraction to your departments as possible. With that in mind, I am sure we can come to an agreement on the purchase of equipment and what is best for the project."	
6	"We have talked about new computers enough. I don't want to get the computers, and that's it!"	
7	"Miguel, you say the project should include the purchase of new computers, and Kathleen, you say the project can use existing equipment. I suggest we perform the following test on the existing equipment to determine if it needs to be replaced."	
8	"Let's see what everyone thinks, and try to reach a consensus."	
9	"Since we cannot decide on the purchase of new computers, we will have to wait until our meeting next month."	
10	"Miguel, what if we get new computers for the design activity on the project and use the existing computers for the monitoring functions?"	

Answer

	Description	Conflict Resolution Technique
1	"Do it my way!"	Forcing
2	"Let's calm down and get the job done."	Smoothing
3	"Let us do a little of what both of you suggest."	Compromising
4	"Let's deal with this issue next week."	Withdrawal
5	"Miguel and Kathleen, both of you want this project to cause as little distraction to your departments as possible. With that in mind, I am sure we can come to an agreement on the purchase of equipment and what is best for the project."	Smoothing
6	"We have talked about new computers enough. I don't want to get the computers, and that's it!"	Forcing

308

	Description	Conflict Resolution Technique
7	"Miguel, you say the project should include the purchase of new computers, and Kathleen, you say the project can use existing equipment. I suggest we perform the following test on the existing equipment to determine if it needs to be replaced."	Collaborating
8	"Let's see what everyone thinks, and try to reach a consensus."	Collaborating
9	"Since we cannot decide on the purchase of new computers, we will have to wait until our meeting next month."	Withdrawal
10	"Miguel, what if we get new computers for the design activity on the project and use the existing computers for the monitoring functions?"	Compromising

Outputs of Manage Team PAGE 350

Plans for releasing team members are included in the resource management plan. Because the length and focus of assigned work varies, team members may be released at different times throughout the project, as their work is completed. Whenever it occurs, the release of team members is considered a part of this process.

As an output of this process, change requests may be needed to reflect changes in resource assignments, costs, schedule, or any other part of the project management plan or project documents. Examples include newly identified needs for team training or changes to plans for recognition and rewards.

During this process, the issue log and lessons learned may be updated based on the results of team management efforts. In addition, the existing systems for human resource management appraisals and evaluations may be updated.

Control Resources PAGE 352

> **Process:** Control Resources
> **Process Group:** Monitoring and Controlling
> **Knowledge Area:** Resource Management

While the previous two processes involved human resources, the Control Resources process relates to the physical resources being used on the project. To control the physical resources assigned to the project, the project manager must ensure that they are available when needed—in the right place and the right quantity.

In this process, the project manager also monitors the quantity, costs, and quality of resources being used, and compares that to what was planned. If there are any discrepancies between the planned versus actual utilization of resources, corrective action may be necessary.

Remember the concept of integration, and how the project processes are related? Imagine a team of construction workers arriving on site, only to find that the building materials and construction equipment have not yet arrived. An issue with the management of physical resources could impact not only the schedule, but also the cost, scope, and quality.

Inputs to Control Resources PAGE 354

Analysis of work performance data, the issue log, and other inputs gives the project manager an idea of how actual resource usage compares to the plan. It's important to note that the resource management plan indicates how physical resources should be utilized, controlled, and eventually released. Other inputs to assist the project manager in controlling resources include project documents, agreements, and work performance data, which are discussed in the following sections.

Project Documents
The following project documents may be used to determine how resources will be controlled throughout the life of a project.

Issue Log
This document provides information about current issues regarding resource usage on the project. Issues may include availability (over- or under-supply), usage (more or less resources being used than what was planned), quality discrepancies, and cost overruns related to resource usage.

Lessons Learned Register
The project manager may be able to benefit from previous project experience with resource control efforts and from historical lessons learned from other similar projects.

Resource Assignments
Resource assignments show anticipated resource usage and where the resources are coming from.

Project Schedule
The project schedule indicates what resources are planned to be used, on which activities, and when they are needed.

Resource Requirements
Resource requirements include what materials, supplies, and equipment are needed.

Resource Breakdown Structure
Resource requirements are usually documented in a resource breakdown structure, which may be referenced by the project manager when a physical resource needs to be reordered or replaced.

Risk Register
The risk register includes information about potential risks related to the acquisition and use of physical resources. The project manager and the team must be aware of these risks, so they are able to recognize risk triggers and initiate risk responses. Newly identified risks to physical resources may be added to the risk register throughout the Control Resources process.

Agreements
If any of the physical resources being used on the project were obtained from an external source, the contract would include details about the procurement as well as the seller's contact information, which can be important in the event an issue arises related to the delivery or quality of the resources, or if additional resources are needed from the same source.

Work Performance Data
This documentation provides a measurement of the resources used, the dates they arrived, and whether they worked as intended.

Tools and Techniques of Control Resources
PAGE 356   The tools and techniques discussed in the following sections are used to evaluate ways to address any variances from the plan. These tools and techniques may be used as part of the Control Resources process.

Performance Reviews
The project manager may undertake a performance review to analyze actual versus planned resource usage and performance. Cost and schedule data may be included in this analysis to determine the possible causes of any variance from the resource management plan.

Trend Analysis
The project manager may compare measurements taken throughout the project to assess resource usage and then use that information to extrapolate potential future usage. This process also compares data to determine whether resource performance is improving or worsening.

Alternatives Analysis   Options for dealing with variances—such as purchasing more or different resources or adding staff to expedite the use of those resources—may be evaluated to determine the most effective way to bring physical resource utilization back to what was planned, or to accommodate improvements in usage. For each option, the project manager might consider factors such as availability, quality, cost, and speed. The options are weighed to determine the most beneficial and cost-effective solution.

Also note that the project manager may use cost-benefit analysis to determine the most cost-effective way to correct a problem or improve a situation. This may be performed as part of alternatives analysis.

Project Management Information System (PMIS)   You have seen throughout this book that the PMIS is used in many areas of project management. In Control Resources, it can be used to track, access, and analyze data on the use of resources and to solve issues regarding resource management. The results of these efforts will be stored in the PMIS so they are accessible throughout the organization.

Problem-Solving Methods   As with many other topics in this chapter, you likely have some experience with problem-solving methods. However, you might not use the terms or processes tested on the exam, and you might not have learned these methods as a science.

Let's look at a preferred problem-solving method that will help you when answering exam questions. Note that the *PMBOK® Guide* includes more than one version of this problem-solving method, although the progression through the steps of the technique are similar in each version.

1. Define the real or root problem, not what is presented to you or what appears to be the problem.
2. Analyze the problem.
3. Identify solutions.
4. Pick a solution.
5. Implement the chosen solution.
6. Review the solution, and confirm that the solution solved the problem.

Outputs of Control Resources PAGE 357   The outputs of the Control Resources process include work performance information, change requests, and updates to project documents and the project management plan.

Work Performance Information   Did you notice that work performance data is an input to this process, and work performance information is an output? The difference is that the work performance data is raw data. It is analyzed in this process and used to compare actual to planned results to create work performance information.

Project Documents Updates   The documents that were inputs to this process may be updated based on the work of monitoring and controlling resources. These documents may include the issue log, the lessons learned register, resource assignments, the project schedule and risk register, and the resource breakdown structure.

Project Management Plan Updates   Components of the project management plan, specifically the resource management plan, may be updated to reflect minor changes in the usage, availability, and quality of resources. In addition to the resource management plan, the project schedule, cost baselines, and quality management plan may be changed as a result of this process.

Resource Management Review

Exercise

This exercise will help you review the key material you need to know for resource management. The Shuffle Game that follows offers another approach to this material. You can use either or both of these study tools, depending on your preference.

Instructions

1. Try to fill in the blanks in the below table using the knowledge and understanding gained after reading this chapter.
2. To review only the material contained in this chapter, focus on the cells that have asterisks. (These are the key topics you need to understand to pass the exam with the minimum amount of study time. The answer table will show only these topics.)
3. To review all the items listed in the *PMBOK® Guide*, fill in the entire table.

Key Inputs	Key Tools and Techniques	Key Outputs
Plan Resource Management Process group:		
*	*	*
Estimate Activity Resources Process group:		
*	*	*
Acquire Resources Process group:		
*	*	*

Key Inputs	Key Tools and Techniques	Key Outputs
Develop Team Process group:		
	*	*
Manage Team Process group:		
*	*	
Control Resources Process group:		
*	*	*

Answer   To save study time and focus on the most important information, this answer table only shows the topics that are covered in this chapter. If you tried to list all inputs, tools and techniques, and outputs, you'll need to check your answers against the *PMBOK® Guide*.

Key Inputs	Key Tools and Techniques	Key Outputs
Plan Resource Management Process group: Planning		
Project management plan Project charter Project documents Enterprise environmental factors Organizational process assets	Data representation • RAM • RACI chart • Organizational breakdown structure • Resource breakdown structure • Work breakdown structure • Text-oriented formats Organizational theory	Resource management plan Team charter
Estimate Activity Resources Process group: Planning		
Project management plan • Scope baseline • Resource management plan Project documents • Activity list • Activity attributes	Bottom-up estimating Analogous estimating Parametric estimating Alternatives analysis Resource histogram	Resource requirements Resource breakdown structure
Acquire Resources Process group: Executing		
Resource management plan Enterprise environmental factors Organizational process assets	Pre-assignment Negotiation Virtual teams Decision making	Physical resource assignments Project team assignments Resource calendars Project management plan updates
Develop Team Process group: Executing		
	Interpersonal and team skills • Team-building • Negotiation • Conflict management • Influencing Training Colocation Virtual teams Communications technology Individual and team assessments	Team performance assessments

Key Inputs	Key Tools and Techniques	Key Outputs
Manage Team Process group: Executing		
Issue log	Interpersonal and team skills • Leadership • Emotional intelligence • Conflict management	
Control Resources Process group: Monitoring and controlling		
Project documents • Issue log • Lessons learned register • Resource assignments • Project schedule • Resource requirements • Resource breakdown structure • Risk register Agreements Work performance data	Performance reviews Trend analysis Alternatives analysis PMIS Problem-solving methods	Work performance information Project documents updates Project management plan updates

Shuffle Game

Some people learn best by doing, which is why we have developed this alternate approach to reviewing resource management. To save you time, only the most important topics for the exam—those covered in this chapter—have been included.

Instructions

1. Cut out the cards on the next pages.
2. Lay out the bold title cards as column headers.
3. Shuffle the remaining cards and try to put them in the columns where they belong. Cards with italic terms must be matched to the corresponding group. For example, a *Cost of Quality* card in italics would match with a Data Analysis card, as cost of quality is a data analysis tool and technique.
4. Check your answers against the material covered in this chapter or the *PMBOK® Guide,* and make note of any gaps in your knowledge.

Note: Be sure to keep all cards for each chapter shuffle game as you will use them again for the final Shuffle Game in chapter 14.

Plan Resource Management *Key Inputs*	**Plan Resource Management** *Key Tools and Techniques*	**Plan Resource Management** *Key Outputs*
Estimate Activity Resources *Key Inputs*	**Estimate Activity Resources** *Key Tools and Techniques*	**Estimate Activity Resources** *Key Outputs*
Acquire Resources *Key Inputs*	**Acquire Resources** *Key Tools and Techniques*	**Acquire Resources** *Key Outputs*
Develop Team *Key Tools and Techniques*	**Develop Team** *Key Outputs*	**Manage Team** *Key Inputs*
Manage Team *Key Tools and Techniques*	**Control Resources** *Key Inputs*	**Control Resources** *Key Tools an0d Techniques*

Control Resources *Key Outputs*	Project management plan	Project charter
Project documents	Enterprise environmental factors	Organizational process assets
Data representation	*RAM*	*RACI chart*
Organizational breakdown structure	*Resource breakdown structure*	*Work breakdown structure*
Text-oriented formats	Organizational theory	Resource management plan

Team charter	Project management plan	*Scope baseline*
Resource management plan	Project documents	*Activity list*
Activity attributes	Bottom-up estimating	Analogous estimating
Parametric estimating	Alternatives analysis	Resource histogram
Resource requirements	Resource breakdown structure	Resource management plan

Enterprise environmental factors	Organizational process assets	Preassignment
Negotiation	Virtual teams	Decision making
Physical resource assignments	Project team assignments	Resource calendars
Project management plan updates	Interpersonal and team skills	*Team-building*
Negotiation	*Conflict management*	*Influencing*

Training	Colocation	Virtual teams
Communication technology	Individual and team assessments	Team performance assessments
Issue log	Interpersonal and team skills	*Leadership*
Emotional intelligence	*Conflict management*	Project documents
Issue log	*Lessons learned register*	*Resource assignments*

Project schedule	*Resource requirements*	Resource breakdown structure
Risk register	Agreements	Work performance data
Performance reviews	Trend analysis	Alternatives analysis
PMIS	Problem-solving methods	Work performance information
Project documents updates	Project management plan updates	

Practice Exam

1. What is the most correct statement about conflict?
   A. The primary source of conflict is personality.
   B. Conflict can be beneficial.
   C. Conflict is best resolved by smoothing.
   D. Conflict is caused by a failure of leadership.

2. Which of the following best describes what is included in the resource management plan?
   A. The results of team performance assessments
   B. The established roles and responsibilities for the project
   C. Project team assignments
   D. Change requests related to the project's physical resources

3. The project manager is reviewing the organization's hiring procedures and policies related to assigning resources to the project. What process are they working in?
   A. Plan Resource Management
   B. Estimate Activity Resources
   C. Acquire Resources
   D. Control Resources

4. The project team is working in an adaptive environment on a complex project that requires a lot of coordination. Under these circumstances, the best strategy is to:
   A. Colocate the team
   B. Hire a contractor
   C. Hold more meetings to get the word out
   D. Gain extra assistance from management

5. What does a resource histogram show that a responsibility assignment matrix (RAM) does not?
   A. The person in charge of each activity
   B. Activities
   C. Interrelationships
   D. Time

6. Which resource management process deals strictly with physical resources?
   A. Plan Resource Management
   B. Estimate Activity Resources
   C. Acquire Resources
   D. Control Resources

7. Which type of hierarchical chart categorizes project work by type of resource?
   A. Organizational breakdown structure
   B. Work breakdown structure (WBS)
   C. Resource breakdown structure
   D. RACI chart

8. Two team members are having a big disagreement over the type of computer hardware to use on the project. Who should resolve the dispute?
   A. The team members and their project manager
   B. The project manager
   C. Management
   D. The sponsor

9. All the following are included in the key outputs of the Plan Resource Management process except:
   A. Training goals
   B. Project organizational charts
   C. Work performance information
   D. Process for acquiring physical resources

10. What is multicriteria decision analysis?
    A. An analytical tool for making decisions about team-building and training activities
    B. A technique used to evaluate potential team members
    C. A quantitative approach to developing recognition and rewards systems
    D. A technique used for designing personnel assessment tools

11. What does "RACI" stand for?
    A. Role, Activity, Communication, Information
    B. Reward, Appraise, Confirm, Invite
    C. Recognize, Act, Check, Identify
    D. Responsible, Accountable, Consult, Inform

12. Preassignment and negotiation are important tools and techniques in which resource management process?
    A. Develop Team
    B. Acquire Resources
    C. Plan Resource Management
    D. Manage Team

13. While working in the Control Resources process, the project manager needs to compare actual versus planned resource usage. Which document would provide the necessary information regarding how physical resources should be utilized?
    A. Lessons learned register
    B. Resource breakdown structure
    C. Work performance information
    D. Resource management plan

14. Which of the following is an input to Develop Team?
    A. Team performance assessments
    B. Project team assignments
    C. Interpersonal skills
    D. Personnel assessment tools

15. Resource requirements documentation and updates to the resource breakdown structure are outputs of which process?
    A. Plan Resource Management
    B. Control Resources
    C. Plan Procurement Management
    D. Estimate Activity Resources

© 2018 RMC Publications, Inc ™ • 952 846 4484 • info@rmcls.com • www.rmcls.com

Answers

1. **Answer** B

   Explanation   Of the choices provided, the most correct statement is that conflict can be beneficial. In fact, conflict on projects often presents opportunities for improvement. The most common source of conflict is schedules, not personality, and conflict is best resolved by collaborating. Conflict is an inevitable consequence of organizational interactions rather than a result of a failure of leadership.

2. **Answer** B

   Explanation   The resource management plan documents the project's roles and responsibilities, as well as other details related to the management of team and physical resources. Project team assignments and change requests related to both team and physical resources are outputs of Acquire Resources; they are not included in the project's resource management plan. The results of team performance assessments are outputs of Develop Team rather than Plan Resource Management.

3. **Answer** C

   Explanation   Inputs to Acquire Resources include organizational process assets such as hiring procedures and policies related to assigning resources to projects.

4. **Answer** A

   Explanation   Colocation helps improve communication and decreases the impact of conflict; it can be particularly useful in adaptive or agile environments and on highly complex projects.

5. **Answer** D

   Explanation   The responsibility assignment matrix (RAM) maps specific resources against the work packages from the WBS. On a resource histogram, the use of resources is shown individually or by groups over time.

6. **Answer** D

   Explanation   Control Resources is the only resource management process that deals strictly with physical resources. Human resources are developed and managed through the Develop Team and Manage Team processes.

7. **Answer** C

   Explanation   A resource breakdown structure, a tool used in the Plan Resource Management process, breaks down the work by type of resource (e.g., people, materials, equipment). It may be updated as part of Estimate Activity Resources, and it serves as an input to Control Resources.

8. **Answer** A

   Explanation   As a rule, those having the problem should resolve the problem. In this case, that means the primary responsibility for working out the problem will fall on the two team members. However, this question indicates the disagreement is big, in which case the project manager should get involved if the team members cannot resolve the problem, so that the conflict does not impact the project.

9. **Answer** C

   Explanation   The resource management plan provides guidance on the management of human resources as well as physical resources; it includes all of the components listed except work performance information, which is an output of Control Resources.

10. **Answer** B

    Explanation Multicriteria decision analysis is a decision-making technique that uses specific criteria (such as availability, cost, experience, location, or skill set) to evaluate possible project resources—whether those are potential team members or physical resources. This decision-making technique can also be used within the integration, scope, stakeholder, and quality knowledge areas.

11. **Answer** D

    Explanation A RACI chart is a type of responsibility assignment matrix (RAM) that uses the letters R for Responsible, A for Accountable, C for Consult, and I for Inform. A RACI chart is used in the Plan Resource Management process; it also serves as an input to the Manage Team process.

12. **Answer** B

    Explanation Preassignment and negotiation are both used in the Acquire Resources process. Some physical resources and team members may be preassigned to the project in the project charter, but the project manager may need to use their negotiating skills to acquire other resources, either from inside or outside the organization.

13. **Answer** D

    Explanation Although the lessons learned register and the resource breakdown structure are important inputs to the Control Resource process, the resource management plan is the document the project manager should review to get information on how physical resources should be utilized. Work performance information is an output of this process rather than an input.

14. **Answer** B

    Explanation Project team assignments, an output of Acquire Resources, are an input to Develop Team. Team performance assessments are an output of Develop Team, and interpersonal skills and personnel assessment tools are tools and techniques used in that process.

15. **Answer** D

    Explanation The Estimate Activity Resources process results in resource requirements documentation, including updates to the project's resource breakdown structure.

Communications
Management

There are 15 questions on this knowledge area on the CAPM exam. Also note, for a full list of all inputs, tools and techniques, and outputs within this knowledge area, please see the table on page 360 in the PMBOK© Guide.

Countless communications issues may occur over the life of a project—for example, a stakeholder deleting a voicemail without listening through to the end of the message, a project manager missing an important email because their inbox is full, or a team member who doesn't receive a key piece of information that could impact their work. Similar issues happen all too often on projects and indicate a need to better plan and manage communications. Think about your experience with real-world projects. How much time is spent planning and managing communications?

When surveyed, project managers typically identify communication-related issues as the problem they experience most frequently on projects. Communication is an incredibly important part of managing a project, so shouldn't a project manager make sure they plan, manage, and monitor their messages?

QUICKTEST

- Communications management process
- Communications management plan
- Communications methods
  - Interactive
  - Push
  - Pull
- Project reporting
  - Types of reports
- Communication models
  - Effective communication
  - Effective listening
- Types of communication
  - Formal written
  - Informal written
  - Formal verbal
  - Informal verbal
- Communication technology
- Communication channels
- Flow of communication on a project
- Meetings

Many beginning project managers only communicate using status reports. As project managers gain experience, they often recognize the need for a more structured approach. Effective project managers create a communications management plan that goes beyond merely sending status reports and includes asking stakeholders what they need communicated to them and identifying what communications need to be received from the stakeholders. Effective project managers also frequently revisit communications at team meetings to limit the potential for problems. To pass the CAPM exam, you should have this type of mindset about communicating on projects.

Although this chapter is not particularly difficult, it is one you should take seriously. Be sure to find your gaps regarding communications, and be aware that communication questions are frequently combined with other topics. For example, a WBS can be used as a communication tool (see the Scope Management chapter), and risk response strategies should be communicated to the stakeholders (see the Risk Management chapter).

You may also see questions linking communications management to stakeholder management. As you might expect, these two are closely related: managing stakeholder engagement and keeping stakeholders informed and involved requires well-thought-out communications. See the Stakeholder Management chapter for more information. The following should help you understand how each part of communications management fits into the overall project management process.

The Communications Management Process	Done During
Plan Communications Management	Planning process group
Manage Communications	Executing process group
Monitor Communications	Monitoring and controlling process group

Plan Communications Management PAGE 366

Process: Plan Communications Management
Process Group: Planning
Knowledge Area: Communications Management

The Plan Communications Management process considers how to develop a plan for project communications activities. This plan should be based on the information needs of stakeholders and the needs of the project. The plan identifies what systems and processes are already in place to support communication needs, as well as what processes and documents must be created to maximize the effectiveness and efficiency of communications on the project. This effort includes planning what information will be communicated, to whom, when, using what method, and how frequently. The major output of this process is the communications management plan, which will guide the project manager and the team in managing and monitoring communications to ensure information is getting to the people who need it, is clear and understandable, and allows stakeholders to take action as necessary.

Project communications occur internally and externally to the core project team–vertically (up and down the levels of the organization) and horizontally (between peers). Planning should include communicating in all directions, as shown in figure 10.1.

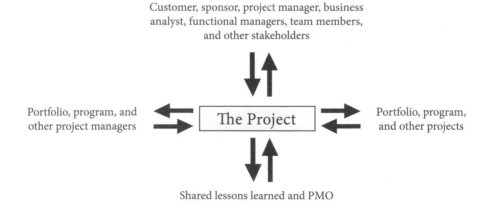

Figure 10.1 Flow of communication on a project

To communicate effectively, you need to handle communications in a structured way and choose the best type of communication for each situation. Information can be expressed in different ways—formally or informally, written or verbal. You need to decide what approach to use for each instance of communication. Make sure you understand the following chart.

Type of Communication	When Used
Formal written	Project management plan, other formal documentation (such as the project charter), and reports; can be both physical and electronic
Formal verbal	Planned meetings and stakeholder briefings; can be face-to-face or remote
Informal written	Email, handwritten notes, text messages, instant messaging, social media, and websites
Informal verbal	Unscheduled meetings, conversations, and other casual discussions

The Five Cs of Communication
Certain qualities of written communication enhance the likelihood that communications will be correctly interpreted and understood by the recipients. The following qualities should be incorporated by the project manager to ensure that messages are effective:

- Correct grammar and spelling
- Concise and well-crafted
- Clear and purposeful
- Coherent and logical
- Controlled flow of words and ideas

Inputs to Plan Communications Management
PAGE 368 The following are key inputs to the Plan Communications Management process.

Project Management Plan
During Plan Communications Management, the project manager will need to consult the project management plan for information on other knowledge areas and management plans, such as those for requirements, configuration, stakeholders, and change. This information will need to be communicated, and it will help the project manager determine how to plan, manage, and monitor communications.

Project Documents
Project documents such as the stakeholder register and any requirements documentation may be utilized as part of Plan Communications Management. The project manager should refer to these documents to plan communications activities and for information about which stakeholders require more specific types of communication.

Enterprise Environmental Factors
To create an effective communications management plan, the project manager must consider the performing organization's environment (enterprise environmental factors), including its culture and expectations.

Organizational Process Assets
The project manager must also take into account the organization's established processes and procedures for communicating about projects, its historical records and lessons learned from previous projects, and any other stored information (organizational process assets).

Tools and Techniques of Plan Communications Management
PAGE 369 In the Plan Communications Management process, the project manager must understand and take a structured approach to using communications technology, methods, and models. Additional tools and techniques

that may be used as part of this process include meetings, data representation, interpersonal and team skills, expert judgment, and communication requirements analysis.

Communication Channels Before moving on to the key tools and techniques of Plan Communications Management, it's important to understand communication channels.

When you add one more person to the team, does the number of communication channels simply increase by one? No. In fact, there is a substantial increase in communication channels. As a result, communication needs can grow rapidly with each added person.

Communication channels can be calculated using the following formula:

$$\frac{n\,(n-1)}{2}$$ n = the number of stakeholders

Note that n equals the total number of people (or communicators).

Let's practice using this formula with an example. If you have four people communicating on your team and you add one more, how many communication channels do you have? To get the answer, you calculate the number of communication channels for four communicators and five communicators, and then subtract to find the difference.

For four communicators, calculate 4 times 3 (which is $n-1$) to get 12, and then divide by 2 to reach the answer, which is 6. For five communicators, calculate 5 times 4 (which is $n-1$) to get 20, and then divide by 2 to reach the answer, which is 10. The difference between 10 and 6 is 4. Simple!

You might not see this formula when taking the exam. But just in case, be sure to understand the concept and know how to calculate the number of communication channels.

Communication Models Many of us don't think scientifically about our communications. We just send an email and expect that it will be read and interpreted properly. The most basic communication model only ensures that a message has been delivered, but excellent project communication requires a more structured approach to communications.

A more comprehensive communication model, interactive communication, includes three main components: the sender, the receiver, and the confirmation that the message is correctly understood (this can also mean feedback from the receiver, such as an acknowledgment of receipt or a general response to a message, for example). Each message is encoded by the sender and decoded by the receiver. The receiver acknowledges receipt of the message, and both the sender and receiver are responsible for confirming that it has been properly interpreted by the receiver.

Factors such as the receiver's perception of the message, everyday distractions, or even a lack of interest can affect the way the receiver decodes a message. Communication models often refer to these types of factors as "noise" because they interfere with the receiver's ability to understand the message.

More complex communication models exist, but for the exam it is assumed that a project manager understands this basic interactive model, as illustrated in figure 10.2. As a result, they will choose methods and tools and techniques that will maximize understanding and responsiveness in project communication. Keep this interactive model in mind when answering communication questions on the exam.

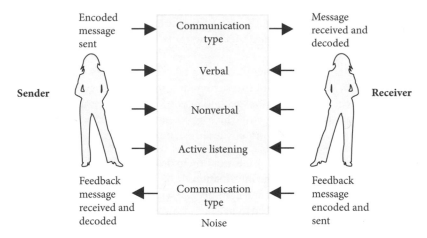

Figure 10.2 The interactive communication model

Effective Communication   The sender should determine which communication method to use to send a message, and then encode the message carefully and confirm that it is understood. When encoding the message, the sender needs to be aware of the following factors.

- **Nonverbal**   A significant portion of in-person communication is nonverbal; this can include gestures, facial expressions, and body language.

- **Verbal**   There are two important aspects of verbal communication:

    - The words and phrases a sender chooses are essential components of the message, but their meaning can be obscured by the accompanying nonverbal factors.

    - Pitch and tone of voice also help to convey a spoken message.

To confirm that a message is understood, it's helpful for the sender to ask for feedback by using questions such as, "Could you rephrase what I've said in your own words?" But it's also up to the receiver to make sure they have received and understood the entire message.

This is especially true in situations involving cross-cultural communication. Senders and receivers of communications must be cognizant of cultural differences, including age, gender, and nationality, and take those factors into account when planning, transmitting, and interpreting communications.

The previous paragraphs apply to individual interactions as well as to project communication. It's possible to plan not just the types of communications to be used, but also ways for the sender to confirm that the receiver has interpreted the message as intended. The communications management plan provides guidance to stakeholders regarding what to communicate and when to communicate it. It also includes direction on how to confirm understanding of communications.

Effective Listening   So what should a receiver do during in-person communication to accurately decode a message and confirm that it has been understood? The receiver should pay attention to the sender's gestures and facial expressions, and try to focus on the content of the message without distraction. It's also important that a receiver practices active listening. Active listening means the receiver confirms they are listening, expresses agreement or disagreement, and asks for clarification when necessary.

If a message is not understood, the receiver should acknowledge the message by saying something like, "I'm not sure I understand. Can you explain that again?" Like the sender, the receiver needs to encode their response carefully, keeping in mind the potential effects of verbal and nonverbal communication, when giving feedback to the sender, as illustrated in figure 10.2.

Communications Technology   Communication can take place in many ways, including face-to-face, over the phone, in writing, through instant messaging, and via email. These means of communicating are collectively referred to as communications technology. Another aspect of planning communications is determining the optimal technology with which to communicate information. To determine the appropriate technology to use, a project manager should ask questions such as:

- Would it be better to communicate this information in person or virtually?
- Would it be better to communicate the information through an email or a phone call?
- What technology is the team familiar and comfortable with?
- How quickly does the information need to be communicated?
- Are there security or confidentiality issues that should be considered when choosing a means of communicating information?
- Would a letter sent through the mail get more attention?

Communication Methods   When planning communications, it's also important to determine the communication method. These methods can be grouped into the following categories:

- **Interactive communication**   This method is reciprocal and involves two or more people. One person provides information; others receive it and then respond to the information. Examples of interactive communication include conversations, phone calls, meetings, instant messaging, and video calls.
- **Push communication**   This method involves a one-way stream of information. The sender provides information to the people who need it, but does not expect feedback from the recipients. Examples of push communication are status reports, emailed updates, blogs, and company memos.
- **Pull communication**   In this method, the sender places the information in a central location. The recipients are then responsible for retrieving the information from that location. This method is often used to distribute large documents or provide information to many people.

In choosing a communication method, a project manager should consider whether feedback is needed or if it is enough to simply provide the information. Where possible, it's worth involving stakeholders in the final decision about which methods will meet their communication needs. Such decisions will support the stakeholder engagement efforts on the project.

Meetings   Early in the project, the project manager is likely to conduct meetings with the team to plan how information will be communicated on the project. Planning for communication should also involve thinking ahead about when, how, and how often meetings will be used throughout the project.

Meetings are a problem in the real world because many project managers manage by doing everything in meetings, and most meetings are not efficient. Thinking ahead about how and when meetings will be conducted, when they're appropriate (or when a less disruptive form of communication could be substituted), and who needs to attend them can go a long way toward addressing this problem.

When planning meetings, a project manager should consider the following rules:

- Schedule recurring meetings in advance.
- Meet with the team regularly, but not too often.
- Have a purpose for each meeting.

Communications Requirements Analysis Requirements analysis will help a project manager correctly understand stakeholders' information requirements. Understanding and fulfilling these requirements will maintain stakeholder engagement by ensuring that communication needs are met. If a project manager skips this step, they risk not meeting the communication needs of stakeholders, and potentially misunderstanding requirements altogether.

The following information may be used to determine and analyze communication requirements:

- Stakeholder register
- Stakeholder engagement plan
- Location of stakeholders
- Number of communication channels

Outputs of Plan Communications Management PAGE 377   The primary output of the Plan Communications Management process is the communications management plan. This plan documents both the communication needs of stakeholders and a strategy for meeting those needs. It should ensure that information gets to the people who need it in a clear and understandable way. For more details about the communications management plan, see the next section. Additional outputs may include updates to the project management plan and updates to project documents, such as the project schedule and stakeholder register.

Communications Management Plan A communications management plan documents how a project manager will manage and monitor communications. Components of the plan may include what communications should be prepared, disseminated, and received among all project stakeholders, how communications should be named and stored, who has access to the communications, who has the ability to edit communications, and who has responsibility for sending and receiving project communications. The plan also includes information on how the effectiveness of project communications will be evaluated. Figure 10.3 shows a portion of what may be found in a communications management plan.

What Needs to Be Communicated	Why	Between Whom	Best Method for Communicating	Responsibility for Sending	When and How Often

Figure 10.3 Sample excerpt from a communications management plan

Because communications are so complex, a communications management plan should be in writing for most projects. It must address the needs of all the stakeholders and should account for any language and cultural differences on the project. The communications management plan becomes part of the project management plan.

Manage Communications PAGE 379

Process: Manage Communications
Process Group: Executing
Knowledge Area: Communications Management

Throughout the life of a project, many stakeholders will require information about the project. The communications needs of stakeholders are determined in planning and documented in the communications management plan. These needs are met in Manage Communications through the distribution of communications artifacts, such as reports, graphics, and emails, as well as through meetings and other in-person communication.

Communications Management

The Manage Communications process also includes making sure information is flowing back and forth on the project in accordance with the communications management plan. This process is about facilitating effective communication and practicing flexible approaches when managing communications. Managing communications also includes providing opportunities for stakeholders to request additional information and clarification.

Inputs to Manage Communications PAGE 381   The inputs to the Manage Communications process include components of the project management plan such as the communications management plan, project documents, work performance reports, enterprise environmental factors, and organizational process assets.

Communications Management Plan   In this process, the project manager will follow the communications management plan, which includes the plans for how to manage communications on the project.

Work Performance Reports   Work performance reports are an output of the Monitor and Control Project Work process in integration management. These reports provide analyzed data and information in a format that can be communicated to stakeholders with their preferred method of communication.

Tools and Techniques of Manage Communications PAGE 383   The tools and techniques of Manage Communications include the communication technology and methods described in the previous process, communication skills, the PMIS, project reporting, interpersonal and team skills, and meetings.

Interpersonal and Team Skills   What communication skills could a project manager use as a tool or technique during the Manage Communications process? Should they use active listening? How should a project manager handle conflict? Should they pay attention to cultural differences between stakeholders? Utilizing a range of communication skills, as well as relying on interpersonal skills can help a project manager better manage communications.

Although the communications management plan may suggest good practices for project communications, it is the responsibility of the project manager and team to tailor their communications approach in response to feedback from stakeholders. Also keep in mind that the culture of the organization and the political environment within which the project and its stakeholders exist will need to be regularly assessed, and the project manager and team must be flexible and adapt to any significant changes. The project manager and all stakeholders on a project must use their skills to reduce or resolve conflicts and promote effective communicating.

Meetings   As discussed in the Plan Communications Management section of this chapter, meetings play a big part in the effort of managing communications. When handled properly, they provide a means to communicate efficiently with stakeholders. Review the following rules for conducting meetings.

- Set a time limit, and keep to it.
- Create an agenda with team input.
- Distribute the agenda beforehand.
- Stick to the agenda.
- Let attendees know their responsibilities in advance.
- Bring the right people together.
- Chair and lead the meeting with a set of rules.

- Assign deliverables and time limits for all work assignments that result from meetings.
- Document and publish meeting minutes.

Project Reporting   A big part of managing communications focuses on project reporting, which involves communicating to stakeholders how the project is going. Much of that information comes from work performance reports, an output of the Monitor and Control Project Work process. It also involves asking for feedback from stakeholders to ensure they have received the information they need and have understood it, and determine whether they need more. This communication may take the form of presentations or reports, as outlined in the communications management plan.

Types of Reports   There are different types of reports used in project management. For the exam, think in terms of a large project, and recognize that a project manager might issue the following types of reports:

- **Status report**   A status report describes where the project currently stands in relation to the performance measurement baseline.
- **Progress report**   A progress report describes what has been accomplished.
- **Trend report**   A trend report examines project results over time to see if performance is improving or deteriorating.
- **Forecasting report**   A forecasting report predicts future project status and performance.
- **Variance report**   A variance report compares actual results to baselines.
- **Earned value report**   An earned value report integrates scope, cost, and schedule measurements to assess project performance.
- **Lessons learned documentation**   Performance reports are used as lessons learned for future projects.

Outputs of Manage Communications PAGE 387   The Manage Communications process results in the distribution of project communications, such as performance reports, status reports, and presentations, as well as other forms of communications. The communications management plan may also be updated to reflect changes in the approach to managing communications on the project.

It's also important to note that the stakeholder engagement plan and stakeholder register may be updated to reflect changes in stakeholder communications requirements or changes in the project's strategy to fulfill their requirements. Lastly, know that issues regarding communications are documented in the issue log and, possibly, in the lessons learned register.

Monitor Communications PAGE 388

> **Process:** Monitor Communications
> **Process Group:** Monitoring & Controlling
> **Knowledge Area:** Communications Management

In the Monitor Communications process, the project manager and team assess how communications are going throughout the project to ensure information is flowing as planned—in the right way, to the right people, and at the right time—to effectively keep stakeholders informed and maintain the desired levels of stakeholder engagement.

Inputs to Monitor Communications PAGE 390   The communications management plan, a component of the project management plan, provides details about how to measure the effectiveness and efficiency of communications. Additional inputs may include project documents such as the issue log and the lessons learned register, work performance data, enterprise environmental factors, and organizational process assets.

Based on what you've learned so far, can you explain how the key inputs to this process may be used to monitor communications? Test yourself by reviewing the information found in the following table.

Input	How Is It Used in Monitor Communications?
Project management plan	The communications management plan and other pieces of the project management plan are important to the Monitor Communications process because they allow you to compare actual communication on the project against planned communication. They provide details on what needs to be distributed, why, how, when, and to whom, along with information on roles and responsibilities.
Project communications	You'll need to compare the actual project communications to the communications management plan. How do the various reports and other communications hold up against what you planned? Are they giving you the intended results?
Issue log	An issue log can be used to document and track issues on the project—areas of confusion, disagreement, conflict, or concern that require attention. It is also updated to reflect resolution of those issues. The issue log helps you assess the causes of the issues and their impacts on the project; it can also help when planning corrective actions. This is a useful tool that lets you capture and communicate issues, so that you're handling them proactively rather than reactively, with the goal of preventing problems and change requests.
Lessons learned register	Actively documenting lessons learned during a project can help you learn from previous problems and avoid repeating the same mistakes. Lessons learned should be shared with other ongoing projects as appropriate. They become part of the historical records of the project and the organization's lessons learned repository, and thereby provide the benefit of past experience with communications issues to future projects.
Work performance data	Work performance data is raw communications data about what has occurred during a project. The data can help you measure the efficiency and effectiveness of communications against planned metrics. You can also use the data in root cause analysis to evaluate the cause of poor communications or analyze variances from the plan to determine if changes are necessary.
Enterprise environmental factors	Organizational culture, existing communications tools and systems, and common practices for communicating are influencing factors that need to be considered when evaluating the effectiveness of communications and the communications management plan.
Organizational process assets	You need to refer to your organization's available or required procedures, reporting formats, standards, tools, and security policies to make sure communications are meeting organizational expectations.

Tools and Techniques of Monitor Communications PAGE 391   This process involves measuring to determine whether the communications management plan is being followed and whether communications are meeting the needs of the stakeholders. If not, the project manager will need to identify where communication is breaking down, and then respond and adjust as necessary to meet the stakeholders' communication needs. How can a project manager tell if communication is breaking down? In addition to the metrics they've established in their communications management plan, the project

manager will need to rely on their soft skills. Some problems will be obvious for the project manager. For example, people will let the project manager know if they're not getting the reports or information they're meant to receive. The project manager will also benefit from encouraging stakeholders to let them know whether the project communications are meeting their needs.

As mentioned earlier, a project manager should ask stakeholders for feedback on the reports and other communications they receive. Also, project team members should report any communication problems they experience and help to identify ways that communication can be improved on the project.

Outputs of Monitor Communications PAGE 392
Outputs that are part of the Monitor Communications process include work performance information, change requests, project management plan updates, and updates to project documents. Can you think of which project documents may need to be updated as part of this process?

Work Performance Information
To understand how communications are performing throughout the life of the project, the project manager will need to compare ongoing project communications to planned communications. This type of data is included in the project's work performance information.

Change Requests
What type of change requests might a project manager encounter during the Monitor Communications process? Stakeholder communication requirements may change as a result of an adjustment to the project, for example. Can you think of another example?

Project Management Plan and Project Documents Updates
Components of the project management plan, such as the communications management plan and stakeholder engagement plan, may need to be updated as a result of the Monitor Communications process. Project documents may need to be updated as well. For example, the issue log may need to include any new issues or resolutions that may have occurred. Or the stakeholder register may need to be updated to reflect any changes to stakeholder communication requirements.

Communications Management

Communications Management Review

Exercise

This exercise will help you review the key material you need to know for communicatons management. The Shuffle Game that follows offers another approach to this material. You can use either or both of these study tools, depending on your preference.

Instructions

1. Try to fill in the blanks in the below table using the knowledge and understanding gained after reading this chapter.
2. To review only the material contained in this chapter, focus on the cells that have asterisks. (These are the key topics you need to understand to pass the exam with the minimum amount of study time. The answer table will show only these topics.)
3. To review all the items listed in the *PMBOK® Guide*, fill in the entire table.

Key Inputs	Key Tools and Techniques	Key Outputs
Plan Communications Management Process group:		
*	*	*
Manage Communications Process group:		
*	*	
Monitor Communications Process group:		
*		*

Answer   To save study time and focus on the most important information, this answer table only shows the topics that are covered in this chapter. If you tried to list all inputs, tools and techniques, and outputs, you'll need to check your answers against the *PMBOK® Guide*.

Key Inputs	Key Tools and Techniques	Key Outputs
Plan Communications Management Process group: Planning		
Project management plan Project documents Enterprise environmental factors Organizational process assets	Communication channels Communication models • Effective communication • Effective listening Communication technology Communication methods Meetings Communication requirements analysis	Communications management plan
Manage Communications Process group: Executing		
Project management plan • Communications management plan Work performance reports	Project reporting • Types of reports	
Monitor Communications Process group: Monitoring and controlling		
Project management plan • Communications management plan Project documents • Issue log • Lessons learned register		Work performance information Change requests Project management plan updates Project documents updates

Shuffle Game

Some people learn best by doing, which is why we have developed this alternate approach to reviewing communications management. To save you time, only the most important topics for the exam—those covered in this chapter—have been included.

Instructions

1. Cut out the cards on the next pages.
2. Lay out the bold title cards as column headers.
3. Shuffle the remaining cards and try to put them in the columns where they belong. Cards with italic terms must be matched to the corresponding group. For example, a *Cost of Quality* card in italics would match with a Data Analysis card, as cost of quality is a data analysis tool and technique.
4. Check your answers against the material covered in this chapter or the *PMBOK® Guide,* and make note of any gaps in your knowledge.

Note: Be sure to keep all cards for each chapter shuffle game as you will use them again for the final Shuffle Game in chapter 14.

Plan Communications Management *Key Inputs*	**Plan Communications Management** *Key Tools & Techniques*	**Plan Communications Management** *Key Outputs*
Manage Communications *Key Inputs*	**Manage Communications** *Key Tools & Techniques*	**Monitor Communications** *Key Inputs*
Monitor Communications *Key Outputs*	Project management plan	*Project documents*
Enterprise environmental factors	Organizational process assets	Communication channels
Communication models	*Effective communication*	*Effective listening*

Communication technology	Communication methods	Meetings
Communication requirements analysis	Communications management plan	Project management plan
Communications management plan	Work performance reports	Project reporting
Types of reports	Project management plan	*Communications management plan*
Project documents	*Issue log*	*Lessons learned register*

Work performance information

Change requests

Project management plan updates

Project documents updates

Practice Exam

1. Inputs to the Plan Communications Management process include:
   A. Project communications
   B. The stakeholder register
   C. Work performance reports
   D. Forecasts

2. The team is assessing how communications are going throughout the project to see if the right information is getting to the right people, at the right time, and in the right way. Which process are they engaged in?
   A. Manage Communications
   B. Monitor Communications
   C. Plan Communications Management
   D. Monitor and Control Project Work

3. The documentation of a project's successes and failures that is produced during the Manage Communications process and then saved for the benefit of other projects is called:
   A. Lessons learned
   B. Status reports
   C. Feedback
   D. Performance appraisals

4. The project manager wants to let the team know that the weekly project status report is now officially due by 4 p.m. on Thursdays. Which form of communication would be most appropriate in this situation?
   A. Formal written communication
   B. Formal verbal communication
   C. Informal written communication
   D. Informal verbal communication

5. Which of the following is not something you need in order to perform Monitor Communications?
   A. Project management plan
   B. Work performance reports
   C. Your firm's procedures, reporting formats, and standards for communication
   D. Issue log

6. Which of the following are all reporting tools used in Manage Communications?
   A. Status reports, quality reports, and lessons learned documentation
   B. Trend reports, forecasting reports, and lessons learned documentation
   C. Payroll reports, status reports, and trend reports
   D. Forecasting reports, payroll reports, and quality reports

7. A report that is focused on predicting future project status and performance is called a:
   A. Forecasting report
   B. Trend report
   C. Status report
   D. Variance report

8. What is one of the most important things for a project manager to keep in mind when developing a plan for project communications activities?
   A. Communication skills are most important during project executing.
   B. The receiver is responsible for making sure communications are clear.
   C. Only the team members need to be concerned about communicating with each other.
   D. The plan should be based on the information needs of stakeholders and on the needs of the project.

9. Change requests are an output of which communications management process?
   A. Manage Communications
   B. Define Communications
   C. Monitor Communications
   D. Plan Communications Management

10. A team of seven people adds two more people to the team. How many communication channels are there now?
    A. 9
    B. 36
    C. 18
    D. 81

11. If the team is analyzing communication requirements and assessing communication models, technology, and methods, which process are they engaged in?
    A. Manage Stakeholder Engagement
    B. Plan Communications Management
    C. Monitor Communications
    D. Manage Communication

12. Which of the following should the project manager be doing as part of Manage Communications?
    A. Preparing and distributing work performance reports
    B. Updating the issue log
    C. Providing opportunities for stakeholders to request additional information
    D. Analyzing communication requirements

13. During Monitor Communications, the project manager will need to rely on metrics established in the communications management plan, as well as _____, to determine if communication is breaking down on the project.
    A. Parametric estimating
    B. Soft skills
    C. Decision tree analysis
    D. Affinity diagrams

14. Which of the following is an example of push communication?
    A. A blog post
    B. A sales meeting
    C. Videoconferencing
    D. An interview

15. Three additional people have been added to the project team. What does the project manager need to keep in mind in terms of project communications?
    A. The number of communication channels on the project will increase by six.
    B. The number of communication channels on the project will triple.
    C. The communication needs of a project grow rapidly with each additional stakeholder.
    D. A formal written introduction should be sent to the existing members of the project team.

Answers

1. **Answer** B
   Explanation The stakeholder register is the only option listed that is an input to Plan Communications Management. Project communications are an output of Manage Communications. Work performance reports and forecasts are inputs to Monitor and Control Project Work.

2. **Answer** B
   Explanation Monitor Communications is the process of assessing how communications are going throughout the project to ensure that the right information is getting to the right people, at the right time, and in the right way—with the goal of keeping stakeholders informed and maintaining the desired levels of stakeholder engagement.

3. **Answer** A
   Explanation The documentation of a project's successes and failures produced during the Manage Communications process is saved as lessons learned so that other projects can benefit from it.

4. **Answer** C
   Explanation While it is important that the project manager document the change in reporting requirements in writing to be sure that everyone gets the message, this situation does not require formal communication. Email—the most likely form of communication in this scenario—is a type of informal written communication.

5. **Answer** B
   Explanation Procedures, reporting formats, and standards for communication are among the organizational process assets that serve as inputs to the Monitor Communications process. The project management plan and the issue log are also inputs to this process. Work performance reports are an input to the Manage Communications process rather than the Monitor Communications process. (The inputs to this process do include work performance data.)

6. **Answer** B
   Explanation Several types of reports are used in the Manage Communication process. In addition to trend reports, forecasting reports, and lessons learned documentation, other commonly used project reports include status reports, progress reports, variance reports, and earned value reports.

7. **Answer** A
   Explanation The key word here is "future." The only choice offered that looks to the future is a forecasting report. A trend report looks at past performance over time. A status report is generally static (relating to a moment in time). A variance report looks at specific project items or activities.

8. **Answer** D
   Explanation To develop an effective communications plan for a project, the project manager must ensure that it is based on the needs of the stakeholder and the project. The communications management plan should document those needs and detail a strategy for meeting them.

9. **Answer** C
   Explanation As an output of Monitor Communications, change requests may relate to changes in stakeholder communication requirements or communications procedures, among other things.

10. **Answer** B

    Explanation The formula for the number of communication channels is $[n \times (n-1)]/2$, where n equals the number of people communicating. Using that formula with the information from the question yields a calculation of $(9 \times 8)/2 = 36$.

11. **Answer** B

    Explanation The activities described here (communication requirements analysis and assessing the appropriate communication models, technology, and methods to use) are all part of developing the communications management plan.

12. **Answer** C

    Explanation Providing opportunities for stakeholders to request additional information is an important part of facilitating effective communication in the Manage Communications process. Work performance reports are outputs of the Monitor and Control Project Work process (and inputs to Manage Communications). Updating the issue log is done in Monitor Communications, not Manage Communications. Analyzing the communication requirements is part of the Plan Communications Management process.

13. **Answer** B

    Explanation Soft skills, such as conversation and observation, and the metrics established in the communications management plan help the project manager determine if communication is breaking down on the project.

14. **Answer** A

    Explanation Push communication is defined as a one-way stream of information from sender to receiver, without feedback. Of the examples listed here, only a blog post matches that description. Although a blogger might provide a comments section where readers could post their feedback, the blog post itself is a push communication artifact.

15. **Answer** C

    Explanation The formula for calculating the number of communication channels is $[n \times (n-1)]/2$; however, we can't use that formula here since we don't know what n is. Although an introduction to the existing members of the project team is a nice touch, that doesn't require formal written communication. What is true is that the communication needs of a project grow rapidly with each additional stakeholder.

Risk Management

E L E V E N

There are 12 questions on this knowledge area on the CAPM exam. Also note, for a full list of all inputs, tools and techniques, and outputs within this knowledge area, please see the table on page 396 in the PMBOK© *Guide.*

Let's start this chapter with a story. A project manager was working on a hardware/software installation in an area where hurricanes are a relatively frequent occurrence, when a hurricane struck during the project.

Not long after the hurricane was over, the project manager was telling people what a great job his team had done, and how quickly they had recovered from the disaster. Would you have been proud of yourself if you were the project manager? Before you answer, consider the following information:

- The activity the team was working on required three days to complete.
- The project manager had warning that the hurricane was coming.
- They had to recover from the disaster.

Instead of being excited about how quickly his team was able to recover from the hurricane, the project manager—and the sponsor—should have questioned the wisdom of scheduling the implementation at a time when there was a strong probability of a hurricane.

A project manager's work does not focus on dealing with problems—it focuses on preventing them. Had the project manager performed risk management on this project, he would have considered the threat of a hurricane and worked with his team as part of the project planning effort to identify possible actions to take if a hurricane was forecast for implementation weekend. Then, when one actually was forecast, the team could have reacted according to the plan, probably by moving the implementation to another weekend and avoiding the damage and rework that resulted from the disaster. This is the value of risk management.

QUICKTEST

- Risk management process
- Definition of risk management
- Threats
- Opportunities
- Risk register
- Risk report
- Risk management plan
- Risk response strategies
  - Avoid
  - Mitigate
  - Transfer
  - Exploit
  - Share
  - Enhance
  - Escalate
  - Accept
- Reserves (contingency)
- Reserve analysis
- Risk appetite
- Risk threshold
- Sensitivity analysis
- Risk audit
- Assumptions analysis
- Documentation reviews
- Probability and impact matrix
- Risk breakdown structure (RBS)
- Expected monetary value
- Contingency plans
- Fallback plans
- Workaround
- Risk owner
- Residual risks
- Secondary risks
- Risk categories
- Monte Carlo analysis
- SWOT analysis
- Checklist analysis
- Risk data quality assessment
- Decision tree
- Risk averse
- Risk factors
- Individual project risk
- Overall project risk

Risk Management ELEVEN

As you read this chapter, make sure you understand that there is a process to risk management. Also try to think about how a project manager would apply risk management throughout the life of a project. That will make it easier to remember the process as well as inputs and outputs. It will also help you discover topics that you do not understand.

As with other chapters in this book, let's look at the risk management process as a whole before we discuss the details. First, risk management must be planned before it's done. Next, the stakeholders help the project manager come up with a long list of all the possible risks for the project. This list is then analyzed subjectively to determine which risks warrant action. The lower-ranked risks are put on a watch list, and the higher risks are assessed quantitatively for their cost and schedule impacts, or moved directly into Plan Risk Responses. The team then reduces the overall risk of the project by implementing specific plans for what to do about the high-probability and high-impact risks. Finally, the overall risk performance of the project is measured and monitored.

Risk management is a process-oriented effort in which one step leads into the next. Therefore, as in many knowledge areas, an output of one process becomes an input to the next.

The following should help you understand how each part of risk management fits into the overall project management process.

If you would like additional training in risk management, please consider our eLearning courses—for more information, visit rmcls.com

The Risk Management Process	Done During
Plan Risk Management	Planning process group
Identify Risks	Planning process group
Perform Qualitative Risk Analysis	Planning process group
Perform Quantitative Risk Analysis	Planning process group
Plan Risk Responses	Planning process group
Implement Risk Responses	Executing process group
Monitor Risks	Monitoring and controlling process group

The Risk Management Process

It is very important to understand the risk management process for the exam. You must know what happens when and understand how risk management can change the way projects are managed. On large, properly managed projects where risk management has been an integral part of planning, the following occurs:

- There are no longer huge "fires" to put out every day—they are eliminated with risk response plans.
- Risks are reviewed in every meeting, triggers are monitored, and risks are addressed before they happen.
- Normally, if a risk event does occur, there is a plan in place to deal with it. Hectic meetings to develop responses are a rarity, and are only needed when an unknown risk event occurs and requires the development of a workaround.

As a result, the project manager has time for efforts such as:

- Monitoring and controlling the various aspects of the project, looking for deviations and trends to find them early
- Implementing a reward system
- Developing the team

- Keeping stakeholders informed of project progress
- Staying ahead of the project

The risk management process is iterative. Although the initiating and planning processes are usually done in sequence, they are repeated frequently during the course of a project. Risks can be identified at any time, as can responses to new risks. If a risk is uncovered after the initial risk identification process, it still must be analyzed, and responses must be planned.

Defining the Concepts

As you read this chapter, remember the basic, yet very important, concepts discussed next. Make sure you are prepared to deal with exam questions that test your knowledge of these concepts.

Risk Management

Risk management is the process of identifying, evaluating, and planning responses to events, both positive and negative, that might occur throughout the course of a project. Through risk management, a project manager can increase the probability and impact of opportunities on the project (positive events), while decreasing the probability and impact of threats to the project (negative events).

Risks are identified and managed starting in initiating and are kept up to date while the project is underway. The project manager and the team look at what has happened on the project, the current status of the project, and what is yet to come—and then reassess the potential threats and opportunities.

Also, given the iterative nature of project management, a response strategy for a newly discovered risk may create other project risks, which must be identified and managed. Be sure to prepare for exam questions that test your knowledge and understanding of these concepts.

Threats and Opportunities

A risk event is something identified in advance that may or may not happen. If it does happen, it can have positive or negative impacts on the project. Project managers often just focus on threats—what can go wrong and negatively impact the project. Don't forget that there can also be positive impacts—good risks, which are called opportunities. Some examples of opportunities include:

- If we can combine orders for the ZYX equipment to buy more than 20 items at once, the cost will be 20 percent less per item than planned.
- If we provide a training class to improve efficiency, work package number 3.4 could be completed two days faster than expected.
- If we can obtain a resource with more experience and a higher level of productivity in May, work on the critical path activity 4.7.2 could be done 10 percent faster.

Up to 90 percent of the threats identified and investigated in the risk management process can be eliminated by changing how the project work is planned and performed. Strategies such as using an adaptive life cycle, outsourcing some or all of the work, or selecting more skilled people within the organization to do the work may reduce risk on a project.

Uncertainty

Uncertainty is a lack of knowledge about an event that reduces our confidence in the conclusions we can draw from specific data. For example, the work that needs to be done, the cost, the time, the quality requirements, and the communication needs might be uncertain. The investigation of uncertainties can help identify risks.

Risk Factors
When assessing risk, it's necessary to determine the following:

- The probability that a risk event will occur (how likely it is)
- The range of possible outcomes (how much it will impact the project; the amount at stake)
- Expected timing for it to occur in the project life cycle (when it might take place)
- The anticipated frequency of risk events from that source (how often it might occur)

Risk Appetites and Thresholds
These terms refer to the level of risk an individual or group is willing to accept. Risk appetite (which is also referred to as risk tolerance) is a general, high-level description of the level of risk acceptable to an individual or an organization. For example, a sponsor is willing to accept little risk to the schedule on this project. Risk threshold refers to the specific point at which risk becomes unacceptable. For example, the sponsor will not accept a risk of the schedule being delayed 15 days or longer. Risk appetites and thresholds vary depending on the individual or organization and the risk area. For example, an organization may have more tolerance for cost-related risks than for risks that affect customer satisfaction or their reputation in the marketplace. Risk areas can include any project constraint (scope, schedule, cost, quality, etc.), as well as risks to reputation, customer satisfaction, and other intangibles.

Risk Averse
A stakeholder who does not want to be negatively impacted by threats is said to be *risk averse*.

Plan Risk Management PAGE 401

> **Process:** Plan Risk Management
> **Process Group:** Planning
> **Knowledge Area:** Risk Management

The project manager, sponsor, team, customer, other stakeholders, and experts may be involved in the Plan Risk Management process. They define how risk management will be structured and performed for the project. Since risk management is critical to the success of a project, a project manager should really think about how they will approach risk management. Ultimately, they should plan before they act. Part of that planning involves determining at a high level the amount and areas of potential risk on the project. Risk management efforts should be appropriate not only to the size and complexity of the project but also to the experience and skill of the project team. Successful risk management cannot be done with just a standardized checklist of risks from past projects. Although such a checklist can be helpful in creating a plan and identifying risks, the necessary risk management effort needs to be performed on each project.

The Plan Risk Management process answers the question of how much time should be spent on risk management based on the needs of the project. This includes the risk appetite of management and other key stakeholders. This process also identifies who will be involved and how the team will go about performing risk management. Organizational procedures and templates related to risk, such as standard probability and impact matrices, are identified as part of this process and then adapted to the needs of the project.

Inputs to Plan Risk Management PAGE 402
The following are the inputs to the Plan Risk Management process.

Project Management Plan The project management plan is an important input to this process, since it includes information about how risk management will be handled in relation to scope, schedule, cost, and so on.

© 2018 RMC Publications, Inc ™ • 952.846.4484 • info@rmcls.com • www.rmcls.com

Project Charter   The project charter indicates the initial high-level risks identified on the project and helps the project manager determine whether the overall project objectives and constraints are generally risky or not.

Stakeholder Register   Stakeholders will view the project from different perspectives and thus will be able to see risks that the team cannot. Stakeholders can be involved in many aspects of risk management.

Enterprise Environmental Factors   In order to plan the risk management effort, it is important to know the areas of risk the organization is willing to accept. This information will later help identify the impact of risks, the highest-ranked risks, and which risk response strategies will be used. It is also important to know the point at which risk becomes unacceptable in the organization.

Organizational Process Assets   For risk, organizational process assets include such things as company templates or procedures for risk management, such as standard probability and impact matrices. These are identified and adapted to the needs of the project. Historical records may include risks from previous, similar projects, including risk categories and formats for stating risks. Lessons learned from other projects can also be valuable in this planning process. In addition to helping plan risk management, these records can help identify, mitigate, and manage risks later in the project as well.

Outputs of Plan Risk Management   PAGE 405   When risk management planning is complete, a project manager should, of course, have a risk management plan.

Risk Management Plan   The risk management plan may include:

- **Risk strategy**   This is an overall approach to managing risk throughout the life of a project.

- **Methodology**   This section of the plan defines how risk management will be performed to meet the needs of a specific project. Low-priority projects will likely warrant less of a risk management effort than high-priority projects.

- **Roles and responsibilities**   This section explains who will do what risk management work. Did you realize that stakeholders outside the project team may have roles and responsibilities regarding risk management?

- **Funding**   This section includes the cost of the risk management process. Yes, there is a cost of doing risk management, but overall, risk management saves the project time and money by avoiding or reducing threats and taking advantage of opportunities. This section also includes a plan for utilizing reserves in response to risks on the project.

- **Timing**   This section of the plan talks about when to do risk management for the project. Risk management should start as soon as the project manager has the appropriate inputs and should be repeated throughout the life of the project, since new risks can be identified as the project progresses and the degree of risk can change over the course of a project. Also note that time needs to be allocated in the schedule for risk management activities.

- **Risk categories**   See the discussion of risk categories on the next page.

- **Stakeholder risk appetite/threshold**   Remember that risk appetite is a high-level description of an individual or group's openness to risk. Thresholds are the measurable amounts of risk that an individual or group is willing to accept within a specific category—such as risk to the project schedule, budget, or the achievement of a particular project objective. The risk appetites and thresholds of key stakeholders are documented and considered in the risk management plan. This information is also considered when ranking risks based on probability and impact, and when prioritizing which risks will be addressed in risk response planning.

- **Definitions of probability and impact**   Would everyone who rates the probability of a particular risk a 7 in qualitative risk analysis mean the same thing? A person who is risk averse might think of 7 as very high, while someone who is risk prone might think of 7 as a low figure. The definitions and the probability and impact matrix (discussed later in this chapter) help the project manager standardize these interpretations and compare risks between projects.

- **Reporting**   This section of the plan describes risk management reports that will be created on the project, what they will include, and to whom they will be sent. In addition, the composition of the risk register for the project is defined here.

- **Tracking**   The tracking section of the plan describes how the risk management process will be audited and how the results of risk management efforts will be documented.

Risk Categories   A standard list of risk categories can help ensure that no areas of risk are forgotten. These categories are broad, common areas or sources of risk that the company or similar projects have experienced. They can include things such as technology changes, lack of resources, regulatory hurdles, or cultural issues. Organizations and project management offices should maintain a standard list of risk categories that all project managers can use to help identify and group individual project risks. When leading risk identification efforts, a project manager should make sure each category is considered. A risk breakdown structure (RBS) is an organizational chart that can help you identify and document risk categories.

Risk can be classified or categorized in many ways, including:

- **External**   Regulatory, environmental, or governmental issues; market shifts; problems with project sites, etc.
- **Internal**   Changes to schedule or budget; scope changes; inexperienced team members; issues with people, staffing, materials, and equipment, etc.
- **Technical**   Changes in technology, technical processes, or interfaces, etc.
- **Commercial**   Customer stability, terms and conditions within contracts, vendors, etc.
- **Unforeseeable**   Only a small portion of risks (about 10 percent) are actually unforeseeable.

The following are additional examples of sources of risk:

- **Schedule**   "The hardware may arrive earlier than planned, allowing work package XYZ to start three days earlier."
- **Cost**   "Because the hardware may arrive later than planned, we may need to extend our lease on the staging area—at a cost of $20,000."
- **Quality**   "The concrete may dry to our quality standards before winter weather sets in, allowing us to start successor work packages earlier than planned."
- **Scope**   "We might not have correctly defined the scope for the computer installation. If that proves true, we will have to add work packages at a cost of $20,000."
- **Resources**   "Our designer may be called away to work on the new project everyone is so excited about. If that occurs, we will have to use someone else, and our schedule will slip between 100 and 275 hours."
- **Customer satisfaction (stakeholder satisfaction)**   "There is a chance the customer will be unhappy with the XYZ deliverable, and the resulting rework of the deliverable and test plans could increase the time required by at least a 20 percent."

Expect the phrases "sources of risk" and "risk categories" to be used interchangeably on the exam.

In addition to risk categories, risks can be classified under two main types:

- **Business risk**   Risk of a gain or loss
- **Pure (insurable) risk**   A risk of loss only (such as fire, theft, personal injury, etc.)

You may also see references to risks described as nonevent risks, which fall under the following categories:

- **Variability**   Risks caused by the inability to predict future changes
- **Ambiguity**   Risks caused by a lack of understanding

Identify Risks

> **Process:** Identify Risks
> **Process Group:** Planning
> **Knowledge Area:** Risk Management

In this process, risks to the project are identified. This effort should involve all stakeholders and might even include literature reviews, research, and communicating with nonstakeholders. Sometimes, the core team will begin the process and then other team members will become involved, or there could be a special, dedicated risk team—a part of the project team focused on risk management efforts.

If you get an exam question about who should be involved in risk identification, the best answer is "everyone"! Each stakeholder has a different perspective of the project and can provide thoughts on opportunities and threats.

Project managers should begin looking for risks as soon as a project is first discussed. In fact, an assessment of overall project risk is included in the project charter. However, the major risk identification effort occurs during planning. The project manager will need to have skills to facilitate the identification of all risks (or as many risks as reasonably possible).

Because risk identification primarily occurs during initiating and planning, most risk identification happens at the onset of a project. But keep in mind that smaller numbers of risks may also be identified later in the project. Risks should be continually reassessed. For the exam, understand that risk identification is done during integrated change control, when working with contracts, when working with resources, and when dealing with project issues.

Tools and Techniques of Identify Risks PAGE 414   The following section discusses some risk identification tools and techniques.

Brainstorming   Brainstorming is usually done in a meeting where one idea helps generate another. Tools such as the risk breakdown structure, risk categories, and prompt lists can help the group identify risks.

Checklist Analysis   Over time, organizations may compile a list of risks encountered on projects, which they review to help them identify relevant sources of risk for current projects. This technique also includes reviewing a checklist of generic risk categories, which is used to help identify specific risks to the project from each category.

Interviewing   Also called "expert interviewing" on the exam, this technique consists of the risk team or project manager interviewing project participants, stakeholders, or experts to identify risks to the overall project or to a specific element of work.

Root Cause Analysis   In root cause analysis, the identified risks are reorganized by their root causes to help identify more risks.

Assumption Analysis   Identifying and analyzing assumptions that have been made on the project, and whether those assumptions are valid, may lead to the identification of more risks.

Constraint Analysis   Constraints such as schedule or budget limitations are examined to determine the level of risk they pose.

Strengths, Weaknesses, Opportunities, and Threats (SWOT) Analysis   This analysis examines the project to identify its strengths and weaknesses, as well as the opportunities and threats that could originate from those strengths and weaknesses.

Documentation Reviews   What is and is not included in project documentation, such as the project charter, contracts, and planning documentation, can help identify risks. Those involved in risk identification might look at project documentation, as well as lessons learned, articles, and other sources, to help uncover risks.

Prompt Lists   This is a list of categories that have been identified as possible sources of risk to the project. The project team can use a prompt list when identifying risks to individual elements of the project as well as risks to the overall project.

Facilitation   Facilitation skills are used by the project manager in conducting meetings to identify individual and overall project risks. As a part of such a meeting, the project manager may use any of the other risk identification techniques discussed earlier in this section.

Outputs of Identify Risks PAGE 417   The Identify Risks process results in the creation of the risk register and the risk report.

Risk Register   Think of the risk register as one document for the entire risk management process that will be constantly updated with information as the risk management processes are completed. The risk register becomes part of the project documents and is included in historical records that will be used for future projects.

 TRICKS OF THE TRADE®   Notice that the risk register, including updates, is an output of several of the risk management processes. (The *PMBOK® Guide* lists the updated risk register under project documents updates.) Read exam questions carefully, and remember that the risk register contains different information at different points in the risk management process. For example, if the project has just started and you are in the Identify Risks process, the risk register will contain the identified risks and potential responses, not the response plans actually selected for the project, which come later.

© 2010 RMC Publications, Inc.™ • 952.952.9101 • info@rmcls.com • www.rmcls.com

At this point in the risk management process, the risk register includes:

- **List of risks**   Risks should be stated as clearly and specifically as possible using a cause-risk-effect format.

- **Potential risk owners**   This information is noted in the risk register as potential risk owners are identified.

- **Potential risk responses**   Although risk response planning occurs later, one of the things experienced risk managers know is that it is not always logical to separate the work of each part of risk management. There will be times when a response is identified at the same time as a risk. These potential responses should be added to the risk register as they are identified; they will be analyzed later as part of risk response planning.

- **Root causes of risks**   The root causes of risks provide valuable information for use in later efforts to plan risk responses and reassess risk on the project, and as historical records on future projects. Until the root cause of a risk is determined and addressed, it is likely to reoccur.

- **Updated risk categories**   You will notice a lot of places where historical records and company records are updated throughout the project management process. Make sure you are aware that documenting lessons learned and communicating information to other projects do not just happen at the end of the project. As part of the risk identification effort, the project provides feedback to the rest of the company regarding new categories of risk to add to the checklist.

Other information that can be documented in the risk register includes risk triggers, the potential impact of identified threats and opportunities, when each risk could occur, and when each risk will no longer present a threat or opportunity.

 A tricky question on the exam might ask, "When in the risk management process are risk responses documented?" The answer is both during Identify Risks (as potential responses) and during Plan Risk Responses (as selected response plans).

Risk Report   A risk report is generated and disseminated to stakeholders to keep them apprised of risk management efforts and outcomes. After the Identify Risks process, contents of the risk register would include an overview of information about the threats and opportunities that have been identified. Updated risk reports will be updates to the remaining risk management processes.

Perform Qualitative Risk Analysis   PAGE 419

> **Process:** Perform Qualitative Risk Analysis
> **Process Group:** Planning
> **Knowledge Area:** Risk Management

At the start of this process, the project manager should have a long list of risks documented in the risk register. But it would be too expensive, and it would take too much time, to plan responses to all these risks. The project manager will need to analyze the risks, including their probability and potential impact on the project, to determine which ones warrant a response. The Perform Qualitative Risk Analysis process involves doing this analysis and creating a shortened list of the previously identified individual project risks. The risks on this list may then be further analyzed in the Perform Quantitative Risk Analysis process, or they may move into the Plan Risk Responses process.

Qualitative risk analysis can be used to do the following:

- Compare the risk of the project to the overall risk of other projects.
- Determine whether the project should be continued or terminated.
- Determine whether to proceed to the Perform Quantitative Risk Analysis process or the Plan Risk Responses process (depending on the needs of the project and the performing organization).

Inputs to Perform Qualitative Risk Analysis PAGE 421   The risk register and the risk management plan are key inputs to Perform Qualitative Risk Analysis that you should know for the exam. Additional project documents that may be used as inputs to this process include the assumption log and the stakeholder register.

Risk Register   One of the primary inputs to this process is the risk register, which at this point in the project includes the list of risks that will need to be assessed in order to perform qualitative risk analysis.

Risk Management Plan   The risk management plan, a component of the project management plan, is also a key input to this process. The project manager can use information such as who will be responsible for what role within the risk management effort, what risk categories exist for the project, and how much money has been allocated to risk management. Additional information may include the schedule for any risk-related activities, the definitions of probability and impact along with the probability and impact matrix, and any risk thresholds.

What if some of the above information isn't available to a project manager? Will the project fail? The answer is no. If the project manager properly plans according to the needs and size of the project, then the project is more likely to be successful. It is important to remember that all project management efforts must be tailored to fit a given project. For the exam, however, you should have only large projects in mind when answering questions, unless otherwise stated.

Tools and Techniques of Perform Qualitative Risk Analysis PAGE 422   The key tools and techniques that can be used in Perform Qualitative Risk Analysis include the following.

Data Analysis   Data analysis techniques that may be used as part of the Perform Qualitative Risk Analysis process include an assessment of other risk parameters, a risk probability and impact assessment, and a risk data quality assessment.

Risk Data Quality Assessment   Before a project manager can use the risk information collected on the project, they must analyze the precision of the data. The project manager will need to assess the accuracy and reliability of the data, determine if the risk is valid, and decide whether more research is needed to understand the risk. Imagine, for example, a risk given to a project manager anonymously. They might allow anonymous contributions during risk identification, but all the identified risks must be defined well enough to perform a qualitative assessment.

A risk data quality assessment may include determining the following for each risk:

- Extent of the understanding of the risk
- Data available about the risk
- Quality of the data
- Reliability and integrity of the data

Risk Parameters Assessment   In addition to creating a short list of risks, qualitative risk analysis includes identifying risks that should move more quickly through the process than others, due to factors that are referred to as risk parameters. Some examples of risk parameters include the following:

- **Urgency**   The urgency parameter indicates if the risk is likely to occur soon or if it requires a particularly long time to plan a response.
- **Dormancy**   Dormancy refers to the anticipated time between when a risk occurs and when its impact is felt on the project.
- **Manageability and controllability**   The manageability and controllability parameter indicates the level of difficulty involved in dealing with an identified risk.
- **Strategic impact**   Strategic impact refers to the degree to which the occurrence of a risk would affect the strategic goals of the performing organization.

Risk Probability and Impact Assessment   Remember that qualitative risk analysis is a subjective analysis of the risks identified in the risk register. Keep in mind that this process is repeated as new risks are uncovered throughout the project.

To perform this analysis, the following must be determined:

- The probability of each risk occurring, using a standard scale; common subjective analysis scales include "Low, Medium, High" and "1 to 10"
- The impact (the amount at stake or the positive or negative consequences) of each risk occurring, using a standard scale, such as "Low, Medium, High" or "1 to 10"

Data Representation   Data representation techniques can be used to perform qualitative risk analysis. These techniques may include hierarchical charts and probability and impact matrices.

Probability and Impact Matrix   Because qualitative risk analysis is based on subjective evaluation, the rating of any one risk can vary depending on the bias of the person doing the rating and how risk averse they are. For example, one person's score of 3 might be another person's 7. Therefore, organizations frequently have a standard rating system to promote a common understanding of what each risk rating means. This standard is shown in a probability and impact matrix.

The probability and impact matrix may be used to sort or rate risks to determine which warrant an immediate response (and will therefore be moved on through the risk process) and which should be put on the watch list (described later). The matrix may be standardized for the company or department, or it may be customized to the needs of the project. Such a matrix results in a consistent evaluation of low, medium, or high (or some other scale) for the project (or all projects). Use of a standardized matrix makes the risk rating process more consistent across projects.

Risk Categorization   Risk categorization examines the question "What will we find if we regroup the risks by categories?" For example, risks might be grouped by source or by work package. Think about how useful it would be to have not only a subjective assessment of the total amount of risk on the project, but also a breakdown of the risks that shows which work packages, processes, people, or other potential causes have the most risk associated with them. Such data will be helpful in risk response planning, potentially allowing the project manager to eliminate many risks at once by eliminating one cause. Risk categories and sources of risks can be organized in a risk breakdown structure.

Outputs of Perform Qualitative Risk Analysis PAGE 427   Projects documents updates are the output of the Perform Qualitative Risk Analysis process.

Project Documents Updates

The updates to project documents that result from Perform Qualitative Risk Analysis may include the risk register, assumption log, issue log, and risk report. Some examples are discussed in the following sections.

Assumption Log

Assumption log updates, or updates to the assumptions in the project scope statement, include new information or clarifications about the project's documented assumptions and constraints.

Issue Log

The issue log should be updated to include any new issues or changes to the issues that have already been included in the log.

Risk Register

The risk register should be updated to add the results of qualitative risk analysis, including:

- **Risk ranking for the project compared to other projects**   Qualitative risk analysis can lead to a number to be used to rank the project in comparison to other projects.
- **List of prioritized risks and their probability and impact ratings**
- **Results of other risk parameter assessments**
- **Risks grouped by categories**
- **List of risks for additional analysis and response**   These are the risks that will move forward into quantitative risk analysis and, potentially, into risk response planning.
- **List of risks requiring additional analysis in the near term**
- **Watch list (noncritical risks)**   These risks are documented in the risk register for observation or later review.

Risk Report

At the end of this process, the risk report includes the results of risk prioritization and a list of the highest-ranking risks.

Perform Quantitative Risk Analysis PAGE 428

> **Process:** Perform Quantitative Risk Analysis
> **Process Group:** Planning
> **Knowledge Area:** Risk Management

The Perform Quantitative Risk Analysis process involves numerically analyzing the probability and impact (the amount at stake or the consequences) of the risks that were ranked highest in qualitative risk analysis. Quantitative risk analysis also looks at how risks could affect the objectives of the project. The purpose of quantitative risk analysis is to:

- Determine which risk events warrant a response.
- Determine overall project risk (risk exposure).
- Determine the quantified probability of meeting the project objectives (for example, "We have an 80 percent chance of completing the project within the six months required by the customer," or "We have a 75 percent chance of completing the project within the $80,000 budget.").
- Determine cost and schedule reserves.
- Identify risks requiring the most attention.
- Create realistic and achievable cost, schedule, or scope targets.

TRICKS OF THE TRADE®   Many people confuse qualitative and quantitative risk analysis. Remember that qualitative risk analysis is a subjective evaluation, even though numbers are used for the rating. In contrast, quantitative risk analysis is a more objective or numerical evaluation; the rating of each risk is based on an estimate of the actual probability and amount at stake (the risk's impact). Therefore, while the rating for a risk in qualitative risk analysis might be a 5, in quantitative risk analysis that same risk might be determined to have a $40,000 cost impact.

The project manager should always do qualitative risk analysis. Quantitative risk analysis is not required for all projects or all risks. It may be skipped in favor of moving on to risk response planning. The project manager should proceed with quantitative risk analysis only if it's worth the time and money. For some projects, the project manager may have a subset of risks identified that require further quantitative analysis. But why spend time quantitatively assessing risks for a low-priority or short-term project, or when the effort will provide minimal return?

Inputs to Perform Quantitative Risk Analysis PAGE 430   Inputs to the Perform
Quantitative Risk Analysis process may include the risk management plan, a component of the project management plan. The risk management plan should indicate whether quantitative risk analysis will need to be performed.

The assumption log, another input to this process, may also be reviewed to determine any assumptions or constraints that have the potential to add a degree of risk that warrants quantitative analysis.

Also note that project estimates and forecasts include milestones that must be achieved. If there is a risk that any of these are unrealistic, or if there is uncertainty that they will be able to be met, that risk may be analyzed in this process. Lastly, the risk register and risk reports include identified risks and the results of qualitative analysis of those risks. The risks with the highest probabilities and impacts are likely to require quantitative assessment.

Tools and Techniques of Perform Quantitative Risk Analysis PAGE 431   Any of
the following techniques can be used to determine quantitative probability and impact.

- Expert judgment from trained risk specialists and team members
- Data gathering techniques, such as interviewing
- Data analysis techniques, such as simulations (like Monte Carlo), sensitivity analysis, decision tree analysis, and influence diagrams
- Interpersonal and team skills
- Representations of uncertainty
- Cost and schedule estimating
- Use of historical records from previous projects

Simulations   What would happen if a project manager could prove to the sponsor that even if the project were to be done 5,000 times, there is only a low probability that the end date they desire would be met? Would this be valuable? This is what the results of simulation techniques such as Monte Carlo analysis can show us. A Monte Carlo analysis uses the network diagram and schedule or cost estimates to "perform" the project many times and simulate its cost or schedule results.

Sensitivity Analysis   Sensitivity analysis is a technique used to analyze and compare the potential impacts of identified risks. A tornado diagram may be used to graphically depict the results of this analysis. Risks are represented by horizontal bars. The longest and uppermost bar represents the greatest risk, and progressively shorter horizontal bars beneath it represent lower-ranked risks. The resulting graphic resembles a funnel cloud or tornado. Figure 11.1 depicts a tornado diagram representing the impact of the threats and opportunities for the milestones involved in the installation of a new computer system.

Risk Management ELEVEN

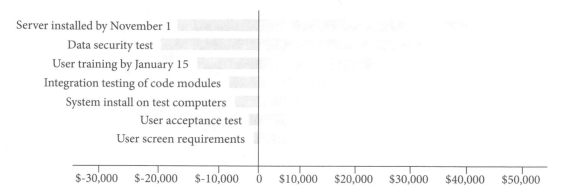

Figure 11.1 Tornado diagram

Decision Tree Analysis   If a project manager has to choose between many alternatives, they should analyze how each choice benefits or hurts the project before making the decision. Decision trees can help with this type of analysis. They are models of real situations that project managers use to make an informed decision about things like, "Which option should I choose?" or "How will I solve this problem?" by taking into account the associated risks, probabilities, and impacts.

There may be a question about decision trees on the exam. You should know what a decision tree is and be able to calculate a simple one from the data given in an exam question. The exam could also ask you to calculate the expected monetary value for cost, the expected value (or just "value") for the schedule of a path, or the value of your decision.

Make sure you understand that a decision tree is analyzed by calculating the value of each branch. The outcome of this calculation will show the best option to select. Let's quickly go through this value calculation.

To evaluate a risk, you can look at the probability or the impact, but the expected value is a better measure to determine an overall ranking of risks. The formula for expected value is simply probability (P) multiplied by impact (I). The calculation for schedule results in the expected value (EV, not to be confused with Earned Value). Expected monetary value (EMV) is used for cost.

$$EMV = P \times I$$

A question on the exam might ask, "What is the expected monetary value of the following?" Expected monetary value can also appear in questions that deal with decision trees and calculating contingency reserves (both described later in this chapter).

Exercise

Don't think of this as another formula you need to memorize—it's too easy. Test yourself! Complete the following chart, and you will understand this calculation for the exam without memorization.

Work Package	Probability	Impact	Expected Monetary Value
A	10%	$20,000	
B	30%	$45,000	
C	68%	$18,000	

© 2019 RMC Publications, Inc.™ • 952.846.4484 • info@rmcls.com • www.rmcls.com

Answer

See the answers in the following table.

Work Package	Probability	Impact	Expected Monetary Value
A	10%	$20,000	$2,000
B	30%	$45,000	$13,500
C	68%	$18,000	$12,240

Note that for opportunities, expected monetary value is often presented as a positive amount (e.g., $3,000), whereas threats are usually presented as a negative number (e.g., –$3,000).

The calculation of expected value is performed during quantitative risk analysis and revised during risk response planning when calculating contingency reserves for schedule and costs.

You should also know the following about decision trees for the exam:

- A decision tree takes into account future events in making a decision today.
- It calculates the expected value (probability multiplied by impact) in more complex situations than the expected monetary value example previously presented. With a decision tree, you could evaluate the costs (or schedule implications) and benefits of several risk responses at once to determine which one is the best option.
- It involves mutual exclusivity (previously explained in the Quality Management chapter).

Outputs of Perform Quantitative Risk Analysis PAGE 436   The Perform Quantitative Risk Analysis process results in updates to the risk register and other project documents.

Risk Register Updates   The risk register and the risk report are updated to add the results of quantitative risk analysis, including:

- **Prioritized list of quantified individual project risks**   What risks are most likely to cause trouble in terms of their effect on the critical path? What risks need the most contingency reserve?
- **Quantified probability of meeting project objectives**   For example, "We only have an 80 percent chance of completing the project within the six months required by the customer." Or, "We only have a 75 percent chance of completing the project within the $800,000 budget."
- **Trends in quantitative risk analysis**   As a project manager repeats quantitative risk analysis during project planning and when changes are proposed, they can track changes to the overall risk profile of the project and see any trends.
- **Initial contingency time and cost reserves needed**   For example, "The project requires an additional $50,000 and two months of time to accommodate the risks on the project." Reserves will be finalized during Plan Risk Responses.
- **Assessment of overall project risk exposure**   Use overall project success (how likely it is that the project will achieve all key objectives) and any variables that may still affect the project to fully understand, at a high level, the overall risk exposure of the project.
- **Possible realistic and achievable completion dates and project costs, with confidence levels, versus the time and cost objectives for the project**   For example, "We are 95 percent confident that we can complete this project by May 25th for $989,000."
- **Recommended risk responses**   After quantitative risk analysis is performed, the risk register may include suggested responses to overall project risks and individual project risks.

Plan Risk Responses PAGE 437

The Plan Risk Responses process involves figuring out, "What are we going to do about each top risk?" In risk response planning, the project manager will need to find ways to reduce or eliminate threats and make opportunities more likely to occur (or increase their impact). The project's risk responses may include doing one or a combination of the following for each top risk.

- Do something to eliminate the threats before they happen.
- Do something to make sure the opportunities happen.
- Decrease the probability or impact of threats.
- Increase the probability or impact of opportunities.

For the remaining (residual) threats that cannot be eliminated:

- Do something if the risk happens (contingency plans). Contingency plans should be measurable so the project manager can evaluate their effectiveness.
- Do something if contingency plans are not effective or are only partially effective (fallback plans).

Stop here for a moment and think about what was just described. To pass the exam, you will need to be able to envision a world that is not a reality for every project manager; you need to envision a world in which proper risk management is done. Think about the power of risk response planning. The project manager eliminates problems (threats) while still in the planning process of their project. Had they not been eliminated, these problems could have caused stress, delays, or added cost to the project. Can you see the value of such efforts?

This is what risk management is all about. If a change to a team member's availability is a top risk, the project manager can investigate the possibility of replacing that team member with another team member who has similar skills. If a work package is causing a large amount of risk, the project manager might look at changing the deliverable, modifying the work to produce it, or removing scope from the project. There are always options to respond to risks.

Risk management goes further than the examples just described, however. In addition to avoiding or exploiting risks, the project manager and the team determine what to do about each of the residual risks (those that cannot be eliminated or exploited through risk response strategies). This might mean accepting these residual risks or planning additional risk responses. The project manager then assigns the work involved in the responses to risk owners—individuals who watch out for the occurrence of a risk and implement preplanned responses.

Inputs to Plan Risk Responses PAGE 439   The primary input to this process is the project risk register. It has been updated throughout the risk management process, and now includes a list of risks that have been qualitatively (and possibly quantitatively) analyzed. The risks have been prioritized based on their probability and impact, among other factors. These are the risks for which responses will be planned. Another important input to this process is the cost baseline, which describes the contingency reserve that will be used in addressing identified risks. (See the discussion of reserves later in this chapter.)

Tools and Techniques of Plan Risk Responses PAGE 441   Expert judgment, interviewing, facilitation, data analysis, and multicriteria decision analysis can all be used to plan risk responses. Additional tools and techniques may include the following risk response strategies.

- Strategies for threats
- Strategies for opportunities

- Contingent response strategies
- Strategies for overall project risk

Risk Response Strategies   When completing risk response planning, a thorough analysis must be done of the potential responses for each risk. The team, guided by the risk owner, may uncover many strategies for dealing with risks. Some of these risk response strategies, also known as risk mitigation strategies or strategies for threats and opportunities, involve changing the planned approach to completing the project, such as changes to the WBS, quality management plan, resources, communications, schedule, or budget. Other strategies, called contingency plans, involve coming up with a plan to be implemented when and if a risk occurs.

For threats, the choices of response strategies include:

- **Avoid**   Eliminate the threat by eliminating the cause, such as removing the work package or changing the person assigned to do work. Avoiding the threat might even involve expanding the scope of the project. Imagine, for example, that a project team estimates there is a 75 percent likelihood of a threat occurring, but an additional level of testing or an additional activity would likely prevent this threat; expanding the scope of the project in this way would help avoid the threat.

  On an overall project level, if the threat is beyond the organization's risk threshold, the project manager will need to take action to make the project acceptable. This could include removing pieces of the project that are too risky in order to avoid cancelling the entire project.

- **Mitigate**   Reduce the probability or impact of an individual or overall project threat, thereby making it a smaller risk and possibly removing it from the list of top risks on the project. Options for reducing the probability are considered separately from options for reducing the impact. Any reduction will make a difference, but the option with the most probability or impact reduction is often the option selected.

- **Transfer (deflect, allocate)**   Make a party outside the project responsible for the threat by purchasing insurance, performance bonds, warranties, or guarantees, or by outsourcing the work. Here is where the strong connection between risk and procurement (contracts) begins. In the world of properly practiced project management, risk analysis is completed before a contract is signed, and transference of risk is included in the terms and conditions of the contract.

Avoidance and mitigation are generally used for high-priority, high-impact risks. Transference, escalation (discussed below), and acceptance (also discussed below) may be appropriate for low-priority, low-impact risks as well as those with higher impact.

One response to pure risks—such as fire, property damage, or personal injury—is to purchase insurance. Insurance exchanges an unknown cost impact of a known risk for a known cost impact. In the example of a risk of fire, the cost impact of the risk is unknown, depending on the extent of the fire. But when insurance is purchased, the cost impact of the risk becomes known—it is the cost of the insurance and the deductible. Transferring the risk by purchasing insurance does not eliminate all impacts. There may still be residual risks. For example, a project could experience schedule delays due to a fire even if fire insurance was purchased, or the cost of damage caused by the fire could exceed the amount of insurance purchased.

Transferring a risk will also leave some risk behind. For example, there is a risk that if the third party has trouble, they could cause a schedule delay. At that point, the project manager will need to decide what to do about any such secondary risks.

For opportunities, the choices of response strategies include:

- **Exploit (the reverse of avoid)**   Add change or work to the project to make sure the opportunity occurs. This could be on the individual project risk level or on the overall project risk level.

- **Enhance (the reverse of mitigate)**   Increase the likelihood (probability) or positive impact of the opportunity. This could be related to the overall approach to scope and schedule, resources used, and project replanning, as well as to individual project risks.

- **Share**   Allocate ownership or partial ownership of the individual or overall project opportunity to a third party (forming a partnership, team, or joint venture) that is best able to achieve the opportunity.

For both threats and opportunities, the potential response strategies include:

- **Escalate**   A threat or an opportunity should be escalated if it is outside the scope of the project or beyond the project manager's authority. Any risks that are escalated will typically be managed at the program or portfolio level—not at the project level. Remember that escalated risk needs to be accepted by the program or portfolio manager, at which point, data on the escalation is documented, and the risk is no longer monitored at the project level.

- **Accept**   Passive acceptance means to do nothing and essentially say, "If it happens, it happens." This leaves actions to be determined as needed if the risk occurs (workarounds). Active acceptance involves creating contingency plans to be implemented if the risk occurs and allocating time and cost reserves to the project.

Whether responding to threats or opportunities:

- The strategy must be timely (implemented at the right time).
- The effort selected must be appropriate to the severity of the risk—a project manager should avoid spending more money to prevent a risk than its expected impact.
- One response can be used to address more than one risk.
- More than one response can be used to address the same risk.
- A response can address the root cause of risk and thereby address more than one risk.
- The team, other stakeholders, and experts should be involved in selecting a strategy.

Watch for questions on the exam about communicating risk-related information. The risk response strategies must be communicated to the sponsor, management, and stakeholders. These parties will need to know that the project manager is in control of the project even if there is a problem, and they may need to approve the resources to make the risk response strategies happen. Communicating about risk is essential for gaining buy-in to the strategy.

Exercise

Now let's see if you can apply what you have learned. Identify the type of risk response strategy being described. The options are to avoid, mitigate the probability, mitigate the impact, transfer, exploit, enhance the probability, enhance the impact, share, escalate or accept.

	Description	Risk Response Strategy
1	Remove a work package or activity from the project.	
2	Assign a team member to frequently visit the seller's manufacturing facilities to learn about problems with deliveries as early as possible.	
3	Move a work package to a date when a more experienced resource is available to be assigned to the project.	
4	Begin negotiation for the equipment earlier than planned to secure a lower price.	

	Description	Risk Response Strategy
5	Outsource a work package to gain an opportunity.	
6	Notify management that there could be a cost increase if a risk occurs because no action is being taken to prevent the risk.	
7	Remove a troublesome resource from the project.	
8	Provide a team member who has limited experience with additional training.	
9	Train the team in conflict resolution strategies.	
10	Outsource difficult work to a more experienced company.	
11	Ask the client to handle some of the work.	
12	Prototype a risky piece of equipment.	
13	Notify the PMO that the testing software needed for the project could be used by three other IT groups if the enterprise solution is purchased.	

Answer

	Description	Risk Response Strategy
1	Remove a work package or activity from the project.	Avoid
2	Assign a team member to frequently visit the seller's manufacturing facilities to learn about problems with deliveries as early as possible.	Mitigate the impact
3	Move a work package to a date when a more experienced resource is available to be assigned to the project.	Exploit
4	Begin negotiation for the equipment earlier than planned to secure a lower price.	Enhance the impact
5	Outsource a work package to gain an opportunity.	Share
6	Notify management that there could be a cost increase if a risk occurs because no action is being taken to prevent the risk.	Accept
7	Remove a troublesome resource from the project.	Avoid
8	Provide a team member who has limited experience with additional training.	Mitigate the probability
9	Train the team in conflict resolution strategies.	Mitigate the impact
10	Outsource difficult work to a more experienced company.	Transfer
11	Ask the client to handle some of the work.	Transfer
12	Prototype a risky piece of equipment.	Mitigate the probability
13	Notify the PMO that the testing software for the project could be used by three other IT groups if the enterprise solution is purchased.	Escalate

TRICKS OF THE TRADE® Potential risk response strategies and contingency plans must be analyzed to determine which strategy or strategies are most cost-effective and most likely to address the risk. Cost-benefit analysis and multicriteria decision analysis are techniques for evaluating and ranking potential risk responses.

Outputs of Plan Risk Responses PAGE 447   The outputs of the Plan Risk Responses
process are change requests, updates to the project management plan, and project documents updates.

Project Management Plan Updates   The efforts spent in risk management can result in updates to the
project management plan. After careful consideration and evaluation, planned risk responses may require
changes to the management plans that were drafted in planning, to address either the overall project risk
or individual project risks, or both. Spend a moment now and think about how risk response planning
might lead to adjustments to the schedule, cost, quality, procurement, communications, and resource
management plans, as well as to the scope, schedule, and cost baselines for the project. This concept is
critical for understanding the impact risk management has on projects.

Project Documents Updates   Other documents a project manager has created to help manage the
project may also change as a result of risk response planning. These documents may include the assumption
log, cost forecasts, the lessons learned register, the project schedule, project team assignments, the risk
register, and the risk report. The risk report is updated to communicate the risks of greatest threat or
opportunity, the overall project risk exposure, and the outcomes of planning related to risk responses
and any anticipated changes. Can you imagine how risk response planning might affect the roles and
responsibilities on a project, including the stakeholder management strategy or quality metrics?

Risk Register Updates   The risk register is updated to add the results of risk response planning, including
the following.

- **Residual risks**   These are the risks that remain after risk response planning. After the project
  manager avoids, exploits, mitigates, enhances, transfers, shares, escalates, and accepts risks
  (and creates related contingency plans and fallback plans), there will still be risks that remain. Those
  residual risks that are passively accepted should be properly documented and reviewed throughout
  the project to see if their ranking has changed.

- **Contingency plans**   Contingency plans describe the specific actions that will be taken if an
  opportunity or threat occurs.

- **Fallback plans**   Fallback plans outline the specific actions that will be taken if the contingency
  plans are not effective. Think how prepared a project manager would feel if they have plans for what
  to do if a risk occurs, and also what to do if the original plan does not work.

- **Risk owners**   A key concept in risk response planning is that the project manager does not
  have to do it all, and neither does the team. Each risk must be assigned to someone who will help
  lead the development of the risk response and carry out the risk response, or "own" the risk. The
  risk owner can be a stakeholder other than a team member. Think about how the application
  of risk management could change real-world projects. The risk occurs; the risk owner takes the
  preapproved action determined in project planning and informs the project manager. No meeting
  is needed—just action! This can be very powerful.

- **Secondary risks**   Any new risks created by the implementation of selected risk responses should
  also be analyzed as part of risk response planning. Frequently, a response to one risk will create
  the possibility of new risks that would otherwise not have occurred. For example, if a portion of
  the project work is outsourced to a seller because the project team does not have the expertise to
  complete the work efficiently, there may be a secondary risk of the seller going out of business. This
  was not a risk to the project prior to outsourcing. The discovery of secondary risks may require
  additional risk response planning.

- **Risk triggers**   These are events that trigger the contingency response. The early warning signs for
  each risk on a project should be identified so risk owners know when to take action.

- **Contracts**   Before a contract is finalized, the project manager should have completed a risk analysis and included contract terms and conditions required to mitigate threats and enhance opportunities. Any contracts issued to deal with risks should be noted in the risk register.

- **Reserves (contingency)**   Having reserves for time and cost is a required part of project management. A project manager cannot come up with a schedule or budget for the project without them.

Reserves are covered in the Cost Management chapter, but let's look at them again here.

Time and cost each have two types of reserves—contingency reserves and management reserves. Contingency reserves account for "known unknowns" (or simply "knowns"); these are items the project manager identified in risk management. Management reserves account for "unknown unknowns" (or simply "unknowns"); these are items the project manager did not or could not identify in risk management. Projects can have both kinds of reserves. As shown in the diagram in figure 11.2 (also shown in the Cost Management chapter), contingency reserves are calculated and become part of the cost baseline. Management reserves are estimated (for example, 5 percent of the project cost), and then these reserves are added to the cost baseline to get the project budget. The project manager has control of the cost baseline and can approve the use of the contingency reserves, but management approval is needed to use management reserves. The same applies to reserves in the schedule.

Make sure you understand that reserves are not an additional cost to a project. The risk management process should result in a decrease to the project's estimated time and cost. As threats are eliminated or their probability or impact reduced, there should be a reduction to the project's schedule and budget. Contingency reserves are allocated for the contingency plans and fallback plans to deal with the accepted opportunities and threats that remain after the risk management planning processes have been completed. No matter what, risks will remain in the project, and there should be a time or cost allotment for them, just as time or cost is allotted to work activities on the project.

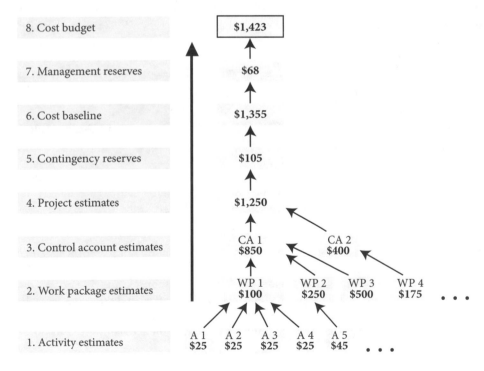

Figure 11.2 Creating a budget

Implement Risk Responses PAGE 449

Process: Implement Risk Responses
Process Group: Executing
Knowledge Area: Risk Management

While implementing risk responses is a new process for the sixth edition of the *PMBOK® Guide*, it isn't new for risk management. Although it wasn't previously called out as a separate process, it is really the heart of risk management, and where the value of proper risk management becomes most apparent. When the preliminary work has been done well, the Implement Risk Responses process can be handled smoothly, since the previously documented plans allow for timely and effective responses to risk events.

Inputs to Implement Risk Responses PAGE 450
The key to success is identifying risks in advance, and then planning and preparing for their potential occurrence. Lessons learned from the current project or past, similar projects provide insight into the success of previous response plans, and valuable input to this process.

Throughout the project, the risk register and risk report are reviewed regularly, ensuring everyone is aware of potential risks and ready to implement the planned responses as needed. Information on triggers enables the project manager, the risk owner, and the team to recognize indications that a risk event is imminent. At that point, the risk owner, supported by the project manager, leads previously assigned resources in performing response activities. The consequences of threats are averted, or opportunities are taken advantage of. Risk thresholds are documented in the plan along with an indication of how much relief is required from risk responses, so that the success of the implementation can be evaluated.

The beginning of this chapter included the story of a project manager who was managing a hardware/software installation during a hurricane. Let's revisit that example.

If the project manager had performed proper risk management, he would have had a plan in place to avoid the risk of a hurricane impacting his project. For example, the scheduled implementation could have been moved to before or after the forecasted hurricane. If the project manager and the risk owners had actively monitored known risk triggers (such as weather reports, including wind speeds and the projected path of the hurricane) and then implemented a risk response plan before the hurricane reached the area, they could have successfully avoided the rework and delays, along with the costs, resulting from the hurricane. Such preparation is critical to successfully implementing a risk response.

Outputs of Implement Risk Responses PAGE 451
Even though we do our best, sometimes our carefully developed plans don't have the expected result. For example, let's assume that a risk owner or the project manager in the previous story implemented a risk response plan to reschedule the implementation, causing the schedule to be extended. Although the plan was executed as intended, the hurricane caused more damage than anticipated, and the schedule had to be extended beyond the planned number of days. Such unforeseen results are managed through change requests to the cost and schedule management plans.

Project documents are updated as a result of the Implement Risk Responses process. The risk register and risk report are updated with information on responses taken, describing details on how well the responses addressed the risk, and suggesting changes to future risk response plans. The project manager adds information to the lessons learned register about what worked and what didn't work when the risk response was implemented. The risk report is updated with changes to the project's risk exposure and planned risk responses. Ongoing issues, such as confusion or disagreement regarding the response as it was implemented, are added to the issue log.

Monitor Risks PAGE 453

Process: Monitor Risks
Process Group: Monitoring & Controlling
Knowledge Area: Risk Management

Risk-related questions on the exam assume that the project manager
has done proper project management, including assigning risk owners, putting contingency plans in place,
and taking actions as outlined in the plan. The exam also assumes the project is substantially less risky
than it would have been if the project manager had not planned the project and properly handled risk
management. If you do not have experience using risk management in the real world, these exam questions
may be difficult. Review the following list of actions involved in the Monitor Risks process, as it will help
you understand what project management is like when it includes risk management.

Actions involved in monitoring risks:

- Look for the occurrence of risk triggers.

- Monitor residual risks.

- Identify new risks, then analyze and plan for them. (Remember, risks can be identified anytime
during the project, along with plans for how to handle the newly identified risks.)

- Evaluate the effectiveness of the risk management plan. Is it working? Does it need adjustment?

- Develop new risk responses. If a plan no longer seems like it will work, based on experience or new
information, an alternate risk response or responses may be more appropriate. This review and
analysis may lead to change requests.

- Collect and communicate risk status. (For example: "Four identified risks occurred last month, and
all risk response plans were implemented successfully. Next month eight other risks may occur. Risk
reserves are still considered adequate for covering the identified risks on this project.")

- Communicate with stakeholders about risks. (For example: "Remember that one of the major risks
on the project could occur next week.")

- Determine if assumptions are still valid.

- Ensure proper risk management procedures are being followed.

- Revisit the watch list to see if additional risk responses need to be determined. (For example: "This
change to the product scope might increase the impact of risk X, currently on our watch list. Let's
analyze it.")

- Recommend corrective actions to adapt based on the severity of the risk events that actually occur.
(For example: "This risk did not have the impact we expected, so let's adjust the contingency plan
and change what we will do if the risk reoccurs.")

- Look for any unexpected effects or consequences of risk events. (For example: "We did not expect
this risk to damage the construction site. We need to decide how to fix the damage after we finish
implementing the already agreed-upon contingency plan.")

- Reevaluate risk identification and qualitative and quantitative risk analysis when the project deviates
from the baseline. (For example: "The project cost is over the cost baseline. This implies that we
missed some major risks. Let's hold another risk identification session.")

- Update risk management and response plans.

- Look at the changes, including recommended corrective actions, to see if they lead to identifying
more risks. (For example: "We keep having to take corrective action related to this problem. Let's
look for the root cause and identify any risks to the remainder of the project that relate to the
problem.")

- Submit change requests to integrated change control.

- Update the project management plan and project documents with approved changes and any relevant information from the analysis of work performance data.

- Create a database of risk data and lessons learned that may be used throughout the organization on other projects.

- Perform variance and trend analysis on project performance data.

- Use contingency reserves and adjust for approved changes.

- Update the risk register and risk report with current risk exposure.

- Reevaluate assumptions and constraints, capture new issues, and update existing ones.

- Close out risks.

Tools and Techniques of Monitor Risks PAGE 456 The following tools and techniques may be used as part of the Monitor Risks process.

Data Analysis Reserve analysis and technical performance analysis fall into the data analysis tool and technique group. Both of these techniques may be used to monitor risks.

Reserve Analysis While the work is being done, reserve analysis is simply a matter of checking to see how much reserve remains and how much might be needed. It is like checking the balance in your bank account. Reserves must be protected throughout the project life cycle.

Now let's talk about a concept that can be tricky on the exam, especially for those who are not experienced in using risk management. People who would like to change the project in response to problems that have occurred may suggest using the reserves instead of adding cost or time to the project. It's important to know that a contingency reserve may only be used to handle the impact of the specific risk it was set aside for. So, if the change is part of the risk response plan that was previously accounted for in the budget, the reserve designated for that response may be used. If it is not, the project manager must take preventive or corrective action, fast track, crash, or otherwise adjust the project to accommodate or make up for the impact of the problem and its resulting changes.

If identified risks do not occur, the associated time or cost reserves should be returned to the company, rather than used to address other issues on the project. Reserves are not a free amount of time or cost that can be used at will by the project manager for any needs. If you are inexperienced with risk management, make sure you understand how reserves are used and protected.

Technical Performance Analysis Technical performance analysis uses project data to compare planned versus actual completion of technical requirements to determine if there is any variance from what was planned. Any variance could indicate possible risks to the project, either opportunities or threats.

Risk Reviews Risk reviews are held regularly to discuss the effectiveness of planned risk responses that have been implemented on the project. They may result in the identification of new risks, secondary risks created by risk response plans, and risks that are no longer applicable. Closing of risks allows the team to focus on managing the risks that are still open. The closing of a risk will likely result in the associated risk reserve being returned to the company.

Risk Audits These audits can be performed during meetings to assess the overall process of risk management on the project. The auditing process is documented in the risk management plan.

Meetings Have you experienced "go around the room" status meetings? Do they seem like an effective use of everyone's time? If there are thirty people in a room, and each person gets a few minutes to report status on activities that do not directly impact others in the meeting, most people in the room will consider the meeting a waste of time. Status updates can often be collected through other means, such as reports or quick one-on-one conversations between the project manager and the team members. Instead, for the exam, think of status meetings as team meetings in which the project manager can perform risk reviews and risk audits.

You can read an article by Rita Mulcahy about status meetings at rmcls.com.

Outputs of Monitor Risks PAGE 457
As with the previous risk management processes, updates to the risk report and other project documents are a result of Monitor Risks, along with the following additional outputs.

Work Performance Information
This is the analysis of the work performance data gathered. Examples include results of risk reviews and audits of how well risk processes are working for the project, performance measurements on schedule progress, comparisons of planned versus actual risk data, determinations of which risks can be closed or are likely to close in the near future, and variance analyses comparing the planned versus actual time and cost of implemented risk responses. This information may be added as updates to the risk register, other project documents, or the project management plan, or it could be the basis of change requests.

Project Documents Updates
Project documents that may be updated as part of the Monitor Risks process include the assumption log, issue log, lessons learned register, risk report, and risk register.

Risk Register Updates The Monitor Risks process will add the following to the risk register:

- Outcomes of risk reassessments and risk audits
- Results of implemented risk responses
- Updates to previous parts of risk management, including the identification of new risks
- Closing of risks that are no longer applicable
- Details of what happened when risks occurred
- Lessons learned

Change Requests
The Monitor Risks process will uncover needed project changes, including changes to the cost and schedule baselines due to overall and individual project risks.

Project Management Plan Updates
This process can result in updates to any component of the project management plan, including the schedule, cost, quality, and procurement management plans, as well as the resource management plan and the scope, schedule, and cost baselines for the project. These changes generally reflect approved preventive or corrective actions or changes to the plans.

Organizational Process Assets Updates
The Monitor Risks process may include the creation or enhancement of risk templates, such as the risk register, checklists, and risk report, as well as updates to risk management processes and procedures. The project's risk breakdown structure and other data may be added to organizational process assets as historical records for future projects.

Risk Management Review

Exercise

This exercise will help you review the key material you need to know for risk management. The Shuffle Game that follows offers another approach to this material. You can use either or both of these study tools, depending on your preference.

Instructions

1. Try to fill in the blanks in the below table using the knowledge and understanding gained after reading this chapter.
2. To review only the material contained in this chapter, focus on the cells that have asterisks. (These are the key topics you need to understand to pass the exam with the minimum amount of study time. The answer table will show only these topics.)
3. To review all the items listed in the *PMBOK® Guide*, fill in the entire table.

Key Inputs	Key Tools and Techniques	Key Outputs
Plan Risk Management Process group:		
*		*
Identify Risks Process group:		
	*	*
Perform Qualitative Risk Analysis Process group:		
*	*	*

Key Inputs	Key Tools and Techniques	Key Outputs
Perform Quantitative Risk Analysis Process group:		
	*	*
Plan Risk Responses Process group:		
	*	*
Implement Risk Responses Process group:		
*		*
Monitor Risks Process group:		
	*	*

383

Risk Management

Answer   To save study time and focus on the most important information, this answer table only shows the topics that are covered in this chapter. If you tried to list all inputs, tools and techniques, and outputs, you'll need to check your answers against the *PMBOK® Guide*.

Key Inputs	Key Tools and Techniques	Key Outputs
Plan Risk Management Process group: Planning		
Project management plan Project charter Stakeholder register Enterprise environmental factors Organizational process assets		Risk management plan
Identify Risks Process group: Planning		
	Brainstorming Checklist analysis Interviewing Root cause analysis Assumption analysis Constraint analysis SWOT analysis Documentation reviews Prompt lists Facilitation	Risk register Risk report
Perform Qualitative Risk Analysis Process group: Planning		
Risk register Risk management plan	Data analysis • Risk data quality assessment • Risk parameters assessment • Risk probability and impact assessment Data representation • Probability and impact matrix Risk categorization	Project document updates • Assumption log • Issue log • Risk register • Risk report
Perform Quantitative Risk Analysis Process group: Planning		
	Simulations Sensitivity analysis Decision tree analysis	Risk register updates
Plan Risk Responses Process group: Planning		
	Risk response strategies	Project management plan updates Project documents updates • Risk register updates

Key Inputs	Key Tools and Techniques	Key Outputs
Implement Risk Responses Process group: Executing		
Project management plan Project documents Organizational process assets		Change requests Project documents updates
Monitor Risks Process group: Monitoring and controlling		
	Data analysis • Reserve analysis • Technical performance analysis Risk reviews Risk audits Meetings	Work performance information Project documents updates • Risk register updates Change requests Project management plan updates Organizational process assets updates

Shuffle Game

Some people learn best by doing, which is why we have developed this alternate approach to reviewing risk management. To save you time, only the most important topics for the exam—those covered in this chapter—have been included.

Instructions

1. Cut out the cards on the next pages.
2. Lay out the bold title cards as column headers.
3. Shuffle the remaining cards and try to put them in the columns where they belong. Cards with italic terms must be matched to the corresponding group. For example, a *Cost of Quality* card in italics would match with a Data Analysis card, as cost of quality is a data analysis tool and technique.
4. Check your answers against the material covered in this chapter or the *PMBOK® Guide,* and make note of any gaps in your knowledge.

Note: Be sure to keep all cards for each chapter shuffle game as you will use them again for the final Shuffle Game in chapter 14.

Plan Risk Management *Key Inputs*	**Plan Risk Management** *Key Outputs*	**Identify Risks** *Key Tools & Techniques*
Identify Risks *Key Outputs*	**Perform Qualitative Risk Analysis** *Key Inputs*	**Perform Qualitative Risk Analysis** *Key Tools & Techniques*
Perform Qualitative Risk Analysis *Key Outputs*	**Perform Quantitative Risk Analysis** *Key Tools & Techniques*	**Perform Quantitative Risk Analysis** *Key Outputs*
Plan Risk Responses *Key Tools & Techniques*	**Plan Risk Responses** *Key Outputs*	**Implement Risk Responses** *Key Inputs*
Implement Risk Responses *Key Outputs*	**Monitor Risks** *Key Tools & Techniques*	**Monitor Risks** *Key Outputs*

© 2018 RMC Publications, Inc.™ • 952.846.4484 • info@rmcls.com • www.rmcls.com

Project management plan	Project charter	Stakeholder register
Enterprise environmental factors	Organizational process assets	Risk management plan
Brainstorming	Checklist analysis	Interviewing
Root cause analysis	Assumption analysis	Constraint analysis
SWOT analysis	Documentation reviews	Prompt lists

Facilitation	Risk register	Risk report
Risk register	Data analysis	*Risk data quality assessment*
Risk parameters assessment	*Risk probability and impact assessment*	Data representation
Probability and impact matrix	Project documents updates	*Assumption log*
Issue log	*Risk register*	*Risk report*

Simulations	Sensitivity analysis	Decision tree analysis
Risk register updates	Risk response strategies	Project management plan updates
Project documents updates	*Risk register updates*	Project management plan
Project documents	Organizational process assets	Change requests
Project documents updates	Data analysis	*Reserve analysis*

Technical performance analysis	Risk reviews	Risk audits
Meetings	Work performance information	Project documents updates
Risk register updates	Change requests	Project management plan updates
Organizational process assets updates	Risk management plan	Risk categorization

Practice Exam

1. For which risk management process is the project charter a required input?
   A. Monitor Risks
   B. Plan Risk Responses
   C. Identify Risks
   D. Plan Risk Management

2. The project manager is assessing the data used to identify the project risks to determine its accuracy and reliability. What tool or technique are they using?
   A. Trigger data analysis
   B. Data quality assessment
   C. A risk rating matrix
   D. Analysis of trends in qualitative risk analysis

3. Which of the following best describes a risk owner?
   A. The person who identified a risk
   B. The department that is the source of the risk and is most knowledgeable about it
   C. The department that will be most affected by the risk
   D. The person who will be responsible for implementing the risk response strategy

4. The team is conducting a risk audit. What process are they working in?
   A. Plan Risk Responses
   B. Manage Risks
   C. Monitor Risks
   D. Plan Risk Management

5. The project manager is performing decision tree analysis to choose between several alternative courses of action. If one risk event has a 90 percent chance of occurring, and its consequences will be $10,000, what does $9,000 represent?
   A. Risk value
   B. Present value
   C. Expected monetary value (EMV)
   D. Contingency budget

6. Which section of the risk management plan defines how risk management will be performed for the project?
   A. Methodology
   B. Definitions
   C. Timing
   D. Roles and responsibilities

7. The risk owner was notified that a risk trigger has occurred, and they are leading the risk response plan to react to the risk event. What process are they working in?
   A. Monitor Risks
   B. Identify Risks
   C. Plan Risk Responses
   D. Implement Risk Responses

8. In response to an identified risk, the project manager meets with the team and management to develop a strategy. After discussions, they decide that it would be best to ensure that the risk happens. This is an example of which risk response strategy?
   A. Share
   B. Exploit
   C. Escalate
   D. Enhance

9. While performing quantitative risk analysis, which tool would the project manager use to simulate the cost or schedule results of the project?
   A. Monte Carlo analysis
   B. Network diagram
   C. Qualitative risk analysis
   D. Precision testing

10. A project manager has just completed subjectively evaluating risks on the project. Which of the following is the most important output of this process?
    A. An assessment of overall project risk exposure
    B. A determination of which risks to process further and which to simply document
    C. The identification of risk triggers
    D. The identification of residual risks

11. When you were first assigned to the project, the sponsor informed you that a schedule delay of 30 days would be unacceptable. What is the term for this kind of constraint?
    A. Risk tolerance
    B. Risk appetite
    C. Risk averse
    D. Risk threshold

12. Which of the following is not included in the risk register as an output of Identify Risks?
    A. List of risk owners
    B. List of potential risk responses
    C. The root causes of the risks
    D. List of risks

13. The project manager is communicating risk status, ensuring that proper risk management procedures are being followed, and closing out risks. What process are they working in?
    A. Identify Risks
    B. Monitor Risks
    C. Plan Risk Management
    D. Implement Risk Responses

14. Which of the following statements is true?
    A. Management approval is needed to use contingency reserves.
    B. Management reserves are for items that the project team was not able to identify.
    C. The project manager can approve the use of management reserves.
    D. Management reserves are calculated and become part of the cost baseline.

© 2010 RMC Publications, Inc.™ • 952.846.4484 • info@rmcls.com • www.rmcls.com

15. What is the difference between risk appetite and risk threshold?
    A. Risk threshold refers to the acceptable level of risk in general, and risk appetite refers to the specific point at which the risk becomes unacceptable.
    B. Risk threshold refers to the acceptable level of risk related to the schedule, and risk appetite refers to a specific amount of acceptable risk related to scope.
    C. Risk appetite refers to the acceptable level of risk in general, and risk threshold refers to the specific point at which risk becomes unacceptable.
    D. There is little difference between the two terms; they can be used interchangeably.

Answers

1. **Answer** D
   Explanation The project charter is an input to the Plan Risk Management process. The charter contains information on the high-level project risks that were identified during project initiating, and it helps the project manager determine if the overall project objectives and constraints are generally risky.

2. **Answer** B
   Explanation There is no such term as trigger data analysis, so that is an incorrect choice. A risk rating matrix helps identify probability and impact. Trends can only be analyzed when the work is ongoing. The purpose of a data quality assessment, which is a tool used in Perform Qualitative Risk Analysis, is to test the value of the risk data.

3. **Answer** D
   Explanation The risk owner is the person who will be looking for triggers and implementing the risk response strategy.

4. **Answer** C
   Explanation Risk audits are a tool used in Monitor Risks to assess the effectiveness of the project's risk management processes.

5. **Answer** C
   Explanation Expected monetary value (EMV) is used in decision tree analysis to determine the best course of action. EMV is computed by multiplying the probability times the impact ($P \times I = EMV$). In this case, $0.9 \times \$10,000 = \$9,000$.

6. **Answer** A
   Explanation The methodology section of the risk management plan defines how risk management will be performed for the project. It can include a list of specific tools and data sources that will be used to manage project risk.

7. **Answer** D
   Explanation In Implement Risk Responses, which occurs during project executing, the plans for responding to risk events are implemented. The risk owner leads the previously assigned resources in performing the risk response activities.

8. **Answer** B
   Explanation This risk must be an opportunity. To exploit the opportunity means to add work or change the project to make sure the opportunity occurs, either at the level of the individual risk or the overall project risk.

9. **Answer** A
   Explanation Monte Carlo analysis is a simulation technique that uses the network diagram and schedule or cost estimates to "perform" the project many times and simulate the cost or schedule results of the project.

10. **Answer** B

    Explanation The activities described in the question take place in the Perform Qualitative Risk Analysis process, and the most important output of that process is a determination of which risks to process further and which to simply document. An assessment of overall project risk exposure is made in the Perform Quantitative Risk Analysis process. Risk triggers and residual risks are identified in Plan Risk Responses.

11. **Answer** D

    Explanation As illustrated by the sponsor's statement in this scenario, the risk threshold is the specific point at which risk becomes unacceptable.

12. **Answer** A

    Explanation Risk owners are not assigned—and therefore cannot be added to the risk register—until Plan Risk Responses. The other items here are all included in the risk register after the Identify Risks process is completed.

13. **Answer** B

    Explanation The activities listed in the question are just a few of the many activities that take place in the Monitor Risk process.

14. **Answer** B

    Explanation The only correct statement here is that management reserves are for items that the project team was not able to identify in risk management. To make the other choices true, you would need to switch the terms "contingency reserves" and "management reserves" wherever they appear. So, the corrected statements would be: "Management approval is needed to use management reserves"; "The project manager can approve the use of contingency reserves"; and "Contingency reserves are calculated and become part of the cost baseline."

15. **Answer** C

    Explanation Risk appetite is a general, high-level description of the acceptable level of risk. For example, "We are willing to accept little risk to the schedule" is a statement of risk appetite. Risk threshold is more specific, referring to a measurable amount of acceptable risk. For example, "We are willing to accept schedule risk of up to 21 days" identifies a risk threshold. It refers to the specific point at which risk becomes unacceptable.

© 2019 RMC Publications, Inc.™ • 952.846.4484 • info@rmcls.com • www.rmcls.com

Procurement Management

There are 6 questions on this knowledge area on the CAPM exam. Also note, for a full list of all inputs, tools and techniques, and outputs within this knowledge area, please see the table on page 460 in the PMBOK© Guide.

A very experienced student in an RMC class was upset about a situation at work. He said he had arranged a meeting with a seller, and the seller did not show up. He then rescheduled the meeting, and the seller still did not show up. When the instructor asked what kind of contract he was working with, the student had to contact his office to find out that he had a fixed-price contract. The instructor then asked him where in the contract it said that the seller had to attend such meetings. After some investigation, the student determined that meetings were not listed in the contract. Why would a seller attend a meeting if he was not getting paid for it?

Think about what procurement management means on a project. We're not talking about the role of an attorney or a contracting or procurement office. Instead, we're talking about the project manager's role.

The basic procurement management skills required of a project manager include being able to help create, read, and manage contracts and any supporting documentation.

Procurement management is one of the hardest knowledge areas on the exam. If you have worked with contracts before, you might have to fine-tune your knowledge and learn new terms for what you already do. You might also have to understand the project manager's role a little better. If you're like many other people, however, you may have little experience in procurement. In any case, this chapter walks you through the procurement process and suggests ways you can most effectively study this topic and prepare for the exam.

QUICKTEST

- Procurement management process
- Procurement management plan
- Procurement strategy
- Agreements (contracts)
- Contract types
  - Fixed price (FP)
  - Time and material (T&M)
  - Cost-reimbursable (CR)
- Advantages/disadvantages of each contract type
- Project manager's role in procurement
- Termination
- Bid documents
- Make-or-buy analysis
- Source selection criteria
- Procurement SOW
- Performance review
- Claims administration
- Closed procurements
- Bidder conferences
- Proposal evaluation
- Risk and contract type
- Make-or-buy decisions
- Independent cost estimates
- Incentives
- Special provisions
- Standard contract
- Terms and conditions
- Change requests
- Breach
- Procurement audit
- Records management system
- Procurement negotiation
- Qualified seller list
- Cost
- Price
- Profit

Procurement Management

TRICKS OF THE TRADE® The *PMBOK® Guide* uses the terms "contract" and "agreement," so you need to be prepared to see both terms on the exam and understand what each means. Contracts can be written or verbal, are typically created with an external entity, and involve an exchange of goods or services for some type of compensation (usually monetary). The contract forms the legal relationship between the entities; it is mutually binding and provides the framework for how a failure by one side will be addressed and ultimately remedied in court.

The broader term "agreement" encompasses documents or communications that outline internal or external relationships and their intentions. A contract is a type of agreement, but an agreement isn't necessarily a contract. Imagine that the international and US divisions of a company want to leverage their resources to achieve a shared strategic objective; they would create an agreement, but likely not a contract. Agreements can be used to express and outline the intentions of projects. The charter and the project management plans are examples of agreements that are not contracts; they are internal agreements. Some other examples of agreements are service level agreements, memos of intent, letters of intent, letters of agreement, emails, "and verbal agreements.

So what does this mean for a project manager? The way a project manager communicates, escalates, and solves problems will vary depending on whether their actions are governed by a contract or an internal agreement. For example, notifying a seller of a default on a contract term or condition should be done through formal written communication to create a record and ensure appropriate legal action can be taken if necessary. In comparison, for an internal agreement, failure to meet a term of the agreement might be handled in a conversation followed up by an email. For the exam, understanding whether a situational question describes an internal agreement or a contract with an outside party might help you select the right answer. In this chapter, we primarily use the term "contract," because the procurement process is used to acquire necessary resources that are outside the project team and involve legal documents between the buyer and seller.

The following should help you understand how each part of procurement management fits into the overall project management process.

The Procurement Management Process	Done During
Plan Procurement Management	Planning process group
Conduct Procurements	Executing process group
Control Procurements	Monitoring and controlling process group

The exam assumes that the project manager is familiar with different contract types, selection criteria, and working relationships with the procurement or legal department. The exam also assumes that the project manager has specific involvement in the procurement process even if they do not lead that process, and that the procurement process cannot occur without the project manager's involvement.

Overview of the Procurement Management Process

Procurement is a formal process to obtain goods and services. To help you better understand it, read the following concepts and imagine what it would take to make this happen in the real world. The rest of this chapter discusses the process in more detail. Make sure you understand procurement management and can generally describe the process before you continue reading the rest of this chapter.

When a project is planned, the scope is analyzed to determine whether the entire project scope can be completed internally, or if any of the work, deliverables, materials, equipment, etc., will need to be outsourced. This analysis results in make-or-buy decisions. If one or more procurements are needed, the procurement department gets involved in the project to manage the procurement process.

When a decision has been made to procure goods or services from an outside source, the project manager facilitates the creation of a plan for the overall procurement process (a procurement management plan), a plan for how each contract will be managed (a procurement strategy), and a description of the work to be done by each seller (a procurement statement of work). The procurement manager determines what type of contract, bid document, and statement of work should be used. At this point, the prospective sellers take action, and the buyer waits for their responses.

The prospective sellers carefully review the buyer's statement of work and all the terms of the proposed contract contained in the bid documents, including the selection criteria. During this review, the sellers develop a full understanding of what the buyer wants. Keep in mind that the amount of time that a prospective seller may need to respond to the bid documents can be substantial (sometimes taking several months), and the buyer's project manager must plan this time into the project schedule.

If a buyer receives competing submissions from many prospective sellers, the buyer might ask for presentations from all the candidates. Or the buyer may just move into negotiations with the preferred seller or sellers. All terms and conditions in the proposed contract, the entire procurement statement of work, and any other components of the bid documents can be negotiated. Negotiations can take a lot of time, and they require the involvement of the project manager.

At the end of the negotiations, one or more sellers are selected, and a contract is signed. The procurement management plan and procurement strategy created earlier may also be updated. Once the contract is signed, the procurement must be managed and controlled. This involves making sure all the requirements of the contract are met. It also means keeping control of the contract and making only approved changes.

Finally, when the procurement work is complete, the procurement is closed.

Could you now describe the procurement process to someone else? Be sure this overview makes sense to you before you continue with this chapter.

Buyers and Sellers
Often, the company or person who provides services and goods can be called a contractor, subcontractor, supplier, designer, or vendor. The *PMBOK® Guide* primarily uses the term "seller," however. It's important to know that the exam may use any of these terms. The company or person who purchases the services is called the buyer. Many companies are a buyer in one procurement and a seller in another.

Read exam questions carefully to see if the situation described in the question is from the buyer's or the seller's point of view. If no point of view is mentioned, assume you are on the buyer's side of the project. Make sure you know the actions that you would take as the project manager for the buyer. This is an especially important concept to understand when taking the exam.

Guidelines for Understanding Procurement
Read the following guidelines to better understand the procurement process.

- Contracts require formality. This means any correspondence, clarification, and notifications related to the contracts should be formal written communication, which can be followed up with verbal communication, if necessary. If issues develop that require arbitration, mediation, or litigation, the formal written communications will be more enforceable and supportable than verbal communications.

- All product and project management requirements for the procurement work should be specifically stated in the contract.
- If it is not in the contract, it can only be required to be done if a formal change order to the contract is issued.
- If it is in the contract, it must be done, or a formal change order to remove it must be approved by both parties.
- Changes to contracts must be submitted and approved in writing.
- Contracts are legally binding; the seller must perform as agreed in the contract, or face the consequences for breach of contract.
- Contracts should help diminish project risk.
- Most governments back all contracts that fall within their jurisdiction by providing a court system for dispute resolution.

The Project Manager's Role in Procurements

You might ask yourself, "If there is a procurement manager, why would a project manager need to be involved in procurements?" This is an important question, and you must fully understand the answer before you take the exam. Here are a few tricks to help you.

Remember that it is the project manager's project. There are certain things that cannot be done effectively without the project manager, and the project manager's expertise is needed so the organization can fully realize the project's benefits. This is so important that typically a large percentage of the questions on the exam are focused on testing whether you know what a project manager should do.

Project managers should be assigned on both the buyer's and seller's sides before a contract is signed. Many companies that sell their services make a huge but common mistake by not involving the project manager in the bidding and proposal process. Instead, only marketing and sales are involved until after the contract is signed. The project manager is then handed a project with a contract that may include unrealistic time or cost constraints. The project starts out in trouble.

Involving the project manager early in the procurement process is so important that the exam will test to see if you know when the project manager should be involved and why. For example, the project manager is often uniquely capable of answering (or getting answers to) many of the technical and project management questions that arise during bidder conferences. If the sellers' questions are answered incorrectly or incompletely, there may be an inadvertent change to a specification or the scope of the contract that was never intended by the buyer.

The remainder of this chapter will follow the procurement process from start to finish. For the exam, you should have a general idea of what happens when, and how the procurement process relates to the project management process.

Plan Procurement Management   PAGE 466

> **Process:** Plan Procurement Management
> **Process Group:** Planning
> **Knowledge Area:** Procurement Management

The Plan Procurement Management process answers the following questions.

- "How will make-or-buy analysis be performed?"
- "What goods and services do we need to buy for this project?"
- "How will we purchase them?"
- "Who are potential sellers to consider?"

In addition to creating a procurement management plan, this process involves putting together the bid documents that will be sent to prospective sellers describing the buyer's need, how to respond, and the criteria the buyer will use to select a seller. Note that the term "bid documents" is used in reference to requests for proposal (RFPs) and requests for quotation (RFQs). You may also see the term used in reference to requests for information (RFIs) as well as invitations for bid (IFBs).

The Plan Procurement Management process includes the following activities:

- Performing make-or-buy analysis
- Creating a procurement management plan
- Creating a procurement strategy for each procurement
- Creating a procurement statement of work for each procurement
- Selecting the appropriate contract type for each procurement
- Creating the bid documents
- Determining the source selection criteria

Inputs to Plan Procurement Management PAGE 468   When planning procurement management, it is important to consider business documents, such as the benefits management plan and the business case. Also keep in mind the project charter, components of the project management plan, project documents, and any relevant enterprise environmental factors and organizational process assets. Review these inputs (described next) to determine what is needed prior to planning procurement management.

Project Charter   The project manager will need to review important information found in the project charter—such as any preapproved financial resources, the overall project description, and the project objectives—in order to create the procurement management plan.

Business Documents   Important business documents that are inputs to the Plan Procurement Management process include the following:

- **Benefits Management Plan**   The benefits management plan lists the benefits of the project and details when they are to be delivered. This information is used to determine what procurements are needed, when procurements must be entered into, and what dates should be included in the bid documents and, ultimately, project contracts.
- **Business Case**   The business case outlines the reason the project was undertaken; the procurement strategy must be in alignment with this.

Project Management Plan   Components of the project management plan, including the scope, quality, and resource management plans, help those involved in the procurement process identify where procurements are necessary and understand any constraints on potential procurement efforts.

Project Documents   Documents such as the milestone list and the requirements traceability matrix can help the project manager plan procurement management. The project schedule and any relevant procurements already in place should be reviewed as well. Other documents used to plan procurements include the following.

- **Project team assignments**   Team assignments will include information on who can help the project manager with procurement planning. If the project team does not have the necessary skills—such as developing bid documents—to complete procurement management activities, team members may require training or need assistance from the procurement department or outside sources.

- **Requirements documentation**   This is where the project manager will find the scope-related requirements that will help define the end product, service, or result provided by a seller. In addition, this documentation includes requirements for compliance, safety, communications, project management practices, reporting, quality, and risk management that are likely to be important to the procurement process.

- **Resource requirements**   Resource requirements describe the skills, number, and type of resources that will be needed on the project. If the required team resources, products, materials, equipment, or services are not available within the performing organization, they will need to be procured.

- **Risk register**   The risk register provides an understanding of the individual and overall project risks uncovered to date, as well as the risk responses that involve procurements. Remember, risk analysis of the project should be done before contracts are signed.

- **Stakeholder register**   The stakeholder register will help identify those who will be impacted by the procurement process as well as those who will have input into or will guide this process, such as the procurement manager, regulatory bodies, and attorneys.

Enterprise Environmental Factors

These factors include the company's culture and existing systems that the project manager will have to use or work around. For procurement, they include marketplace conditions, the services that are available to be purchased, and the culture and structures surrounding the organization's approach to procurements.

Organizational Process Assets

The organizational process assets that are used in procurement can include procurement procedures and documents, standard contract types used by the organization, statement of work templates, lessons learned from past procurements and projects, and lists of prequalified sellers. Note that selecting the right contract type for each procurement is critical to the success of the project. The following pages include descriptions of the contract types, along with an exercise to help you understand when each is best to use. Take your time with this section; it includes a lot of information you will need to know for the exam.

Types of Contracts

Different types of contracts can be used to acquire goods and services on a project. The types of contracts or agreements that are approved for use within an organization are considered organizational process assets. From those contract types, the procurement manager will select the contract type for each procurement based on the following considerations.

- What is being purchased (a product or service)
- The completeness of the statement of work
- The level of effort and expertise the buyer can devote to managing the seller
- Whether the buyer wants to offer the seller incentives
- The marketplace or economy
- Industry standards for the type of contract used

The three broad categories of contracts are:

- Fixed price (FP)
- Time and material (T&M)
- Cost-reimbursable (CR)

TRICKS OF THE TRADE®   Some contract types can be referred to by more than one name, which can make it difficult to learn them. Here is a trick. Start by learning the three main categories of contract types shown in the previous list. Then, when the exam asks a question relating to contract type, check whether knowing the contract category helps you answer the question. In most cases, it will.

You must understand the contract types and be able to recognize the differences between them. Questions on the exam may require you to recognize that the project manager's responsibilities and actions will vary depending on the type of contract being used. There may also be questions that require you to pick the most appropriate contract type based on a particular situation. Think through this section carefully!

Fixed Price (FP) A fixed-price contract should be used for acquiring goods, products, or services with well-defined specifications or requirements. In general, with a fixed-price contract, a clearly defined statement of work along with competing bids means the project manager is likely to get a fair and reasonable price. This is one of the most common types of contract, though it's less likely to be used in something like information technology than in construction. If the costs are more than the agreed-upon amount, the seller must bear the additional costs. Therefore, the buyer has the least cost risk in this type of contract because the scope is well-defined. (Note, however, that when fixed-price contracts are entered into and the statement of work is not sufficiently detailed, claims and disputes over what is in and out of the contract create higher risk of cost overruns or delay.) The seller is most concerned with the procurement statement of work (SOW) in a fixed-price contract. This is going to help them accurately estimate time and cost for the work involved, and allow them to determine a price that includes a fair and reasonable profit. The amount of profit is not disclosed to the buyer in this contract type. Types of fixed-price contracts include firm fixed price, fixed price incentive fee, fixed price award fee, and fixed price with economic price adjustments. Purchase orders are also a type of fixed-price contract.

For the exam, be aware that even though the buyer may prefer a fixed-price contract as a way to control costs, it is not always the best choice, and in some cases it may be inappropriate. Sellers in some industries may not have the detailed accounting records of past project activities required to accurately estimate future projects. Buyers may not have the expertise to prepare the clear and complete procurement statement of work required for a fixed-price contract.

Because many buyers are not knowledgeable about contracts, they often ask the seller to provide a fixed price, even when the scope of work is incomplete. In such a case, the procurement statement of work is not really adequate for the seller to make a reasonable estimate of required costs and time. Think for a minute about the consequences of doing this, which include the following.

- The seller is forced to accept a high level of risk.
- The seller needs to add a significant amount of reserves to their price to cover their risks; therefore, the buyer pays more than they otherwise might have.
- The seller can more easily try to increase profits by cutting scope or claiming that work the buyer wants is outside the contract and thus requires a change order. The buyer will not be able to state with certainty if something is within the scope of the work or outside it (and, therefore, needs a change order and additional payment to the seller) if there is not a complete procurement statement of work.

If a fixed-price contract is used when it shouldn't be and the seller realizes they will not be able to make any profit on the project, the seller might try to take their best people off the project, cut work that is specifically mentioned in the contract, cut work that is not mentioned in the contract but is needed, decrease quality, or take other actions to save themselves money.

The following sections discuss some of the most common forms of fixed-price contracts.

Fixed Price (FP) Before creating a FP contract, all requirements must be clearly described. Then a fixed total price is set for the project, and no changes to scope should occur.

Example: Fixed-Price Contract
Contract = $1,100,000.

Fixed Price Incentive Fee (FPIF)   In a FPIF contract, profits (or financial incentives) can be adjusted based on the seller meeting specified performance criteria, such as getting the work done faster, cheaper, or better. The final price is calculated using a formula based on the relationship of final negotiated costs to the total target cost.

Example: Fixed Price Incentive Fee Contract
Contract = $1,100,000. For every month the project is finished early, an additional $10,000 is paid to the seller.

Fixed Price Award Fee (FPAF)   In a FPAF contract, the buyer pays a fixed price plus an award amount (a bonus) based on performance. This is similar to the FPIF contract, except that the total possible award amount is determined in advance and apportioned based on performance. For example, the buyer might say there is a maximum $50,000 award fee available, and it will be apportioned at the rate of $5,000 for every month that production exceeds a certain amount. This is a type of incentive contract. In many instances, the award paid is judged subjectively. Therefore, procedures must be in place in advance for determining the award.

In the decision to use this type of contract, the cost to administer the award fee must be weighed against the potential benefits.

Example: Fixed Price Award Fee Contract
Contract = $1,100,000. For every month performance exceeds the planned level by more than 15 percent, an additional $5,000 is awarded to the seller, with a maximum award of $50,000.

Fixed Price with Economic Price Adjustments (FPEPA)   If a contract will cover a multiyear period, there may be uncertainties about future economic conditions. The future cost of supplies and equipment that the seller might be required to provide under contract might not be predictable. In such cases, a buyer might choose a fixed-price contract with economic price adjustments. Think "economy" whenever you see this on the exam, and you should remember it.

Example: Fixed Price with Economic Price Adjustments Contract
Contract = $1,100,000, but a price increase will be allowed in year two based on the US Consumer Price Index report for year one.

Purchase Order   A purchase order is the simplest type of fixed-price contract. This type of contract is normally unilateral (signed by one party) instead of bilateral (signed by both parties). Most other contract types are bilateral. A purchase order is usually used for simple commodity procurements. Purchase orders become contracts when the buyer accepts the terms. The seller then performs or delivers according to those terms (for example, providing equipment or products). Although unilateral purchase orders are most common, some companies will require the seller's signature on a purchase before the buyer will consider the purchase order official. In that case, it is the signature that forms the acceptance needed to make a contract.

> **Example: Purchase Order**
>
> Contract = 30 linear meters of wood at $9 per meter.

Time and Material (T&M)   In this type of contract, the buyer pays on a per-hour or per-item basis. Time and material contracts are frequently used for service efforts in which the level of effort cannot be defined when the contract is awarded. It has elements of a fixed-price contract (in the fixed price per hour) and a cost-reimbursable contract (in the material costs and the fact that the total cost is unknown). Compared to other types of contracts, time and material contracts typically have terms and conditions that are simpler, to allow for quick negotiations so that work can begin sooner.

Imagine you're the project manager on a project where you will have to pay someone on a contract basis for every hour they work, no matter how productive they are, and no matter what they are doing Would you want to do this for a long period of time? Remember, the seller's profit is built into the rate, so they have no incentive to get the work done quickly or efficiently. For this reason, a time and material contract is best used for work that is valued at a small dollar amount and lasts a short amount of time. Knowing when it's best to use a time and material contract can help you correctly answer exam questions.

To make sure the costs do not grow higher than budgeted, the buyer may add a "Not to Exceed" clause to the contract, and thus limit the total amount they are required to pay. With a time and material contract, the buyer has a medium amount of cost risk as compared to cost-reimbursable and fixed-price contracts.

> **Example: Time and Material Contract**
>
> Contract = $100 per hour plus expenses or materials at cost.

Cost-Reimbursable (CR)   A cost-reimbursable contract is used when the exact scope of work is uncertain and, therefore, costs cannot be estimated accurately enough to effectively use a fixed-price contract. This type of contract provides for the buyer to pay the seller allowable incurred costs to the extent prescribed in the contract. Such contracts also typically include an additional fee or award amount added to the cost to allow for seller profit. Types of cost-reimbursable contracts include cost, cost plus fixed fee, cost plus incentive fee, cost plus award fee, cost plus fixed fee, and cost plus percentage of costs.

A cost-reimbursable contract requires the seller to have an accounting system that can track costs by project. With a cost-reimbursable contract, the buyer has the most cost risk because the total costs are unknown. The seller provides an estimate to the buyer; the buyer can use the estimate for planning and cost management purposes, but it is not binding. What is binding is the buyer's responsibility to compensate the seller for their legitimate costs of work and materials as described in the contract. Research and development and information technology projects in which the scope is unknown are typical scenarios where a cost-reimbursable contract may be used. The following sections discuss some of the most common forms of cost-reimbursable contracts.

Cost Contract   A cost contract is one in which the seller receives no fee (profit). Cost contracts are typically used by nonprofit organizations.

> **Example: Cost Contract**
>
> Contract = Cost of work and materials. There is no profit. With this type of contract, the seller is reimbursed but does not make a profit.

Cost Plus Fixed Fee (CPFF)   A cost plus fixed fee contract provides payment to the seller of actual costs plus a negotiated fee that is fixed before the work begins. (This is the seller's profit; it's usually a percentage of the estimated cost of the project.) The fee does not vary with actual costs; thus, the seller does not have an incentive to increase or inflate costs. The fee may be adjusted as a result of changes to the procurement statement of work.

Example: Cost Plus Fixed Fee Contract
Contract = Cost plus a fee of $100,000.

Cost Plus Incentive Fee (CPIF)   A cost plus incentive fee contract provides for the seller to be paid for actual costs plus a fee that will be adjusted based on whether specific performance objectives stated in the contract are met. In this type of contract, an original estimate of the total cost is made (the target cost) and a fee for the work is determined (a target fee). The seller gets a percentage of the savings if the actual costs are less than the target cost, or if the actual costs are more than the target cose, the seller shares the cost overrun with the buyer. The ratio is often 80 percent to the buyer and 20 percent to the seller. (See more on incentives later in this section.)

Example: Cost Plus Incentive Fee Contract
Contract = $500,000 target cost plus $50,000 target fee. The buyer and seller share any cost savings or overruns at 80% to the buyer and 20% to the seller.

Cost Plus Award Fee (CPAF)   In a cost plus award fee contract, the buyer pays all costs and a base fee plus an award amount (a bonus) based on performance. This is similar to the CPIF contract, except that the incentive is a potential award, and there is no possibility of a penalty. The award amount in a CPAF contract is determined in advance and apportioned depending on performance. This is a type of incentive contract. In some instances, the award to be paid is judged subjectively. Therefore, procedures must be in place in advance for determining the award.

As with a FPAF contract, when deciding whether to use cost plus award fee contract, the cost to administer the award fee must be weighed against the potential benefits.

Example: Cost Plus Award Fee Contract
Contract = Cost plus a base fee plus award for meeting buyer-specified performance criteria. Maximum award available is $50,000.

Cost Plus Fee (CPF) or Cost Plus Percentage of Costs (CPPC)   A CPF or CPPC contract requires the buyer to pay for all costs, plus a percentage of the costs as a fee. In the United States, this type of cost-reimbursable contract is generally not allowed for federal acquisitions or procurements under federal acquisition regulations—and it is bad for buyers everywhere. Can you figure out why?

If seller profit is based on a percentage of everything billed to the buyer for the project, what incentive is there to control costs? Say a seller has to purchase materials from one of two suppliers. Although the materials from both suppliers meet the quality requirements, one supplier charges $4 per unit and the other charges $40 per unit. A seller might be tempted to choose the $40 per unit charge because they will make more profit. It is possible for the buyer to construct the contract so that the seller will need to prove they pursued the least expensive path in completion of the procurement statement of work when selecting materials or subcontracting portions of work. This contract type requires the buyer to carefully monitor and control all invoices.

© 2019 RMC Publications, Inc ™ • 952 846 4484 • info@rmcls.com • www.rmcls.com

Example: Cost Plus Fee or Cost Plus Percentage of Costs Contract
Contract = Cost plus 10 percent of costs as fee.

A trick for the exam is to realize that buyers must select the appropriate type of contract for what they are buying. Test your understanding of the different types of contracts using the following table. Knowing the advantages and disadvantages of each type of contract will help you select the appropriate type of contract when answering exam questions.

Fixed-Price Contract

Advantages	Disadvantages
• This type of contract requires less work for the buyer to manage. • The seller has a strong incentive to control costs. • Companies usually have experience with this type of contract. • The buyer knows the total price before the work begins.	• If the seller underprices the work, they may try to make up profits by charging more than is necessary on change orders. • The seller may try to not complete some of the procurement statement of work if they begin to lose money. • This contract type requires more work for the buyer to write the procurement statement of work. • A fixed-price contract can be more expensive than a cost-reimbursable contract if the procurement statement of work is incomplete. In addition, the seller needs to add to the price of a fixed-price contract to account for the increased risk.

Time and Material Contract

Advantages	Disadvantages
• This type of contract can be created quickly, because the statement of work may be less detailed. • The contract duration is brief. • This is a good choice when you are "hiring bodies" (adding people to augment your staff).	• There is profit for the seller in every hour or unit billed. • The seller has no incentive to control costs. • This contract type is appropriate only for work involving a small level of effort. • This contract type requires a great deal of day-to-day oversight from the buyer.

Cost-Reimbursable Contract

Advantages	Disadvantages
• This contract type allows for a simpler procurement statement of work. • It usually requires less work to define the scope for a cost-reimbursable contract than for a fixed-price contract. • A cost-reimbursable contract is generally less costly than a fixed-price contract because the seller doesn't have to add as much to cover risk.	• This contract type requires auditing the seller's invoices. • This contract type requires more work for the buyer to manage. • The seller has only a moderate incentive to control costs. • The total price is unknown.

The exam may also ask questions that correlate risk with the different types of contracts. Figure 12.1 shows the amount of cost risk that the buyer and seller have with each contract type. Use this diagram to better understand the different contract types and answer questions such as the following.

Question   Who has the risk in a cost-reimbursable contract—the buyer or the seller?
Answer   The buyer. If the costs increase, the buyer pays the added costs.

Question   Who has the cost risk in a fixed-price contract—the buyer or seller?
Answer   The seller. If costs increase, the seller pays the costs and makes less profit.

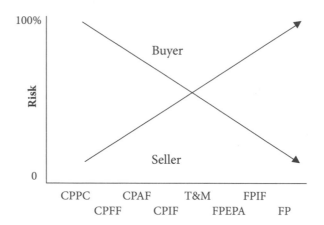

Figure 12.1 Risk to buyer and seller according to contract type

Exercise

After going through all these pages, you should start to feel like you understand the different types of contracts. Use this exercise to help you put it all together. However, keep in mind the questions on the exam are unlikely to test this level of detail. So if you can complete this exercise successfully, you should be well prepared for any questions about contracts.

Answer the questions in the following table for each contract type.

	Question	Cost-Reimbursable	Time and Material	Fixed Price
1	Generally, what is being bought? (product or service)			
2	How might the costs to the buyer be stated in the contract?			
3	How might the profit be stated in the contract?			
4	What is the cost risk to the buyer? (high, medium, low, none)			

© 2010 RMC Publications, Inc.™ • 952.846.4484 • info@rmcls.com • www.rmcls.com

	Question	Cost-Reimbursable	Time and Material	Fixed Price
5	How important is a detailed procurement statement of work? (high, medium, low, none)			
6	What industry uses this contract type most frequently?			
7	How much negotiation is usually required to sign the contract after receipt of the seller's price? (high, medium, low, none)			
8	What level of effort and expertise will the buyer need to devote to managing the seller? (high, medium, low, none)			
9	How are costs billed to the buyer?			
10	How much auditing of the seller's costs will the buyer need to do? (high, medium, low, none)			

Answer

To make sense of this exercise, review the answers in the following table.

	Question	Cost-Reimbursable	Time and Material	Fixed Price
1	Generally, what is being bought? (product or service)	Service (some products may be included)	Service	Product
2	How might the costs to the buyer be stated in the contract?	Costs are variable, but the fee or profit is fixed (as a set amount or a percentage).	Hourly rate or price per unit	As a set currency amount (e.g., $1 million)
3	How might the profit be stated in the contract?	Listed separately, and known to the buyer	Included in the hourly rate, and may be unknown to the buyer	Included in the price, and unknown to the buyer

	Question	Cost-Reimbursable	Time and Material	Fixed Price
4	What is the cost risk to the buyer? (high, medium, low, none)	High; increases in costs are reimbursed by the buyer	Medium; although the costs are not fixed, they are known per unit, and this contract type is used for small purchases for a limited time.	Low; increases in costs are borne by the seller.
5	How important is a detailed procurement statement of work? (high, medium, low, none)	Low; the procurement statement of work only needs to describe the performance or functional requirements, since the seller provides the expertise on how to do the work, The buyer pays all costs, so there is less need to finalize the scope.	Low; this type traditionally has very little scope, and may only describe skill sets required.	High; the procurement statement of work must be complete so the seller knows exactly what work needs to be done in order to come up with an accurate price to complete the work.
6	What industry uses this contract type most frequently?	IT, research and development, and knowledge work. When the work has never been done before (as is often the case in these industries), the seller cannot fix a price, and therefore, this is the best form to use.	When hiring people for an hourly rate, you are usually hiring services, such as legal, plumbing, or programming.	Complete scope of work is most common in the construction industry.
7	How much negotiation is usually required to sign the contract after receipt of the seller's price? (high, medium, low, none)	High; all estimated costs are looked at to calculate the fee to be paid.	Low or none	None
8	What level of effort and expertise will the buyer need to devote to managing the seller? (high, medium, low, none)	High	Medium	Low
9	How are costs billed to the buyer?	Actual costs as incurred; profit at project completion, or apportioned as allowed in the contract	Hourly or per unit rate (which includes all costs and profit)	Fixed price (which includes profit) according to a payment schedule as work is completed and as allowed in the contract

	Question	Cost-Reimbursable	Time and Material	Fixed Price
10	How much auditing of the seller's costs will the buyer need to do? (high, medium, low, none)	High; all costs must be audited, and there will be a large number of invoices.	None; there may be an audit of work hours completed against those billed, but that will take little effort.	Low; since the overall contract costs are fixed, auditing usually focuses on making sure work is completed, not looking at detailed costs and receipts.

Tools and Techniques of Plan Procurement Management PAGE 472

There are two primary types of analysis that can be useful during the Plan Procurement Management process: make-or-buy analysis and source selection analysis. Let's review both.

Make-or-Buy Analysis

During planning, the project manager must decide whether the project team will do all the project work, or if some or all of the work will be outsourced. They also need to determine if all required materials or equipment are available within the performing organization. They need to ask questions such as, "How are resources currently distributed?" and "What are the capabilities of each resource?" The answers to these types of questions can help the project manager determine what can be done internally, and what will need to be done by or procured from outside resources. Make-or-buy analysis is completed early in the planning process to avoid wasted time planning work that will ultimately be outsourced. Also note that this analysis triggers make-or-buy decisions, which are documented in the procurement management plan.

Source Selection Analysis

Determining the criteria that will be used to select a seller is an important part of procurement planning. To make this determination, the project constraints must be analyzed. For example, is schedule the most important criteria, or is cost the critical factor?

If the buyer is purchasing a commodity, such as linear meters of wood, the source selection criteria may just be the lowest price. If the buyer is procuring construction services, the source selection criteria may be price plus experience. If the buyer is purchasing services only, the source selection analysis will be more extensive. In this case, the source selection criteria may include:

- Number of years in business
- Financial stability
- Understanding of need
- Price or life cycle cost
- Technical expertise
- Quality of past performance
- Ability to complete the work on time

If the organization has a preferred seller list, or a master services agreement with an outside source, that information is also considered when analyzing source selection options.

Outputs of Plan Procurement Management PAGE 475

The Plan Procurement Management process results in the outputs discussed in the following sections. Additional outputs may include information on qualified sellers, which is an organizational process asset update, and updates to project documents such as the lessons learned register, milestone list, requirements documentation, and requirements traceability matrix.

Procurement Management

Procurement Management Plan

The procurement management plan documents how procurements will be planned, executed, and controlled. Enterprise environmental factors and organizational process assets will significantly influence this plan. They include the governing approach to procurements for the project, information about how to perform the make-or-buy analysis, and the policies and procedures that will be used in the procurement processes.

The planning portion of the procurement management plan includes standards for selecting the best type of contract to use for each procurement, details of how procurement documents will be created or tailored to meet the needs of the project, and guidelines for establishing selection criteria.

The executing portion of the plan documents how the Conduct Procurements process will flow. It also outlines the roles and responsibilities of team members as well as the rules for bidder conferences and negotiations.

The control portion of the plan indicates how contract stipulations will be monitored and controlled. It also provides metrics and information on when and how measurements will be taken, guidelines for resolving disputes, the process for accepting deliverables, and the payments to be made.

Make-or-Buy Decisions

Make-or-buy decisions are the result of make-or-buy analysis. Any decisions to "buy" will require the team to follow the procurement management process to obtain needed products, equipment, or services. As the planning process continues, make-or-buy decisions may be adjusted; they may also necessitate changes to other parts of the project management plan.

Procurement Strategy

A procurement strategy is developed for each procurement after the make-or-buy-analysis has been completed and the goods or services to be acquired from outside the organization have been identified. The acquisition of these goods or services must be incorporated into an overall procurement strategy for the project. This strategy has three basic elements: how goods or services will be delivered to the buyer, what type of contract will be used, and how the procurement will be carried out throughout each phase. The project manager must manage the procurement to achieve the objectives of each phase, and also manage the transitions between the phases.

Procurement Statement of Work (SOW)

The project manager facilitates the creation of a scope of work to be done on each procurement. This is done by breaking down the project scope baseline into the work the project team will do and the work that will be purchased from the seller(s). The work to be done on each procurement is described in a procurement statement of work.

Each statement of work must be as clear, complete, and concise as possible, and it must describe all the work and activities the seller is required to complete. This includes all meetings, reports, and communications. It must also detail the acceptance criteria and the process of gaining acceptance. The cost of adding activities later is typically more than the cost of adding them at the beginning of the procurement. Does this make you think about the amount of work required to create a complete procurement statement of work?

What does the word "complete" mean? It depends on what you are buying. For example, if a project manager is buying expertise (such as software design or legal services), their procurement statement of work will include a detailed description of functional and performance requirements, a completion timeline, and evaluation criteria, in addition to required meetings, reports, and communications.

If they are buying the construction of a building, their requirements will be extremely specific, outlining things such as the materials to be used, the process that must be followed, and even a work schedule. If the project manager is hiring staff that they will direct (for example, a programmer to be added to the team), their procurement statement of work will likely contain more details about what they want the person to create or achieve.

The project manager should ask themselves, "If I were the seller, how comfortable would I be signing a legally binding contract to complete this work for a certain price?" They should put themselves in the seller's shoes, and make sure the scope of work is as descriptive and as complete as possible. The level of detail required will influence the selection of the contract type and the creation of the bid documents.

The procurement statement of work may be revised during contract negotiation, but it should be finalized by the time the contract is signed. A procurement statement of work can include drawings, specifications, and technical and descriptive wording. Also note that the phrase Terms of Reference (TOR) is sometimes used in relation to the procurement statement of work, as these two phrases share common qualities and therefore may contain similar components. No matter what it contains, however, the procurement statement of work becomes part of the contract.

Remember that a contract is a document used to manage a procurement activity. It does not just sit in a drawer. Therefore, both parties to the contract should always be asking, "What does the contract say?" If the procurement statement of work is not complete, the seller may frequently need to request clarification or ask for change orders, which can get expensive, and the project manager or procurement manager may find themselves constantly dealing with questions about whether a specific piece of work is included in the original cost or time estimates submitted by the seller.

Source Selection Criteria   Source selection analysis results in finalized source selection criteria. Often, the criteria are assigned numerical percentage values (weighted) to enable evaluation of proposals based on each criterion. The criteria are included in the bid documents to give the seller an understanding of the buyer's needs and help the seller decide whether to bid or make a proposal on the work. When the buyer receives the sellers' responses during the Conduct Procurements process, source selection criteria such as cost, quality, and expertise become the basis for the evaluation of the bids or proposals.

Independent Cost Estimates   The buyer may prepare an internal estimate, or use the input of experts, to come up with a benchmark against which to validate the bids provided by outside sellers during Conduct Procurements.

Bid Documents   After the contract type is selected and the procurement statement of work has been created, the buyer can put together the bid document, which describes the buyer's needs to sellers. The following are some types of bid documents.

- **Request for proposal (RFP)**   An RFP (sometimes called a request for tender) requests a detailed proposal that includes information on price, how the work will be accomplished, who will do it (along with résumés, in some cases), and the company's experience.

- **Invitation for bid (IFB)**   An IFB, sometimes called a request for bid (RFB), usually requests a total price to do all the work. Think of an IFB as a form of RFP where the work described in the procurement statement of work is detailed enough for bidders to determine a total price.

- **Request for quotation (RFQ)**   An RFQ requests a price quote per item, hour, meter, or other unit of measure.

- **Request for information (RFI)**   An RFI might be used before bid documents are created. Responses to the RFI help the buyer identify which companies are qualified to handle the procurement. Buyers can also use RFIs to collect information on what work is possible, for later inclusion in RFPs or IFBs. Remember that the purpose of an RFI is to gather information, whereas the purpose of an RFP or RFQ is to buy something.

To provide the seller with as clear a picture as possible of what the work involves and what needs to be done to win the work, bid documents may include the following information for sellers:

- Background information about why the buyer wants the work done
- Procedures for trying to win the work (such as whether there will be a bidder conference, when the responses are due, and how the winner will be selected)
- Guidelines for preparing the response (such as maximum length and topics to address in the response)
- The exact format the response should be in (such as which forms must be filled out and whether email submissions are allowed)
- Source selection criteria—the criteria the buyer will use to evaluate responses from the sellers (such as number of years in business, quality of the response, or price)
- Pricing forms (forms to adequately describe the price to the buyer)
- Procurement statement of work
- Proposed terms and conditions of the contract (legal and business)

Note that the proposed contract is included in the procurement documents. Do you know why? The terms and conditions of the contract are also work that needs to be done, and there are costs associated with that work, including such things as warranties, ownership, indemnification, and insurance requirements. The seller must be aware of all the work that needs to be completed to adequately understand and price the project.

Well-designed bid documents can have the following effects on a project:

- Easier comparison of sellers' responses
- More complete responses
- More accurate pricing
- Decreased number of changes to the project

Sellers may make suggestions for changes to the procurement documents, including the procurement statement of work and the project management requirements included in the documents, before the contract is signed. When approved, these changes are issued by the buyer as addenda to the bid documents, and ultimately become part of the final contract.

Change Requests
Keep in mind that many procurements do not begin for months or years after the initial project planning is completed. Therefore, the procurement management plan is likely to be iterated, and possibly changed through integrated change control, as each procurement is needed. This is often accomplished through change requests.

Additional Terms To Know
The following sections discuss some additional terms a project manager should know when working with procurements.

Standard Contract
The contract terms and conditions are most commonly created by the buyer, who may have even put their terms and conditions into a standard format that is used over and over on similar procurements. Standard contracts are usually drafted—or at least reviewed—by lawyers, and they generally do not require additional review if used for the purpose for which they were intended. You should understand standard contracts, but also understand the project manager's role in special provisions (described next).

Special Provisions (Special Conditions)
The project manager must be able to not only read and understand standard terms and conditions, but also determine when additions, changes, or deletions from the standard provisions are required. By facilitating necessary adjustments, the project manager can

make sure the resulting contract addresses the particular needs of the project. The project manager meets with the procurement manager (if there is one) to discuss the needs of the project and to determine the final contract terms and conditions. (Remember that when taking the exam, you are the buyer's project manager, unless a question states otherwise.)

Additions, changes, or deletions are sometimes called special provisions and can be a result of any of the following:

- Risk analysis
- The requirements of the project
- The type of project
- Administrative, legal, or business requirements

Terms and Conditions

Terms and conditions (either standard or special) in a contract differ depending on what the project manager is buying. If they are buying work that includes equipment, they will need terms that describe when ownership of the equipment will be transferred to the buyer, as well as terms that require insurance for damages in transit. If the project manager is buying professional services, they will need terms that require professional liability insurance or insurance for errors and omissions. The required terms are usually determined by the procurement manager—however, the project manager should be generally familiar with the most common terms.

The following list outlines some general terms and conditions that are used in standard or special provisions. You do not need to know specific examples. Instead, you should be generally familiar with what all these concepts mean and what impact they would have on a project manager. The exam questions will simply test your understanding of these concepts; keep in mind that you are unlikely to see more than a couple of questions that relate to these concepts.

- **Acceptance** How will the project manager specifically know if the work is acceptable?
- **Agent** Who is an authorized representative of each party?
- **Arbitration** This is a method for resolving disputes that relies on a private third party to render a decision on the dispute.
- **Assignment** This refers to the circumstances under which one party can assign its rights or obligations under the contract to another.
- **Authority** Who has the power to do what?
- **Bonds** These are the payment or performance bonds, if any, that must be purchased.
- **Breach/default** This occurs when any obligation of the contract is not met. Watch out—a breach on the seller's part does not provide an excuse for a breach on the buyer's part.
- **Changes** How will changes be made? What forms will be used? What are the timeframes for notice and turnaround?
- **Confidentiality/nondisclosure** What information must not be made known or given to third parties?
- **Dispute resolution** How will any disputes regarding the contract be settled? Some options for dispute resolution are to use the courts or an arbitrator.
- **Force majeure** This refers to a situation that could be considered an "act of nature," such as a fire or freak electrical storm; it is an allowable excuse for either party not meeting contract requirements.
- **Incentives** These are benefits the seller may receive for achieving the buyer's objectives of schedule, cost, quality, risk, and performance.
- **Indemnification (liability)** Who is liable for personal injury, damage, or accidents?

- **Independent contractor**   This term means the seller is not an employee of the buyer.
- **Inspection**   Does anyone have a right to inspect the work during execution of the project? If they do, under what circumstances?
- **Intellectual property**   Who owns the intellectual property (such as patents, trademarks, copyrights, processes, source code, books, etc.) used in connection with or developed as part of the contract?
- **Invoicing**   When will invoices be sent? What supporting documents are required? To whom will they be sent?
- **Liquidated damages**   These are estimated damages for specific defaults, described in advance.
- **Management requirements**   Examples of management requirements include attendance at meetings and approval of staff assigned to the project.
- **Material breach**   This is a kind of breach that is so large that it may not be possible to complete the work under the contract.
- **Notice**   To whom should certain correspondence (information) be sent?
- **Ownership**   Who will own the tangible items (such as materials, buildings, or equipment) used in connection with or developed as part of the contract?
- **Payments**   When will payments be made? What are the late payment fees? What are reasons for nonpayment?
- **Procurement statement of work**   If it is not a separate document, this will be included as part of the contract.
- **Reporting**   What reports are required, how frequently, and who will send and receive them ?
- **Retainage**   This is an amount of money, usually 5 percent or 10 percent, that is withheld from each payment, and then paid when the final work is complete.
- **Risk of loss**   This allocates the risk between the parties to a contract in the event goods or services are lost or destroyed during the performance of a contract.
- **Site access**   This describes any requirements for access to the site where the work will be performed.
- **Termination**   Termination is stopping the work before it is completed.
- **Time is of the essence**   This term means that the delivery dates are strictly binding. The seller is on notice that time is important and any delay will be a material breach.
- **Waivers**   These are statements saying that rights under the contract may not be waived or modified other than by express agreement of the parties.
- **Warranties**   These are promises of quality for the goods or services delivered under the contract, usually restricted to a certain time period.
- **Work for hire**   The work provided under the contract will be owned by the buyer.

Conduct Procurements PAGE 482

> **Process:** Conduct Procurements
> **Process Group:** Executing
> **Knowledge Area:** Procurement Management

This process involves getting bid documents, including the procurement statement of work and other documents, to prospective sellers, answering the sellers' questions, and receiving and evaluating sellers' responses. The project manager will also need to select a seller using the source selection criteria specified in the procurement management plan, and then negotiate the contract.

Inputs to Conduct Procurements PAGE 484

The project manager and team will utilize many important inputs in this process. For instance, the procurement management plan gives direction on the work that will be done during this process. Other management plans provide information on how project work will be done, including the work that will be performed by outside sellers. Also note that the cost baseline provides direction regarding the approved budget for costs related to procurements. The schedule indicates the dates within which procurements must be completed.

Because the process to finalize procurements is ongoing throughout the project, the project manager and team may be able to make use of lessons learned from prior procurements on the current project. Lessons learned documentation may provide insight into the organization's previous experiences with potential sellers. This information might enable the team to select a seller based on the seller's past performance, eliminating the need for additional evaluation, and making the process more efficient and effective.

Of course, the procurement documentation created in planning is also a key input. However, before the project manager can send bid documents to prospective sellers, they need to know who those sellers are. A buyer may use techniques such as advertising to find possible sellers or may send the bid documents to a select list of sellers preapproved by the organization (an organizational process asset). Or, the organization may already have an existing agreement with a particular seller. In this case, they could work with that seller to negotiate terms to add new work to the contract.

Seller Proposal (Price Quote or Bid)

This is a seller's response to the bid documents. A proposal is usually the response to a request for proposal (RFP); a price quote is usually the response to a request for quote (RFQ); and a bid is usually the response to an invitation for bid (IFB). The proposal (or price quote or bid) represents an official offer from the seller. RFPs and RFQs describe how the buyer will meet the seller's request. A potential seller's response to an RFI provides information to help the buyer better define their procurement need. Responses to a seller's request for information may trigger the creation of an RFP or RFQ.

Keep in mind that sellers may have many RFPs, RFQs, and IFBs sent to them. They need time to review them and determine which they are interested in responding to. To ensure that the best sellers will be interested, the bid documents should be as complete and straightforward as possible.

When a seller decides to respond, they need to form a team, evaluate the buyer's needs, attend the bidder conference, and create a response. This can sometimes take a month or more. The buyer's project manager should allow for this time—and the time required for the rest of the procurement process—in the project schedule.

Independent Cost Estimates

The buyer should compare the seller's proposed cost with an estimate created in-house or with outside assistance during procurement planning efforts. This allows the buyer to discover any significant differences between what the buyer and seller are including in the procurement statement of work. The buyer must have their own estimates to check reasonableness and cannot rely solely on the seller's cost estimates. Responses that are significantly different from what is expected may indicate an issue with the sellers' understanding of the procurement statement of work.

Tools and Techniques of Conduct Procurements PAGE 487

The tools and techniques of the Conduct Procurements process may include expert judgment, advertising, proposal evaluation, bidder conferences, and interpersonal and team skills, such as negotiation.

Advertising

To attract sellers, an advertisement may be placed in newspapers, magazines, online, or in other types of media. Not all advertising costs money: the need for sellers could be announced on the company's website, through media releases or professional associations, or through free online advertising.

Bidder Conferences

Once the prospective sellers have been identified and have received the bid documents, the buyer controls who can talk to the sellers about the work, and what can be discussed. This control allows the buyer to maintain the integrity of the procurement process and to make sure all sellers are bidding or proposing on the same work.

To make sure all the sellers' questions are answered, the buyer may invite the sellers to attend a meeting called a bidder conference (or contractor conference, vendor conference, or prebid conference) in which they can tour the buyer's facilities (if relevant to the project) or attend an online forum and ask questions about the procurement. The questions asked during the bidder conference, along with the buyer's responses, are documented and sent to all prospective bidders to make sure they all have the same information. The questions and answers asked during the bidder conference are also added to the bid documents as addenda.

Getting answers to questions can be important because many bid documents will include a provision saying that by submitting a bid or proposal, the seller warrants that the bid covers all the work. The bidder conference is also an opportunity for the buyer to discover anything that is missing in the bid documents.

A bidder conference can be key to making sure the pricing in the seller's response matches the work that needs to be done and is, therefore, the lowest price. Bidder conferences benefit both the buyer and seller. It is a good practice for the project manager to attend the bidder conference. The exam often asks what things the project manager must watch out for in a bidder conference. The answers include:

- Collusion
- Sellers not asking questions in front of the competition
- Making sure all questions and answers are put in writing and issued to all potential sellers by the buyer as addenda to the bid documents

Proposal Evaluation

After receiving the proposals, the buyer (represented by an evaluation committee) may first use a screening system to eliminate sellers who do not meet the minimum requirements of the source selection criteria. Then, the buyer uses the source selection criteria identified in the Plan Procurement Management process to assess the ability and willingness of the sellers to provide the requested products or services. This data analysis technique provides a basis for quantitatively evaluating proposals and minimizeingthe influence of personal prejudices.

To select a seller:

- The buyer may simply select a seller and ask them to sign a standard contract.
- The buyer may ask a seller to make a presentation, and then, if all goes well, move on to negotiations.
- The buyer may narrow down ("shortlist") the sellers to a small group.
- The buyer may ask the shortlisted sellers to make presentations, and then ask selected seller(s) to go on to negotiations.
- The buyer may negotiate with more than one seller.
- The buyer may use some combination of presentations and negotiations.

The choice of methods depends on the importance of the procurement, the number of interested sellers, and the type of work to be performed. The sellers' proposals are usually reviewed and compared by the evaluation committee using one or a combination of the formal, structured processes discussed next.

Negotiations

Don't get worried about this topic. You do not have to be an expert negotiator to pass the exam. But, as you have seen in other chapters of this book, the ability to negotiate is an important interpersonal skill for a project manager. The exam assumes that the project manager is involved in contract negotiations, although the procurement manager generally leads the negotiations.

Negotiations are not usually needed in a fixed-price contract because the scope is complete and the lowest bidder is selected based on price. If negotiations are needed, they cover only parts of the proposed contract.

If a cost-reimbursable or time and material contract is used, there will likely be negotiations to finalize the contract price and other issues. After the contract is signed, however, in all contract types there will be negotiations whenever there are proposed changes to any part of the contract.

The buyer's and seller's project managers must be involved in negotiations, because they are responsible for facilitating project management and the resolution of technical issues on the project. The project managers must be involved in negotiating any issues that affect the key objectives of the project or how the project will be managed. Without the project managers' involvement in negotiations, it is common for a contract to be signed that the project managers later discover cannot be completed.

Objectives of Negotiations   It is important for everyone involved in negotiations to understand that the objectives of the negotiations are to:

- Obtain a fair and reasonable price.
- Develop a good relationship between the buyer and the seller.

The second item surprises most people, because they think of negotiations as win-lose. In a win-win situation, the buyer gets the work completed and the seller makes a reasonable profit. What's wrong with that? If negotiations turn from a win-win situation (preferable) to a win-lose situation, the seller will be less concerned with completing the work than with recovering what was lost in the negotiations. If negotiations are win-lose (in favor of the buyer), the buyer's project manager will have to spend time making sure the seller does not add extra costs, propose unnecessary work, or initiate other activities through claims or changes to "win" back what they lost during the negotiations. Many projects go bad because of the way negotiations were handled, not because of project problems.

Main Items to Negotiate   The main items to address while negotiating a contract can be vastly different, depending on what is being purchased. To achieve a signed contract, the following are usually negotiated in order (see if the order makes sense to you):

- Scope
- Schedule
- Price

Many people who are new to procurement management do not realize that price may not be the primary selection criteria or the major concern while negotiating. Often price is not a factor at all. Schedule may be more important, and a buyer might sacrifice a lower cost to gain speed. Perhaps the procurement is intended to solve a problem rather than complete specific work activities. In that case, the negotiations might involve detailed discussions of the feasibility of the proposed solution.

Outputs of Conduct Procurements PAGE 488   When negotiations are complete, the procurement contract is awarded to the selected seller. Note that the *PMBOK® Guide* refers to this output using the broader term "agreement," but we'll continue to use the more specific term, "contract," as the most appropriate term for the document describing the legal relationship entered into by the buyer and seller.

Agreements (Contracts)   When you think of the word "contract," what comes to mind? If you are like many others, you think of all the legal words, such as indemnification, intellectual property, and other fine print. People often think of the preprinted or standard contracts (boilerplate contracts) supplied by the contracting or legal department. This is only partially correct.

The word "contract" actually refers to the entire agreement between both parties. Therefore, it does include the boilerplate language (with the terms and conditions previously described), but it also includes business terms regarding payments, reporting requirements, marketing literature, the proposal, and the procurement statement of work—all the requirements of the project.

What Is the Purpose of a Contract?

- To define roles and responsibilities
- To make things legally binding
- To mitigate or allocate risk

Many project managers and business professionals think the only relevant part of a contract is the procurement statement of work because they are most familiar with that aspect of the contract. However, the procurement statement of work does not include all the requirements. In fact, some of the boilerplate language can be more important. For example, think of a project to develop new software. Who owns the resulting program? Who owns the resulting program if it contains modules or pieces of programs previously used and planned for future reuse? How does the buyer protect their rights and ensure that all source code is delivered? The ownership clause in a contract for such services might be more important than the procurement statement of work itself.

A contract is a legally binding document. Therefore, all the terms and conditions in the contract must be met. A change process is negotiated and documented as part of the contract, so neither the buyer nor the seller can choose not to conform—or not to do something required in the contract. Changes to the contract must be made formally in writing, and submitted to integrated change control.

What Do You Need in Order to Have a Legal Contract?

- An offer
- Acceptance
- Consideration (a transfer of something of value, not necessarily money)
- Legal capacity (separate legal parties that are legally competent)
- Legal purpose (you cannot have a legal, enforceable contract for the sale of illegal goods or services)

A contract, offer, or acceptance may be verbal or written, although written is preferred.

Imagine that you need plumbing work done on your home. You contact a plumber who sends you a price with a notice that says, "If you want me to do the work on your home, send me a copy of the design drawings." Three weeks later, that plumber shows up at your home to start work. You are surprised, as you signed a contract with another plumber. The plumber says you also have a contract with him because you sent the drawings. Is the plumber right? Yes; acceptance can be an action, or it can be verbal. You have a difficult situation on your hands, and you will likely have to pay this plumber something. The trick is to avoid these situations by understanding contracts.

The key outputs of the Conduct Procurements process are discussed in the following sections.

Selected Sellers After all the work of evaluating responses and negotiating with one or more prospective sellers is complete, a seller is chosen for each procurement. This means that the buyer and seller have agreed and signed off on all terms and conditions of the contract, and they will move forward to create the product or service during the Control Procurements process.

Change Requests Sometimes during project executing, problems that arise related to the procurement process (for example, a seller who isn't performing) or other areas of the project (such as risk, quality, schedule, or scope management) require reevaluation of the procurement management plan and make-or-buy decisions. So, it may be necessary to revisit the work previously done in Plan Procurement Management, which can lead to a decision to contract for resources or goods and make other changes to the project management plan or other aspects of the project. Such changes need to be submitted through integrated change control, where they are evaluated against the entire project, and then approved, rejected, or deferred.

This is important enough to state again that contracts may be finalized after other project plans are completed and approved. This could trigger the need for changes to any part of the overall project, potentially including the schedule or cost baselines (to address the availability or cost of procured resources), or other components of the project management plan or project documents.

Project Management Plan and Project Documents Updates   The finalized agreement may also necessitate changes to the planned approach to quality or communications management, as agreed upon in the contract between the buyer and seller.

Resource calendars and the requirements traceability matrix may be updated to reflect the responsibilities of new sellers for specific project requirements. The risk register may need to be updated with information regarding risks associated with particular sellers. The preapproved seller list may also need to be updated based on work done in Conduct Procurements.

Control Procurements PAGE 492

> **Process:** Control Procurements
> **Process Group:** Monitoring & Controlling
> **Knowledge Area:** Procurement Management

The Control Procurements process involves managing the legal relationship between the buyer and seller, ensuring that both parties perform as required by the contract, and closing each contract when it is completed or terminated. Throughout this process, the seller is focused on completing the work while the buyer is focused on measuring the performance of the seller and comparing actual performance to the contract, other procurement documents, and the management plans.

You should understand the following points covered in the Control Procurements process.

- What the project manager should be doing at any point in time
- What problems and issues to watch out for that might affect the management of the project under each contract type
- That all work and legal requirements in the contract must be accomplished, however small and seemingly unimportant
- That the project manager must help uphold all parts of the contract, not just the procurement statement of work

Inputs to Control Procurements PAGE 495   The procurement management plan includes the actions the project manager and team will take to oversee the procurements and ensure they are completed in accordance with the contract. The project manager may also review lessons learned to avoid the recurrence of issues experienced in the past. Also note that approved change requests from integrated change control are implemented in this process.

The project manager will use the milestone list and the schedule, scope, and cost baselines to confirm that the project is progressing as planned. The requirements documentation describes the technical and other requirements the procurement is expected to meet. Quality reports indicate whether the work of the procurement is within the established quality metrics. Work performance data from the Direct and Manage Project Work process gives the project manager information on costs and the status of project activities, and is used to evaluate seller performance.

Remember that monitoring and controlling is ongoing throughout the project. The project manager is continually measuring and assessing project progress compared to the contract, the procurement documentation, and the management plans. The tools and techniques described later in this section include many ways in which this is accomplished.

When variances are identified, they are analyzed and may need to be managed using the integrated change control system. Approved changes will be integrated into the management plans or the contract. Contract changes are handled using the organization's contract change control system, which is an enterprise environmental factor. This system includes change procedures, forms, dispute resolution processes, and tracking systems, and is described in the contract. These procedures must be followed, and all changes should be made formally.

Tools and Techniques of Control Procurements PAGE 497   The following tools and techniques can be used during the Control Procurements process.

Performance Reviews   During the Control Procurements process, the buyer's project manager analyzes all available data to verify that the seller is performing as they should. This is called a performance review. Often, the seller is present to review the data and, more importantly, to discuss what the buyer can do differently to help advance the work. The purpose of this review is to determine if changes are needed to improve the buyer-seller relationship, what processes are being used, and how the work is progressing compared to the plan. Formal changes to the management plans or the contract may be requested as a result of this meeting.

Inspections   Inspections may involve walkthroughs of the project work site or reviews of deliverables produced to verify compliance with the procurement statement of work. Do the deliverables meet specifications? Variances or deviations may trigger change requests.

Audits   An audit is performed by a team that includes representatives of both the buyer and the seller. The purpose of the audit is to confirm that the seller's activities are in compliance with approved procurement policies and processes. Variances are identified, and adjustments are made accordingly. The results of such an audit can be used to improve the procurement process and to capture lessons learned.

Earned Value Analysis   Earned value analysis metrics can be used to identify scope, schedule, or cost variances from the performance measurement baseline. Variances are analyzed to determine their impact on the project. The results may be used to generate reports, forecast future performance, or predict actual completion dates and costs. Change requests may be requested based on the results of this analysis.

Trend Analysis   Trend analysis determines whether performance is getting better or worse; it can be used to develop forecast estimates and estimate at completion.

Claims Administration   Conflict can also occur between the buyer and the seller, and this may result in the seller submitting a claim against the buyer. A claim is an assertion that the buyer did something that has hurt the seller, and the seller is now asking for compensation. Another way of looking at claims is that they are a type of seller-initiated change request. Claims can get nasty. Imagine a seller that is not making as much profit as they had hoped, issuing claims for every action taken by the buyer. Imagine the number of claims that can arise if you are working with a fixed-price contract and an incomplete procurement statement of work.

Claims are usually addressed through the contract change control system. The best way to settle them is through negotiation or the dispute-resolution process specified in the contract. Many claims are not resolved until after the work is completed.

Outputs of Control Procurements PAGE 499   The following sections outline the primary outputs of the Control Procurements process.

Change Requests   While the work is underway, the buyer's needs may change, and, as a result, the buyer may issue a change order to the contract. The impacts of the contract changes are then negotiated by the two parties. Changes to the contract may be requested throughout the procurement process, and are handled as part of the project's integrated change control efforts, along with all other project changes. Any changes need to be analyzed for their impact on the rest of the project.

If you do not have experience working with contracts, you should be aware of the concept of constructive changes, which do not result from formal change requests. Rather, constructive changes occur when the buyer, through actions or inactions, limits the seller's ability to perform the work according to the contract. This can include over-inspection or failure to cooperate. The buyer can also cause the seller to file a claim for damages if the buyer fails to uphold their end of the contract (for example, by failing to review documents or deliverables on time). Project managers need to be particularly sensitive to constructive changes. Such changes often happen during the course of managing a procurement. A simple direction to the contractor to perform certain work that may seem minor can result in a constructive change that costs the company a lot of money if that change is outside the scope of the contract.

Procurement Documentation Updates   Throughout the Control Procurements process, data on the contract and contract performance by both the buyer and the seller is gathered and analyzed. This information needs to be updated and archived.

Because a contract is a formal, legal document, thorough records relating to the contract must be kept. A records management system may need to be used to keep the procurement documentation complete, organized, and accessible. Record keeping can be critical if actions taken during a procurement are questioned after the procurement is completed, such as in the case of unresolved claims or legal actions. Records may also be necessary to satisfy insurance requirements. For many projects, every email, every payment, and every written and verbal communication must be recorded and stored. On other projects, information about the weather and the number of people on the buyer's property each day might need to be recorded. Whatever information is appropriate for the particular industry and project is saved.

On large or complex projects, a records management system can be quite extensive, with one person assigned just to manage these records. A records management system can include indexing systems, archiving systems, and information retrieval systems.

Closed Procurements   Closing procurements consists of tying up all the loose ends, verifying that all work and deliverables are accepted, finalizing open claims, and paying withheld retainage for each of the procurements on the project. The buyer will provide the seller with formal notice that the contract has been completed. There may be some obligations, such as warranties, that will continue after the procurement is closed.

Procurements are closed:

- When a contract is completed
- When a contract is terminated before the work is completed

Many people who are new to procurement do not realize that a contract can be terminated before the work is complete. The contract should have provisions for termination, which can be done for cause or for convenience.

When many changes to a procurement are required, it may be best to terminate the contract and start fresh by negotiating a new contract with the existing seller or finding a new seller. This is a drastic step that should be taken only when the existing contract no longer serves the purpose of defining all the work, roles, and responsibilities.

The buyer may terminate a contract for cause if the seller breaches the contract (i.e., does not perform according to the contract). This illustrates another reason the contract should clearly identify all the work required by the buyer. The buyer can also terminate the contract before the work is complete if they no longer want the work done (termination for convenience). Sellers need to realize that this can happen.

A seller is rarely allowed to terminate a contract, but it could be appropriate on some projects. In any case, termination can result in extensive negotiations on what costs the buyer will pay. This is controlled by the language of the contract. In a termination for convenience, the seller is usually paid for work completed and work in process. If the contract is terminated for cause due to a default, the seller is generally paid for completed work but not for work in process. The seller may also be subject to claims from the buyer for damages. In any case, termination is a serious issue, and one that has lasting effects on the project. Termination negotiations can be drawn out long after the work has stopped—highlighting yet another reason why the details of the project must be documented on an ongoing basis.

All procurements must be closed out, no matter the circumstances under which they stop, are terminated, or are completed. Closure is a way to accumulate some added benefits, such as lessons learned. It provides value to both the buyer and the seller and should not be omitted under any circumstances.

Procurement Management Review

Exercise

This exercise will help you review the key material you need to know for procurement management. The Shuffle Game that follows offers another approach to this material. You can use either or both of these study tools, depending on your preference.

Instructions

1. Try to fill in the blanks in the below table using the knowledge and understanding gained after reading this chapter.
2. To review only the material contained in this chapter, focus on the cells that have asterisks. (These are the key topics you need to understand to pass the exam with the minimum amount of study time. The answer table will show only these topics.)
3. To review all the items listed in the *PMBOK® Guide*, fill in the entire table.

Key Inputs	Key Tools and Techniques	Key Outputs
Plan Procurement Management Process group:		
*	*	*
Conduct Procurements Process group:		
*	*	*
Control Procurements Process group:		
	*	*

Procurement Management

Answer To save study time and focus on the most important information, this answer table only shows the topics that are covered in this chapter. If you tried to list all inputs, tools and techniques, and outputs, you'll need to check your answers against the *PMBOK® Guide*.

Key Inputs	Key Tools and Techniques	Key Outputs
Plan Procurement Management Process group: Planning		
Project charter Business documents Project management plan Project documents Enterprise environmental factors Organizational process assets • Types of contracts	Make-or-buy analysis Source selection analysis	Procurement management plan Make-or-buy decisions Procurement strategy Procurement statement of work Source selection criteria Independent cost estimates Bid documents Change requests
Conduct Procurements Process group: Executing		
Seller proposal Independent cost estimates	Advertising Bidder conferences Proposal evaluation Negotiations	Agreements Selected sellers Change requests Project management plan updates Project documents updates
Control Procurements Process group: Monitoring and controlling		
	Performance reviews Inspections Audits Earned value analysis Trend analysis Claims administration	Change requests Procurement documentation updates Closed procurements

Shuffle Game

Some people learn best by doing, which is why we have developed this alternate approach to reviewing procurement management. To save you time, only the most important topics for the exam—those covered in this chapter—have been included.

Instructions

1. Cut out the cards on the next pages.
2. Lay out the bold title cards as column headers.
3. Shuffle the remaining cards and try to put them in the columns where they belong. Cards with italic terms must be matched to the corresponding group. For example, a *Cost of Quality* card in italics would match with a Data Analysis card, as cost of quality is a data analysis tool and technique.
4. Check your answers against the material covered in this chapter or the *PMBOK® Guide,* and make note of any gaps in your knowledge.

Note: Be sure to keep all cards for each chapter shuffle game as you will use them again for the final Shuffle Game in chapter 14.

Plan Procurement Management *Key Inputs*	**Plan Procurement Management** *Key Tools & Techniques*	**Plan Procurement Management** *Key Outputs*
Conduct Procurements *Key Inputs*	**Conduct Procurements** *Key Tools & Techniques*	**Conduct Procurements** *Key Outputs*
Control Procurements *Key Inputs*	**Control Procurements** *Key Tools & Techniques*	**Control Procurements** *Key Outputs*
Procurement documentation updates	Closed procurements	Project charter
Business documents	Project management plan	Project documents

Enterprise environmental factors	Organizational process assets	*Types of contracts*
Make-or-buy analysis	Source selection analysis	Procurement management plan
Make-or-buy decisions	Procurement strategy	Procurement statement of work
Source selection criteria	Independent cost estimatess	Bid documents

Change requests	Seller proposal	Independent cost estimates
Advertising	Bidder conferences	Proposal evaluation
Negotiations	Agreements	Selected sellers
Change requests	Project management plan updates	Project documents updates

Performance reviews	Inspections	Audits
Earned value analysis	Trend analysis	Claim administration
Change requests		

Practice Exam

1. With which type of contract is the seller most concerned about project scope?
   A. Fixed price (FP)
   B. Cost plus fixed fee (CPFF)
   C. Time and material (T&M)
   D. Purchase order

2. Which of the following activities occurs during the Plan Procurement Management process?
   A. Make-or-buy decisions
   B. Answering sellers' questions about the bid documents
   C. Advertising
   D. Proposal evaluation

3. The contract for the project specifies that the seller will be paid for actual costs plus a percentage of any cost savings if the actual costs are below a targeted amount. What type of contract is being used?
   A. Fixed price incentive fee (FPIF)
   B. Time and material (T&M)
   C. Cost plus incentive fee (CPIF)
   D. Purchase order

4. Which of the following should the project manager do in the Conduct Procurements process?
   A. Evaluate risks.
   B. Select a contract type.
   C. Perform market research.
   D. Answer sellers' questions about procurement documents.

5. What is the main purpose of a procurement audit?
   A. Settle any outstanding claims from the buyer
   B. Loosely review the project before signing a contract with a selected seller
   C. Confirm that the seller's activities comply with approved processes
   D. Acknowledge substantial completion

6. A team is in the Plan Procurement Management process. Which of the following are they working on?
   A. Evaluating proposals received
   B. Awarding a procurement contract
   C. Creating a request for proposal (RFP)
   D. Conducting a procurement audit

7. What is one of the buyer's key objectives during contract negotiations?
   A. Obtain a fair and reasonable price.
   B. Negotiate a price under the seller's estimate.
   C. Ensure that all project risks are thoroughly delineated.
   D. Ensure that an effective communications management plan is established.

8. Which of the following is an example of a contract price that might be included in a cost plus fixed fee (CPFF) contract?
   A. $10,000 plus fee
   B. Costs plus $10,000 as a fee
   C. $10,000
   D. $150 per hour

9. Source selection criteria are an output of which procurement management process?
   A. Control Procurements
   B. Plan Risk Responses
   C. Plan Procurement Management
   D. Estimate Costs

10. Which input to Conduct Procurements is a response to the project's bid documents?
   A. Independent cost estimates
   B. Change requests
   C. Selected sellers
   D. Seller proposals

11. Which of the following statements about contracts and agreements is true?
   A. An agreement is a type of contract, but a contract isn't necessarily an agreement.
   B. Contracts can only be in writing.
   C. Contracts are generally used within an organization rather than in connection with procurements with external entities.
   D. A contract is a type of agreement, but an agreement isn't necessarily a contract.

12. Work performance data is an input to which procurement management process?
   A. Acquire Resources
   B. Control Procurements
   C. Plan Procurement Management
   D. Conduct Procurements

13. Which tool or technique of Control Procurements involves negotiating a form of seller change requests?
   A. Contract change control system
   B. Inspections and audits
   C. Performance reporting
   D. Claims administration

14. The project manager has determined that a consultant is needed to immediately begin working on a part of the project. The work is expected to last a few weeks. What is the most appropriate contract type in this situation?
   A. Fixed price (FP)
   B. Fixed price with economic price adjustments (FPEPA)
   C. Time and material (T&M)
   D. Cost plus fixed fee (CPFF)

15. Bidder conferences are used during which procurement management process?
   A. Conduct Procurements
   B. Control Procurements
   C. Plan Procurement Management
   D. Plan Procurements

© 2018 RMC Publications, Inc ™ • 952.846.4484 • info@rmcls.com • www.rmcls.com

Answers

1. **Answer** A

   Explanation With a fixed price (FP) contract, the seller has the cost risk and therefore needs to completely understand the procurement statement of work (SOW) before bidding. Fixed-price contracts are most appropriate on projects with well-defined requirements and specifications.

2. **Answer** A

   Explanation Make-or-buy decisions are one of the critical activities of Plan Procurement Management. Advertising to attract sellers, answering sellers' questions, and evaluating proposals are all activities that take place later, during the Conduct Procurements process.

3. **Answer** C

   Explanation A cost plus incentive fee (CPIF) contract, which is typically used on projects with an uncertain scope of work, specifies that the seller will be paid for actual costs up to a set amount. Costs savings below that amount are shared by the buyer and seller, as are cost overruns above that amount.

4. **Answer** D

   Explanation During the Conduct Procurements process, the project manager answers questions submitted by prospective sellers. Risk analysis is done before the Conduct Procurements process begins. Selecting a contract type is part of Plan Procurement Management. Market research is also performed in the Plan Procurement Management process, to enable selection of the appropriate sellers for the needs of the project.

5. **Answer** C

   Explanation Procurement audits, which take place during Control Procurements, are used to confirm that the seller's activities are in compliance with approved procurement policies and processes; the results of audits can also be used to improve procurement processes.

6. **Answer** C

   Explanation A request for proposal (RFP) is created in the Plan Procurement Management process. Proposals are received, and the contract is awarded, in the Conduct Procurements process. Procurement audits are a tool of Control Procurements.

7. **Answer** A

   Explanation Although thorough risk identification and an effective communications management plan are important, they are not the buyer's key objectives in contract negotiations. Negotiations should be win-win, so negotiating a price below the seller's estimate is not the best choice. A fair and equitable price will help to create a good working relationship between the buyer and the seller, which is the best outcome for the project.

8. **Answer** B

   Explanation In a cost-reimbursable contract, the buyer pays all costs. If there is a fixed fee added to the contract, the buyer pays the actual costs and the fixed fee ($10,000 in this example).

9. **Answer** C

   Explanation Source selection criteria are used to rate or score proposals. They are determined in the Plan Procurement Management process, and they are included in the bid documents to give the seller an understanding of the buyer's needs and to help the seller decide whether to bid on the work.

10. **Answer** D

    Explanation A proposal, which represents an official offer from the seller, is the seller's response to the bid documents. Typically, a proposal is a response to a request for proposal (RFP), while a price quote is a response to a request for quote (RFQ). A bid is a seller's response to an invitation for bid (IFB). Independent cost estimates (an output of Plan Procurement Management) are used in Conduct Procurements to evaluate and compare seller's cost estimates. Change requests and selected sellers are outputs of Conduct Procurements.

11. **Answer** D

    Explanation A contract, which is a type of agreement, can be written or verbal, and is typically used in connection with procurements from external entities. "Agreement" is a broader term than "contracts"; it encompasses documents or communications that outline internal or external relationships between buyers and sellers and their intentions.

12. **Answer** B

    Explanation Work performance data from the Direct and Manage Project Work process is an input to Control Procurements. Work performance data gives the project manager information about how the procurements are progressing so they can determine if changes to the procurements are required.

13. **Answer** D

    Explanation Claims administration involves negotiating and settling claims, which can be thought of as a form of seller change requests. (Remember that when a seller makes a claim they are asserting that something the buyer did hurt the seller in some way. In return, the seller wants compensation.)

14. **Answer** C

    Explanation Time and material (T&M) contracts typically have fairly simple terms and conditions, allowing for shorter negotiations so that work can begin more quickly. They are also typically used for relatively small levels of work effort.

15. **Answer** A

    Explanation Bidder conferences are a tool used in Conduct Procurements. They provide an opportunity for prospective bidders to ask questions about the procurement and ensure that all prospective bidders have the same information.

Stakeholder Management

THIRTEEN

There are 13 to 14 questions on this knowledge area on the CAPM exam. Also note, for a full list of all inputs, tools and techniques, and outputs within this knowledge area, please see the table on page 504 in the PMBOK© Guide.

Some topics might seem easy to you—so much so that you might be inclined to skip studying them. Does the topic of stakeholders fall into this category for you? Do you already know that a project manager needs to be the expert in project management during a project, while relying on certain stakeholders to serve as experts in what needs to be done and how it should be accomplished? A project manager is much like an orchestra conductor in that regard. As the leader of the orchestra, the conductor doesn't play any of the instruments, but rather provides the sheet music and the guidance to help the musicians put on a great performance. Similarly, a project manager does not do all the work activities within a project—that is the job of the project team. The project manager facilitates, motivates, coordinates, and integrates all those work activities into a successful outcome. Failing to understand the importance of planning, managing, and continuously evaluating stakeholder engagement will make a huge impact on your understanding of project management.

> **QUICKTEST**
> - Stakeholder management process
> - Stakeholder definition
> - Stakeholder involvement
> - Stakeholder analysis
> - Stakeholder register
> - Stakeholder expectations
> - Stakeholder engagement
> - Stakeholder engagement plan
> - Stakeholders engagement assessment matrix
> - Stakes

Do you have experience in properly involving stakeholders? What kind of complaints have you heard from key stakeholders? Have you ever witnessed a project manager deliver a product, but later discover that their stakeholders did not use it? A project won't be successful without significant, continuous interaction with stakeholders. A project team can build a great product or service, but if the project manager is not in close contact with the stakeholders who will use it, they may not realize they've missed the mark until it's too late.

Let's consider another scenario. Imagine you are a project manager who has been assigned a new project. The director of your department provides you with a 200-page scope of work and a charter, and tells you to get started. What do you do next?

Before you answer that question—and before you take the exam—you need to make sure you understand a simple concept: proper project management requires a project manager to identify all stakeholders, analyze their power, interest, and level of engagement, elicit their requirements and expectations (for product, project, project management, quality, communications, etc.), and then evaluate and incorporate all of that

447

information into the product and project scope as needed. A project manager cannot simply accept a scope of work or project charter without considering the project's stakeholders and their requirements. And stakeholder involvement doesn't end there—the need to engage stakeholders continues throughout the life of the project. This means the project manager will need to build and maintain a positive relationship with the stakeholders, and make sure they continue to be involved in the project at the level necessary to make the project a success.

The following should help you understand how each part of stakeholder management fits into the overall project management process.

The Stakeholder Management Process	Done During
Identify Stakeholders	Initiating process group
Plan Stakeholder Engagement	Planning process group
Manage Stakeholder Engagement	Executing process group
Monitor Stakeholder Engagement	Monitoring and controlling process group

Stakeholder Involvement in Projects

Let's look at how a project manager should involve stakeholders throughout the life of a project. You may notice that some of this discussion touches on processes that fall outside the stakeholder management process, such as Collect Requirements, Plan Communications Management, Manage Communications, and Plan Resource Management. This demonstrates the important role that stakeholders play in all aspects of a project.

So, what should a project manager do with stakeholders throughout a project?

- **Identify all of them.**   The first step in working with stakeholders is identifying all of them as early as possible. Stakeholders who are discovered later in the project will likely request changes; this can impact the project and lead to delays.

- **Determine their requirements.**   This is neither easy nor fast, but the project manager must make every effort to obtain as many requirements as possible before work begins. This applies to both plan-driven and change-driven projects. The level of detail of the requirements may differ between plan-driven and change-driven projects, but it's essential to determine as many requirements as possible up front for both. Do you try to do this? Many project managers don't even attempt it.

  To understand why this is important, think about the effects of starting a project without all the requirements. Those effects would likely include changes, delays, and possibly even project failure. How would it look if you had to say to your sponsor, "I didn't know about that stakeholder's requirement. Now that I know, I need to extend the schedule to accommodate their needs or cut another stakeholder's needs out of the project." This is just bad project management, and it can be avoided with proper stakeholder management.

  There are many ways to make sure you have the requirements—from just asking if you do, to conducting requirements reviews, to explaining to people what the negative consequences to the company and the project will be if a requirement is found later.

- **Determine their expectations.**   Expectations are beliefs about (or mental pictures of) the future. These expectations include what stakeholders think will happen to them, their department, and the company as a whole as a result of the project. Expectations tend to be much more ambiguous than stated requirements—or they may be undefined requirements. They may be intentionally or unintentionally hidden. For example, the expectation that a project will not interrupt other work, or that it will produce dramatic improvements, could affect its likelihood of success. Expectations that remain unidentified can have a major impact on all project constraints. Once the project manager has captured the stakeholders' expectations, they are analyzed; they may be converted to requirements and become part of the project.

The difference between what a stakeholder thinks will happen and what actually happens might cause conflict, rework, and changes. Why wait for a change request? Why not prevent as many changes as possible by asking stakeholders what they expect and clarifying any expectations that are inaccurate or poorly defined? This might involve walking stakeholders through what will occur to make sure there are no undiscovered expectations or requirements that could be unrealistic.

- **Determine their interest.**   It's important to determine the level of interest each stakeholder has in the project. Does the stakeholder care about the project? Are they likely to be engaged? Once a project manager gathers and analyzes that information, they can use it to plan a strategy for maintaining or increasing that stakeholder's interest and level of engagement. They may also find that certain stakeholders are especially interested in working on a particular part of the project—to learn new skills or prove their skills—or that they need attention and support from a key stakeholder for deliverable reviews and acceptance. An effective project manager will determine each stakeholder's interests and engagement related to the project and will structure the work, roles, and responsibilities to maximize engagement.

- **Determine their level of influence.**   Each stakeholder is able to negatively or positively affect the project to some degree. This is their level of influence, and it should be identified and managed.

- **Determine their level of authority.**   Each stakeholder's level of authority will impact their effect on the work and outcome of the project.

- **Plan to engage stakeholders**.   Project management focuses on planning before taking action. A project manager needs to plan ahead! How will they keep stakeholders involved in the project? How will they engage with stakeholders' interests, influence, and expectations? How will they include stakeholders in project decision making?

- **Plan how to communicate with them**.   Planning communications with stakeholders is critical, and closely related to stakeholder engagement. How can a project manager keep stakeholders involved and get them to communicate their thoughts and concerns if they haven't planned how information will be shared on the project? Remember that poor communication is the most frequent cause of problems on projects—careful communication planning can help prevent those problems.

- **Manage their expectations, influence, and engagement**.   Involving stakeholders doesn't end after initiating or planning. The project manager will need to work with stakeholders and manage relationships throughout the life of the project.

- **Communicate with them**.   Stakeholders are included in project presentations and receive project information, including progress reports, updates, changes to the project management plan, and changes to the project documents, when appropriate.

- **Monitor communications and stakeholder engagement**.   Good communication and relationships with stakeholders are critical to success, so it's essential to monitor these two areas of the project. The project manager will need to determine if and where communication or relationships are breaking down, and adjust their approach as necessary.

One key to a project manager's success is how they handle stakeholder relationships. Stakeholders must be involved, and their involvement must be managed by the project manager. That involvement may range from minor to extensive, depending on the needs of the project and the performing organization.

Identify Stakeholders   PAGE 507

> **Process:** Identify Stakeholders
> **Process Group:** Initiating
> **Knowledge Area:** Stakeholder Management

Stakeholders are identified during project initiation, and the first identified stakeholders are likely to be those who pinpoint a problem or need. They may be involved in developing the business documents for a project to provide a solution, for example. The business case and benefits management plan, which are created before project initiating, may include lists of stakeholders who will benefit from, or be affected by, the project.

Why is it so essential to identify all stakeholders? Any stakeholders who are missed will likely be found later. When they are discovered, they will probably request changes, which may cause delays. Changes made later in the project are much more costly and harder to integrate than those made earlier. Identifying all stakeholders helps to create a project that considers all the interests, influence, and interdependencies of stakeholders. That said, changes within a project or organization may introduce new stakeholders, or a project manager may simply miss stakeholders in the initial identification. It's important, therefore, to reassess the list of stakeholders throughout the project to determine whether anyone needs to be added and, if so, what that will mean for the project.

Many project managers fail to consider the broad range of potential stakeholders. Remember, stakeholders are any people or organizations whose interests may be positively or negatively impacted by the project or its product, as well as anyone who can exert positive or negative influence over the project. This diverse group can include the sponsor, team members, senior management, subject matter experts, end users of the product or service, other departments or groups within the organization, functional or operational managers, vendors, consultants, regulatory agencies, customers, financial institutions, and many more. If the project includes procurements, the parties to those contracts are also stakeholders.

Keep in mind that a project manager should not do the work of identifying stakeholders alone. The project team should be involved in this process as well. Subject matter experts, other project managers in the organization who have worked on similar projects, and professional associations can also be consulted during stakeholder identification. And as new stakeholders are identified, they may be able to suggest other stakeholders to add to the list.

Inputs to Identify Stakeholders   PAGE 509
The following are key inputs to the Identify Stakeholders process. Additional inputs may include the business case, benefits management plan, components of the project management plan, and agreements.

Project Charter   The project charter contains information about the project's key stakeholders, including the sponsor, customer, and others who are known at the time of creating the project charter. It may also include information about the responsibilities of each key stakeholder. This document serves as a starting point for identifying all the stakeholders on the project.

Project Documents   What project documents would you use as part of the Identify Stakeholders process, and why? Try to answer the question before reading the next paragraph.

Did you determine which documents would be most useful, based on what information is included within those documents? For example, the change log, as well as the issue log, may include information that introduces new stakeholders or changes an existing stakeholders' relationship to the project. Requirements documentation may also have information about potential stakeholders.

Tools and Techniques of Identify Stakeholders   PAGE 511
The following tools and techniques can be used during the Identify Stakeholders process.

Questionnaires and Surveys   Stakeholders, team members, and subject matter experts may be asked to name other potential stakeholders and provide input regarding the management of particular stakeholders or stakeholder groups.

Brainstorming and Brain Writing   Participants may take part in brainstorming sessions to help identify additional stakeholders. Brain writing is an individual effort, while brainstorming involves a group of people interacting and working together.

Stakeholder Analysis   When identifying stakeholders, the project manager will need to consider the stakeholders' roles and responsibilities on the project, as well as their level of authority and influence within the organization. Every stakeholder has expectations and attitudes toward the project that must be uncovered. The project manager must also determine the interest level of each known stakeholder—that is, what is at stake for them.

There are several kinds of interest (stakes) that a stakeholder may have in the project.

- **Ownership**   A stakeholder may have to sell property for the new freeway expansion that is beign proposed.
- **Knowledge**   A stakeholder may be the expert who designed the legacy inventory management system that is being replaced.
- **Rights**   A stakeholder may be concerned that the new development will endanger the community by destroying the watershed.
- **Rights**   A government official may be responsible for ensuring that the safety practices on the construction site comply with state and federal laws.
- **Interest**   The community may be concerned that additional traffic will come into their residential neighborhood if the new commuter rail stop does not have adequate parking facilities.
- **Contribution**   A resource manager may be concerned that the team members they are providing to the project will not be able to complete their normal operational work in addition to their project work.

Document Analysis   This technique involves assessing all project documents and reviewing any lessons learned as well as other historical information (organizational process assets) from past projects. This analysis can be used to identify stakeholders and collect information about the stakeholders and their stakes in the project.

Stakeholder Mapping   In addition to analyzing each stakeholder's potential impact and influence, the project manager will need to identify ways to manage them effectively. Stakeholder mapping, which groups stakeholders into categories, is a data representation technique that project managers can use to analyze and plan how the project team will build relationships with stakeholders. Creating a stakeholder map with categories and classifications can help the project manager determine how to prioritize their efforts to engage stakeholders on the project.

The following are examples of stakeholder mapping.

- **Power/interest grid**   This grid is used to group stakeholders based on their level of power and their interest in the project's outcome. Variations of this tool emphasize other stakeholder attributes, such as power/influence or impact/influence.
- **Stakeholder cube**   This three-dimensional model is used to represent aspects or dimensions of a stakeholder group.
- **Salience model**   This model is used to group stakeholders based on their need for attention, authority level, or level of involvement.

Stakeholders can also be grouped by directions of influence (upward, downward, outward, and sideward).

Outputs of Identify Stakeholders   PAGE 514   The Identify Stakeholders process results in a stakeholder register, change requests, and updates to the project management plan and project documents such as the assumption log, issue log, and the risk register. These outputs are outlined in the following sections.

Stakeholder Register   Information about stakeholders is compiled in the stakeholder register, which is a key output of the Identify Stakeholders process. The stakeholder register may include each stakeholder's name, title, supervisor, project role, contact information, major requirements and expectations, assessment information, impact and influence, attitude about the project, stakeholder classification, and other relevant information. Figure 13.1 shows an example of a stakeholder register.

Stakeholder Register

Project Title: _____   Project Number: _____

							Assessment Data Results			
ID	Name	Title	Contact Information	Major Requirements	Main Expectations	Roles/ Responsibilities	Influence (1 to 5)	Power (1 to 5)	Interest (1 to 5)	Classifications
1										
2										
3										
4										

Shaded area = IMPACT

Figure 13.1 Sample stakeholder register

The stakeholder register is an important input to the Plan Stakeholder Engagement process, as well as several other planning processes, including Plan Communications Management. Remember that the register will be added to and updated throughout the life of the project.

Change Requests   As additional stakeholders are identified after the first iteration of stakeholder identification, changes to the project management plan and project documents may be required to reflect how we plan to manage their involvement and meet their needs. The project plans that may be impacted include the requirements, communications, risk, and stakeholder engagement plans.

Project Management Plan Updates   The identification of new stakeholders, or new information about known stakeholders, may prompt changes in the project's approach to stakeholder engagement, risk, requirements, or communications management.

Project Documents Updates   Assumptions about stakeholders may be updated in the assumption log. The issue log and the risk register may also be updated to include any issues or risks associated with project stakeholders.

Plan Stakeholder Engagement PAGE 516

Managing the impact, relationships, and engagement of the stakeholders that have been identified and analyzed during the previous process is essential to project success, but it can take a lot of time. That's why it's so important, as with much of project management, to think and plan ahead before taking action.

Stakeholders can be an asset or a problem on a project, depending on how well the project is planned. To effectively manage relationships with this many people, the project manager will need to develop a stakeholder engagement plan and think ahead about how the project will impact stakeholders. Additional considerations to ensure that stakeholders are an asset on the project include how the project manager and the project team will interact with stakeholders, how they will involve stakeholders in making decisions, how they will manage stakeholders' expectations, and how they plan to keep each stakeholder satisfied.

Planning stakeholder engagement requires a strategy that will determine the project manager's approach to stakeholder involvement, which will result in actionable plans. This means the project manager should schedule time to get to know the stakeholders and check in with them throughout the project. If the project manager knows a stakeholder well, they will have more success managing their engagement and be better able to predict what that engagement will look like throughout the project.

Often, project managers have hundreds of stakeholders on a given project, located all over the world. Can you image how those project managers build and maintain relationships with their stakeholders? This is exactly why they need a plan. Project managers may not be able to have a close relationship with every stakeholder, but they can't afford not to have relationships with key stakeholders and as many project team members as they can. It's also important to plan ways in which the project manager and the project team can develop relationships with stakeholders who are not team members.

Imagine you are a project manager managing a project. It's important to know that the closer you are to stakeholders, the more comfortable they will be coming to you with problems and concerns, and the easier it will be for you to pick up on verbal and nonverbal cues that can tell you when something might be wrong. This can be an early warning system for problems on your project. How can you build positive and powerful relationships with your stakeholders? The same way you build them with your friends and family—by spending time getting to know them and allowing them to get to know you. The more time you spend with someone, the better you'll be able to ascertain their impressions and concerns.

During planning, the project manager will need to determine which stakeholders will require the most time and effort. These decisions require the project manager to think about the role of each stakeholder, the environment within which they operate, and the specific needs of the project. If there are any procurements in place, keep in mind that the project manager will need to coordinate with the procurement department to plan stakeholder engagement efforts related to parties of the contract.

Let's consider an example. Imagine you are a project manager managing a project to replace the online application process for open positions in your company. Your sponsor is the human resources director, who wants to streamline the process and encourage candidates with advanced technical experience to apply for jobs. Even though your stakeholders include anyone who is a potential job candidate (possibly millions of people), there are a few key stakeholders with whom you will plan to spend most of your time: your sponsor and the managers within the company who evaluate candidates. As the project team is designing and building the new website to satisfy stakeholder requirements, you will ask for frequent feedback from your key stakeholders about how the design meets their expectations. You might also identify a few newly hired employees who could help the team understand problems with the existing application process. Your stakeholder engagement plan might include formal review meetings where you discuss progress and get feedback on the progress of the website development.

Your experience on other projects and historical records of similar projects can help you anticipate and plan to meet stakeholder needs on the project. However, you should make use of the expertise of others as well. If you'll be working with a stakeholder for the first time, talk to another project manager or team member who knows this person. Meet with professional organizations, consultants, and subject matter experts to hear valuable insight on working with various stakeholders and stakeholder groups. Ask questions about how best to work with the stakeholders, and then meet with them as soon as possible to initiate these important relationships. Make sure the stakeholders themselves understand how important it is for you to meet their needs, and encourage them to communicate frequently as the planning and project work proceed. These preliminary meetings and conversations are critical for you to get an impression of how to best work with each stakeholder.

Not every stakeholder will be as engaged in the project as you might like, and some might be more engaged than you would wish. Stakeholder engagement can range from being unaware of (or resistant to) the project, to feeling neutral about it, to being supportive—even interested in taking a leading role on the project. Think about each stakeholder's attitude and interest in the project, as this will help you determine the level of engagement required to make the project successful. You should also consider how much engagement you require from stakeholders during each phase of the project. You may require some stakeholders to be more involved during planning, for example, while others will take on a more prominent role during executing. Identify and analyze variances between the current and desired level of engagement, and work with the team to identify ways to achieve the right engagement level.

Inputs to Plan Stakeholder Engagement PAGE 518 The following are key inputs to the Plan Stakeholder Engagement process. Additional inputs may include the project charter, components of the project management plan (such as the resource, risk, and communications plans, for example), and agreements.

Project Documents Which project documents would be considered a part of the Plan Stakeholder Engagement process? What would a project manager review prior to planning engagement? Documents such as the assumption log, change log, and issue log may include information about the following.

- Any assumptions or constraints that are associated with a specific stakeholder will be included in the assumption log.
- Any issues that impact a specific stakeholder or stakeholder group and need to be properly communicated will be included in the issue log (including information about any specific stakeholder communications that will need to occur in the event of an issue).
- Any stakeholders who request changes will be listed in the change log.

The project schedule, risk register, and stakeholder register may also be helpful project documents when planning stakeholder engagement.

Stakeholder Register As discussed in the Identify Stakeholders process, the stakeholder register includes vital information about the particular stakeholders on a project, including their requirements and level of influence. A project manager will use this information to plan the best way to manage stakeholder engagement.

Tools and Techniques of Plan Stakeholder Engagement PAGE 520 The following
are key tools and techniques of the Plan Stakeholder Engagement process.

Stakeholder Engagement Assessment Matrix
A stakeholder engagement assessment matrix is a data representation tool used to compare the stakeholders' current and desired level of engagement (see fig. 13.2). The stakeholder engagement plan documents how adjustments to the stakeholders' level of engagement will be achieved. This matrix is revisited as the project progresses to evaluate ongoing stakeholder engagement. Analysis of updates to this matrix may indicate the need to further plan or alter the stakeholder engagement strategy.

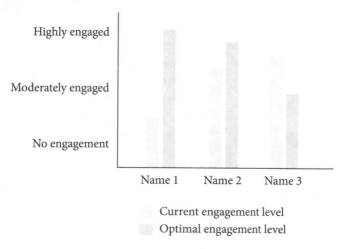

Figure 13.2 Stakeholder engagement assessment matrix

Assumption and Constraint Analysis and Root Cause Analysis
Evaluating assumptions about stakeholders' attitudes toward the project enables the team to determine the actions necessary to adjust the stakeholders' levels of engagement to benefit the project. Analysis of project constraints can provide insight into determining strategies to adjust the stakeholders' levels of engagement.

Root cause analysis is a way for the project manager and team to analyze the cause of the current level of stakeholder support and engagement. Doing so will help them determine how to best facilitate a change to bring the stakeholders' engagement level to what is desired.

If you've never planned stakeholder involvement on a project before, it can be difficult to imagine how a project manager would go about doing this on an individual level. Think about the various stakeholders involved in a large project. How would a project manager plan to manage the involvement of all those stakeholders?

The following are some suggestions that a project manager may use to manage stakeholder involvement. These are generalized descriptions and answers, but if you don't work on large projects in your real world, reviewing this information will help you better understand the work that needs to be done for large projects.

Stakeholder Description	Options for Managing Stakeholder Involvement
• High interest in the project, low influence, highly knowledgeable expert on high-risk areas	• Invite the stakeholder to participate in analyzing the risks on the project.
• Low interest, the source of major requirements on the project (high influence), not easy to work with	• Determine why the interest is low. Ask the stakeholder about their engagement preferences and how they would like to be involved with the project. • Identify ways to elicit requirements as efficiently as possible. • Make sure requirements are clearly captured and approved by the stakeholder as accurate. • Send reports.
• High interest, high influence, not a supporter of the project	• Ask why the stakeholder is not a supporter. Use your understanding to base your plan for engaging this stakeholder on dealing with those reasons.
• High interest, high influence, a supporter of the project	• Ask the stakeholder what is most important to them, involve the stakeholder in team meetings, report project performance to this person, and include information as the stakeholder requests.
• Moderate interest, high influence, completing many activities on the project, a supporter of the project	• Invite the stakeholder to officially join the project management team. Identify the stakeholder's preferred level of involvement; use this information to continue to get their support throughout the life of the project.
• Moderate interest, high influence because the stakeholder has identified a large number of potential risks for the project, a supporter of the project	• Plan to meet with the stakeholder periodically throughout the project to potentially identify any other risks. Keep the stakeholder informed about the effectiveness of risk efforts, and involve the stakeholder in risk reviews and audits.
• Moderate interest, nervous about completing assigned activities	• Plan to find and forward relevant literature to help the stakeholder, and arrange for training if necessary.

Output of Plan Stakeholder Engagement PAGE 522   The result, or output, of this process is the stakeholder engagement plan. This plan documents the existing and desired levels of engagement for all stakeholders, including plans to achieve the desired levels. It also provides details about the ways in which stakeholders will be involved in the project and includes guidelines and metrics for monitoring and evaluating how well the plan is meeting the needs of stakeholders and the project.

Stakeholder engagement plans generally have a component that addresses how communication will be used on the project to help manage stakeholder engagement and expectations. This means that the stakeholder engagement plan and the communications management plan can be repositories of some similar information about stakeholder communication requirements and who needs to receive what information on a project. However, these two plans have a different focus.

- The communications management plan emphasizes the details of the technology, methods, and models of communication—the what, when, and how of communication.

- The stakeholder engagement plan, on the other hand, explains the why of communications—why certain stakeholders need to receive certain information, and how the sharing of that information will help in managing stakeholder engagement and expectations. As you might expect, portions of these two plans are often created together.

Keep in mind that the stakeholder engagement plan will likely require adjustment throughout the project. We've already discussed how a project manager will reevaluate their list of stakeholders during the project. The discovery of new stakeholders may require changes to the plan, and there may be changes to the project that require more, or less, involvement from various stakeholders.

It's important to note that a project manager should be very careful with information about stakeholders. Thinking carefully before they share the stakeholder engagement plan, stakeholder register, or other verbal and written communication about stakeholders will ensure proper stakeholder management. Consider all the potentially sensitive information that is documented about stakeholders' attitudes and personalities, or the obstacles and challenges related to working with some stakeholders. Given how important it is to maintain good relationships with stakeholders, a project manager should be aware of how damaging it would be to their project for someone to find a list of stakeholders along with negative comments about them (particularly if that person is on the list).

A project manager should always maintain a positive attitude toward stakeholders, even those who are resistant or difficult to work with. A good leader is encouraging and supportive of everyone involved with the project. This means that when they discover an obstacle or challenge associated with a stakeholder, they may decide not to share it with others or write it down: so, some portions of the stakeholder engagement plan may reside only in the project manager's mind.

Manage Stakeholder Engagement PAGE 523

> **Process:** Manage Stakeholder Engagement
> **Process Group:** Executing
> **Knowledge Area:** Stakeholder Management

To meet stakeholder needs, resolve their issues, and make sure they remain interested and active in the project, it's essential to encourage stakeholder engagement and manage their expectations. Although this is an executing process, managing stakeholder engagement is ongoing throughout the life of the project.

Imagine the following scenario.

> *A project manager knows that a particular stakeholder is dissatisfied because one of his requests was not included in the scope of the project. The rest of the stakeholders agreed upon the scope, but the project manager anticipates that this person will continue pressing to add his request. The project manager schedules a meeting with the stakeholder to talk about why this request was not a high priority for the other stakeholders and to suggest this stakeholder build a business case for it being included in another project.*

How about this situation?

> *During requirements gathering, a stakeholder expresses concern about how much the project would impact her department's other work. The project manager contacts her to say, "I have kept your concern in mind while planning the project. You know we could not do this project without impacting your department, but because of your concerns, I have put together a report telling you when we will impact your department's regular work." As the project moves forward, the project manager continues to check in with the stakeholder to discuss any unforeseen impacts.*

Or this one?

> *A project manager notices that a stakeholder who used to provide helpful input regularly has become less involved in the project lately. The project manager touches base with the stakeholder to say, "I've really missed getting your feedback on the status reports. I've always appreciated your comments. Is there a reason you've been holding back lately? Is there anything I can do to get you more involved again?"*

Why bother doing such work? These actions are proactive, and they let the stakeholder know that their input is important and their needs and concerns are being considered, even if they are not agreed to. These efforts are likely to encourage stakeholder support of the project, and they also serve the valuable role of keeping the communication channel with that stakeholder open, so they can inform the project manager of potential changes, newly discovered risks, and other information.

Do you think project managers do not have the time it takes to do these things? As with many other areas of project management, such efforts can actually help a project manager be more efficient by reducing the amount of time they are forced to spend dealing with problems. When taking the exam, assume, unless stated otherwise, that the project manager has followed the best practices of project management. Therefore, the project manager has time to continuously encourage stakeholder engagement and manage expectations.

Inputs to Manage Stakeholder Engagement PAGE 525   The project manager reviews the stakeholder engagement plan, other management plans, and project documents, such as the stakeholder register, issue log, and change log, to find and address any issues that could be impacting stakeholder engagement. This review may identify sources of confusion or misunderstanding. For example, a deferred or rejected change request could decrease the engagement level of the stakeholders who supported the change.

Given how important good communication is to stakeholder management, it's also critical to follow the communications management plan. How can a project manager keep people involved and informed if they're not communicating? Managing stakeholder engagement also requires attention to stakeholders' needs while work is being done. It's also essential for the project manager to maintain trust, help resolve conflicts, prevent problems, foster agreement among stakeholders to meet the needs of the project, and generally encourage stakeholder support of the project and its overall outcome.

Tools and Techniques of Manage Stakeholder Engagement PAGE 526 In addition to the communication methods described in the Communications Management chapter (interactive, push, and pull), as well as expert judgment and meetings, the following are tools and techniques used in the Manage Stakeholder Engagement process.

Interpersonal and Team Skills   Much of a project manager's job involves interacting and communicating with people, so it's important for project managers to have good interpersonal and team skills, including cultural awareness and conflict management. They should be leaders, motivators, and team builders. They need to be able to establish trust on a project, be approachable and influential, consider cultural differences, and be effective listeners. Without these skills, a project cannot operate smoothly, and the project manager will lose opportunities to learn about issues before they become serious problems.

In addition, project managers need to be willing to address conflict directly and in a timely manner. Conflict is inevitable; project managers should approach dealing with conflict as an opportunity to improve the project and relationships with stakeholders.

Ground Rules   As mentioned in the Resource Management chapter, ground rules are part of a working agreement (team charter) that outlines any behavioral expectations a project manager may have for their project team, along with other stakeholders. These rules may apply when managing stakeholder engagement.

Communication Skills   What communication skills would best help a project manager when managing stakeholder engagement? Different stakeholders will require the project manager to utilize a variety of communication methods. Formal and informal conversations, meetings, and progress reporting are all examples of communication methods that may be used as part of the Manage Stakeholder Engagement process.

Outputs of Manage Stakeholder Engagement PAGE 528

The Manage Stakeholder Engagement process can result in requested changes to the project or product scope as well as updates to components of the project management plan. It can also lead to updates to project documents. The following are key outputs of the Manage Stakeholder Engagement process.

Change Requests

To effectively manage stakeholders' expectations and prevent future issues, the project manager may need to request changes to the project, including corrective or preventive actions.

Project Management Plan and Project Documents Updates

As in many other executing processes, Manage Stakeholder Engagement may result in updates to affected areas of the project management plan, such as the communications management plan and the stakeholder engagement plan, and project documents, such as the stakeholder register, lessons learned register, issue log, and change log. The issue log may need to be updated to document stakeholders' concerns and their final resolution. Lessons learned may be documented to reflect the results of efforts to engage stakeholders.

Monitor Stakeholder Engagement PAGE 530

> **Process:** Monitor Stakeholder Engagement
> **Process Group:** Monitoring & Controlling
> **Knowledge Area:** Stakeholder Management

Maintaining stakeholder relationships and monitoring stakeholder engagement are ongoing responsibilities of the project manager. Monitoring stakeholder engagement will help the project manager understand stakeholder perceptions of project progress. This will allow the project manager to make minor adjustments to ensure continuous stakeholder engagement and support. In addition to evaluating stakeholder engagement and improving or refining strategies for engagement, this process also involves reassessing the stakeholder register, updating stakeholder information, adding stakeholders as appropriate, and noting when a particular stakeholder's involvement is no longer necessary.

Inputs to Monitor Stakeholder Engagement PAGE 532

The components of the project management plan that are inputs to this process include the resource management plan (remember that all team members are also stakeholders), the communications management plan, and the stakeholder engagement plan. In addition to these plans, the issue log tracks any concerns, disagreements, confusion, or unresolved questions that arise during the project. This log can provide direct or indirect information about stakeholder engagement. Other project documents include the lessons learned register and the risk register. Note the inclusion of the risk register as an input here. It's important to realize that a lack of stakeholder engagement adds risk to the successful completion of the project. Such risks must be identified and managed.

It's important to know that monitoring stakeholder engagement requires you to collect and analyze data. For example, work performance data from the Direct and Manage Project Work process in integration includes measurements of project performance and the engagement levels of specific stakeholders. That data is then used to compare actual engagement efforts against the project management plan, to identify any variances. Any such variances may indicate a potential problem with stakeholder engagement. The stakeholder management plan specifies how this work of analysis and evaluation will be accomplished, who should be involved, how the results should be documented and presented, and how changes will be handled.

Tools and Techniques of Monitor Stakeholder Engagement PAGE 533

Imagine you are the project manager on a project. How would you analyze the work performance data related to relationships? You would establish, in your stakeholder engagement plan, some measurable performance metrics regarding stakeholder engagement. You might, for example, use a data analysis technique such as root cause analysis or alternatives analysis to assess stakeholder engagement. You could also use the stakeholder engagement assessment matrix to further analyze stakeholder engagement levels. These types of tools will help you figure out if any adjustments or changes need to be made to maintain stakeholder engagement.

Although work performance data and metrics are useful for giving you information about the quality of relationships, keep in mind that some of your assessment will also be subjective. For example, if an activity is behind schedule because a stakeholder has not provided needed information, the percent complete data will reflect the delay. This might point to a lack of stakeholder engagement or a problem with a relationship on the project. These indicators require you to clarify and analyze the problem, and then work to correct or improve the situation. If the stakeholder in this example is not returning phone calls, you will want to find out why. If the stakeholder is engaged, but having difficulty providing the information or getting the work done, you may need to revise the strategy for engaging this stakeholder and reevaluate the work assignment or the time estimate. This type of assessment can be immensely helpful in monitoring stakeholder engagement.

Communication, Interpersonal, and Team Skills

Communication plays a large role in helping a project manager discover and correct relationship problems. To maintain strong relationships, a project manager will need to spend time talking with stakeholders to determine methods for information gathering. This information may include data about the stakeholder's ongoing (and evolving) feelings about the project and other stakeholders. To get feedback, direct questions such as, "How do you think things are going?" can be used. However, assessing the success and strength of relationships often requires a more complex and subtle form of communication. This is when interpersonal skills can really make a difference. To further understand how stakeholders feel, a project manager can use techniques such as active listening, monitoring body language, leadership, facilitation, and emotional intelligence. These skills will help identify issues or concerns that need attention.

Outputs of Monitor Stakeholder Engagement PAGE 535

As a project manager learns about problems or issues from individual stakeholders, they should consolidate this information, look for patterns, and make adjustments as necessary. Conversations with stakeholders may also reveal the need for a change request. These changes could be recommendations for solving a problem, risk mitigation suggestions to prevent future potential problems, or ways to improve the engagement of various stakeholders.

The Monitor Stakeholder Engagement process results in work performance information (an analysis of the work performance data gathered through stakeholder engagement efforts) and possibly updates to the project management plan and the project documents, such as the issue log and the stakeholder, risk, and lessons learned registers.

Stakeholder Management Review

Exercise

This exercise will help you review the key material you need to know for stakeholder management. The Shuffle Game that follows offers another approach to this material. You can use either or both of these study tools, depending on your preference.

Instructions

1. Try to fill in the blanks in the below table using the knowledge and understanding gained after reading this chapter.
2. To review only the material contained in this chapter, focus on the cells that have asterisks. (These are the key topics you need to understand to pass the exam with the minimum amount of study time. The answer table will show only these topics.)
3. To review all the items listed in the *PMBOK® Guide*, fill in the entire table.

Key Inputs	Key Tools and Techniques	Key Outputs
Identify Stakeholders Process group:		
*	*	*
Plan Stakeholder Engagement Process group:		
*	*	*
Manage Stakeholder Engagement Process group:		
	*	*

Key Inputs	Key Tools and Techniques	Key Outputs
Monitor Stakeholder Engagement Process group:		
	*	

Answer   To save study time and focus on the most important information, this answer table only shows the topics that are covered in this chapter. If you tried to list all inputs, tools and techniques, and outputs, you'll need to check your answers against the *PMBOK® Guide*.

Key Inputs	Key Tools and Techniques	Key Outputs
Identify Stakeholders *Process group: Initiating*		
Project charter Project documents	Questionnaires and surveys Brainstorming and brain writing Stakeholder analysis Document analysis Stakeholder mapping	Stakeholder register Change requests Project management plan updates Project documents updates
Plan Stakeholder Engagement *Process group: Planning*		
Project documents • Stakeholder register	Stakeholder engagement assessment matrix Assumption and constraint analysis Root cause analysis	Stakeholder engagement plan
Manage Stakeholder Engagement *Process group: Executing*		
	Interpersonal and team skills Ground rules Communication skills	Change requests Project management plan updates Project documents updates
Monitor Stakeholder Engagement *Process group: Monitoring and controlling*		
	Communication skills Interpersonal and team skills	

Shuffle Game

Some people learn best by doing, which is why we have developed this alternate approach to reviewing stakeholder management. To save you time, only the most important topics for the exam—those covered in this chapter—have been included.

Instructions

1. Cut out the cards on the next pages.
2. Lay out the bold title cards as column headers.
3. Shuffle the remaining cards and try to put them in the columns where they belong. Cards with italic terms must be matched to the corresponding group. For example, a *Cost of Quality* card in italics would match with a Data Analysis card, as cost of quality is a data analysis tool and technique.
4. Check your answers against the material covered in this chapter or the *PMBOK® Guide,* and make note of any gaps in your knowledge.

Note: Be sure to keep all cards for each chapter shuffle game as you will use them again for the final Shuffle Game in chapter 14.

Identify Stakeholders *Key Inputs*	**Identify Stakeholders** *Key Tools & Techniques*	**Identify Stakeholders** *Key Outputs*
Plan Stakeholder Engagement *Key Inputs*	**Plan Stakeholder Engagement** *Key Tools & Techniques*	**Plan Stakeholder Engagement** *Key Outputs*
Manage Stakeholder Engagement *Key Tools & Techniques*	**Manage Stakeholder Engagement** *Key Outputs*	**Monitor Stakeholder Engagement** *Key Inputs*
Monitor Stakeholder Engagement *Key Tools & Techniques*	Project charter	Project documents
Questionnaires and surveys	Brainstorming and brain writing	Stakeholder analysis

Document analysis	Stakeholder mapping	Stakeholder register
Change requests	Project management plan updates	Project documents updates
Project documents	*Stakeholder register*	Stakeholder engagement assessment matrix
Assumption and constraint analysis	Root cause analysis	Stakeholder engagement plan
Interpersonal and team skills	Ground rules	Communication skills

Change requests	Project management plan updates	Project documents updates
Communication skills	Interpersonal and team skills	

Practice Exam

1. The stakeholder engagement plan, the change log, and _____ are inputs to the Manage Stakeholder Engagement process.
   A. Stakeholder questionnaires
   B. Brainstorming
   C. The communications management plan
   D. Formal and informal conversations

2. Stakeholder assessment and classification information is documented in an output of which process?
   A. Plan Stakeholder Engagement
   B. Identify Stakeholders
   C. Manage Stakeholder Engagement
   D. Monitor Stakeholder Expectations

3. What is a stakeholder engagement assessment matrix?
   A. A tool used in Manage Stakeholder Engagement
   B. An input to Monitor Stakeholder Engagement
   C. An output of Identify Stakeholders
   D. A tool used in Plan Stakeholder Engagement

4. Which of the following is not true about the stakeholder engagement plan?
   A. It is part of the project management plan.
   B. It should be sent out to everyone on the team or posted in an accessible location.
   C. It will be re-evaluated and updated throughout the project.
   D. It provides the specifics about how and why various project information will be distributed to stakeholders.

5. In which of the following would the project manager document any concerns, disagreements, confusion, or unresolved questions that arise during the project?
   A. Stakeholder engagement assessment matrix
   B. Issue log
   C. Work performance report
   D. Stakeholder register

6. Which part of the team charter outlines the behavioral expectations for the project team and other stakeholders?
   A. Ground rules
   B. Stakes
   C. The stakeholder cube
   D. Stakeholder register

7. Which of the following is an input to Identify Stakeholders?
   A. Stakeholder register
   B. Change requests
   C. Updates to the assumption log
   D. Project charter

8. Which of the following is true about the communications management plan and the stakeholder engagement plan?
   A. The communications management plan identifies the communications technologies that will be used, and the stakeholder engagement plan identifies the methods that will be used for specific stakeholders.
   B. The stakeholder engagement plan addresses the how of communication, while the communications management plan addresses the why.
   C. The stakeholder engagement plan needs to completed before the development of the communications management plan can begin.
   D. The stakeholder engagement plan explains why stakeholders need to receive certain information, while the communications management plan explains the models of communication that will be used.

9. One of the project stakeholders is an expert in the accounting processes that are at the core of the software being developed by the project team. What type of stake does this represent?
   A. Ownership
   B. Knowledge
   C. Interest
   D. Contribution

10. The team is in the process of assessing the engagement of their stakeholders and categorizing them as unaware, resistant, neutral, supportive, or leading. Which stakeholder management process is the team involved in?
    A. Plan Stakeholder Engagement
    B. Identify Stakeholders
    C. Manage Stakeholder Engagement
    D. Monitor Stakeholder Expectations

11. The team is analyzing data they have gathered about stakeholders and comparing it to their stakeholder engagement metrics. Which process are they engaged in?
    A. Identify Stakeholders
    B. Monitor Stakeholder Engagement
    C. Manage Stakeholder Engagement
    D. Analyze Stakeholders

12. All of the following are potential outputs of the Manage Stakeholder Engagement process except:
    A. Change requests
    B. Updates to the issue log
    C. Expert judgment
    D. Updates to the stakeholder engagement plan

13. Which of the following statements best explains why it is important to identify all stakeholders on the project as early as possible?
    A. The stakeholder register should be continuously updated throughout the project.
    B. Changes made later in the project are more expensive than those made earlier.
    C. Stakeholder engagement must be documented in the stakeholder engagement plan.
    D. The project manager is responsible for encouraging stakeholder support of the project and its outcome.

14. In the project's power/interest grid, a stakeholder has been categorized as _____. Because of that, the project manager has identified ways to elicit requirements from the stakeholder as efficiently as possible and intends to get the stakeholder to approve those requirements to ensure their accuracy.
    A. High influence/low interest
    B. Low influence/high interest
    C. High influence/high interest
    D. Low influence/low interest

15. Which stakeholder management process may result in change requests, updates to the project management plan, and work performance information?
    A. Identify Stakeholders
    B. Plan Stakeholder Engagement
    C. Manage Stakeholder Engagement
    D. Monitor Stakeholder Engagement

Answers

1. **Answer** C
   Explanation Good communication is critical to encouraging and managing stakeholder engagement; therefore, the communications management plan is a key input to the Manage Stakeholder Engagement process. Brainstorming and stakeholder questionnaires are data gathering tools and techniques used in the Identify Stakeholders process, while formal and informal conversations are tools rather than inputs for Manage Stakeholder Engagement.

2. **Answer** B
   Explanation Information about project stakeholders, including assessment and classification information, is documented in the stakeholder register, which is an output of Identify Stakeholders.

3. **Answer** D
   Explanation The stakeholder engagement assessment matrix is one of the analytical tools that may be used in Plan Stakeholder Engagement. It is used to compare the current level of stakeholder engagement with the desired level of engagement.

4. **Answer** B
   Explanation The stakeholder engagement plan often includes candid assessments of stakeholders' attitudes and personalities, as well as details regarding obstacles or challenges related to working with specific stakeholders. So, it should be shared with discretion and certainly not posted publicly. The other choices are all true statements.

5. **Answer** B
   Explanation The issue log, which serves as an input to Monitor Stakeholder Engagement, is where any concerns, disagreements, confusion, or unresolved questions that arise during the project are documented.

6. **Answer** A
   Explanation Ground rules help reduce the level of conflict on a project by defining the behavioral expectations for the project team and other stakeholders. Ground rules are included in the team charter and may be applied as part of managing stakeholder engagement.

7. **Answer** D
   Explanation The project charter is a critical input to Identify Stakeholders. It identifies the key project stakeholders and includes information about their responsibilities. The list of stakeholders is then expanded through the work of the Identify Stakeholders process. The stakeholder register, change requests, and updates to the assumption log are all outputs of Identify Stakeholders.

8. **Answer** D
   Explanation The stakeholder engagement plan addresses the why of communication (why certain stakeholders need certain information), while the communications management plan addresses the how (the methods, models, and technology that will be used). Often, it is most efficient to develop some portions of these two plans together.

9. **Answer** B
   Explanation Part of stakeholder analysis is determining the interest level of each stakeholder, each of whom may have a different stake in the project. Someone with a knowledge stake in the project can benefit the project through their specialized knowledge and expertise. Other types of stakeholder's stakes include contribution, interest, ownership, and rights (including legal or moral rights).

10. **Answer** A

    Explanation In Plan Stakeholder Engagement, the team uses the stakeholder engagement assessment matrix to compare the current and desired levels of stakeholder engagement. Using such a matrix, the team can classify the engagement levels of stakeholders into categories, such as unaware, resistant, neutral, supportive, and leading.

11. **Answer** B

    Explanation The work described in the question relates to analyzing work performance data and turning it into work performance information, which is done during Monitor Stakeholder Engagement. Note that the data is an input to this process, and the information is an output.

12. **Answer** C

    Explanation Expert judgment is one of the tools and techniques used in the Manage Stakeholder Engagement process. The other answer options are all possible outputs of Manage Stakeholder Engagement.

13. **Answer** B

    Explanation Although all of these statements are true, the best explanation for why is it important to identify stakeholders early in the project is that changes made later in the project are likely to be more expensive. When a stakeholder is missed, their requirements are likely to be missed as well. When those requirements are eventually identified, any resulting change requests will likely add more cost to the project.

14. **Answer** A

    Explanation The power/interest grid is used to group stakeholders based on their level of power or influence and their interest in the project's outcome. It can be used to determine the best way to engage those stakeholders. When working with a stakeholder who has been identified as high influence/low interest, the project manager should attempt to determine why their interest is low, ask the stakeholder about their engagement preferences, use the stakeholder's time efficiently, and make sure their requirements are accurately documented.

15. **Answer** D

    Explanation Although change requests and updates to the project management plan may be outputs of several stakeholder management processes, work performance information, which can include details about the current status of stakeholder engagement, is only an output of Monitor Stakeholder Engagement.

Exam Study Tools

F O U R T E E N

This chapter will provide additional study tools, including tables, games, and exercises, to help you review everything we have covered. These tools offer different approaches, from formulas to memorize for your download sheet, to a fun matching game, to a tricks quiz that will help you remember the relationships between the knowledge areas and process groups. Although each tool offers value in preparing for the exam, some of these tools may fit your preferred style of studying better than others. With that in mind, feel free to use only the tools that appeal to you most.

Formulas to Know for the Exam

There will be very little calculation on the exam; the only formulas you are likely to need are listed below. Although as a rule memorization won't be very helpful, knowing these formulas will allow you to answer a handful of questions correctly. Consider listing these formulas on your download sheet at the start of the exam, especially if you are uncomfortable with math.

Name	Formula	Covered in Chapter
Total Float	LS − ES or LF − EF	Schedule Management
Cost Variance (CV)	EV − AC	Cost Management
Schedule Variance (SV)	EV − PV	Cost Management
Cost Performance Index (CPI)	EV / AC	Cost Management
Schedule Performance Index (SPI)	EV / PV	Cost Management
Estimate at Completion (EAC)	AC + (BAC − EV)	Cost Management
Estimate to Complete (ETC)	EAC − AC	Cost Management
Variance at Completion (VAC)	BAC − EAC	Cost Management
Communication Channels	$\dfrac{n(n-1)}{2}$	Communications Management
Expected Monetary Value	EMV = P × I	Risk Management

Commonly Occurring Inputs and Outputs

Many of the items discussed in this book are inputs to or outputs of several project management processes. The following section is a summary of some of the most commonly occurring inputs and outputs. Although these inputs and outputs were not listed in this book every time they occurred, all the instances are listed here. It's also important to note that many of the inputs and outputs listed in this section have components. For example, the scope baseline is a component of the project management plan. To study these components, review the knowledge area chapters in this book and compare your understanding to the figures at the beginning of each process in the *PMBOK® Guide*.

Instead of memorizing this information, look for patterns that are easier to recall (and that you might want to record on your download sheet). This will be helpful, since many of the exam questions will offer one or more of these commonly occurring inputs or outputs as an answer option, and knowing whether that item is an input or output of that process will give you an advantage in identifying a correct answer.

Commonly Occurring Inputs

- Enterprise environmental factors
- Organizational process assets
- Project management plan
- Project charter
- Project documents
- Agreements
- Work performance information, data, and reports
- Business documents

The following table shows when these inputs occur in the process of managing a project.

Input	Knowledge Area	Processes
Enterprise environmental factors	Integration Management	All processes except Close Project or Phase
	Scope Management	Plan Scope Management, Collect Requirements, Define Scope, and Create WBS
	Schedule Management	All processes except Control Schedule
	Cost Management	All processes except Control Costs
	Quality Management	All processes except Manage Quality
	Resource Management	All processes except Control Resources
	Communications Management	All processes
	Risk Management	All processes except Implement Risk Responses and Monitor Risks
	Procurement Management	All processes
	Stakeholder Management	All processes

Input	Knowledge Area	Processes
Organizational process assets	Integration Management	All processes
	Scope Management	All processes except Validate Scope
	Schedule Management	All processes
	Cost Management	All processes
	Quality Management	All processes
	Resource Management	All processes
	Communications Management	All processes
	Risk Management	All processes except Monitor Risks
	Procurement Management	All processes
	Stakeholder Management	All processes
Project management plan	Integration Management	All processes except Develop Project Charter and Develop Project Management Plan
	Scope Management	All processes
	Schedule Management	All processes
	Cost Management	All processes
	Quality Management	All processes
	Resource Management	All processes
	Communications Management	All processes
	Risk Management	All processes
	Procurement Management	All processes
	Stakeholder Management	All processes
Project charter	Integration Management	Develop Project Management Plan and Close Project or Phase
	Scope Management	Plan Scope Management, Collect Requirements, and Define Scope
	Schedule Management	Plan Schedule Management
	Cost Management	Plan Cost Management
	Quality Management	Plan Quality Management
	Resource Management	Plan Resource Management
	Communications Management	Plan Communications Management
	Risk Management	Plan Risk Management
	Procurement Management	Plan Procurement Management
	Stakeholder Management	Identify Stakeholders and Plan Stakeholder Engagement

Input	Knowledge Area	Processes
Project documents	Integration Management	All processes except Develop Project Charter and Develop Project Management Plan
	Scope Management	All processes except Plan Scope Management
	Schedule Management	All processes except Plan Schedule Management and Define Activities
	Cost Management	All processes except Plan Cost Management
	Quality Management	All processes
	Resource Management	All processes
	Communications Management	All processes
	Risk Management	All processes
	Procurement Management	All processes
	Stakeholder Management	All processes
Agreements	Integration Management	Develop Project Charter, Monitor and Control Project Work, and Close Project or Phase
	Scope Management	Collect Requirements
	Schedule Management	Develop Schedule
	Cost Management	Determine Budget
	Quality Management	No processes
	Resource Management	Control Resources
	Communications Management	No processes
	Risk Management	Identify Risks
	Procurement Management	Control Procurements
	Stakeholder Management	Identify Stakeholders and Plan Stakeholder Engagement
Work performance data, information, or reports	Integration Management	Monitor and Control Project Work and Perform Integrated Change Control
	Scope Management	Validate Scope and Control Scope
	Schedule Management	Control Schedule
	Cost Management	Control Costs
	Quality Management	Control Quality
	Resource Management	Manage Team and Control Resources
	Communications Management	Manage Communications, and Monitor Communications
	Risk Management	Monitor Risks
	Procurement Management	Control Procurements
	Stakeholder Management	Monitor Stakeholder Engagement

Input	Knowledge Area	Processes
Business documents	Integration Management	Develop Project Charter, and Close Project or Phase
	Scope Management	Collect Requirements
	Schedule Management	No processes
	Cost Management	Determine Budget
	Quality Management	No processes
	Resource Management	No processes
	Communications Management	No processes
	Risk Management	No processes
	Procurement Management	Plan Procurements Management
	Stakeholder Management	Identify Stakeholders

Commonly Occurring Outputs

- Enterprise environmental factors updates
- Organizational process assets updates
- Project management plan updates
- Project documents updates

The following table shows when these outputs occur within the process of project management.

Output	Knowledge Area	Processes
Enterprise environmental factors updates	Integration Management	No processes
	Scope Management	No processes
	Schedule Management	No processes
	Cost Management	No processes
	Quality Management	No processes
	Resource Management	Acquire Resources, Develop Team, and Manage Team
	Communications Management	No processes
	Risk Management	No processes
	Procurement Management	No processes
	Stakeholder Management	No processes
Organizational process assets updates	Integration Management	Direct and Manage Project Work, Manage Project Knowledge, and Close Project or Phase
	Scope Management	No processes
	Schedule Management	No processes
	Cost Management	No processes
	Quality Management	No processes
	Resource Management	Acquire Resources and Develop Team
	Communications Management	Manage Communications
	Risk Management	Monitor Risks
	Procurement Management	All processes
	Stakeholder Management	No processes

Output	Knowledge Area	Processes
Project management plan updates	Integration Management	Direct and Manage Project Work, Manage Project Knowledge, Monitor and Control Project Work, and Perform Integrated Change Control
	Scope Management	Control Scope
	Schedule Management	Define Activities, Develop Schedule, and Control Schedule
	Cost Management	Control Costs
	Quality Management	All processes
	Resource Management	All processes except for Plan Resource Management and Estimate Activity Resources
	Communications Management	All processes
	Risk Management	Plan Risk Responses and Monitor Risks
	Procurement Management	All processes
	Stakeholder Management	All processes except Plan Stakeholder Engagement
Project documents updates	Integration Management	Direct and Manage Project Work, Monitor and Control Project Work, Perform Integrated Change Control, and Close Project or Phase
	Scope Management	Define Scope, Create WBS, Validate Scope, and Control Scope
	Schedule Management	All processes except Plan Schedule Management and Define Activities
	Cost Management	All processes except Plan Cost Management
	Quality Management	All processes
	Resource Management	All processes
	Communications Management	All processes
	Risk Management	All processes except Plan Risk Management
	Procurement Management	All processes
	Stakeholder Management	All processes except Plan Stakeholder Engagement

Process Review

Here is another tool to help you prepare for the CAPM exam. Many of the exam questions will test your comprehension of the *PMBOK® Guide* processes using everyday language, rather than using the more technical descriptions. If you are able to fill in this table on your own, you will be well prepared to answer those kinds of questions.

Exercise

For each project management process listed, fill in the appropriate information in the remaining columns.

Process	Knowledge Area	Process Group	What Does It Mean?
Define Activities			
Sequence Activities			
Plan Procurement Management			
Develop Project Management Plan			
Collect Requirements			
Direct and Manage Project Work			

Process	Knowledge Area	Process Group	What Does It Mean?
Develop Schedule			
Perform Qualitative Risk Analysis			
Define Scope			
Validate Scope			
Identify Stakeholders			
Conduct Procurements			
Monitor and Control Project Work			
Perform Integrated Change Control			

Answers

Process	Knowledge Area	Process Group	What Does It Mean?
Define Activities	Schedule Management	Planning	Create an activity list from each work package
Sequence Activities	Schedule Management	Planning	Create a network diagram
Plan Procurement Management	Procurement Management	Planning	Create the procurement statement of work, procurement strategy, bid documents, and the procurement management plan
Develop Project Management Plan	Integration Management	Planning	Create a project management plan that is bought into, approved, realistic, and formal
Collect Requirements	Scope Management	Planning	Finalize and document detailed requirements and determine how they will be managed
Direct and Manage Project Work	Integration Management	Executing	Produce work according to the project management plan (also called deliverables); create an issue log to track and record issues that have the potential to impact the project
Develop Schedule	Schedule Management	Planning	Create a bought into, approved, realistic, and formal project schedule and schedule baseline
Perform Qualitative Risk Analysis	Risk Management	Planning	Analyze the probability and impact of potential risks to determine which risks might warrant a response or further analysis
Define Scope	Scope Management	Planning	Create the project scope statement
Validate Scope	Scope Management	Monitoring and controlling	Meet with the customer to gain formal acceptance of interim deliverables
Identify Stakeholders	Stakeholder Management	Initiating	Identify and document information (in the stakeholder register) about the stakeholders on the project
Conduct Procurements	Procurement Management	Executing	Select a seller based on the seller responses and obtain a signed contract
Monitor and Control Project Work	Integration Management	Monitoring and controlling	Measure performance against the project management plan; change requests may be a result of this comparison
Perform Integrated Change Control	Integration Management	Monitoring and controlling	Evaluate the impact of change to the project and approve, reject, or defer change requests

Matching Game

Many of the CAPM exam questions will focus on testing your comprehension of basic project management terms. To check your understanding of the *PMBOK® Guide* terms listed on the next page, match each numbered term to its definition. (The Answer Key follows the game.)

Terms	Definitions
1. WBS dictionary	A. An assessment done by the project management team to evaluate and enhance the effectiveness of the team as a whole
2. Manage Quality	B. The degree to which the project fulfills requirements
3. Enterprise environmental factors	C. A description of what is and is not part of the project, deliverables, acceptance criteria, and constraints and assumptions; this description is used to manage and measure project performance
4. Corrective action	D. A method to measure project performance against the project baselines; it can be used to forecast future performance and project completion dates and costs
5. Precedence diagramming method	
6. Risk register	E. Threats and opportunities that may impact the project
7. Project scope statement	F. Using the range of optimistic, pessimistic, and most likely estimates to estimate an activity
8. Team performance assessment	G. Scope, schedule, and cost baselines against which project performance can be managed, measured, and controlled
9. Issue log	H. Action taken to bring expected future project performance in line with the project management plan
10. Risks	I. Meeting with the customer to gain formal acceptance of interim deliverables
11. Three-point estimating	J. The longest duration path through a network diagram—the shortest time to complete the project
12. Performance measurement baseline	K. Using mathematical relationships found in historical information, industry requirements, standard metrics, or other sources to create estimates (e.g., dollars per foot)
13. Parametric estimating	
14. Project documents	L. A document containing all management plans and the performance measurement baseline; this document describes how the project will be executed, monitored and controlled, and closed
15. Decomposition	M. A record of what was done right, what was done wrong, and what would be done differently if the project could be redone
16. Validate Scope	N. Breaking the project work into smaller, more manageable pieces
17. Constraints	O. Company culture and existing systems (conditions) that may impact the project in a positive or negative way
18. Organizational process assets	P. A graphic representation in which nodes (or boxes) are used to represent activities, which are then linked to show their sequence
19. Integrated change control	Q. A record of issues to be monitored until resolved
20. Lessons learned	R. Ensuring that the project work, the processes followed, and the deliverables that are produced conform to the quality management plan
21. Earned value	S. The process of implementing risk response plans, which includes ensuring proper execution of all agreed-to responses
22. Critical path	T. A description of the work to be done for each work package
23. Project management plan	U. The document where most of the risk information is kept; it is updated constantly throughout the risk management process
24. Implement Risk Responses	V. The process where recommendations for changes are evaluated for their impact across all knowledge areas and either approved, rejected, or deferred
25. Quality	W. Any documentation used to manage the project that is not part of the project management plan
	X. Existing processes, procedures, and historical information
	Y. Limiting factors

Answer Key for Matching Game

1.	**T**	14.	**W**
2.	**R**	15.	**N**
3.	**O**	16.	**I**
4.	**H**	17.	**Y**
5.	**P**	18.	**X**
6.	**U**	19.	**V**
7.	**C**	20.	**M**
8.	**A**	21.	**D**
9.	**Q**	22.	**J**
10.	**E**	23.	**L**
11.	**F**	24.	**S**
12.	**G**	25.	**B**
13.	**K**		

Review Shuffle Game

Understanding the inputs, tools and techniques, and outputs of each process is essential for passing the CAPM exam. The shuffle games at the end of each chapter reinforce this information. This game uses the same cards as the shuffle games. However, it is more difficult. It's a way for you to really challenge yourself, and analyze what information you have retained and truly learned.

Instructions

1. Gather together all the cards you cut out for the chapter shuffle games.
2. Pick out the bold header cards and lay them out first, then mix up the remaining cards thoroughly.
3. Try to recreate the tables that you built in the chapter shuffle games. Remember to use the understanding this book has given you, and try to logically determine any gaps in your knowledge.
4. Check your answers against the *PMBOK® Guide* or the relevant chapter, and make a note of any gaps for further review.

© 2018 RMC Publications, Inc.™ • 952.846.4484 • info@rmcls.com • www.rmcls.com

Process Tricks Quiz

Knowing which processes fall into which process group and knowledge area is key for the CAPM exam. The purpose of this tool is to show specific patterns that will help you remember the relationships between the processes, process groups, and knowledge areas without memorization. If you have trouble with this quiz, spend more time reviewing the table on page 556 in the *PMBOK® Guide* and pay special attention to which processes occur within which process group, as the CAPM exam will likely test your understanding of those relationships.

1. What are the only two processes in the Initiating process group?

2. What is the only process in the Closing process group?

3. Which two process groups have more processes than the other groups?

4. Which seven knowledge areas include at least one Executing process?

5. What are the only two knowledge areas that include more than one Executing process? (Extra credit: What are those processes?)

6. Which process is the only process in the monitoring and controlling process group that does not include either "monitor" or "control" in its name?

7. Which two knowledge areas have all but one of their processes in the planning process group? What process group do the outlying processes fall into? (Extra credit: What are those outlying processes?)

8. What is the only knowledge area that has at least one process in every process group?

9. Out of the twenty-four Planning processes, which seven don't include the terms "plan," "define," "estimate," or "create"?

10. Out of the ten Executing processes, which two don't include the terms "manage," "conduct," or "team"?

Answers

Here are the answers to the quiz questions on the previous page, with their associated tricks.

1. Develop Project Charter and Identify Stakeholders
   Trick: There are only two processes in the Initiating process group, in integration management and stakeholder management (the first and last knowledge areas covered in this book).

2. Close Project or Phase
   Trick: There is only one process in the Closing process group, in integration management (the first knowledge area covered in this book).

3. Planning (24 processes) and Monitoring and Controlling (12 processes)
   Trick: The majority of processes fall in either the Planning or Monitoring and Controlling process groups. If you need to decide which process group a process falls into, the choice will most often be between these two groups.

4. Integration management, quality management, resource management, communications management, risk management, procurement management, and stakeholder management.
   Trick: Only about half of the 10 knowledge areas include even one executing process. (Note: This doesn't mean there aren't any executing tasks in other process groups; however, their primary executing task, gathering work performance data, is part of Direct and Manage Project Work.)

5. Integration management, and resource management (Direct and Manage Project Work, Manage Project Knowledge, Acquire Resources, Develop Team, and Manage Team)
   Trick: Integration management and resource management are the only two knowledge areas that include more than one Executing process.

6. Validate Scope
   Trick: There is only one process in the monitoring and controlling process group that isn't monitored or controlled by a project manager.

7. Schedule management; cost management; and monitoring and controlling (Control Schedule and Control Costs)
   Trick: All the processes in schedule management and cost management fall into the Planning process group except for those that include the keyword "control."

8. Integration management
   Trick: Only one knowledge area covers all the process groups—the one that involves integrating all the aspects of project management.

9. Collect Requirements, Sequence Activities, Develop Schedule, Determine Budget, Identify Risks, Perform Qualitative Risk Analysis, Perform Quantitative Risk Analysis
   Trick: The keywords for the Planning process group are "plan," "define," "estimate," and "create."

10. Acquire Resources, Implement Risk Responses
    Trick: The keywords for the Executing process group are "manage," "conduct," and "team."

Process Matrix Shuffle Game

Here's an opportunity to apply the tricks you've just learned in the above quiz. Use the cards on the following five pages to create a map that assigns each process to the correct knowledge area and process group.

Instructions

1. Cut out the cards on the next pages.
2. Start building your map across the top, laying out the five bold title cards for the process groups (Initiating, Planning, etc.).
3. On one side of your map (left or right), lay out the ten bold title cards for the knowledge areas (Integration, Scope, etc.).
4. You should now have a map showing the process groups across the top and the knowledge areas down the left or right side. Shuffle the remaining cards and try to put them in the correct location based on your knowledge and understanding gained after reading this book.
5. Check your answers against page 25 of the *PMBOK® Guide*.

Note: The cards for this game are printed in a larger font to help you distinguish them from the Shuffle Game cards, in case they get mixed together.

Initiating	Planning	Executing
Monitoring & Controlling	Closing	Integration
Scope	Schedule	Cost
Quality	Resource	Communications
Risk	Procurement	Stakeholder

Develop Project Charter	Identify Stakeholders	Develop Project Management Plan
Plan Scope Management	Collect Requirements	Define Scope
Create WBS	Plan Schedule Management	Define Activities
Sequence Activities	Estimate Activity Durations	Develop Schedule
Plan Cost Management	Estimate Costs	Determine Budget

Plan Quality Management	Plan Resource Management	Estimate Activity Resources
Plan Communications Management	Plan Risk Management	Identify Risks
Perform Qualitative Risk Analysis	Perform Quantitative Risk Analysis	Plan Risk Responses
Plan Procurement Management	Plan Stakeholder Engagement	Direct and Manage Project Work
Manage Project Knowledge	Manage Quality	Acquire Resources

Develop Team	Manage Team	Manage Communications
Implement Risk Responses	Conduct Procurements	Manage Stakeholder Engagement
Monitor and Control Project Work	Perform Integrated Change Control	Validate Scope
Control Scope	Control Schedule	Control Costs
Control Quality	Control Resources	Monitor Communications

Monitor Risks	Control Procurements	Monitor Stakeholder Engagement
Close Project or Phase		

CONCLUSION

Congratulations, you have reached the end of this book!

As noted in chapter 1, we recommend that you review the information in this book several times to really retain what you have learned. So read through this book again, focusing on the areas where you have identified gaps in your knowledge. During your second pass through this book, you will find that you understand some topics better than you did the first time, and other concepts will stand out to you that you previously missed.

In particular, make sure you review the PMI-isms in chapter 1, the most commonly used tools and techniques in chapter 2, and Rita's Process Chart™ in chapter 3. Having a solid understanding of the project management process and the material presented in this book will not only help you pass the exam, it will also enable you to apply what you have learned to real-world projects.

Thank you for taking this journey with us. We hope you will come back to RMC Learning Solutions® after you have earned your CAPM certification. We can help you continue your training and earn PDUs to maintain your certification through our advanced instructor-led classes, eLearning courses, and products. We can also help you study for and pass the PMP® exam.

Good luck, and we look forward to seeing you again!

Index

Index

Index

Index

Index

Index